RE-IMAGINE SANTA

Re-Imagine Santa

YVONNE VISSING

Vissing and Associates

Dedication
For those who want to believe that the impossible could be possible

Re-Imagine Santa © by Yvonne Vissing
First edition 2020   All rights reserved. No part of this book may be reproduced without author consent.
Copyright 2020 Yvonne Vissing
ISBN 978-1-7358304-8-3
978-1-7358304-9-0 ebook
Publisher: Vissing and Associates
Vissing & Associates, LLC.   PO Box 273 Chester NH 03036
Email vissingandassociates@gmail.com

Contents

Dedication   iv

1   The Big Question   1

PART 1 SANTA OF YESTERDAY

2   Winter Festivals & the Santa Connection   12

Washington Irving Quote   41

3   Historical Figures Morphed Into Santa Claus   42

Hamilton Wright Mabie Quote   69

4   St. Nicholas & the Religious Co-optation of Santa Claus   70

Martin Buber Quote   82

5   The Female Santas   83

Mary Engelbreit Quote   103

| 6 | Santa Comes to the United States | 104 |

Jan Miller Girando Quote — 118

| 7 | Santa as Political Psychological Warfare | 120 |

Jill Jackson Miller & Sy Miller Quote — 144

| 8 | Big Biz & Santa | 145 |

Glen MacDonough And Victor Herbert Quote — 169

| 9 | The War Between Santa and Jesus | 170 |

V. V. Deloria Quote — 190

| 10 | Science & Santa | 191 |

John Greenleaf Whittier Quote — 219

PART 2 SANTAS OF TODAY

| 11 | Questions about You | 222 |

Washington Irving Quote — 243

| 12 | Santa and the Inner Life of Children | 244 |

Charles Dickens Quote — 260

| 13 | Santa, Peers, and Play | 261 |

David Grayson Quote — 279

| 14 | Santa Over the Child's Lifespan | 281 |

Mary Ellen Chase Quote — 295

| 15 | Santa, Symbols and Families | 296 |

Rachel Field Quote — 334

| 16 | Santa and the Community | 335 |

Bob Hope Quote — 358

| 17 | Santa in Contemporary Events | 359 |

Mary Engelbreit Quote — 370

| 18 | Santa Around the World | 371 |

Antoine De Saint-Exupery Quote — 381

PART 3 WHO WILL SANTA BECOME TOMORROW?

| 19 | Santa In Transformation | 384 |

M. Kathleen Haley Quote — 410

| 20 | Rethinking Gifting | 412 |

Mahatma Gandhi Quote — 442

| 21 | How To Explain Santa To Children | 443 |

Emerson, Lake And Palmer Quote — 470

| 22 | Where This Leaves Me | 472 |

Final Quote To Remember — 491

References — 492

Picture Credits — 518

About The Author — 520

About The Book — 522

Santa — 524

Chapter 1

The Big Question

The Big Question

Santa Claus poses a problem for a diverse contemporary society. On one hand, he is a character that has brought joy, lessons of altruism and generosity, as well as presents to children for hundreds of years. Millions of parents and children have loved him. More recently, he has become criticized for encouraging childhood greed, consumerism, Christianity, and white northern European male supremacy. He is now found around the world, but if someone is Muslim, Hindu, or Buddhist, from Africa, South America, Oceania, then why should Santa be of interest to them? No matter who you are or where you come from, sooner or later as parents we have to address the question – should we encourage or discourage children from believing in Santa Claus?

This question gets complicated because the issue isn't really about Santa at all. Rather, he a reflection of larger social issues that are quite political and symbolic in nature. The debate about Santa Claus is far from a children's issue. Santa is, in fact, an adultified issue - and always has been.

The stories we tell children about Santa Claus aren't mere stories to be discounted. They say a lot more than they may seem on the surface. Santa Claus embodies adult issues that reflect what we as parents and society value as priorities. It is adults who are choosing who Santa Claus is. We have the power to decide who he will become in the lives not just of our children but to his meaning around the globe. Whether we see him as a good guy, hero, victim, scapegoat, or a bad-guy perpetrator of social ills is up to us.

What is the story we want to tell our children about Santa Claus? Does Santa have a place in the world today, and if so, what should it be? I have struggled with these questions as both a parent and a scholar. My primary interest is how to ensure child well-being according to a human rights framework. Children's lives seem to be more complex and complicated. Despite the rhetoric that childhood is the best time of life, many children struggle with health challenges, abuse, exposure to violence, poverty, as their little lives suffocate in suffering. I believe that children benefit from having exposure to a joyful universal gift-giver whose primary benefit is to teach altruism and who reinforces the idea that all children are special. Children have a right to have hope, to feel loved, to use their imaginations, and look forward to the future when dreams might come true. What figure that all children know about can deliver that?

Santa Claus sprang to mind as the primary figure, with all of "his" different iterations and depictions. I grew up familiar with him. But are there other figures that can fulfill this role of making children's joy a priority while delivering messages of generosity and kindness to others? I wanted to find out. As background, I was curious about who the "gift-giving figures around the world" were. In a simple Google search of that keyword, there were over 4 million hits. Almost all of them dealt with the winter solstice, Santa Claus-type characters. There were a few others who I met who will be shared in this book, but few who had crossed the cultural boundaries to be more universally familiar to children around the world other than Santa Claus. Therefore, how should Santa be addressed by those who find value in him, those who don't, and those who are ambivalent towards him?

I needed to figure this out. Frankly, Santa Claus didn't seem like much more than an excuse for celebration until I became a parent. That was when I figured I'd better sort through what Santa Claus was going to mean in the lives of my own children. It was clear that the world of children today is different than the one I experienced when I was little when believing in Santa was accepted and expected. The world has become more diverse. Children seem smarter and more culturally aware at an early age. "Political correctness" had become a pervasive sentiment and believing in Santa Claus seemed a casualty of it. Communities and schools started forbidding the celebration of any and all holidays in order not to offend anyone, or trying to include them all, and then never pleasing any of them. Professionals and politicians hotly debated how to handle Santa Claus, Christmas, Hanukkah, Kwanza, and other December celebrations.

I was aware of varied religious views, disparate household economic conditions, and different ideological perspectives, all that made blanket acceptance of Santa questionable and complicated my decision of how to handle Santa Claus. I grew up on the Mason-Dixon line learning the mantra "be nice", so was it nice to let my children believe in Santa when others didn't or might get offended? But was it nice to deny them an ages-old custom that had brought me so much joy just because someone didn't like this fantasy figure? I wrestled with whether I would be a better parent if I encouraged my children to believe in Santa Claus or if I didn't. As a parent who wanted to do everything possible to raise good children who were respectful of others, what was the right way to answer the question – should I let my children believe in Santa?

It was important to me to figure out how to respond to this seemingly simple-on-the-surface but deeply complicated question. How I chose to answer it seemed to have huge implications for my children, my family, and me. I'm a mom-scholar; my three children are my raison d'etre, my joys, my teachers, my reason for getting up each day. I adore them. I am a college professor, a pediatric sociologist who is 95% confident that I can figure out most things if I conduct thorough research. Little did I know that my journey in researching the Santa Claus question would open up so many fascinating dimensions not just of history but also my own psyche. In the process of doing my research, I became a Santaologist.

Santa's arrival was the highlight of my year and a source of joyful expectation. My folks struggled financially to make ends meet and as children, we looked forward to Christmas morning. It wasn't just the presents we enjoyed – it was the growing anticipation of the season, the decorations, music, holiday foods, and having the opportunity to get together with friends and family that we didn't see most of the year. We always were gifted, but we didn't get many or expensive presents. Year after year, I never got a pony, but there were always sweets to eat, games, or toys to play with, a new outfit to wear, and socks. Always socks. Our Santa had a definite practical side, but he made sure we had a couple of gifts that would entertain or make us giggle.

Santa was not associated with religion in our eyes. The arrival of Santa and Christmas coincided chronologically but as children, we saw them as entirely different entities. There was church and then there was Santa. Santa was secular and quite distinct from religion. Santa Claus was altruistic, joyful, accepting of all, and created an opportunity for us children to have fun and bond together as a community. God was, well, God! God was abstract and invisible, Santa was tangible and real. They weren't competitors. They gave us different things.

My parents read me stories and I watched TV shows about the magical man who lived with elves at the North Pole, working all year to make toys that he brought to all the children of the world in a single night as he flew through the sky in a reindeer-pulled sleigh. He was rich with thrilling images and fantastic stories that engaged my brain in mental gymnastics of "how did he do that?" But I also learned that Santa was a real person. My father was American Legion friends with a fellow-soldier named Jim Yellig. During World War II, Yellig had been ordered by his commander to be Santa Claus for local children because he came from the town of Santa Claus, Indiana. This turned out to be a life-changing event for Yellig, who became called the Santa of all Santas, who came back from the war to create Santa Claus Land, the nation's first themed amusement park. Dad drove Yellig in his Santa suit all around the country to be in parades and wave at children. I remember being very little and going to the park and Santa Yellig coming over and warmly greeting my dad. It's a pretty awesome thing for a child to see Santa Claus in his fuzzy red suit and long white beard talking to my dad as if they were best friends who knew all his wishes. Santa Yellig came to my house one summer day and brought my brother and me a hundred Christmas tree seedlings in his pick-up truck (not a sleigh) so we could keep Christmas with us all year round. He wore jeans and a work shirt, with sweat beads rolling down his face as he dug his shovel in the ground to show us how to plant the trees, but even without his red suit, he was clearly Santa Claus. Fifty years later, Yellig's Christmas trees grow tall in our yard. We grew up aware of the legacy of Santa Claus as a fantastic-fantasy character, but we also knew he was real - because he was! We talked with him. He smiled and patted us on the head. He personally put presents directly into our hands. He and my dad hung out and laughed together; I guess my dad could be considered his elf. There was no problem in my mind integrating Santa as a real person who lived down the road and the fantasy being who lived at the North Pole with elves. Believing he was both seemed perfectly logical to me.

But times have changed. It is clear that not everyone believes in Santa Claus. Even back when I was a child, not everyone believed in Santa. I was friends with a Jehovah's Witness boy at school who announced that his family didn't celebrate holidays, which was perplexing to my young self. The girl was known as "one of the poor kids" said that Santa didn't come to her house. This bothered me. Big kids in the elementary school took delight in telling the younger ones that Santa wasn't real, which made some of us cry. How could they be correct, when I had the firsthand experience of knowing he was real? Middle-schoolers pompously announced how science and Santa were incompatible, and no smart person could ever believe in him. But I did.

It occurred to me that the idea that science, God, or Santa, are from different realms of consciousness. In high school, I sent Christmas cards to people to wish them happiness, but one year my former camp counselor returned it with a tart note, saying that he was Jewish, didn't celebrate Christmas and that I had not been respectful of his tradition. I remember feeling hurt and confused since being rude to him was the last thing I wanted to be. I sent him the card to let him know I liked him and wanted to wish him joy. I didn't understand. Years later I recall going to the city's Christmas parade followed by the all-community holiday-song-in-the-park gathering afterward and found myself uncomfortable. I expected songs everyone could appreciate and sing along to, like Frosty the Snowman, but instead, only religious songs like Away in the Manger and O Little Town of Bethlehem were sung by a church choir. Community members of all different persuasions had come to celebrate the winter season together, but within minutes the crowd dispersed because what was promoted as an inclusive event wasn't. A third-grade teacher-colleague recalled how her student told her she wasn't really a good person because people of her faith "didn't believe in Jesus"; her response was to refuse to let her class celebrate any December holidays. She wasn't trying to be punitive, but she didn't know how to build diverse holidays that were inclusive, not alienating. I've watched community members engage in nasty fights about whether the town should light up a tree, have a menorah, Kwanza candles, or put up "pagan" symbols like holly. Santa is no longer allowed to show up in many schools or at public events. Yellig's Santa Claus Land has become relabeled as Holiday World. It is clear that in some people's minds Santa stands for a whole lot more than a jolly gift-giver, and that not everyone thinks children should be encouraged to believe in him.

It seemed to me that Santa and I were standing at a crossroads. Which direction should I have my children take – to believe or not believe? To see him as a joyful, caring community-builder or someone who alienated neighbors and friends we care about? What was Santa Claus going to become – beloved, irrelevant, or Public Enemy #1? I had to figure it all out.

As a university professor, pediatric sociologist, founding director of a Center for Childhood & Youth Studies and the child rights policy chair for the United Nations Convention on the Rights of the Child and author of eight books, I decided to use my scholarly background to help me understand how to deal with the Santa Claus question. Methodologically, I have read everything I can find on Santa

Claus, including scholarly articles, books galore, news articles, and social media accounts. I've interviewed children and parents who believe and those who don't in order to better understand the issue. I have conducted observations and participant observations of people who are pro-Santa and anti-Santa. I have run focus groups with students in my university classes about their experience of Santa Claus. I have analyzed the way communities handle the issue of the December holidays and Santa. I have interviewed people from cross-cultural backgrounds to look for similarities and differences in how they view Santa Claus. I have looked at different theoretical paradigms to try to explain the Santa dilemma and have consulted with scholars from around the world to sort out this issue. In the pages that follow is what I learned.

I have divided this book into three sections to help organize my thoughts. The first is about the history of Santa. The second part of this book is about our contemporary understandings of who Santa Claus is and his relationship to children and childhood. The third section is about how Santa Claus can be transformed in the future – to either become meaningful or meaningless.

I've divided each chapter into three sections – the first focuses on the dilemma that parents face as they consider what to tell their children about Santa Claus. The second is the bulk of the chapter that explores what I learned. Sometimes I have given direct citations to certain materials or people, but often the points I learned came from multiple sources so I created an extensive list of references I used in the back of the book. The third section of each chapter will be my take-away from what I learned. The material integrates some of my many selves – my child self, my mom self, and my scholar self. It is my hope that my research and journey in answering the question – should children believe in Santa Claus – will be helpful to you in constructing your own answers.

At the end of this book, I will synthesize all the pieces I learned to share my take-away of what I learned about Santa Claus and how I recommend him to be handled by parents and the community as we venture forward into the future. The information will help you to better understand who Santa Claus has been in the past, how he is being cast in the present, and it will give you thoughts to consider for his place in the future of your family, and the family of humankind. I hope you will enjoy the journey and that you, like me, will discover things about Santa Claus, history, the world, and yourself that never dawned on you before.

Part 1 Santa of Yesterday

Chapter 2

Winter Festivals & the Santa Connection

The Dilemma

Can parents introduce children to Santa Claus without connecting him to Christmas as a religious holiday? How did Santa get connected to Christmas in the first place? Why does Santa Claus come on Christmas Eve? Can Santa's arrival be viewed independently from Christmas – and if so, wouldn't that become more inclusive for people who wanted to enjoy a festive holiday without it being seen as Christian? Finding answers to these questions seemed like a good place for me to start my research.

What I Discovered

What I learned is that it was no accident that this philanthropic, merry-maker arrives on December 24. There are a variety of reasons for this timing that have nothing to do with Christmas and nothing to do with Christianity at all.

In order to allow Santa Claus to transform in a relevant way into the future, his historical underpinnings must be understood in context. It is important to see the commonalities among different December celebrations and how they combined around the arrival of Santa Claus. Ancient festivals all focused upon the importance of family, giving to others, self-sacrifice, as well as the pleasure of food, lights, beauty, and joy gained from being together. Some festivals incorporated central figures to be their bringers of presents and merriment. Many are easily seen as transformations of the Santa spirit. Santa, as we have come to know him, has incorporated wonderful attributes from all kinds of histories and cultures from around the world around the same time of the year – winter, particularly December - for several common purposes.

In the northern hemispheres of the world, winter brings darkness, cold, and the end of a growing season. These pose life-challenges. People share a universal need for hope when confronted with adversity. How can we create hope? Community bonding and festivities are a commonly used strategy. Winter celebrations were designed to bring a sense of light into the lives of the community. Festivals pulled people out of their homes, into familial and public gatherings where they shared delicious foods that often contained sweets, carbohydrates, and fats, foods that would help sustain them through the winter. They often consumed drinks that had some alcohol content. The sharing of food and drink encouraged happy social moments and opportunities to exchange stories that could help build and solidify relationships. People engaged in singing, dancing, game-playing, theatrical performances, and playing tricks. Irrespective of which festival or culture one comes from, merriment has been an ingrained part of all of the celebrations. Many had an emphasis on love, romance, or sexuality. As people attempted to get through the challenges of the winter, festivals helped them to turn their minds to spring, the return of light, warmth, the growing season, and the creation of new life. The North American Basque Association (Nabasque 2013) sums it up this way:

> "In many cultures where the seasons change and winter is harsh, there is oftentimes a winter celebration figure or mythical personage around whom the festive revelries of midwinter revolve. This ritual serves as the hub of activities around which the clan, the community and the nation identifies in their collective attempt to break the wintry chill of outdoor inactivity and to fill the still, sometimes foreboding silence of the snowclad countryside. Whether this figure is called "Papa Noel," "Santa Claus," or "Olentzero," the motif is the same... The pre-Christian era celebrated the end/beginning of a year, while for Christians their year-end/beginning was Easter. So the older tradition was assimilated and Christians moved the celebration of the birth of Christ to this season".

Some main midwinter festivals include the following:

Winter Solstice: The winter solstice is the shortest day of the year when the night is longest and there is the least amount of daylight. The term solstice originates from the Latin words sol stitium, which means the sun stands still. The significance of the solstice is the moving out of the dark into the light, with winter being over and days lengthening so a new growing season could occur. Life was challenging for early peoples and they used all year to prepare for survival during the cold winter months. Celebrating the winter solstice was a way to give them hope that easier and more plentiful times lay ahead.

The winter solstice tends to fall around December 21 in the Northern hemisphere, although the Roman Julian calendar found it falling on December 25. The Romans did not celebrate the winter solstice but put more emphasis on Saturnalia, which was observed from December 17-23, or Kalends from January 1-5. The Egyptians used a different calendar and celebrated the sun god on the day of the winter solstice, and their celebration of the birth of the gods Osiris and Aeon occurred on January 6. Neolithic and Bronze Age remnants such as England's Stonehenge or Ireland's Newgrange point to the importance of solstices. The Roman emperor Aurelian (215-275 AD) decided to use the winter solstice date to create a festival to honor the arrival of the sun god, and this holiday became known as the Birth of the Invincible Sun. Later this holiday and its date were co-opted by Christian leaders in the mid-fourth century to persuade people to move away from their traditional festivals to incorporate a focus on Jesus as the "light of the world" (John 8:12). The birth of Jesus became associated with December 25 and the date of January 6 became Epiphany. But the winter solstice as an astrological event has been incorporated into celebrations around the world.

Look at the wide range of winter solstice type festivals that existed around the world in the ancient days! They include:

Amaterasu, a 7th-century Japanese celebration commemorating the emergence of the sun goddess from her seclusion in a cave and restoring sunlight to the world.

Beiwe Festival, celebrated by the Saami people of Scandinavia, to worship Beiwe, the sun goddess of fertility and sanity who travels through the sky in a structure made of reindeer bones to heard back to the greenery which is the reindeer's major source of food.

Chawmos is a winter solstice festival for the Kalash people in Pakistan. It is a celebration of nature, mountain spirits, deities, ancestors, community, and incorporates prayers that may be delivered to the supreme being Dezao, and a celebration for the start of a new year.

Maidyarem is an Iranian mid-winter festival in the Zoroastrian tradition. It occurs at the solstice and is connected with Vahman, the Amesha Spenta, or Holy Immortal, who is associated with good plans and intentions. It is celebrated in Dey, the month when the sun returns.

Dongzhi Festival occurs in China and other East Asian cultures around December 21, and it traces its origins to the yin and yang nature of the universe since this is the time when there will be more daylight, hence more positive energy, flowing into the lives of people. Families join together and may have rituals at the houses to protect them from ghosts who may haunt innocent villagers during the winter solstice.

Goru is the winter solstice celebration of the Dogon people of Mali and celebrates the arrival of humanity from the sky god, Amma.

Hogmanay is a Scottish celebration that celebrated the end of winter and the arrival of the sun.

Inti Raymi is a festival of the sun found among the Inca in South America and that honored the Inca god Inti. It also celebrated the winter solstice and new year in the Andes. In Machu Picchu priests performed a tying of the sun ceremony where they tried to hitch the sun to a stone column so it could not escape. While the Spanish conquest of the area eradicated most memories of the festival, memories of it remained, including through the Monte Alto culture, and may be seen in current day plays.

Junkanoo in the Bahamas and Jamaica is a late December celebration of costumes, music, and festivities that have similarities to Saturnalia.

Karachun is a Slavic holiday at which Hors, the old sun dies on December 22 and is resurrected as the new sun, Koleda on December 23. The festival of Koleda is a winter solstice festival and lasts for ten days when families invited their household gods to join them in singing, dancing, visiting, wishing each other good luck, and giving little gifts to each other in a tradition called Kolyadovanie.

La an Deroilin or Wren Day in Ireland and Wales is celebrated on December 26 and is a time of visiting, singing, dining, and merriment.

Lenaea is a Greek midwinter ritual influenced by Brumalia that celebrated women, rebirth, and miracles.

Lohri is an Indian winter solstice celebrated in the Punjab area.

St. Lucy's Day in Scandinavia is held on December 13. Women wear a crown-like wreath on their heads that has candles on it as a symbol of chasing away winter and bringing back the sun. They pass out sweets and gifts to children on this day.

Makara Sankranti is a Hindu festival held in India and Nepal that occurs around January 14, when the sun enters the zodiac sign of Capricorn. Offerings are made to the sun god during this time and it is 3 days of joyous festivities that include eating special sesame candy balls and doing ritualized activities to hope for a good future.

Maruaroa o Takurua is a mid-winter festival for New Zealand's Maori people when the sun turns from the northern journey with his winter bride Takurua to begin his journey back to his summer bride Hinerumati.

Mean Geimhridh is a Celtic solstice festival that occurs around December 19 to 23 when according to Welsh mythology, Rhiannon gave birth to the sacred son Pryderi (around 3200 BC). The festival contains rituals and gift-giving to the needy.

Modraniht was a December 24 event known as the night of the mothers when a sacrifice was made by Anglo-Saxon pagans.

Montol or Mummer's Day was an ancient Cornish or Celtic midwinter festival held every December 26. Costumes, dancing, and blackening faces or wearing masks were common at it.

Rozhanitsa Feast was a 12th century late December Russian and Slavic observance where the mother goddess

Rozhanista offered deer-shaped cookies, honey, bread, and cheese as gifts to others.

Shab-e-Chelleh was celebrated on the first day of winter at the solstice around the second millennium BC in the Persian Empire that is now Iran. Mitha was born at the end of this night after a defeat of darkness against light and people celebrate the birth of light as a family time of fun, feasting, merriment, listening to poems and stories.

Sewy Yelda is known as the Night of Winter holiday that is celebrated by some Kurdish peoples in honor of the rebirth of the sun, a victory of light over darkness. It is a time when children play games and are given sweets in a community-wide celebration that included feasts.

Sol Invictus is the December 25 festival of the birth of the unconquered sun (Dies Natalis Solis Invicti) introduced by Roman Emperor Elagabalus around 218-222. The folk tradition of worshiping a sun god was linked with the birth of Jesus.

Soyalangwul is the winter celebration of the Zuni and Hopi people and is held on December 21 to bring the sun back from its long winter sleep.

We Tripantu is celebrated in Chile as the re-emergence of the sun comes back to earth after the longest night of the year. It was associated with mother eth coming to fertilize the earth so it can again bloom.

Zagmuk is a festival of Babylonian or Iranian origin that lasted 11 days at the winter solstice to observe the sun god Marduk's battle over chaos and darkness. It was a time of revelry, celebration, parades, feasts, bonfires, gifting, and wearing costumes. Sumerians called their version of the festival Zagmuk, while the Babylonians called it Akitu. It has striking resemblances to European celebrations of the Twelfth Night and twelve days of Christmas traditions.

Ziemassvetki in Latvia is a December 21 winter festival that celebrated the birth of Dievs, the highest god of Latvian mythology. It is a time when fires are extinguished to signal an end to unhappiness and the beginning of a new year of opportunity. During their feasts, a space at the table was reserved for ghosts who were thought to arrive on a sleigh. Caroling was common at each other's houses; this holiday was later co-opted to become part of a Christmas celebration.

This list of winter solstice related festivals shows that the birth of the sun, and with it hope for the new year, was a common worldwide occurrence, long before there were mass communication systems available for them to disseminate information. The convergence of the solstice festival times and the December 24 arrival of Santa Claus is noticeable. So are many of the rituals people experienced. The early Christian leaders undoubtedly recognized that the winter solstice – December 25 date was important to peoples worldwide. If they co-opted it to be seen as the birth date of Jesus, then they had a better chance of replacing agrarian and naturalistic celebrations with a Christian one. Rumor has it that no one knows for sure when Jesus was born, but spring has been a frequently mentioned time, not December. It is important to remember that most stories of the ancients were told orally and were handed down from generation to generation. The art of writing is a relatively recent phenomenon, especially in forms that could be kept over long periods of time. Thus, all ancient history is subject to variation.

Other notable winter festivals associated with the creation of Santa Claus include:

Kalends: Kalends is a Roman new year festival that was thought to occur from January 1-55. Many of its traditions were incorporated into Christmas customs. These included decorating homes and temples with greenery, as greenery was associated with the goddess Strenia. People also exchanged gifts, ate honey and cakes to symbolize a sweet year ahead, giving coins to each other as a sign of abundance, and the used lights to commemorate the holiday. Costume wearing, fortune telling, music, dancing, feasting, mumming, playing dice, and celebrating in a joyous, visible way on the streets occurred as part of the celebration. People used this time period to be abundant with life, with eating better foods, becoming more extravagant and generous by giving to themselves and others. It was a holiday that everyone, everywhere celebrated, and taking time off the mundane activities of life to be joyful and indulgent was expected (Miles 1990).

These rituals were so engrained and enjoyable that the people did not want to part with them when people who were Christian wanted them rejected. The boisterousness, drunkenness, gambling, masquerading, and merriment associated with Kalends was looked down upon by leaders of the emerging faiths and great attempts were made between the fourth to the eleventh centuries to stamp it out. Little by little their diligence was successful in either eradicating the Kalends celebration altogether or transforming it into other forms of more acceptable ritual. These included the second provincial Council of Tours in 567 ordering it as a time of fasting and penance, it became a time of greater thoughtfulness and sobriety, the 7th century the Christian January 1 holy day of the Feast of the Circumcision, and the advent of Christmas itself.

Birth of the Invincible Sun: In the first century, the Roman culture consisted of a variety of religions that worshiped different gods in different types of rituals, ceremonies, and festivals. The followers of a one-god faith focused on the Persian sun god, known as Mithras or Sol, and his association with the sun transformed into the god who created the world and all things in it, a god who would never age or die. He was a god who demanded truth and justice in a world that would last forever. His December 25 festival was known as the Natalis Sol Invicti, or the Birth of the Invincible Sun. Mithraism members were inducted into the faith in a form of baptismal ceremony, after which they were to learn seven levels of knowledge or sacraments. The members shared meals and bonded together as a community, and believed that upon their death, blissful immortality awaited them. Over time Sol became associated with the supremacy of the Roman Empire and in 274 the Roman emperor Aurelian named the sun god the sole protector of the Empire. But as Christianity became the dominant religion, by the fifth century this faith had dwindled. Many of the sol or Mithras traditions became incorporated into Christmas traditions.

Saturnalia: The Roman counterpart to Christmas was Saturnalia, the time intersected with both the winter solstice and Advent, and was a time of festivities, merry-making, dancing, eating and drinking, sensuality, and gifting one another. In ancient Rome, the god Saturn was honored in this midwinter festival. It was originally a festival of Kronia or Cronus in Greece. This festival celebrated the building of a temple for Saturn. Festivities began on December 17 and lasted for a week until the 23rd. Saturn and Kronos were thought to be the same figure, and the word Saturn came from the Latin words for "to sow" or "to satisfy". Saturn was thought to rule over the kingdom of Katium and taught people how to plant, enjoy the world's bounty, and live in harmony. Equality was an important value associated with Saturn, as was a sense of abundance. During Saturnalia, there were private, public, temple, and school celebrations. Businesses closed down as people were expected to use this week for enjoyment. Markets emerged to sell special items that people could gift to each other. It was a time of merriment and justice, and slaves were treated well, given a banquet served by their masters in their honor, and sometimes switching places to mock the existing social hierarchy as a form of fun. People wore special and colorful clothes and children were expected to play, and men and women may cavort in each other's clothing during a time of excesses of all types, including drinking and eating, music and dance, noises of all sorts, misbehavior, sex, and gambling (Miles 1990).

Brumalia: This Greco-Roman holiday was generally held on December 24 and was related to both to the winter solstice and the ancient Greek Lenaia. Bruma means a short day or winter. This celebration included drinking wine, playing games, feasting, and being joyful. Even Emperor Justinian I, who was known to persecute pagans, allowed for this well-loved holiday. It was celebrated until the 6th century AD.

Yule: Yule is a pagan winter solstice festival often associated with Nordic and Germanic peoples that is celebrated in late December. Yule is one of the sabbats or spokes of the wheel on the pagan calendar and occurs around Dec. 21 or the winter solstice. At the time of the winter solstice, the world is reborn as the wheel (yule) of the sun turned slowly around. The word "Yul" means wheel and the day of Yul was the first day the sun visibly turned in its long drop toward the horizon, the day the sun-wheel turned. The month of December was also called Yule from the word Geol or feast. The Yule notion of the circle of seasons is also reflected by the use of wreaths during the holiday season. Yule has also become a term that has become associated with Christmas, especially in more English traditions. It was also referred to as Jul or Jol, which means wheel. It is thought that peoples who lived in those northern geographic lands dreaded the cold, short days of winter when food could be scarce and looked forward to the lengthening days and return of the sun. Greenery was used as decorations, and festivities included singing, exchanging gifts, celebrating around bonfires, and eating special foods. The boar or boar's head was often present as a symbol of the god Frey, who represented sunlight, fertility, peace, and plenty. As Christianity became more prevalent in Scandinavia, pagan rituals, and Christian observances meshed together; tenth-century King Haakon the Good of Norway ordered that Yule celebrations should be held around the time of Christmas and overtime Yule traditions of feasting and merrymaking were absorbed into the celebration of Christmas. English monk

St. Bede (672-735 AD) wrote that Yule was also known as Giuli, which refers to the turning of the earth to have longer days and that Anglo-Saxons in Britain had their own pagan midwinter festivals around this time, festivals that became incorporated into Christmas traditions later on, such as greenery, mumming, and wassailing.

Other Gifting and Winter Holidays

Kwanza: Kwanza is a joyous week-long holiday designed primarily by people of African descent between the dates of December 26 and January 1 that focuses on the importance of community, family, responsibility, and self-improvement. The holiday is built upon the notion that people within the family are the sources of joy for each other. Gifts are often exchanged. There is no central Santa figure per se for Kwanzaa.

It began around 1966 in response to the US Civil Rights Movement. Professor Maulana Karenga at California State University researched festivals in various African cultures and combined their traditions into the new celebration of Kwanza. The holiday combines the unique traditions in a holiday that allows people to celebrate their similarities. Kwanza may look different everywhere as each family or community adds their unique components to the celebrations. Symbolically, candles are lit to remind people that in these dark days, whether in winter or the challenges of life, there is always hope and light. The kinara holds seven candles, one black, three red and three green, which represent the people, the struggle and the future. They also represent the seven principles: unity (umoja), self-determination (kujichagulia), collective responsibility (ujima), cooperative economics (ujamaa), purpose (nia), creativity (kuumba) and faith (imani) (Elfster 2019; Trammell 2017).

Hanukkah: Hanukkah is an ancient holiday known as the Jewish festival of lights. It is sometimes referred to as a winter solstice holiday since it occurs in mid-winter. Because they use a calendar that is neither solar nor lunar, some allege it is not a winter solstice transformation. Regarded as the festival of lights, seven nights of gifting can be found in Jewish homes around the world where it is custom for family members to give each other small but emotionally significant gifts on each of the nights as they light candles on the menorah. It is a time of celebrating hope. Dreidel games are played, songs are sung, and foods cooked in oil, such as donuts or potato pancakes called latkes, are consumed. There is no Santa figure.

Boxing Day: Boxing Day, December 26, is the day that many people of English background choose to open their gifts, instead of doing so on Christmas Eve or Christmas Day. Boxing Day is historically the day in which the alms boxes for the poor were opened and distributed among the needy, so some people prefer to open holiday gifts then in remembrance of the common threads that bind us all. The tradition of giving alms to the poor is built upon the charity influences of ancient festivals, and inevitably inspired authors like Washington Irving and Charles Dickens to write about the importance of giving to the needy. The notion that wealthy people should help the poor during the holiday season is a common characteristic in almost all of the ancient festivals.

Eid al Fitr: Ramadan is a time of peaceful prayer, reflection, and charity where Muslims pray for the world and to find one's inner quietness for answers to spiritual matters. It is a time of fasting when food cannot be eaten between dawn and dusk. Ramadan ends with the holiday Eid al Fitr, when family feasts and celebrations occur. It could occur in December or at other times of the year since it is determined by the lunar calendar and cycles of the moon. A lunar month moves forward by 10-11 days each year, so while it is not necessarily a winter solstice holiday, it is certainly related to the lunar calendar. During this holiday, small but meaningful gifts may be exchanged between family and friends. Charitable contributions may be made to others, including strangers. Children often receive eidia offerings in money bags or sweets like cookies and date. Family members will also buy one another presents, although most are directed towards the youngest members of the family. Fireworks and lights may also be used to celebrate Eid-al-Fitr (Elfster 2019; Simpson 2019).

Diwali: Diwali is an Indian Hindu fall festival of lights celebration that in many ways is the equivalent as Christmas and winter solstice festivities in its importance to the community. Families join together to enjoy each other's company, share food, and a sense of abundance. Lakshmi, the goddess of prosperity. Diwali symbolizes the spiritual awakening, a victory of light over darkness, good over evil, and knowledge over ignorance and gets its name from the row of clay lamps that Indians light outside their homes to symbolize the inner light that protects them from spiritual darkness. Houses, shops, and community displays of lights are found everywhere. Sharing celebratory foods and festivities with family, friends, and neighbors is common. Fireworks are an important part of this five-day celebration where people pray that goodness will be blessed upon them. (BBC 2018; National Geographic 2019).

Pancha Ganapati: This five-day, Dec 21-25 Hindu holiday is a family-centered substitute for Christmas. Ganapati or Ganesh, the elephant-headed god of new beginnings and prosperity, is a symbol of the holiday. During these days, families get together at each other's homes or go on picnics and outings. Family members are to make up for past mistakes and bring Ganesh's gifts of joy and harmony into their lives. Each day a tray of sweets, incense, and fruits are offered to Ganesh, preferably by the children. Families will sing and chant and give children colorful presents. Sending others holiday cards and decorating homes with pine, bamboo, palm or banana boughs, hanging colorful ornaments, garlands of limes or sweet modaka, and lights are traditional. Special holiday foods are prepared, like vadai (spicy donuts).

The first day the family is to create a vibration of love and harmony among all members and making amends for past misdeeds, insults, mental pain, and injuries caused and suffered. They conclude by extolling one another's best qualities. The color is yellow. Day 2, color blue, is devoted to creating or restoring a vibration of love and harmony among neighbors, relatives and close friends by presenting heartfelt gifts and offering apologies to clear up any ill-will that may exist. Relatives and friends in far-off places are written to or called, forgiveness is sought, apologies made and tensions released. In day 3, red, people are encouraged to establish love and harmony among business associates and the public. Day 4, color green, is to bring forth joy and harmony coming from music, art, drama and dance. At day 5, orange: the discipline of the day is for love and harmony that comes from charity and religiousness. As the gifts are opened, people celebrate Ganesh's abundant, loving presence that inspires them to do good for the coming year. This holiday began in 1985 by Satguru Sivaya Subramuniyaswami so children and families could celebrate the essence of the holiday season without compromising their Hindu values. Santa Claus is not present, but Ganesh is.

Feast of Our Lady of Guadalupe: This festival is celebrated on December 12 and is a time when people in Mexico celebrate their distinct cultural heritage while at the same time affirming their distinctness. Its origins hail from the Virgin Mary appearing to Juan Diego, who was reportedly a regular-type-of-guy who became Mexico's first saint. The Lady of Guadalupe is thought to incorporate characteristics favorable to the indigenous, polytheistic members of Mexico and brings people together, irrespective of their differences culturally, racially, and religiously. One theory is that she was created, in part, by the Aztec people who had an elaborate, coherent symbolic system for making sense of life. When Spaniards came in to destroy their culture, the image of the Lady of Guadalupe filled that void (Harrington 1988).

Oseibo: Oseibo is a Japanese holiday that falls around the 20th of December (by the 20th). It is a holiday that focuses on telling someone how much they mean to you. The summer festival of Ochugen and the winter festival of Oseibo began near the start of the Edo Period in the 1600s when it was considered a duty to give gifts to those you felt indebted to, like your boss or a government leader. Over time it has become transformed away from a day where you give gifts out of obligation to one where you do so because you want to show someone that you care about them. It isn't debt. It is love. That spirit has always been there, and is now being revived. Beyond the ritual, there is joy. And that joy can come in many forms, but often with sweets and art (Elfster 2019).

Omisoka: The Japanese new year's holiday of Omisoka is celebrated on Dec. 31, and families place a kadomatsu (pine branch decoration) on each side of the front door to attract good fortune inside the house, and some hang a shimekazari, which is a decoration that will welcome the new year's divinities, or toshigami, and bring happiness. Families share foods like toshikoshi soba to ensure longevity and prosperity and go off to make an offering to divinities to let them know their wishes for the year to come. This fits the criteria of family and community-centered holidays in December in which gifts are given to children. Hope for a better future also fits the winter solstice dimensions.

Chinese New Year: The Chinese New Year is traditionally celebrated in late January or early February. Lasting two weeks, it is a time of fun and festivities for young and old alike. People may give others gifts, often money in red envelopes. Red is considered a lucky number in China and is thought to bring happiness, beauty, vitality, good luck, success, and good fortune. There are fireworks, lights, decorations, and community members may join together to put on performances, such as dragon dances. While it is not exactly at the time of the winter solstice, it is determined by the Chinese lunar calendar. Its zodiac represents twelve animals to correspond to a given year. The end of the two-week period results in the Lantern Festival and many lights of different types (Quinn 2019).

Las Posadas: This holiday starts the Christmas season for people in Mexico, and many other Spanish-speaking countries. It is celebrated for nine days during which reenactments of Mary and Joseph's trip into Bethlehem take place. Costumes, food and treats, and star-shaped piñatas are part of the celebration. Each night a different quality is focused upon when families get together, including humility, strength, detachment, charity, trust, justice, purity, joy, and generosity. Afterward, people enjoy festive foods such as tamales, poche or atole. Children may then break candy and toy-filled pinatas (Barbetz 2019).

Advent, Christmas and Epiphany date selection

With so many festivals occurring about the same time, it would have been difficult for leaders of a new religious ideology to dissuade people from their desire to celebrate these customary and cherished festivals. The creation of Advent and Epiphany were alleged to be a political maneuver to co-opt members of different religions into emerging Christianity. In 567 the Council of Tours declared the days that fell between December 25 and January 6 be considered a festal tide. The January 6 date became known as Epiphany and was considered to be the end of the holiday season. King Alfred the Great of England in the ninth century made it law that his subjects observe the twelve days between December 25 and January 6, and King Haakon the Good of Norway followed suit. Work, legal proceedings, and excessively boisterous behavior were forbidden during this time when people were expected to sing, feast, drink, make merry, tell stories, and simply have fun. In the 1300s King Richard II of England organized a Christmas jousting tournament that drew knights from all over Europe and was a cause of much enjoyment by the citizens.

The word "epiphany" is thought to originate from the Greek word epiphaneia, which means appearance, to manifest or show something previously unseen. Epiphany has been referred to as Theopahia, playing on the Greek word, theophaneia, which means the appearance of a god, and the Feast of Lights, or a time of spiritual illumination which marked the end of the holiday season. But there are also numerous other legends about Epiphany that do not seem associated with Jesus of Christianity at all. January 6 was thought to be the birthday of Egyptian god Osiris or the birth of the god Aeon, whose mother Kore was alleged to have been a virgin. The winter solstice was thought to occur on January 6 in ancient Egypt, and a festival in honor of the god of the sun occurred there for years. Others believe that the winter solstice occurred on that day, according to the Egyptian calendar.

Around the 2nd century AD, the Christian church identified the January 6 date to commemorate a variety of different events, and over the next few centuries, Epiphany became celebrated by most Christian groups around the world. It slowly transformed to focus on the story of the Magi, and its tale was recanted in processions and plays, similar to processions and theatrical events shared in ancient festivals. The story contained elements common in ancient plays as well: the presence of a villain (King Herod), giving of gifts (gold, frankincense, and myrrh), music, noise, color, costumes, and revelry.

It is clear that midwinter and solstice festivals were common from many different cultural backgrounds. While Kalends, Saturnalia, Zagmuk, and the Birth of the Invincible Sun were celebrated by the masses for generations, the aspects that people liked about them became woven into the celebration of advent or the twelve days of Christmastime. Aspects of the drunken, sensual, singing, dancing, costuming, and revelry of the original festivals became sidelined. To this day there is a bifurcation in people's views about how this season of the year is to be celebrated – with color, music, song, drinking, and eating and merriment OR with sober days filled with pensive reflection, prayer, and self-sacrifice.

Importance of Trees

Hope for renewal is seen again and again in the winter festivals. Trees were often used in folk celebrations and faiths, and the evolution of the Christmas tree to be the decorated spot where gifts are left is an example of its cultural evolution. The most common story about the creation of a Christmas tree probably comes from the Nordic areas where greenery was a coveted resource. The winter solstice celebrations pointed to hope for spring and the growth of plants. In the eighth century, St. Boniface tried to persuade Druid peoples to abandon the worship of an oak tree thought to be the sacred oak of Odin. This Donar oak tree was the site of sacrifices, and it was cut down and replaced by a fir tree which was thought to be a sign of new life. It was decorated as signs of thankfulness and slowly became part of Christian customs in Germany, and later this tradition spread elsewhere.

But another version of the Christmas tree exists. It is thought that thousands of years before the birth of Jesus, Nimrod was associated with evergreen trees and gift-giver. According to ancient Babylonian legends, a woman named Semiramis (who is also known as the goddess Astarte, Asherah, Ashtoreth, Isis, Ishtar, and Easter) married her son, Nimrod. When he died, an evergreen tree sprang up overnight from a dead tree stump. Nimrod was thought to visit the tree and leave gifts there each year on the anniversary of his birth, December 25. Nimrod later became known as the god, Baal. Therefore, the celebration of December 25 is a day of acknowledging Nimrod's birthday.

Solstice Importance

The Winter Solstice has been the impetus around the world as a source of celebration, but the way most of these winter festivals are celebrated today seem to have less to do with their historical origins of the solstice and more to do with religious or cultural holidays. Scholars have observed that pieces of these worldwide festivals, customs, and rituals were incorporated into Christmas traditions over time. It is important to realize that the ancient and pagan festivities came first, and that contemporary understanding of Christmas is a result of the cooptation, transformation, and evolution of these folk festivals. Herbert Armstrong's classic work on "the plain truth about Christmas" (date) indicates that Christmas was not observed until about 300 AD and that the festival of Saturnalia (December 24) and Brumalia (December 25) and the Birth of the Invisible Sun (December 25) continued to be observed well into the fourth century.

December 25th was a celebration day among the sun-worshippers of Mithraism, who regarded it as "the birthday of the invincible sun." Tammuz, the Babylonian pagan sun deity, was honored during the solstice. Some religious scholars allege that the Christian cross symbol is actually the letter " t " the symbol for the pagan god tammuz, thus the cross itself is of pagan origin and date thousands of years before the birth of Jesus.

The methodical morphing of folk festivals into religious holiday traditions was strategic. So was making the winter solstice estimated date of around December 25 as the birth of the sun god, which transformed into the birth of the Son of God. The *New Catholic Encyclopedia* (1967) alleges that most scholars accept the hypothesis that the birth of Jesus was assigned to the winter solstice dates of either December 25 (Julian calendar) or January 6 (Egyptian calendar) because these were the days when the sun began its return to the northern sky. December 25 is also thought to be the birthday of the twins, Heru Sa Aset and Bast, who were the children of Aset, or Isis. It was thought that at the winter solstice she died, but she had been magically impregnated and the twins continued to grow in her until December 25. That day is special because it is a reminder of the transformation of the parents into a new form and being. The green tree is a symbol of the green-skinned Asar, God of fertility and vegetation. The colored lights are symbols of Aset, Goddess of magick, and divine light. Red, green, and white are the traditional candle colors of Bast (this was Her birthday alone for several thousand years of early Kemetic history), later being adapted to red for Aset (the color of the Mother's menstrual flow), green for Asar (the color of vegetation), and white for the Twins (the color of pure light).

In the 5th century, the Roman Catholic Church ordered that the birthdate of the Christ child should be observed on December 25, the day of the Roman feast of the sun god, Sol. Martin G. Collin's writing of *Syncretimas* indicates that there was not necessarily a known date for the birth of Jesus and that the evolution of Christmas has more to do with political determinism than biblical fact. Other dates for the birth of Jesus were advanced, such as March 25, April 19, November 17, or likely in late September or early October during the Feast of Tabernacles, but there is no evidence of any sort that supports any of these dates. It appears that coordinating the birth of the new leader of the Christian faith with the beloved folk festivals of the day was the impetus. In Riedel, Tracy and Moskwitz's The *Book of the Bible*, these authors allege that Roman emperor Aurelian selected December 25 for the winter solstice holiday in AD 274 and the early Christians adopted this day for their Christ-mass so that they would be less conspicuous in the observance of their holiday. The New Schaff-Hezog *Encyclopedia of Religious Knowledge*'s article on Christmas confirms the association between Brumalia, Saturnalia, and Christmas. It alleges that these festivals were too deeply entrenched in popular custom to be set aside because of Christian influence. They were so filled with merrymaking that even new converts to Christianity didn't want to leave these beloved festivals behind. Merging the festivals into a social context of the new religion of Christianity was palpable to both converts who didn't want to leave their old ways behind, and traditionalists who came to view the new faith as less of a threat if they could keep their old rituals and festivals. December 25th was thought to be the date of the winter pagan Brumalia festival in Rome. It was preceded by the Saturnalia festival that ran a week before, usually from December 17 to 24, which honored the winter solstice, or the day the sun begins its return to northern skies. The Saturnalia and Brumalia festivals were so popular that Emperor Constantine chose to incorporate their festivities into those of the Roman Catholic Church. Emperor Constantine was largely responsible for placing Christianity and paganism on equal footing. Similarly, the shift of making Sun-day the first day of the week occurred, giving honor to the importance of the sun; the decision to make this the designated day for holy worship within the Christian church was strategic and designed to win over the hearts and minds of the non-Christian community.

The importance of winter solstice celebrations in the creation of Christmas is thus worthy of close attention. They tended to share uniformity with the presence of revelry, lights, family and community sharing, desire for the increase of sunlight to come, and use of greenery to represent the coming of spring and times for growth and return of the sun. They coincide with the appearance of a benevolent figure like Santa, who are often figureheads in these celebrations. In many parts of the world, especially those most traditionally associated with the arrival of Santa and his reindeer, December is a time of darkness, cold, and hibernation. But through Santa and these festivals come light, warmth, and joy born out of merry-making, sharing, and caring. Instead of being depressed that there is so little light, the Winter Solstice points to the beauty of the darkness and the knowledge that even a glimmer of sunshine can inspire joy within us. It has been celebrated by people for thousands of years across the planet.

It is clear that the December 25 holiday is not a Christian one originally, but a universal celebration of the victory of light over darkness. There is a universal appreciation of the importance of merrymaking, feasting, and fellowship. The giving of gifts, the decorating with greens and lights as symbols to welcome spring, and the sharing of special, delicious foods seem to be universally embraced in these festivals and celebrations.

Ancient cultures shared celebrations and honored certain characters that had significance for them. Festivals like Saturanalia and figures like Odin were important and people appreciated what they contributed to their life. There was a strategic attempt by governmental and religious leaders to impose new norms and ideologies to get people to give up alignments to old customs and characters around the time of the rise of Christianity. It is important to note that the spread of Christianity had as much to do with the political conquering of peoples as it did the religious conversion. It was easier for leaders to control the masses by changing their minds and significant community events than it was for them to slaughter them. From his earliest days, Santa Claus was born out of ideological conflict – and the debate over him continues.

What I Concluded

I knew about a couple of these December winter festivals holidays, but I had no idea how many there were or that they were commonplace around the world and in different cultures. They were all designed to help people survive the challenges of winter and darkness. They gave people hope for spring and the return of the light. All these festivals shared common features, including feasting, revelry, drinking, decorating with greens and lights, parading, costumes and special clothes, singing, dancing, and theatrical performances in community-wide events. They all had an emphasis on taking time to enjoy life, family and friends. Gifting was encouraged in all of the festivals. Gifting was especially directed at a) children; b) the poor or needy; c) family, and d) friends and neighbors with whom one shared regular contact.

There is no record that the birth of Jesus occurred during the Winter Solstice season, but there are plenty of records that the find December has been filled with a variety of celebrations around the world. Linking Santa with the birth of Jesus isn't historically validated by fact. It is obvious that winter celebrations and the birth of Jesus are two entirely separate occurrences. The facts should diffuse the argument among people who believe that Santa is a vehicle of Christians to either convert or exclude children. The December 25 date was assigned by political and religious leaders to merge winter solstice festivals with the newcomer Christian ideology in order to garner public acceptance of their new regimes. The festivals occurred first; the focus from the birth of the sun god to the birth of the son of God is not accidental.

In my mind, the winter solstice and December holidays have all morphed together, almost indistinguishable from each other in the spirit, if not the rituals and details, to be a time of celebration and love. Having something that everyone in the community can bond around was the function of all these festivals. But over the years, Santa got connected with Christmas which got connected with Christianity, which ended up fragmenting the community instead of uniting it. Something went amiss, so I wanted to figure out why.

Washington Irving quote

Tis the season for kindling the fire of hospitality in the hall, the genial fire of charity in the heart

Washington Irving

Editorial, Gas Age-Record. 12.24.1921

Chapter 3

Historical Figures Morphed Into Santa Claus

The Dilemma

Is Santa Claus a Christian symbol or not? Instead of taking people's word for whether he was or whether he wasn't, I used my research skills to find out. And why does Santa Claus go by so many different names? There's Father Christmas, Kris Kringle, St. Nicholas, and a bunch of other things he's called. Are they one-in-the-same, or do they refer to different people, with different stories and different ideas, values, and traditions? Most people have been told that Santa Claus and St. Nicholas are one-and-the-same. This is the party-line, the most-regaled superficial story. But is that true?

And there is this theme that Santa evaluates who's "naughty or nice", who rewards good children and punishes bad ones. The Elf on the Shelf became a hot-seller for parents who used him as a ploy to tell children that they were always being spied upon. Moving the elf to different locations was designed to convey to children a modified version of George Orwell's (1977) character of Big Brother in his book, *1984*, where their behavior is under constant surveillance and if they don't act "appropriately" that they could get in trouble with the authorities (aka – parents or Santa himself).

I needed to get a better handle on who this guy known as Santa Claus was, where he came from, and what he was really like. So let me tell you what I found out.

What I Discovered

First, I wanted to know **where does Santa Claus come from**? The obvious answer that even young children have been socialized to announce is that Santa comes from the North Pole! Indeed, Santa is often assumed to come from the North Pole - but is it the North Pole at the very top point of the planet, North Pole, Alaska, or is he from North Pole, Idaho, North Pole, Oklahoma or North Pole, New York? There are a host of other cities that claim to be the official home of Santa Claus; there is a town named Santa Claus found in Indiana, another in Georgia, and even one in the Mohave Desert in Arizona. His home is reportedly located in Norway, Finland, Sweden, Greenland as well as Iceland. The town of Velikiy Ustjug in the Vologda region of Bulgaria is also proclaimed to be his permanent residence. A Swedish logistics firm calculated that Santa probably comes from Kyrgyzstan, in Eurasia, since that location would enable him to deliver the gifts to children everywhere in the shortest period of time. Santa is also thought to come from Turkey if one sticks with the Santa Claus-St. Nicholas story. There is a rumor that he also comes from Cyprus.

Just as there are multiple North Poles from whence Santa Claus could hail, there are also multiple characters associated with who we think Santa Claus is and what he looks like. St. Nicholas is often thought of as the main contributor to our perception of Santa Claus – but actually, he's not, which I will discuss in the next chapter. The real story about Santa Claus started long, long before St. Nicholas. He just happened to have a powerful and influential publicity agent – the church. In reality, there have been a host of characters worldwide throughout time that has combined and evolved into our understanding of Santa Claus.

The festivals that I discovered and told you about in the previous chapter were embedded with characters (real or mythical) who helped deliver gifts and messages about what was important. Historically, winter festivals and their accompanying expressions of joy, feasting, and decorations with tree branches were targets for co-optation by the church and state. So were key beloved figures of different cultures (Miles 1990). The Santa character as we know him today has a history that is entangled with a variety of other traditions and stories, as you will learn here.

The Santa character as we know him today has a history that is entwined with a variety of other cultures, traditions, and stories. He has gone by different names at different times and in different places. He has been known as King Frost, Pere Noel, Lord Snow, Odin, Thor, Wodin, Winterman, Father Winter, Kris Kringle, Sinter Klaas, Sintirklass, Christkindlein, Kerstman, Papai Noel, Viejo Pascuero, Lam Khoong-Khoong, Santy, Dun Che Lao Ren, Old Man Christmas, San Nicolás, Ded Moroz, Shakhta Babah, Colacho, Hoteiosho, Samichlaus, Weihnachtsmann, Christmas Man, and Father Christmas, and many others whose origins are far from being Christian. It appears that the notion of having a benevolent elder watching out for children and gifting them when they are good is a cultural universal.

Some of the most influential historical pre-St. Nicholas figures that have shaped the Santa Claus character include the following:

Thor: Thor was the god of the peasants and the common people (Grueber (2011). Thor was usually portrayed as an elderly man, jovial and friendly, of heavy build, with a long white beard. Greek gods often had natural elements they claimed and Thor's element was the fire, thus his color was red. Thunder was thought to be caused by the rolling of his chariot, for he alone among the gods never rode on horseback but drove in a chariot drawn by two white goats named Cracker and Gnasher. He fought the giants of ice and snow, and thus became the Yule-god. He was said to live in the "Northland" where he had his palace nestled among icebergs. He was considered a cheerful and friendly god, never harming the humans but rather helping and protecting them. The fireplace in every home was especially sacred to him, and he was said to visit and protect them by coming down through the chimney into his element, the fire. At Yule, which is regarded as the pivotal or turning point in the calendar year as the earth moves from darkness to light, Thor would visit every home with a fireplace and bring gifts to children, who would put out their sabots, or wooden shoes, the night before. Good children would receive gifts of fruit, candy, and pieces of coal to burn in the fireplace. Coal was considered a good gift because it kept children warm and brought them light during harsh, cold, dark winters.

Thor was an elderly man, jovial and friendly, of heavy build, with a long white beard, as is the traditional image of Santa Claus. It is interesting to note that in later years, Santa would be referred to as Christ of the Wheel, with the wheel being a pagan term for the calendar year. Thor lived amongst icebergs, and Santa at the North Pole where it has ice and snow. Thor dressed in red, and Santa dressed in red. Thor flew through the air on a chariot pulled by named goats while Santa flies through the sky in a sleigh pulled by reindeer. Thor arrives down the chimney, and so does Santa. Thor and Santa brought children gifts, including candy; Thor put gifts in children's shoes, Santa in their stockings. Thus these are remarkable similarities, are they not?

Odin and Wodan: Santa Claus is also associated with the gods Odin and Wodan. By 800 AD the Vikings had traveled extensively around the world, bringing with them their beliefs in the Northern deities and nature Elementals. The Vikings had traveled extensively around the world and merged different cultural notions together into their understanding of the physical and supernatural world. Their main god was Odin, who came to earth dressed in a hooded cloak to sit and listen to his people and see if they were contented or not. Odin had a genial personality and had the ability to cure diseases and predict the future. He allegedly brought with him a large satchel full of all kinds of things that would delight both the needy and the worthy.

Odin was portrayed as a Sage with a long flowing white beard and hair who would fly through the skies on his eight-legged white horse, Sleipnir. It was common for children to leave their boots outside their house filled with carrots, hay, or sugar for Sleipnir in hopes that Odin would reward their kindness and good deeds.

Odin is often referred to as Wodin or Wodan (for which Wednesday or Wodan's day is named). He was the god of wisdom and magic and his name means "the inspired one". He could travel to other worlds to gather more insight while his two black ravens Huginn (Thought) and Muninn (Memory) kept him informed about the news in the world. It is likely that Huginn and Muninn influenced the creation of Santa's elves, and may have contributed to Santa's ability to know what children wanted for Christmas.

Odin is often portrayed as an energized or enlightened being who was beloved and had a large following of friends. He trained warriors for the battle in the underworld at Ragnarok, the Norse judgment day. His warriors may have painted their bodies black and fought in the middle of the night. Black is not thought to be evil or bad, as his ravens and warriors are sources of support and spiritual insight. The black-white themes represented in the Odin/Wodan tales illustrate the knowledge that good can be manifest differently. Odin could perform magick or miracles, but also paralyze his enemies with his sight, insight, or knowledge of the truth (Heij 2012).

In ancient Norse tradition, solstice events included an emphasis on celebration, the drinking of beer to honor the gods, and a time for family, friends, and neighbors to join together and feast with good food and drink. People who loved Odin and their winter celebrations didn't want to let them go when there were cultural changes occurring that could diminish his importance, such as the encroaching of Christianity. Whether it was strategic in terms of official power brokers, or informal influences in the minds of the masses, often beloved characters who people didn't want to lose had their essences transformed into new figures. This exportation of belovedness seems to be another cultural universal.

Similarities between Odin and Santa Claus are obvious. Odin and Santa are dressed in hooded cloaks or warm garb with long hats. They both sit and listen to people to see what they need in order to be content. Both have pleasant personalities and carry bags full of items to delight people to whom they visited. Both are wise, have long flowing white beards and fly through the sky pulled by chariots with steeds that have the number 8 in common. Odin had magic and could travel to other worlds, and Santa can travel all across the world in a single night. Odin has raven helpers, as Santa as elven helpers.

King Frost and Lord Snow: A variety of stories exist that explain why Santa exists and most of these explanations have nothing to do with religion, especially Christianity. For instance, by 600 AD when the Saxons had invaded and settled Britain, they brought along their celebration of spirits who were thought to influence the weather, such as King Frost and Lord Snow. They were beloved. Back in their day, it was customary for actors to dress up in costumes that represented those weather conditions. King Frost and Lord Snow dressed in warm, furry cloaks and had a sense of majesty about them. Often pointed caps and capes were worn that were draped with seasonal flowers such as Holly or Ivy. By encouraging these 'spirits' to join in the Saxton's feasts, where there was extensive eating, drinking, and merry-making, it was hoped that the harsh weather would be kinder to them. These costumes, decorations, and merry-making were merged into the common people's understanding of Santa Claus.

Father Winter and Father Christmas: The European figures of Father Winter and Father Christmas have been incorporated into our understanding of what Santa Claus does and what he looks like. Father Winter supposedly came down from the northern mountains with the snows, dressed in furs and skins, heralding winter. This character was well known in Scandinavia, where the Laps believed that when he herded the reindeer down to lower pastures it was a sign that the winter snows were coming. Some reindeer ran so fast down the mountains it seemed they were flying. There are legends that allege flying reindeer are actually manifestations of the Greek god, Hermes, the messenger.

Father Christmas is related to Father Winter, who was a key figure in Winter Solstice celebrations and is related to the Roman and Greek gods. It is documented that by 600 AD, the Saxons had invaded and settled Britain and brought with them their celebration of spirits who bring the weather, including King Frost and Lord Snow. It was customary for adult actors to dress up in costumes that represented particular weather conditions. Often, they wore pointed caps and cloaks/capes. They could be draped in seasonal flowers like ivy. By encouraging these 'spirits' to join in the Saxton's feasts where there were extensive eating and drinking, it was hoped that harsh winter weather would be kinder to them.

There is a close analogy between Father Winter, Father Christmas, and Santa. Father Winter supposedly came down from the north mountains with the snows, dressed in furs and skins, with his reindeer. Like Thor, Father Winter's element was fire and he too entered homes through the fireplace. Laps had dome-shaped homes with one opening, which was both door and smoke hole. Thus it would be logical that Father Winter, like Thor or Santa, would enter houses through the chimney. All three shared the attribute of caring for others and were thought to be benevolent protectors of the people and a lover of children.

Agios Vasilis: Agios Vasilis is the Greek Santa Claus. He was born in the town of Pontus in 330 AD to wealthy parents who had ten children. His grandfather was reported to be executed during days of the Christian persecution. Agios moved to Athens, and eventually traveled around the area to Egypt, Mesopotamia, Syria, and Palestine and eventually settled in Caesarea where he taught law. The story goes that he met Eustathius of Sebaste, who was a bishop and ascetic who mentored Agios to turn towards God. He and one of his brothers founded a monastery near Annesi which other members of his family and members of the community joined. Over time he was elected to be a bishop and focused on helping people who were poor, sick, or suffering in some way by giving away his family inheritance and creating a soup kitchen during a time of famine so the hungry would have something to eat.

Beyond the generosity aspect, he was reportedly little like the Santa Claus that he has become called. He was tall and thin, he had a black beard and black eyes that were thought to penetrate people's souls. His reputation is one of not being jolly and amicable; rather he was regarded as having a hot temper and being imperious. Legend holds that Agios met a powerful prefect who ordered the people in the community to give him all of their money and treasures. Agios supposedly told the prefect that the people were poor and did not have treasures to give, which made him so angry he threatened to kill Agios. The community was so worried that they ran to their homes and brought forth all their wealth to save Agios. In what is seen as a miracle, St. Mercourios emerged with an army which forced the greedy prefect to withdraw. The grateful Agois sought to return the treasure but did not know who gave what, so he had hundreds of cakes baked, and into each, he put a gold coin, and then each person in the community could share the wealth. This led to a custom of baking a cake in his name at New Year feasts, with a coin baked inside.

How exactly he became known as the Greek Santa Claus is unclear. What seems to be known is that his giving practical aid to the poor was considered a gift, and legends from different groups of people morphed into him being regarded as the Orthodox church's gift-giver. He died on January 1, 379 and this has become celebrated as his feast day. His feast day became regarded as a time to give charity (hence gifts) to others. Families join together for meals that include a sweet bread named after him (Vassilopita). After the children go to bed, the custom is for mothers to put under the Christmas tree a piece of vasilopitta and a glass of wine for Santa. This is done because he would arrive at the home exhausted and consume the cake and drink the wine, after which he places presents for the children of the family under the tree. Children awake early in the morning and cut Santa's cake to find out who gets the piece with the coin in it, after which they open Santa's presents.

Olentzero: All Santa figures have undergone a transformation, and Olentzero, of the Basque region of Europe, is no exception. Stories about him hail back at least to the 16th century in the forests of the Pyrenees near the village of Leska. Olentzero was one of the tribes of jentilak, or giants, who lived there. He was reported to be an irritable, thick glutton who ate large amounts of meat that he washed down with strong alcohol. He became a famous figure in local lore, but his dark side was revamped to make him more civilized and loveable and to maneuver pagan beliefs towards Christianity.

The new version of Olentzero was that he was abandoned in the woods. Little goblins, called Prakagorri, or "red-pants," who helped a blond, long-haired fairy, found him. Two versions of the story exist, one that the fairy raised him and the other was that she delivered him to a childless couple to raise as their own son. He became a strong charcoal maker who carved wooden animals, toys, and dolls. He grew into a happy adult and when his parents passed away, he was lonely and thought that other children may be lonely too, so he decided to spend his life helping children, especially those who had no parents. He carried the toys he made in a big bag and give them to local children when he went into the village. Legend has it that during one visit he saw a house afire and he dashed into it to save the children inside. The burning house collapsed upon him but the fairy flew in to save him, saying that he should not die, rather, he should live forever as the maker of toys for all the children in the country that he should deliver on December 24. He arrives not wearing red like Santa, but in peasant farmer attire of dark pants tucked into knee socks, a dark shirt, black hat and wears a beret (Compoy 2016; Nabasque 2013).

Let's take a breath for a minute to recall the common themes between these characters. They were older, male, often had beards, may travel in chariots or sleighs, had animals like deer, horses, or goats transport them, and they could travel through the sky, reinforcing their god-like status. They were wise. They listened to what people needed and tried to help them out. They also liked to have fun, and enjoyment and community benefit seemed to live in harmonious balance with each other. It was common for them to bring gifts and they carried presents sometimes in bags. They appreciated getting a snack when they arrived to deliver gifts, and their animals did as well. There was a fondness for the color red, and a preoccupation with fire in some way, either to bring light or warmth. Arrivals coming down chimneys or leaving gifts by the fireplace were typical. Santa was obviously constructed by merging many different characters and stories.

Santa's Entourage: Those who are "Nice"

All around the world, it seemed like the early Santa figures had helpers. A common assumption is that Santa is able to deliver toys to children throughout the world because he is helped by elves. The theme that Santa does not work alone is important. We see through viewing a variety of mythological and historic Santa contributors that seldom were they solitary beings. As the Beatles chimed, Santa and his predecessors "got by with a little help from his friends". These helpers have their own traditions and have contributed to contemporary perceptions of Santa Claus. These "subordinate Clauses" are present in tales to help Santa Claus to do his work. The most common ones are elves, Christkindl, or the controversial Zwarte Piet.

Elves. The most common companions are elves. The nisse, nisser, tomte, and Yule Lads hail from Scandinavia and Iceland and are the prototype for elves. Their names may be used interchangeably; they are not the same but they contribute to the Santa character as he is known today. The nisser are elves or gnomes who existed long before the birth of Christ. According to Danish lore, the nisse is a small mythical, little old gentleman dressed in red and grey. He is hundreds of years old, as his long white beard shows. Danish legend often shows him carrying a wooden spoon. The nisse likes to play tricks, and this behavior has been incorporated into traditional Santa giving surprises or unexpected gifts for children. Nisse are traditionally considered to be small.

The Julenisse, or Yule nisse, is an older, adult-sized man with a white beard. He has a good nature, wears a red suit and hat, and carries a sack of toys on his back that he delivers to children in their homes on Christmas Eve. People today continue to dress up as Julenisse and visit children. It is custom for him to ask, "Are there any good children here?" before he hands out gifts. He does not come down the chimney in the middle of the night, but comes in through the door and looks the children directly in the eye as he speaks with them.

Nisse is derived from the name Nils which is the Scandinavian form of Nicholas. There are several types of nissers in Norway. The most well-known is the Fjøsnisse who take care of the animals on the farms where they live. The Fjøsnisse are very short, usually bearded, and wear wool clothes and a red knitted hat. They often play tricks on people. The Norwegian/Danish nisse and the Swedish Tomte are similar; they are all mischievous little sprites that tend to work alone for the protection and welfare of the home and farm. The word "tomte" means "homestead man", derived from the word tomt, which means homestead or building land. The tomtar and nisse do not expect gifts for themselves; they demand only respect and trust of those with whom they visit, and a simple snack, such as a bowl of julegrøt (Christmas porridge) with butter on Christmas Eve. In Sweden the Jultomte arrives at children's homes to deliver gifts by a sleigh pulled by his Christmas goat. The leader may be accompanied by helpers; the Jolasveinar are referred to as the 13 Yule Men (or elves) and have been known to be pranksters. Today the head nisse is sometimes referred to as Santa Klaus.

There are other elfin references that exist. For instance, the Menehune are dwarf or elfin like figures that come not from the North Pole but Hawaii. According to their folklore, the menehune, like elves, were a small race of nocturnal people. They tended to keep to themselves, were excellent craftspeople, they could work at fantastic speeds, tended to be stealth. They were helpful but had a tendency to appreciate merriment and mischief. Rumor holds that they were once prevalent in Hawaii but disappeared in the 1800s about the same time that North Pole elf legends developed. The notion that Hawaii was home to elves is another example of how widespread Santa-type figures can be found.

Christkindl. Sometimes it wasn't elves but or angels who accompanied Santa Claus but humans, dwarves, or animals. For instance, in some European and Latin American countries gifts are brought by Christkind or Christkindl, which is a sprite-like child, usually depicted with angel wings and blonde hair. There are variations to the Christkind character, with some having him/her coming with St. Nicholas to be his helper to deliver gifts. Other versions have Christkind, not Santa, bringing presents to children. Christkind was reportedly promulgated by the Protestant reformer, Martin Luther, to promote Jesus, or Christ, as the one who delivers all gifts to children. This figure was evidently created to encourage a religious view of the holiday and make children link Christmas with Christkind. Christkind, like Santa, doesn't let children see him/her. In some traditions, Christkind lets children know that he/she has arrived by the ringing of a bell. Sometimes parents ring the bell or tell children that they heard one ring, after which they hurry off to see if presents were delivered. While I can find no official link to this, I can't help but wonder if this bell depiction was the motivation for the bell the child finds in his pocket on Christmas morning in the book, *The Polar Express*.

Black Pete, or Zwarte Piet, was a companion of Sinterklaas who was seen as positive but in recent years has become very controversial. There are mixed accounts of Black Pete's origin. One story holds that Odin relied upon black ravens, Huginn and Muninn, to perch at the chimneys of children's homes to listen to learn if the children were acting good or bad. It morphed into an account that Pete helped Santa by going down the chimney to listen to children and report back to him about whether they were naughty or nice. By doing so, his skin became dark because he became covered with soot. Some versions hold that Sinterklaas was strict and as a religious figure, very stern, but that Zwarte Piet was a beloved companion because he was joyful, laughed, talked with children, wore brightly colored Moorish clothes with puffy shirt sleeves, and was the one who actually handed out gifts to the children. Stories indicate that Zwarte Piet was actually more well-liked and popular than Sinterklaas.

Other variations of Black Pete emerged, helpers such as a Hoofd Piet, or Head Piet, who carries the book of Sinterklaas, a Rijm Piet, or Rhyme Piet, who may read Sinterklaasgedicht poems of a teasing nature to amuse both children and adults during their arrival. Black Pete is curiously similar to Haji Firuz, who is the herald of Nowruz, the Persian new year, and has a black face that is covered in soot, wearing bright red clothes and a hat, perhaps as a manifestation of an ancient Zoroastrian fire-keeper. He arrives with a Santa Claus figure known as Amoo Nowruz, who is an elderly man with a white beard who brings gifts to children. Haji Firuz sings and makes merry for people on this "one day a year" celebration. Pete was often the one who gave children gifts, according to some stories. These associations were not necessarily negative and were regarded as some to be more positive than the strictness of Sinterklaas.

Historically, one version of his story indicates that Zwarte Piet was once a slave who became freed by St.

Nicholas and he chose to be his lifelong friend and companion as a result. Another is that Black Pete was a slave but when he was liberated he was required to be the servant for Sinterklass. Another is that he was a fire-scorched demon or a sort of bogeyman. An 1850 book by Jan Schenkman is thought to have contributed significantly to the image of Zwarte Piet being a servant and a reinforcement for Colonial racist oppression. At one point Black Pete was seen to be the one who punished bad children, whipped them, or even put them into burlap bags to whisk them away because they were acting in evil ways. Over time Pete was stereotyped to act stupid, dumb, doing silly things, and have no autonomy as he had to do whatever Sinterklaas demanded. There are other variations that held that Black Pete delivered punishments to naughty children while Sinterklaas rewarded nice ones. The stories, hence, are all over the board.[1]

Black Pete has become commonly a part of festivities in the Netherlands, where people dress up like him and act joyfully. While Santa Claus traditionally is viewed to come from the North Pole by reindeer in the US, in the Netherlands, Sinterklaas rides a white horse and comes from Spain on a boat with his helper, Black Pete, or a group of black servants called the Zwarte Pieten. This is an occasion where families flock to the wharf to watch the mayor celebrate their arrival. Their arrival became such a big deal that their arrival was televised. The custom holds that Sinterklaas will visit all the houses by traveling over the roofs on his horse; children leave carrots and hay for the horse in their shoes. Black Pete is thought to be the one who enters their homes through the chimney to exchange gifts for the carrots.

Studies vary: some have found that he is regarded by many locals to be an important traditional character who conveys joy, kindness, altruism, and therefore should be maintained. However, Black Pete has become identified by others as a racist, oppressed character of servitude who is negatively stereotyped and is not a positive role-model for children. While people can dress up like Santa without controversy, dressing up like Black Pete has become regarded as racist behavior, especially by white-skinned people who wear black make-up on their faces. Assertions that he is a racist figure can be seen in the presence of people today wearing black-face make-up. The trend is that Black Pete should go. But like the transformation of Santa Claus, the transformation of Zwarte Piet is not unanimous or readily embraced.

There is concern that children will subconsciously associate negative attributes with black people, even though it is often white people today who are the ones dressing in black-face as they pretend to be Zwarte Piets. The Global African Congress filed a petition in 2003 to the Dutch Parliament calling for the abolishment of Black Pete that was rejected. The Black Pete character has triggered international outrage and debate on racism and there was even a court case in the Netherlands to address it. In a detailed article on Black Pete in the *International Journal on Human Rights*, Lemmens (2017), a professor of human rights law at the University of Leuven in Belgium, argues that

> "There is no consensus on the appearance and the origins of Zwarte Piet, the tradition has changed over time and there seems to be geographical differences between the various European regions. As a consequence, multiple readings and interpretations of the Zwarte Piet figure are possible. Both the opponents of Zwarte Piet and his defenders have good ar-

guments to back their interpretation of the tradition. Under these circumstances, it is not for the law to decide which interpretation should prevail: *in dubio, pro libertate*. A solution can only be found through societal debate".

Izalina Tavares (2004), a fellow a Humanity in Action, argues that the Sinterklaas-Black Pete relationship is one based in white supremacy and nurtures age-old Western stereotypes of black people's inferiority. Tavares argues that "what needs to be addressed is not whether this tradition is racist but why the majority of Dutch society is denying the truth that it is."

The debate over both sides of the Black Pete issue continues, as shown in the comments on blogs like Rachel's Ruminations (2020). Black Pete, like Santa Claus himself, was never a real person. He too is a product of social construction. While once he was seen as a beloved "hero", he is now regarded as a symbol of oppression and racism. As Lemmens points out, there is no clear historical or legal position for what Black Pete was/is – social debate determines how he is regarded, just as for Santa Claus. He, like Santa, has come to symbolically represent certain characteristics that have changed across time. One thing is for sure – just as Santa Claus is undergoing a social transformation, so is Black Pete.

Santa's Entourage: Those who are "Naughty"

Whether children are naughty or nice is a theme often repeated in the traditional Santa Claus story. The song Santa Claus Is Coming To Town lyrics assert "he knows if you've been bad or good so be good for goodness sake".

There is the notion that good children get presents and bad children don't. Getting coal instead of toys in your stocking is regarded as a sign of punishment for being bad, but curiously, coal was seen as a good present long ago because it helped people to stay warm in cold climates. This naughty-nice thing is troublesome for me. Historically, Santa figures were designed to be kind to every child. But somewhere along the line, he was transformed to convey authoritarianism, with the "you better do what I say or else" message.

I worry tremendously about what the "getting-gifts-means-you're-good" and the "if-you're-naughty-you-won't-get-presents" message means to poor children or children who do not live in homes where Santa comes. As a child, I remember trying to be good, but being a child is hard and sometimes I made mistakes no matter how good we try to be. I was really scared by being threatened by adults to "be nice" or else there may be Hell to pay, and Santa wouldn't come. So I was intrigued by the host of Santa's "helpers" who existed to keep naughty children in line.

Pelznickel/Belsnckle: Earlier it was mentioned how Christkindlein was seen to be a positive gift-giver, but evidently didn't come alone. He/she reportedly had a dwarf-like helper known as "Pelznickel" or "Belsnickle", meaning "Nicholas with furs". The German words pelzen/belzen means to wallop, and the word nickel is a variation of the name Nicholas. Christkindlein quietly visited while everyone was asleep but Pelznickel was visible. Together they morphed St. Nicholas with the emerging figure of Santa Claus.

Originally Pelznickel appeared as a frightening character who wore furs and tattered clothes who would show up at children's homes at dark a week or so before Santa's arrival. He carried a switch to beat bad children. Pelznickel was sometimes referred to as the Christmas woman, as the character's face was often hidden but wore female clothes (no doubt a disparaging message about the role of women). She would supposedly act "with masculine force and action" as she threw gifts of nuts and fruits onto the floor out of a sack slung around her shoulders, while she whipped children scrambling to get them with a hazel switch (Brown 1896). Petznickel was described as being a frightening devil-like character. Over time he/she came to be seen as an adult wearing furs and fake whisker disguises to a short human or tall elf or totem who wasn't terribly intimidating. **Pelznickel would entertain children with a sometimes scary performance.** Over time Pelznickle's bundle of switches morphed into a bag of toys and gifts.

Krampus: Krampus is a mythical figure thought to accompany St. Nicholas when he visits the home of children. The origins of Krampus are varied. One is that Krampus was the son of Hel, in Norse mythology, who resided over Hell, the land of the dead.[2] He is thought to drag bad children into the realm of the underworld. A predominant version is that as St. Nicholas triumphed over evil, and the devil (or in this case, the devil's son) was made into his slave on the eve of his feast day. Krampus was thus seen as a variation of the devil. Another version was that he was reportedly shackled to St. Nicholas and forced to do his bidding. While St. Nicholas is thought to reward good children, Krampus arrives wearing rusty chains and bells to warn naughty children that they better be good, and if they're not he will punish them. His appearance is of a black or brown hairy creature with cloven hoofs, goat type horns, and a long forked tongue. Krampus may carry birch switches to swat bad children. In an extreme case, Krampus is thought to take a naughty child and stuff him or her into a sack to devour it for Christmas dinner, throw them into the river to drown, or transport them to the underworld.

Commonly found in Austria, Bavaria, Hungary, Croatia, Slovenia, and other Alpine area countries, historically, Krampus was to show up at children's homes on Dec. 5, known as Krampusnacht or Krampus Night. The following day, Dec. 6, is St. Nicholas Day or Nikolaustag. Sometimes St. Nicholas and Krampus visit children together to talk together with each child directly and ask them questions that would help each child to examine his or her conscience.

Krampus has taken on popularity in recent years. There are more movies or shows starring Krampus, sales of Krampus chocolates, figurines, greeting cards, comic books and collectible horns. There are Krampus parties, festivals, and events where people who tend to drink heavily and dress like devils in a Karmpus Run, or Krampuslauf. Townspeople chase the "devils" through the streets in an event that seems fun for all. In northern Italy, there is an annual December Krampus festival where just before the sun sets, Krampus comes out of a cave to chase children with whips, called ruten. Bundles of birch bark ruten are sold in many stores. There are Krampus parades in Europe. Some Krampus festivals rival Mardis Gras in the US. Thus Krampus, like Santa, has been commercialized to be both big business and big fun throughout the globe.

Pre Foucettard: A similar Krampus character, travels with St. Nicholas during St. Nicholas's feast day of December 6. While Nicholas delivers gifts to good children in the eastern parts of France, Pre Foucettard, or the "whipping father" delivers lumps of coal or ruthlessly flogs naughty children who have misbehaved His origin hails back to at least 1150 AD, when supposedly he captured three boys, drugged them, slit their throats, cut them into pieces and put them into a stewpot. St. Nicholas came and saved them and made Pre Foucettard his servant to repay for his crimes. He is depicted as a dark-faced man with a sinister appearance, fangs, frowny-angry face, scraggly unkempt hair, a long beard, and wearing dark (black or brown) clothes. He carries a whip, large stick, or bundle of switches. Sometimes he is portrayed wearing a wicker basket on his back so he can place bad children in it and carry them away. His face may have been dark from going down chimneys with St. Nicholas, although some versions liken him to be similar to Zwarte Piet.

Over time his character changed as he assumed a slightly different presentation. During the 1930s Le Père Fouettard first appeared in the United States under the names of Father Flog or Spanky. Although almost identical to the original French personification, Father Flog had nothing to do with Christmas and also had a female accomplice named Mother Flog. The two doled out specific punishments for specific childhood crimes, such as cutting out children's tongue for lying. It is rumored that the man on the cover of Led Zeppelin IV is Le Père Fouettard, but I cannot say that with certainty.

Knecht Rupnecht originally represented an archetypal manservant who had no connection with Christmastime (Tille 1899), but now he has been transformed to be a helper-companion of St. Nicholas. The earliest accounts of him occur during the 17th century (Siefker 1997). He has been described as a farmhand, a foundling, a household sprite, a devil, St. Rupert, and Ru Clas, or Rough Nicholas. He also goes by the name of Hans Muff. His appearance is male with a long beard and he wears fur that may have soot or straw on them. He is thought to arrive on a white horse. He may be accompanied by faeries, elves, house-spirits, or men with blackened faces who are dressed as old women. He would visit the homes of children with St. Nicholas and good children, or those who could pray, would receive apples, nuts, and gingerbread while those who could not gift him and demonstrate their goodness may be beaten or given 'gifts' such as lumps of coal, sticks, switches or stones.

Others. In Czechoslovakia an angel and a demon, called a Cert, may accompany St. Nicholas to deliver gifts on Dec. 6. The cert wears black clothing, carries a whip and chain, and frightens children with a reminder to be good or be punished. This figure is similar to other dark companions of St. Nicholas. These dark companion figures emerged over different times and places to instill in children the notion that Santa Claus was not always a jolly, all-giving and all-forgiving character. If they were not good, there may be repercussions.

Cypriots share another commonality with Santa, that of having a form of elves show up. They are tricksters, mischievous and sometimes dangerous sprites called "Kalikantzari" or Calicantzari. They prey upon people during the twelve days of Christmas, from Christmas Eve to

Epiphany. Unlike Krampus or Le Père Fouettard, these Cyprus elves are more mischievous than mean.

What I Concluded

I never realized how many of Santa Claus's particular behaviors, appearances, and arrival schemes have been based on different figures from around the world and across time. His altruistic visits through chimneys, when he brings items to delight, come from many different people and traditions. His appearance of being elderly, bearded, and wearing red and furs does as well. Similarly, his being wise, knowing what people needed and wanted was a cultural universal, as was an emphasis on kindness, joy, and understanding that there were consequences for our behavior. Arriving via flying chariots in the sky pulled by animals to bring gifts in portable sacks or packs to children was something found in many traditional stories. The use of gifts to encourage appropriate social behavior, especially among children, became seen as a way to ensure the transmittal of valued social norms.

The notion that bad things could happen to misbehaving children, from being punished, snatched, whipped, or receiving lumps of coal occurred as a juxtaposition to receiving sweets, toys, and enjoyable trinkets. There was a dichotomous, yin and yang quality of goodness and badness constructed; Santa figures were often seen as nice, wise, and kind; but they may be accompanied by figures who harsh. The Santa figure was portrayed in more heavenly or kingly ways, while the messenger of punishment for ill behavior was mean, ugly, frightening demons.

Santa's appearance of being male fit the power position of the day; men were in charge of organized religious and political institutions. Santa was universally portrayed as being elderly, with a long white beard, giving credence to the importance of the aged leaders. Wearing red had symbolic importance across cultures. Wearing of furs and stately hats were commonplace and were important for warmth but also for demarcating position. Being able to fly in the sky above homes and the heads of commoners was a consistent theme. There was also a not-so-subtle common theme of ugly women being mean to children.

By this time in my research, I concluded that a convincing argument has been made for Santa not being a singular real person. His arrival on December 24 is actually associated with a variety of ancient festivals. His history began long before Christianity was around. The fact that people have assumed that St. Nicholas was the prototype for Santa Claus is simply a major stretch of one's imagination, as shown in the next chapter.

Notes:

1. You may find this article to be of interest on Black Pete's history: Jeroen Rodenberg & Pieter Wagenaar (2016) Essentializing 'Black Pete': competing narratives surrounding the Sinterklaas tradition in the Netherlands, International Journal of Heritage Studies, 22:9, 716-728, DOI: 10.1080/13527258.2016.1193039

2. For more information of Krampus, you may want to go to these websites: https://www.nationalgeographic.com/news/2018/12/131217-krampus-christmas-santa-devil/ Or https://blog.vkngjewelry.com/hel-norse-goddess/

Hamilton Wright Mabie quote

Blessed is the season
Which engages the whole world
In a conspiracy of love.

Hamilton Wright Mabie

Project Gutenberg

Chapter 4

St. Nicholas & the Religious Co-optation of Santa Claus

The Dilemma

Like many people, I learned that Santa Claus originated from a monk named St. Nicholas, and it is the legend that most people associate with the creation of Santa Claus. Except that's not correct. There is a link, but from a chronological and historical point of view, the origins and essence of Santa Claus were long in place before St. Nicholas came along. Therefore, assuming that St. Nicholas = Santa Claus is inaccurate, wrong if you are going to factually understand Santa's origin.

What I Discovered

As shown in previous chapters, there were a variety of winter festivals around the world that communities enjoyed. What I learned is that as the Christian church was emerging, it needed to gain members in order to survive and become seen as a dominant religion. It tried to gain foot-hold in its recruitment and conversion of members but people were not eager to join. It seems like people's community-based nature celebrations were enjoyable and requirements to be a member of this new faith were strict and foreign. People were not eager to give up their joyful community festivals to join a more solitary, rule-driven, less fun group. Leaders of the church felt they had to do something to win over the hearts and minds of potential members.

The church swooped in and co-opted the pagan and winter solstice festivals and tried to embed Christian themes into them. Beloved figures around the world associated with festivals or sharing altruism and joy were morphed into new personas in order to propel the growth of Christianity around the world. Essentially, church leaders took a little bit of this and a little bit of that from festivals and beloved figures and merged them together into the construction of a new character, Santa Claus, and a new festival, Christmas. These festivals and figures originally had nothing to do with the church. They were anything but Christian. But the Christian church saw the great benefit to tagging itself to the original Santa figures and festivals. Over time, the church's ability to transform winter festivals into Christmas and altruistic figures into Santa Claus made people forget their pagan and international origins. This means that there was originally no direct association between the Santa or winter festivals and the social construction of Christmas as we know it. This is a huge and important piece of information to synthesize as we grapple with who Santa originally was and how the Santa Claus story was created.

So how did a stern, religious bishop named Nikolaos get morphed into a joyful, gift-giving symbol of Christmas? People are generally not consecrated into sainthood until at least five years after their death, whereupon Nikolaos, whose name means victor of the people, became known as St. Nicholas. Accounts of his early life were written after his death, but it appears that Nikolaos was born sometime around 280 A.D. in Patara, near Myra, in modern-day Turkey. His parents were devout Christians who raised their only child to practice faith through actions. His parents were quite wealthy and the child lived a comfortable lifestyle. But an epidemic, perhaps like COVID-19, set upon the land, and even their money could not protect them from dying of what is thought to have been the plague. As an orphan, the young Nikolaos grew up in a monastery which reinforced the faith taught to him by his parents. He became a priest at age 17 and dedicated his life to faithful action, giving away all the money he inherited from his parents as well as everything he owned. His generosity continued throughout his life. He had a fondness for helping a peculiar population of people - children, sailors, prostitutes, criminals, and the needy.

People within the community, as well as people within his church, were so touched by the young priest's kindness that Nikolaos was rewarded by being made the bishop of his home-town. As a bishop, Nikolaos wore the traditional bishop's hat, or miter, and a long flowing white robe covered by a red cape. He did not cut his facial hair and his beard became progressively long and grey as he aged. Bishop Nikolaos traveled the countryside helping others, giving gifts of money, and other presents that he carried in a sack slung over his back. As was his custom, Nikolaos chose to remain hidden while giving these gifts and he liked to keep his good deeds anonymous. Often he delivered his gifts while people slept.

One of the more famous stories of Nikolaos's generosity focuses on a poor man who had no money to take care of his three daughters. Bishops had the opportunity to know about the struggles of people, and Nikola0s allegedly dropped little bags of gold into stockings that the girls had left to dry by the fire. Because the golden balls resembled oranges, it has become a customary Christmas symbol for St. Nicholas to put oranges into the toe of children's stockings on Christmas Eve. There are other versions of why Nikolaos gave the family gold. One indicates that the money was for the daughters' dowry for their wedding days since otherwise, the father could never have otherwise afforded to marry them off. Other stories indicate the gold was to keep the girls from being sold into slavery, while another indicates the money was given to keep the girls from being forced into prostitution. A version of the story told is that while the poor family was away begging, Nikolaos threw a bag of gold through their window. He did this for two nights in a row. But on the third night, the father hid in order to see the secret benefactor. He caught Nikolaos in the act. When the father told Nikolaos that he had thought the money had been sent by God, not a human, Nikolaos replied that God had indeed sent him. This notion that people are vehicles to carry out God's work is woven throughout the St. Nicholas story. Whenever people received anonymous gifts, they would say that St. Nicholas had left them. His fame quickly spread to many lands.

Stories about St. Nicholas often focus on the protection of children. There was a young boy named Basilios, who supposedly was in the church when it was raided by pirates who stole Basilios as booty along with the church treasures. He was sold to an emir as a slave. Reportedly Nikolaos was able to miraculously whisk the boy out of his enslavement and return him home to the arms of his grateful parents. Another tale describes how three boys were murdered by an evil innkeeper who were then magically revived by St. Nicholas.

Nikolaos's religious up-bringing taught him that goodness was the right path to follow. But he reportedly had a less kind side that caused him trouble and even his benevolent actions sometimes led to his misery. He lived during the days of Roman Emperor Diocletian, who ruthlessly persecuted Christians. There are reports that he slapped the face of Arius, who he thought was a heretic, which led to him being temporarily defrocked and imprisoned. Under the emperor's rule he was exiled and imprisoned, along with countless other early Christians who outnumbered criminals in the prison during those days. Nikolaos defied Roman law and kept preaching Christianity and was arrested and tortured for disobeying laws and spent more than a decade in jail. Among his punishments, according to Saint Simeon's

10th-century account, were starvation and thirst, which resulted in his becoming quite thin and gaunt.

Over a decade later, around 312 AD, Constantine became the leader. Across the empire, bishops and priests returned to work and Bishop Nikolaos was released from jail. Reports indicate that he did not find this new world comfortable and he decided to take action to institute his version of religiosity in Myra, which was a seat of Artemis worshipers. Nikolaos reportedly prayed for vengeance (and maybe did more than just pray), and his prayers were answered with the falling of Artemis's temple. The priests who lived in Artemis's temple ran in tears to the bishop and appealed to his Christian mercy. They wanted their temple restored but Nikolaos was not to be moved. Prison had left him in no mood for compromise. "Go to Hell's fire," he is reported to said to have said, "which has been lit for you by the Devil" (Pope 2010). Thus St. Nicholas's fury against Artemis worshippers is an important but often unknown link to understanding Santa Claus and how he and his helpers are almost always portrayed as males while powerful women were phased out.

Religious scholars (Pope 2010) have observed that "the real St. Nicholas was nothing close to the St. Nick (Santa Claus) of the modern age. He was a thin curmudgeonly man with a zeal for the Lord that caused flairs of anger. Compromise was unknown to him. The slow transformation of him into "Jolly ole' St. Nicholas is a remarkable recasting of him centuries in the making." So the actual Bishop Nikolaos, who was later made into a saint, looked nothing like what we conceive Santa to look like today, except for the fact that he wore a long cape/robe, some red clothing, and a tall cap (that flopped down in contemporary pictures of Santa.

Msg. Pope explains that "Paintings show (St. Nicholas as) a thin man. He was spare of frame, flinty of eye, pugnacious of spirit. In the Middle Ages, he was known as a brawling saint. He had no particular sense of humor that we know of. He could be vengeful, wrathful, an embittered ex- con....No doubt, Saint Nick was a good man. A noble man. But a hard man."

He is thought to have died on December 6, 343, or 346 AD in Myra and was buried in his cathedral church, where a unique relic, called manna, formed in his grave. This liquid substance was said to have special healing powers, which fostered the continued growth of devotion to St. Nicholas. Many people came to his tomb to pay homage, but in the year 1087 sailors removed his bones from that tomb and buried them in a new crypt in Bari, Italy, where people even today make pilgrimages to ask for his help.

The anniversary of his death became a day of celebration, St. Nicholas Day. His feast day is celebrated on the anniversary of his death, December 6. This was traditionally considered a lucky day to make large purchases or to get married. While St. Nicholas's day is still celebrated by some people, there was a strategic move by the church to morph St. Nicholas's day with the winter solstice celebrations. This took years to accomplish, but resulted in St. Nicholas, aka Santa Claus, ushering in Christmas day with gifts. Over time, the legend of St. Nicholas and his gift-giving evolved into more of a social tradition than a religious one.

The secularization of St. Nicholas into Santa Claus came slowly, but methodically. The early Christian church didn't observe Christmas since it was associated with the observance of the feast days of pagan gods. The word Christmas, or "Cristes Maesse," or Christ's mass, does not appear in

English until 1038 and appears to be an attempt, for the church to co-opt the pagans who still preferred their naturalistic spirituality to that of the organized Christian religion. In 1057 AD Dom Ytherius refused to allow a musical rendition of St. Nicholas's life be performed in his French church, but the popularity of Nikolaos's "golden legend" forced him to later change his mind (Hakim 1996). In the year 1119 a monk wrote the first known history of St. Nicholas, and afterward, in commemoration of his kind acts, nuns in Belgium and France began leaving candy in the shoes of children on his December 6 Feast Day. In 1150 AD, Guace, a Norman French scribe to the royal household, wrote the life of St. Nicholas as metric poems for use as sermons and Hilarius wrote the first musical play about him in 1200. By the year 1400, there were over 500 songs and hymns written in honor of St. Nicholas.

St. Nicholas's name was modified after his sainthood to meet the language of the local communities who heard tales of his generosity. Over time his name was changed from "Saint" to "Santa," and from Nikolaos to Nicholas to Klaus which later became Claus. On his feast day, he may arrive with his sidekick, Krampus or Black Peter. Krampus was thought to frighten or punish children who were bad. St. Nicholas and Black Peter were thought to talk with each child directly, and in the conversation ask questions that would help each child to examine his or her conscience, which became a part of the Santa "naughty and nice" tradition. Haladewicz-Grzelak (2011) discovered how images of St. Nicholas changed over time, showcasing the development of a theme that included altruism. Many focused on addressing people's needs, especially those who were poor and children who were well-behaved.

To this day, in some households, the father of the family may dress up as St. Nicholas on the eve of his feast. Since St. Nicholas Day arrives on December 6, some families use its celebration as a way to set into motion Advent events that help children to prepare for the arrival of Christmas in a happy and thoughtful way. He has been portrayed to deliver particular messages, such as the importance of generosity and giving to others, to remember children, those who are alone, those in financial need, and those who may be ignored or looked down upon by others. St. Nicholas is used to deliver a message that our daily deeds can be a reflection of a higher way of being filled with goodness for all.

Ironically, after the Reformation, St. Nicholas became forgotten in most of the Protestant-faith countries of Europe except Holland. There he became known as Sinterklaas, a kindly wise old man with a white beard, wearing a white dress and red cloak riding in the skies and over the rooftops of houses on his white horse, accompanied little helpers. It takes little imagination to see the association between the name Sinterklaas and Santa Claus. The different variations of Santa and his helpers have morphed into our current understanding of what Santa is, what he looks like, and what he does (Heij 2012).

The name "Santa Claus" appears to have come from the Dutch "Sinter Klass" pronunciation of St. Nicholas. In Europe, Christkindlein, or the Christ child, was thought to accompany St. Nicholas on some of his gift-giving visits, or gifts came from Christkindlein. The word Christkindlein over time mutated into "Kriss Kringle", another name for the gift-bearer we have come to know as Santa. Thus, Santa Claus was originally a combination of two religious figures – St. Nicholas and Christkindlein, as well as a host of pagan influences. Just as the Christ child was thought to be loving and forgiving, these attributes became synonymous with Kris Kringle, St. Nicholas, or Santa Claus as well. Thus Nikolaos's name was changed from "Saint" to "Santa," and from Nikolaos to Nicholas to Klaus which later became Claus, or Sinterklass.

What appears to have happened is that over time St. Nicholas's image of an altruistic gift-giver became interwoven with stories from a variety of cultural, religious, and folk behaviors that came from all over the world. As pointed out earlier, St. Nicholas ended up being a gaunt, angry, embittered man who was very little like the Santa Claus figure that we usually envision today. We know that there was a merging of St. Nicholas with the images of other winter and benevolent characters. Until 1300 AD, St. Nicholas was described to have a short dark beard, as would be common for a Bishop in the eastern part of Europe doing those days. But over time his beard turned long and white, probably incorporating images of the noted figures of Odin, Thor, and Winterman.

By the time of the Renaissance, St. Nicholas had become the most popular saint in Europe. But religious tensions led to a concern about the devotion that should be given to saints. Yet even after the Protestant Reformation, when the veneration of saints began to be discouraged, St. Nicholas maintained a positive reputation, especially in Holland. By the 1500s people in England became less focused on St. Nicholas and favored another gift-giving figure known as Father Christmas. During that time there were more than 700 churches dedicated to St. Nicholas in Great Britain alone and in Britain, but the churches realized that parishioners were devoted to their traditional folk beliefs as well.

In order straddle the pagan and Christian worlds, each parish would employ a man from outside the parish to dress in a long hooded disguise to go to each home leaving a small gift and taking back to the priests any important news they had learned or the plight of the needy who needed help. From the 17th to the 19th century, country mummers put on annual plays which kept the gift-giving visitor of Father Christmas alive in Britain, focusing on more of a pagan than a religious theme, as was the spirit of the times. The mummers would wear masks and costumes and dance in ways that were reminiscent of times gone by in pagan and localized rituals, thereby helping keep traditional celebrations and community festivities alive.

What I Concluded

I was pretty flabbergasted by what I learned about ole' St. Nick. He is almost always portrayed as "the man" when it comes to explaining who Santa Claus is. After learning about the other cast of characters, and who St. Nicholas was, all I can figure is that he had a heck of a public relations firm behind him to promote him as the one and true Santa Claus. Now I can say with confidence that despite rhetoric to the contrary, St. Nichols was not the foundational figure for the construction of Santa Claus.

The evolution of an orphan boy into St. Nicholas then into Santa Claus has taken generations to occur. Reports were that St. Nicholas's physical appearance was nothing like that of Santa Claus's. In a Washington Post article (Hakim 1996), the question is pondered – how did a vengeful, thin, ex-con turn into jolly, kindly old Santa Claus who lives at the North Pole with Mrs. Claus and a host of devoted elfin assistants and doting reindeer? Clearly, the primary influences for Santa as we know him came from sources other than St. Nicholas, origins that were not Christian at all. That fact may be unnerving, or comforting to people, depending on how they feel.

Martin Buber quote

*God made so many
different kinds of people
Why would he allow
only one way to serve him?*

Martin Buber

1952, *Eclipse of God*, New York: Harper and Bros.

Chapter 5

The Female Santas

The Dilemma

Where are the women in the construction of Santa Claus? It's curious that in my own home, it was my mother, and grandmothers, who "made" Santa Claus. They were the ones who thought about what others needed or wanted, they were the ones that went shopping, wrapped presents, hid them, decorated the home, sang carols, and baked cookies. In my own home with my children, I have become Santa doing exactly all of those things. In fact, I took it to an even higher level as I tried to give my children the most extraordinary, magical experience of Santa and the holidays.

Yet where were the men in all this? While I know a few men who really get into making Christmas special, often it seems their holiday contribution is singular – getting and putting up the tree. Then their Santa role seemed to vanish until Christmas morning when they seemed to take pride in what their wives had quietly created. I recall my mom and me buying, wrapping, and putting presents into the bag that my father, dressed as Santa, would carry as he made his enthusiastic appearance, Ho-Ho-Ho-ing, and passing out the gifts. We stood in the shadows, smiling, pleased that others were so happy with the experience, and receiving no acknowledgment for our role at all. So as I conducted this research, I wondered – why is it that female Santas are never acknowledged since women are the ones who I see most actively making Santa. They just aren't the ones depicted as doing so.

If in many homes, it is the mother, rather than the father, who gets, makes, wraps, and delivers presents to children, if women are the ones who typically do the majority of cooking, decorating, and festivity planning, if they are the people helping children write letters to SC, and working with them to figure out how to be altruistic to others, why is Santa Claus always portrayed as being male? I decided to find out where the women were in the Santa story.

What I Discovered

While male dominance prevailed, there were a variety of women who were associated with Santa. While Santa Claus is depicted as male in pictures, stories, and personas, there have been a variety of women who have contributed to our understanding of Santa, yet they are starkly absent in most portrayals or discussions of Santa Claus.

I learned that the most commonly associated women in history who are thought to have contributed to the spirit of Santa Claus include Artemis Ephesus, La Befana, and Saint Lucy. And then there is Mrs. Claus. I really wanted to understand how they contributed to our understanding of Santa

Claus and how they have been portrayed or transformed to represent either women's best or worst forms.

Artemis: Going back in time, Artemis was considered a Greek deity, and her Roman counterpart was Diana. Artemis was the daughter of Zeus and Leto and the twin sister of Apollo. She was the goddess of the forest, fields, and harvest. Artemis was overseer of those who were vulnerable. Gifted with healing powers, she was a woman who had a great love for animals. She was sometimes depicted as a powerful, multi-breasted figure who protected women and babies during childbirth. Her temple was famous for revelry, dancing, and consumption of delicious foods and drink at ritualized festivals. She was regarded as a cornucopia analogous to the Earth Mother's abundance.

Stories hold that Artemis's popularity, beauty, sexuality, and love of food, dance, and merriment was appalling to St. Nicholas. He became so angry at her pagan worshipers and her ongoing influence that he destroyed her temple in a ruthless manner. However, her female believers continued on, under the guise of being Christian nuns. They carried forward many of her traditions in subtle ways that could not be directly associated with Artemis. St. Nicholas attempted to usurp Artemis's popularity and authority by aligning himself with groups she had protected, such as children, sailors, and women. The attribute of protecting the vulnerable and needy became increasingly associated with Nicholas, not Artemis, as time went on. "Over centuries, St. Nicholas replaces Artemis, Santa Claus replaces St. Nicholas" (Curtis 1995:19). This is akin to Joseph Campbell's notion that in patriarchal societies, male dominance often usurps the position of divine motherhood (Campbell... Masks).

But it is more than that, Curtis states. The conflict between Artemis, St. Nicholas, and Santa Claus is really an ancient discourse of opponents in league with supernatural components, whether mythological, pagan, or religious. People's understanding of the Santa figure, who he is, what he looks like, what he does, and what he represents, is keenly interrelated to time and culture. Usurping female authority has ancient, as well as contemporary, realities.

I went into ancient history books and learned more about Artemis. She was the original feminist. She was the patron protector of young girls. Artemis fought against women being raped. She helped women to have their babies successfully and helped establish the importance of midwifery. She swore never to marry and relished in her independence. She chose to be a virgin and keep her own power. She had five golden horned deer called Elaphoi Khrysokeroi that she harnessed to drive her chariot, in a reindeer-pulled Santa-sleigh image that is not to be dismissed. Sacred symbols associated with her today are the bow and arrow, deer, and the cypress, or greenery. She knew how to find beauty in people and the world; she knew how to wield her power, and was beloved and respected. Her temple, before St. Nicholas destroyed it, is now thought to be one of the Seven Wonders of the Ancient World.

No wonder Nicholas and the men of the day were threatened by her.

Berchta or Perchta: Another female influence in the construction of Santa Claus is Berchta, a pagan winter and mother goddess who was the wife of Wodan or Odin. Also known as Perchta, this Teutonic goddess hailed from what is now Bavaria and was known as the white lady who spins destiny. Her name means bright, luminous, or glorious. She was thought to live in the forests and winter snow and she was accompanied by 24 hounds leading spirits through the wintertime to resting places in the spring. She was thought to descend to earth on Mother's Night, a festival held the night before the Winter Solstice (or December 20). She may also travel on nights between December 22 and January 6 bestowing gifts to those who have been generous or punishing those who have been greedy or lazy. Stories vary about how she travels, including by wagon, pushing a plow, or flying on a broom accompanied by spirits, fairies, and elves. She arrived in the still of the night, unrecognized, and went up and down chimneys in order to bring gifts to children. She is thought to make snow by shaking her feather bed and fog from the smoke of her fire.

Originally described as a beautiful dark-haired woman dressed in white, over time descriptions of her appearance changed considerably. Instead of being powerful and beautiful, she was transformed into being portrayed as an old woman with long teeth and tangled hair. It is thought that the change in her image had to do with Christian promoters not wanting her to be seen as a beautiful goddess that would be endearing to the masses. They methodically changed stories about her so she would be seen as ugly, frightening to children, and mean. This left Berchta as no longer a Goddess but rather an ugly old woman and patron of witches.

Transforming her from a goddess into a demon witch wife was another example of the evolution of positive winter characters into evil-doers in order to promote Christianity. She was recast as a witch queen who claimed the souls of unbaptized children for God. She was also known to punish women for working at Christmastime, which is curious because women around the world and across time have always worked to take care of their families, especially at holidays. Tales of her wickedness were disseminated in order to frighten children into behaving, as she may leave lumps of coal in stockings of bad children, instead of sweets for good ones, when she visited their homes on January 6. It is fascinating how once coal was considered a good gift because it enabled people to stay warm, but became re-cast over time to be a bad gift, while toys and sweet treats were identified as more desirable.

Berchta's transformation is another ironic portrayal of how a pagan goddess could have her story changed to promote Christianity or give a new message to old customs and behaviors. Her alteration from being beautiful and kind to someone who is ugly and wicked diminished the role of women as it emboldened the importance of older men being the gatekeeper to delivering goodness.

Frau Gaude: The mysterious Frau Gaude (sometimes referred to as Frau Harke) was thought to be a member of Berchta's entourage or the wife of Wodan/Odin who rides alone beside him as he travels across the sky There is also the rumor that Frau Gaude is Odin in drag. Frau Gaude was thought to lead a procession of ghosts and spirits across the night skies during the twelve days of Yule, either in a cart or carriage. She is thought to be accompanied by a pack of phantom dogs. People are encouraged to keep their doors and windows shut, otherwise, the dogs will come and settle in front of the fireplaces in homes.

She is regarded as a spirit of healing, who can place, or remove curses. Only by removing curses on Christmas Eve that were placed on the world can she be venerated (Illed 2009). She rewards those who have been kind with gifts of prosperity.

Snegurochka: Another female Santa character is Snegurochka. She is often referred to as the Snow Maiden and is thought to be the daughter of Spring and Frost and the grand-daughter and helper of Ded Moroz, the Russian version of Father Christmas. She reportedly lives with Ded Moroz in Veliky Ustyug and helps him deliver gifts to good children in celebration of the new year. Spring supposedly gave her a wreath to help open her heart to loving others. Ded Moroz may appear in different forms during the holiday season, so Snegurochka also assumes guises as she delivers gifts.

There are other versions of who Snegurochka is and how she came into being. There is a Russian fairy-tale that tells the story about a man and woman who regretted that they never had children, and one winter's day made a girl out of snow. They used two blue beads as her eyes, a piece of red ribbon for her mouth, and took their fingers to craft dimples in her cheeks. Through their desire, she became a real child. Her dress was long and white, glittering with snow sparkles. She was reported to be one of the most beautiful children alive; sometimes she is depicted by wearing a gold crown or a fancy hat that is edged in fur. She lived with them through the winter but was lonely. When summer came, she wandered into the woods and fields to pick flowers with the village girls. As the sun started to wain they built a fire and played games jumping over the fire. But when Snegurochka took her turn jumping over the flames, she melted and evaporated into a white cloud. Her memory is kept by children burning a straw figure in a bonfire as winter turns to spring.

Another version of this story is that she's the daughter of Father Frost and the Snow Queen and that she is immortal, living in the forests, and it is thought she would give up her immortality to live and love like normal humans, but if she does legend hints that she would dissolve into mist.

Snegurochka has become a popular character in some parts of the world at New Year, where children dress up like her. Father Frost may arrive in communities in a horse-drawn sled to bring gifts to children, and she communicates gently with the children and helps him interact with them as they deliver the presents.

A common figure in Russian winter tales, she is also the prototype for Russian nesting dolls. She is typically depicted wearing a long silver-blue robe and a furry cap. She is not to be confused as the same character as the Snow Queen described in the Hans Christian Anderson story.

La Befana: The female figure most often associated with Santa Claus is La Befana. Historically, her legend begins as an old Italian woman who was sweeping her house one day when three men stopped to rest. They said they were following a bright star in the sky, which was to lead them to the infant Jesus in Bethlehem. They invited her to join them on their journey. She longed to go but refused as she had much cleaning to finish. This was a decision that she soon regretted. In her tattered clothes and worn-out shoes, she ran after them, broom in hand, but could not catch them.

La Befana's tale and appearance have changed over time. The most common version is of her flying over the roofs of children at Christmastime, in particular on the January 6 celebration of Epiphany, bringing them gifts that she would put into shoes or stockings that the children leave out for her to fill. Shoes or stockings are traditionally left by the fireplace since she can come into the house down the chimney. She doesn't have a sleigh and reportedly travels on foot. She carries her gifts to children over many miles in order to deliver the presents. A basket or bag are usual descriptors for how she brings the gifts, which are simple toys, trinkets, or sweets.

Another version is that she roams the world in hopes of finding the Christ Child. Since no one can never tell for sure who is holy, she leaves gifts for all the children. While she brings sweets and pleasant presents to good children, she is known to bring cinders and coals to naughty ones. This is a curiosity because cinders and coal were essential for people to start a fire and stay warm or cook food. How coal and cinders were transformed into something bad is unclear. Still, another view is that Le Befana was once a Roman goddess who grew old and was transformed. There is yet another version that holds she was a traditional witch, striving for kindness and balance in the world.

To this day, children often write notes to La Befana, telling her that they have been good. Daring children may suggest gifts that they would appreciate her bringing to them. These notes are sent up through the chimney, where she can retrieve them as she flies over the roof-tops. La Befana resembles Santa in still other ways, such as her arriving at in the still of the night. It is custom for children to leave her food and drink to sustain her on her journey, such as a plate with an orange or mandarin on it and a glass of wine. When the children awake they find the fruit is gone, the wine is drunk, and a handprint in ashes on the plate, proving that La Befana had been there. Before going to bed on Epiphany, children are supposed to be sweet and say a chant or rhyme that La Befana may hear. A traditional one, found at http://italophiles.com/la_befana.htm, is:

> Sleep, child, this is the night,
> the Befana comes from her cave,
> and carrying candies and sweets
> she goes over the rooftops.
> Slowly, slowly, gently gently
> she puts her ear to the chimney
> and if she hears tantrums
> or someone moves, she moves on.
> And to the children who are rude,
> mean, or don't want to go to bed,
> and to the children who are bad,
> she leaves only lumps of coal.
> But if when she listens,
> she hears everyone asleep
> then with a skill that would surprise you
> she slides into your home.
> And she takes from her sack
> all the goodies, and all the
> beautiful things, like dolls and flowers,
> and candies and cookies for the children.

St. Lucy: Another gift-giving female figure during the December holidays is St. Lucy. She also goes by Santa Lucia and Saint Lucia and lived from 283-304 AD in Italy. Her name in Latin means "light". She is particularly popular in Scandinavia, Italy, Czechoslovakia, Austria, Denmark, and Sweden. December 13 is her feast day, where it is common for girls to dress in white gowns with candles on a crown. At her feast day, she delivered gifts to children, which is still carried on today by giving gifts to children and to charity institutions. French nuns became renowned for displaying the spirit of St. Nicholas or Santa by leaving treats in children's shoes on St. Lucy's day.

Like Artemis, she was an early feminist. She is mentioned in literature as having courage, but her story reflects a far darker story than her feast days would now portray. Legends have it that Lucy's widowed mother wanted her to marry a wealthy man that Lucy did not want to marry. She was under much pressure to do so and devised a plan to get out of the marriage. She told her ill mother that she had a vision that Christ was a better life-partner and if she dedicated her life to God her mother's ailment would be cured. She gave away her dowry to the poor. The rejected bridegroom was so angry he sought assistance from the governor, Paschasius, who ordered that she be moved to a brothel where she would be defiled. She warned Paschasius that he would be punished for his actions. Guards who came to take her there were unable to move her. He ordered the guards to gouge out her eyes. They tied her to a team of oxen, but still, she would not go. The guards piled bundles of wood around her but she would not burn. They eventually took their swords and plunged them into her throat, killing her.

Thus Lucy was a woman so dedicated to not marrying someone she didn't want that would be brutally attacked for her actions. She became transformed into a figure who wore white and a beloved gift-giver in the month of December. Throughout Scandinavia, Italy, and the Philippines families celebrate her by baking sweets, making big pasta family dinners, singing songs, and engaging in rituals like planting wheat to show that life continues. Her candles represent bringing light out of the darkness. It is curious that little girls continue the tradition of wearing white, wearing crowns with candles to show illumination.

I found it fascinating that I had so little familiarity with these women. Why hadn't I learned about them in any more than a superficial way? They were beautiful, powerful, kind, independent, fun, and well-liked. But men tried to oppress them, exploit them, reduce their power, or engage in campaigns to make them seem unattractive or bad in some way. Is that why women were not considered to be contenders for the Santa Claus character? My research yielded little about women as Santa Clauses until WWII. Again, I discovered information that I never knew about.

World War II Female Santas: When men went off to war, women were left to take over their traditional jobs in order to keep the country running and their families functioning. Women like Rosie the Riveter worked in factories, operated machinery, drove cabs, farmed, and worked in almost every part of the business world. But a Smithsonian article (Daughtery 2017), excerpted below, acknowledged that World War II opened the door for public recognition of female Santa Clauses – but not without public complaint.

Many men were drafted into the war. As a result, most of the fundamental jobs in the US became occupied by women. Farmers were women. Factory workers like Rosie the Riveter were women. And when the men were away, women were "allowed" to be Santa Clauses. A St. Louis

Times article in 1941 acknowledged First Lady Eleanor Roosevelt's observation that women could successfully take over jobs conventionally reserved for men when they were away during wartime. But the article drew a line in the snow at Santa, saying "There is one male domain, however, that should be defended at all costs. A woman Santa Claus? Heaven forbid! That would be stretching the credulity of guileless little children too far."

But change was already underway. Filene's in Boston had hired a Mrs. Claus back in 1906 to help its male Santa work with the children, even though there had been little information that Santa had a wife. Soon after World War II war began the first female department store Santa appeared in Chicago. She was dressed in red and looked like the traditional Santa Claus, except without the whiskers. It was reported that children seemed happy to tell her what they wanted for Christmas. A Woolworth store in Union New Jersey hired Anna Michaelson to be their female Santa and she wore traditional Santa attire and a white wig and beard. Charlie Howard, a department store Santa who also trained other Santas endorsed the idea of having female Santa Clauses in a 1937 Associated Press interview where he announced plans to graduate two Mrs. Clauses that year, whose job would be to "greet little girls, learn what they want in their Christmas stockings, teach them how to play with dollies, dollhouses, dishes, and clothes." Howard required that the female Santas had to be good looking. Soon department stores around the country hired women to play Santa, sitting in thrones previously monopolized by men or ringing bells on street corners for charity.

While the Washington Post announced in 1942 that it was better to have a female Santa than no Santa at all, other reactions, like that of the Wichita Daily Times accused women of invading another male bastion, the sacred world of Santa Claus. Reactions included rage over women's audacity to pretend to be Santa Claus, fear over their taking over jobs that could go to older men who weren't sent off to war, and allegations that seeing a female Santa could pose irreparable psychological damage to children. A syndicated newspaper columnist named Henry McLemore is reported by Daughtery to have gotten "the shock of my life" when he saw a female department store Santa, saying "If there is such a thing as a minor horror, then a minor horror of this war is female Santa Clauses," he wrote. "Kristine Kringle! Sarah St. Nicholas! Susie Santa Claus! Holy Smoke!"

But by 1943 there were so many female Santas that Hollywood make-up artist Max Factor Jr., decided he would put forward recommendations on how to standardize their look. He reportedly believed that seeing too many different looking Santas would be confusing for children. He tried to standardize the appearance of Santas to be bearded males.

Female Santas became so commonplace that they were topics of conversation by comedians and reporters. Bob Hope is reported to have said that "a lot of the Hollywood actresses are playing Santa Clauses this year and when you think about it, it isn't as silly as it sounds after all. Who can do a better job of filling a stocking than [actress] Betty Grable?"

When the war ended in 1945, so did women's opportunities to be recognized and hired as Santa Clauses. Even today, as I will show later about Santa Claus organizations, there is still institutionalized resistance for women to be recognized as Santa Clauses. When women want to participate, they are relegated to the lower ranks of Mrs. Claus.

Mrs. Claus: The character of Mrs. Santa Claus embodies stereotypes of what women were "supposed" to be like, according to standards of the late 1800s and into the twentieth century. Her identity is so entwined with that of her husband that she had no identity of her own, not even known by a first name. In recent days she has been sometimes called Mary, Merry, or Carol, in keeping with the Christmas theme, but in most coverage of her, she is only known as Mrs. Claus, with her identity solely as Santa's wife.

Since the first mention and depictions of her since the 1880s, she has been depicted as elderly, heavy-set, with white hair and a pleasant disposition. Her pictures typically have her in a red dress or cape trimmed in fur, and her dress is on the long side and poofed out with a crisp petticoat. Her job is to serve Santa and elves. One never sees her portrayed as having any life of her own; she is always in the shadow of her busy husband. Her actions focus on cookie-baking, keeping the elves in line, having her husband's suit ready, helping paint toys or dressing dolls, engaging in secretarial duties, and, of course, waiting on her husband. Her personality is calm, patient, reasoning, supportive, kind, and a source of stability at the North Pole.

Reportedly, she was never mentioned until an 1849 short story, A Christmas Legend, by James Reese. Then she was mentioned again in an 1851 *Yale Literary Magazine*, an 1862 essay in *Harper's Magazine*, and the 1878 children's book, *Lill's Travels in Santa Claus Land*.

Her invisibility evidently caught the ire of Katherine Bates in 1889 when she wrote the poem, Goody Santa Claus. Around this time, Mrs. Claus took on an aggressive, carping, and complaining persona in several writings. In Bates' poem, Goody Claus laments, "Why should you have all the glory of the joyous Christmas story, And poor little Goody Santa Claus have nothing but the work?.... Santa, wouldn't it be pleasant to surprise me with a present? And this ride behind the reindeer is the boon your Goody begs...Would it be so very shocking if your Goody filled a stocking just for once? Oh, dear! Forgive me. Frowns do not become a Saint.....But I'll mend that sock so nearly it shall hold your gifts completely. (Let me) Take the reins and let me show you what a woman's wit can do."

Casting Mrs. Claus as subservient seems not dissuaded authors in the decades to come. She didn't become a visible part of the Santa celebrations until the 1950s. The song, Mrs. Santa Claus in 1953 and Phyllis McGinley's 1963 children's book *How Mrs. Santa Claus Saved Christmas*, helped create the expectation that she might be present. In the 1970s, undoubtedly influenced by the Women's Movement, Mrs. Claus became more apparent in television films, including a 1996 musical in which actress Angela Lansbury played Mrs. Santa Claus.[1] Despite her increased appearance, when given the opportunity to be a forceful partner to Santa Claus or a major character in the Santa Claus story, she instead is relegated into the shadows as a compliant, never-complaining, sweet lady who is content in her role of doing for others. Seldom is there a romantic interest conveyed in the Santa Claus-Mrs. Claus relationship. They seem to have a working, platonic, business relationship in which his needs are met, but hers are nowhere in the picture.

Mrs. Claus as a transition character to Santa as gay?: In the evolution of the character of Santa Claus, there is a newer version to explain his transformation. This view holds that Santa Claus's primary relationships are with men, particularly elves. There is an assertion that the Mrs. Claus character is actually his beard, or cover-up for his homosexuality. Daniel Kibblesmith's book, *Santa's Husband*, (2017) portrays Santa in two ways – as a white Santa who is married to a black man who is also a Santa. Samantha Allen (2017) alleges that "The right-wing are getting mightily upset about a sweet children's book which imagines a gay Santa. But historically, Santa's heterosexuality is just as imaginary."

Allegations that Santa Claus could be gay are not new. As documentation of that perspective, the following points in the traditional Santa story are pointed out. Santa is a warm, nurturing person who doesn't mind wearing furs or red velvet and routinely sports tall black leather boots. He has never fathered a child with Mrs. Claus, or anyone else. He is an artist, craftsman, who makes toys and paints them. He works with a variety of elves, who are almost always portrayed as male. He has chosen to travel not by horses or oxen, but by graceful, beautiful, and delicate reindeer who are named things like Dancer, Prancer, and Vixen. His favorite reindeer, Rudolph, has been alleged to be gay too, as "all the other reindeer used to laugh and call him names. They never let poor Rudolph join in any reindeer games." He travels by starlight and puts sweets and treats into stockings. Other comparisons abound, but you get the idea.

The transformation of Santa Claus into a gay man reflects other changes in society. This portrayal has been met with different responses. One has been resistance and re-sentiment, with allegations that that isn't who Santa Claus is. The other has been to embrace diversity and honor the positive attributes of being gay. In this sometimes heated debate on who Santa Claus is, it is wise to remember that he is, and always has been, a product of social construction. It reminds us that there has always been jockeying for the position of people who want to present their image of Santa Claus as the dominant, right, and true version. The fact remains, that one can reasonably argue that there have been many different genders and figures across time who have contributed to our understanding of who Santa is. If this is a natural evolution of society, then why should we expect his transformation to be stagnant and stuck in the past? As he transforms, what will "he" look like, and what will that say about the larger society and where we are headed?

What I Concluded

Studying the history of Santa Claus puts us smack into studying the role of gender in society. There have been women who were gift-givers and female representations of the Santa figure throughout time. Gift-giving, merriment, kindness, travel by sometimes magical ways, or trudging through cold terrains carrying bundles of presents for children are common threads among them. There is undoubtedly a causal relationship of how female and male attributes from different characters morphed together to transform into the Santa Claus that we know today.

Gender stereotypes abound in the presentations of female Santas. Powerful, beautiful women were often transformed into unattractive women, hags, or witches. Historically, portraying women who had the power to be unattractive may have been strategic. Turning pretty women into those with characteristics deemed unattractive may have been as well. Turning women into witches made powerful women feared. Whether they were "a good witch or a bad witch" (homage to the Wizard of Oz), appeared to be debated, as many were kind and giving but transformed to be frightening figures. The chubby, sweet Mrs. Claus figure who has no life of her own except to serve her husband set a standard for children in the twentieth century to live by. In the 1970s, during the heyday of the Women's Liberation Movement, she started to take on a little more attractive and active role. But the stereotypes of her complaint-self remain dominant.

Portraying female Santas as subservient to men, or using force to keep them down, is a common theme. Artemis and Lucy were put to death for being uppity. These messages are not to be missed. Except growing up I missed them. When my father dressed up like Santa Claus, my mom by default became Mrs. Claus. She was the prototype of the subservient woman who gave up her life to advance that of her husband's. She was cookie-baker extraordinaire. Right after Thanksgiving, she began her baking and by the time December 25 came around, she had made dozens of different kinds of cookies and sweets. She put them into containers on a card table in the corner of the dining room and everyone who came to visit left with a plate full of goodies. There were Springerlies and pfeffernusse from Germany, Mexican Wedding Cakes, Bourbon balls from Kentucky, Chow-Mein noodle butterscotch "spiders", and of course, iced sugar cookies, to name but a few. She was smiley and chubby, and kind to everyone who knocked at the door. In short, she WAS Mrs. Claus. And she, like Goody

Santa in Katherine Bates' 1889 poem, she regretted and resented pushing her life aside while her husband got all the glory. That was a fascinating thing to realize. And then I thought of all the women of my generation who had done exactly the same thing, me included...

Note:

1. https://historybecauseitshere.weebly.com/mrs-santa-claus--a-strong-and-supportive.html

Mary Engelbreit quote

We shall light
a candle of understanding
in our hearts
which shall not be put out

Mary Engelbreit

Believe. 1998. Andrews McMeel Pub.

Chapter 6

Santa Comes to the United States

The Dilemma

Santa Claus is often associated with his persona in the United States. It seemed to me that Santa Claus has been exported as an American product to people around the world. I knew that there were European influences on the construction of Santa Claus, but I never thought too much about how it happened. I learned he was found in other parts of the world long before he arrived in the US. His journey and transformation here is a fascinating reflection of social forces in the building of a nation that I had never really considered before this project. I would be you will find things that surprise you too in this chapter!

What I Discovered

There was no Santa Claus in the early days of what would become the United States. In the 1600 and 1700s, the celebration of Christmas was haphazardly celebrated if acknowledged at all. Remnants of folk festivals and pagan rituals that people celebrated in their home countries were still present, even into the early 1900s. In order to understand the evolution of Santa in Colonial America, it is necessary to go back in time and remember what was occurring. The new nation was founded, at least in part, on a desire for religious freedom. The individuals coming to found what would become the United States hailed primarily from Europe. Europe had been experiencing tremendous religious conflict, and tensions between the Christian and pagan or folk communities took a back seat to those between the Protestants and the Catholics. Serious problems erupted over religion in Britain, Germany, France, Spain, and the Netherlands. Vigorous arguments occurred over the nature of God, core beliefs and values, the appropriate type of worship, and how faith should be structured. Some people wanted a rigid orientation toward faith while others were more secular and flexible. In all likelihood, the people who first immigrated to America must have been the most dissatisfied with their former countries and hoped to create a new world where it would be easier for them to practice their beliefs. The notion of religious tolerance and freedom of expression entered into the public fray. Humanistic philosopher John Locke helped shape the thinking of the day. At that point in time, there would have been no universal agreement on if there was a Santa Claus, or what he should be like.

The earliest records of Christmas in the colonies indicated that there was a tremendous geographic variation that reflected the cultural and religious orientations from which its new citizens came. In the more southern colonies there tended to be a heavy Anglican orientation, and worship services combined traditions from folk festivals, such as feasting, drinking, gaming, noise-making, fireworks, and small gifting. The holiday season lasted through the twelve days until Epiphany. Homes embraced the custom of decorating with greenery and lights.

But in the New England colonies, the Puritans disdained the notion of Christmas in general, and especially the frivolity surrounding it. Despite the new nation's alleged concern with religious tolerance, Puritans tried to enforce their views on others. During the 1600s, laws were created to forbid people from feasting and frolicking, behaviors that were essential in ancient folk festivals. It even became illegal to mention St. Nicolas' name. People were not allowed to exchange gifts, light a candle, or sing carols. Christmas was regarded as a totally religious, not secular, experience if it was acknowledged at all.

But others felt it was possible that God would want people to celebrate and give gifts, just as St. Nicholas had so many years before. This religious tension about the nature of God and how he wanted people to behave is longstanding. Minister Cotton Mather, of the famed Salem Witch Trials, warned congregants that if they engaged in secular aspects of the holiday that they would suffer the "burning wrath of God". Therefore, no Santa dared be found in Massachusetts.

It was in the New York and Pennsylvania colonies that Santa Claus first made his appearance. In an accidental twist of fate, Santa's popularity was increased in New York City during the melting pot era of immigration as the city experienced cultural and technological development because of the new mix of ideas. In 1626, a fleet of ships, led by the Goede Vrowe (Goodwife), left Holland for the New World. The Goede Vrowe's masthead was none other than St. Nicholas. The Dutch purchased some land from the Iroquois for $24, named the village New Amsterdam and erected a statue of St. Nicholas in the town square. That village was renamed overtime to be New York. The New York Historical Society was founded in 1804 and Nicholas was made its patron saint. Its members embraced the gift-giving tradition brought to the US during the 1700s by Dutch immigrants.

New York and Pennsylvania were heavily populated by Dutch and German immigrants, and many of them had developed versions of Santa and Christmas that made the religious, pagan, and secular compatible. Also, even within Protestants, there was wide variability in their religious denominations, with some like the Amish and Quakers who didn't celebrate Christmas, or the Moravians who traditionally celebrated elegant Christmas love-feasts and Lutherans who enjoyed baking cookies and fancy gingerbread houses. Some traditions brought with them the notion of Sinterklaas, Christkindlein, and Knecht Ruprecht, and they incorporated them into the new traditions here.

When Washington Irving was made a member of the New York Historical Society around 1810, he saw a woodcut of a bearded man in the building - an image that he later incorporated into his writings. Writing under the pseudonym Diedrich Knickerbocker, Irving included describes Saint Nicolas riding into town on a horse in his book "A History of

New York." Two years afterward (1812), he revised the book to show Nicholas riding over the trees in a wagon. This image undoubtedly influenced William Gilly who wrote an 1821 poem about "Santeclaus" who was dressed in fur and drove a sleigh drawn by a single reindeer as he delivered gifts. Gilly reportedly wrote this poem after he actually observed Santa and his flying reindeer.

New Yorker Clement Moore is credited for creating the famous poem, best known as The. However, it is unclear if Moore really wrote the poem. Foster in his book, "Author Unknown," argues that "A Visit From St. Nicholas," was first published anonymously in a Troy, N.Y. newspaper in 1823 and it closely matches the views and verse of Henry Livingston Jr., a gentleman-poet of Dutch descent. Livingston, who lived in Poughkeepsie, N.Y., who died before Moore was ever named as the poem's author. However, there is information from Moore that he actually saw Santa and his reindeer, which is what prompted his writing the poem in the first place. Irrespective of who actually wrote it, the poem filled our heads with images about what Santa may look like, and how he may behave. The citation for it can be found in the References:

The Night Before Christmas

Twas the night before Christmas, when all through the house
Not a creature was stirring, not even a mouse.
The stockings were hung by the chimney with care,
In hopes that St Nicholas soon would be there.

The children were nestled all snug in their beds,
While visions of sugar-plums danced in their heads.
And mamma in her 'kerchief, and I in my cap,
Had just settled our brains for a long winter's nap.

When out on the lawn there arose such a clatter,
I sprang from the bed to see what was the matter.
Away to the window I flew like a flash,
Tore open the shutters and threw up the sash.

The moon on the breast of the new-fallen snow
Gave the luster of mid-day to objects below.
When, what to my wondering eyes should appear,
But a miniature sleigh, and eight tinny reindeer.

With a little old driver, so lively and quick,
I knew in a moment it must be St Nick.
More rapid than eagles his coursers they came,
And he whistled, and shouted, and called them by name!

"Now Dasher! now, Dancer! now, Prancer and Vixen!
On, Comet! On, Cupid! on, on Donner and Blitzen!
To the top of the porch! to the top of the wall!
Now dash away! Dash away! Dash away all!"

As dry leaves that before the wild hurricane fly,
When they meet with an obstacle, mount to the sky.
So up to the house-top the coursers they flew,
With the sleigh full of Toys, and St Nicholas too.

And then, in a twinkling, I heard on the roof
The prancing and pawing of each little hoof.

As I drew in my head, and was turning around,
Down the chimney St Nicholas came with a bound.

He was dressed all in fur, from his head to his foot,
And his clothes were all tarnished with ashes and soot.
A bundle of Toys he had flung on his back,
And he looked like a peddler, just opening his pack.

His eyes-how they twinkled! his dimples how merry!
His cheeks were like roses, his nose like a cherry!
His droll little mouth was drawn up like a bow,
And the beard of his chin was as white as the snow.

The stump of a pipe he held tight in his teeth,
And the smoke it encircled his head like a wreath.
He had a broad face and a little round belly,
That shook when he laughed, like a bowlful of jelly!

He was chubby and plump, a right jolly old elf,
And I laughed when I saw him, in spite of myself!
A wink of his eye and a twist of his head,
Soon gave me to know I had nothing to dread.

He spoke not a word, but went straight to his work,
And filled all the stockings, then turned with a jerk.
And laying his finger aside of his nose,
And giving a nod, up the chimney he rose!

He sprang to his sleigh, to his team gave a whistle,
And away they all flew like the down of a thistle.
But I heard him exclaim, 'ere he drove out of sight,
"Happy Christmas to all, and to all a good-night!"

This poem had a monumental impact on the public's perception of Santa Claus. Pagan images of Santa being dressed in brown or green garb went by the wayside as a result of this poem. Charles Dickens had published "A Christmas Carol" in 1843, and while Santa Claus wasn't exactly in it, the tale had a big impact on the public's desire to live generously to others.

Soon the combined image of St. Nicholas the elf-like gift-bringer described by Moore, and a friendly "Kriss Kringle" amalgam of the Christkindlein and Pelznickel figures had permeated the American collective mind. In 1841 Philadelphia merchant J.W. Parkinson hired a man to dress in "Criscringle" clothing and climb the chimney outside his shop in order to encourage shoppers to visit his store. This view of an adult-sized Santa soon became the dominant image. In 1863, a caricaturist for *Harper's Weekly* named Thomas Nast developed his own image of Santa as a figure with a flowing set of whiskers dressed in fur from head to toe. By 1866 his drawing of "Santa Claus and His Works" established Santa as a *maker* of toys. Three years later a book of the same name combined Nast drawings with a George Webster poem that identified the North Pole as Santa's home.

During this time, there was no consistent image of how big Santa was supposed to be. Sometimes he was described as large – tall and fat, sometimes he was normal or slight build, while other times he was portrayed as small and elf-like. His clothing also varied, from being dressed in furs like Belsnickle, or in cloth suits of red, blue, green, or purple. Sinter Klaas was described as everything from a "rascal" with a blue three-cornered hat, red waistcoat, and yellow stockings to a man wearing a broad-brimmed hat and a "huge pair of Flemish trunk hose." Germanic images were more likely to show Santa as a saint in bishops robes, as a winter man in furs, as a saintly old man, often seen in the company of the Holy Child, and as a gift-bringer in robes of every color from brown, white, green, blue to golds, pinks, and red.

Even in this latter guise, his countenance was serious more often than jolly, though laughing Santas did appear. These were usually influenced by American imagery. A Boston printer named Louis Prang introduced the English custom of Christmas cards to America, and in 1885 he issued a card featuring a red-suited Santa that was similar to Nast's 1881 drawing of "Merry Old Santa Claus." The chubby Santa with a red fur-trimmed suit began to replace the Belsnickle image and the multicolored Santas. This view is in contrast to that provided by Santa historian Robert Sullivan who alleges that Santa is really only about three feet tall and weighs only 150 pounds.

Thus the role of Santa Claus changed significantly over the first hundred years of the new nation. The Puritan resistance to frivolity and revelry eventually gave way to the characterization brought to New York and Pennsylvania by the Dutch and Germans. They offered people with a framework in which they could feast and frolic on festivals, in ways that were not dissimilar from their ancient relatives who celebrated Saturnalia, Yule, and other holidays. The dissemination of different cultural images of Santa type characters occurred due to the massive influx of immigrants who came about that time to America. During that time there was cultural negotiation about what Santa should look like.

Add into this equation the benefits of the Industrial Revolution and the greater financial security that it brought. Suddenly, with a bit of discretionary income, the idea of gifting others became part of the custom. Santa became a perfect vehicle for stores of the day to encourage sales. During holidays even back in the days of the ancient celebrations like Kalends, Saturnalia, Brumlina, or other Winter Solstice celebrations, key components shared by them included gift-giving, which often included sweets, games, or money. The Industrial Revolution helped provide a free flow of money, and entrepreneurs quickly found creative ways to help people find ways to spend it. At that point in time candy and toys were commonly advertised items but it didn't take long for corporations to see the importance of molding Santa and Christmas into potentially lucrative associations. This continues to be the case, which will be explored later.

By the turn of the 20th century, Santa Claus had taken his place in dominant American culture. His presence was used by businesses, by politicians, by newspapers, and the public embraced a figure that brought happiness and a sense of affluence. However, the question of "is there really a Santa?" has always been present in the collective mind. The most predominant example of this is the 1897 letter that eight-year-old Virginia O'Hanlon wrote to the New York Sun. She had reportedly asked her father if there was a Santa, and her father (undoubtedly hedging the issue), encouraged the child to write to the newspaper, which was obliged only to state the truth. The newspaper's editor, Francis P. Church, wrote an editorial to the child in the paper – an editorial (details in References) that has now become famous. Here it is:

Yes, Virginia, There is a Santa Claus

I am 8 years old. Some of my little friends say there is no Santa Claus. Papa says, "If you see it in The Sun, it's so." Please tell me the truth, is there a Santa Claus? Virginia O'Hanlon

Virginia, your little friends are wrong. They have been affected by the skepticism of a skeptical age. They do not believe except what they see. They think that nothing can be which is not comprehensible by their little minds. All minds, Virginia, whether they be men's or children's, are little. In this great universe of ours, man is a mere insect, an ant, in his intellect as compared with the boundless world about him, as measured by the intelligence capable of grasping the whole of truth and knowledge.

Yes, Virginia, there is a Santa Claus.

He exists as certainly as love and generosity and devotion exist, and you know that they abound and give to your life its highest beauty and joy. Alas! how dreary would be the world if there were no Santa Claus! It would be as dreary as if there were no Virginias. There would be no childlike faith then, no poetry, no romance to make tolerable this existence. We should have no enjoyment, except in sense and sight. The external light with which childhood fills the world would be extinguished.

Not believe in Santa Claus! You might as well not believe in fairies. You might get your papa to hire men to watch in all the chimneys on Christmas eve to catch Santa Claus, but even if you did not see Santa Claus coming down, what would that prove? Nobody sees Santa Claus, but that is no sign that there is no Santa Claus. The most real things in the world are those that neither children nor men can see. Did you ever see fairies dancing on the lawn? Of course not, but that's no proof that they are not there. Nobody can conceive or imagine all the wonders there are unseen and unseeable in the world.

You tear apart the baby's rattle and see what makes the noise inside, but there is a veil covering the unseen world which not the strongest man, nor even the united strength of all the strongest men that ever lived could tear apart. Only faith, poetry, love, romance, can push aside that curtain and view and picture the supernal beauty and glory beyond. Is it all real? Ah, Virginia, in all this world there is nothing else real and abiding.

No Santa Claus? Thank God he lives and lives forever. A thousand years from now, Virginia, nay 10 times 10,000 years from now, he will continue to make glad the heart of childhood. Merry Christmas and a Happy New Year!!!! (Church 1992).

The war against believers and nonbelievers was quashed, at least for a while, by this editorial. It was now safe to believe in Santa. *The Yes Virginia There Is A Santa Claus* editorial was one of the first widely disseminated views that there really was a Santa Claus. It led the way for motion pictures such as The Miracle on 34th Street, in which a little girl who disbelieves in Santa has a personal experience that changes her mind. Since that film, movie companies have found Santa to be a big money-maker. The 1947 film version of The Miracle on 34th Street was not the first public questioning of whether Santa existed, or whether anyone who believed in him might actually be crazy. Actually, a book published in London in 1678, The Examination and Tryal of Old Father Christmas and his clearing by Jury, was the first public analysis of whether Santa existed. The verdict – he does. The message that Santa Lives was re-cast in the remaking of The Miracle on 34th Street in the 1990s with the same theme.

By the 1920s, there had become a socially accepted picture of what Santa Claus looked like. Norman Rockwell created portraits of Santa Claus that combined attributes of both the saintly and jolly when he created a picture for the Saturday Evening Post in 1922. Some Santa experts allege that the pictures of Santa we most readily embrace are those designed by the Coca-Cola Company. From 1931 to 1964, Haddon Sundblom created a new Santa picture for each Christmas for Coca-Cola advertisements that appeared world-wide on the back covers of Post and National Geographic magazines. The Coca-Cola image is the one that most people associate with Santa – a large, jolly-looking man wearing a red suit trimmed with white fur, leather boots and belt, long white beard, and a pack of toys slung onto his back.

What I Concluded

The Santa Claus most people continue to visualize was created largely through the efforts of early nineteenth-century New Yorkers, artists, and authors. He was particularly inspired by the Dutch gift-giving Sinterklaas. Pagan traditions that people enjoyed were slowly incorporated into festivities surrounding the arrival of the gift-giving December figure we have come to know as Santa Claus. The American Santa is a secular visitor who arrives at Christmas, not the 6 December. He dresses not in a bishop's robe and hat, but in furs and red clothes, the resemblance of pagan fire-gods. He is not stern and thin like St. Nicholas but jolly and chubby. He arrives driving a team of flying reindeer rather than a flying horse or walking on foot carrying a bag of toys.

When I started this project, I never realized how the New Englanders didn't allow Santa or Christmas. In Portsmouth NH there is the Strawberry Banke historical site of colonial houses, each with its own story. It was there I first learned that houses weren't decorated for Christmas, and frivolous festivals that included songs and the pre-cursors to Santa Claus were forbidden. I'd heard that New York was originally named New Amsterdam, but I never realized the implications when it came to Santa Claus. Growing up in Southern Indiana where Germans were a predominant group, we always had celebratory holiday foods and decorations. Looking at the history of how Santa was introduced into the US made me realize what a socially constructed figure he was.

Jan Miller Girando quote

Dear Santa,
Here's my Christmas list
I hope I'm not too late.
If you could help with some of this
That really would be great.
To start with, I'd like brotherhood
And peace throughout the land
And gifts of faith and hope for those
Who need a helping hand.
Could you deliver dreams come true
Fill lonely hearts with love,

And ring us close (at least in thought)
To those we're fondest of?
I know this list is getting long
(I'm almost out of space)
But could you put a Christmas smile
On every child's face?
With all of your commitments,
This may see a daunting task,
But I've been good...and anyway,
It never hurts to ask.

Jan Miller Girando
In *Believe* by Mary Engelbreit
1997, Andrews McMeel Pub.

Chapter 7

Santa as Political Psychological Warfare

The Dilemma

Some people don't like Santa for political reasons. When Santa Claus is viewed exclusively as a December gift-giver it neutralizes the notion that he could be a political figure. I like history but I am not a historian. Yet I thought I better go back in time and figure out the politics of Santa Claus. This turned out to be a worthwhile thing to do, because what I discovered really shocked me.

What I Discovered

Because Santa Claus became popular with the people in early America, he also became a convenient figure to be used by political leaders to advance their agendas. Certainly, government leaders back in the time periods of ancient winter solstice type celebrations knew this and they used holidays to either appease the population or to deny them access to celebrations in favor of "more important" agendas. As political leaders and religious ideologies meshed together, they saw the opportunity to manipulate and exploit local holidays and figures for their own purposes. And as I learned, he continues to be a political tool.

Anthropologists and Santaologists have studied the role of Santa cross-culturally and found that he has often been associated with differences of opinion over who he is and what he represents and that his presence has often been tinged with conflict among adults over the ages (Stronach 2011). Santa has always been a symbol of bipolarism. On one hand, he is seen as the epitome of altruism, love, and play created to delight children. On the other, he is seen as embodying a complex set of adult political and ideological agendas that have absolutely nothing to do with the well-being of children. This bifurcation of who he is has contributed to the confusing love/hate relationship that people seem to have with him.

It's hard to come up with a time when there wasn't controversy about Santa. The heated discussions people that share today are merely part of an ongoing historical debate over the role, function, and authenticity of the character we have come to know as Santa Claus. The evolution of the figure we have come to know as Santa Claus has become markedly different over the last 200 years. The foundations for Santa Claus were embedded into a variety of different cultures over hundreds of years, as shown in the previous chapter. There was never a Santa Claus per se but there were many different figures that gave rise to his attributes, as well as the construction of his name.

It appears that the positive attributes of Santa Claus have been co-opted by four major constituencies over time. These include cooptation by religious groups; cooptation by governments; cooptation by the corporate industry; and cooptation by ideologues. In a previous chapter, it was shown how the Christian church and political rulers strategically maneuvered folk beliefs into formalized rituals and events that were designed to support a new status quo. Variations of these forces are still at work, as is his exploitation by a host of corporate industries. This chapter will include an analysis of how different ideological factions over time have attempted to co-opt a contemporary understanding of who Santa Claus is and what he means.

Ancient Warfare and Santa

The history of the winter solstice festivals clearly conveys their dates were co-opted into the new Christian calendar of events, with December 25 becoming regarded as the birth of Jesus and January 6 becoming known as Epiphany. It is of utmost importance to realize that both December 25 and January 6 were festival dates shared by not one, but many different ancient groups. They originally had nothing to do with the birth of the baby Jesus or Christianity. Therefore, the date for that which has come to be known as

Christmas is not at all Christian in origin. They were chosen for political reasons.

It appears that many of the prototypes for Santa Claus were a combination of a variety of Greek, Roman, and pagan figures. These figures had social power and influence, figures whose power had to be subdued or eliminated in order for new religious and political ideologies to take hold. During that time, there was no separation between church and state. God and government were one and the same.

How does one system of power seek to overthrow a pre-existing one? One technique is by force, which may include torture or death. Another technique is imprisonment. None of these techniques win the hearts and minds of the people. When the Roman Empire sought to convert the masses to Christianity, religious leaders quickly identified that conversion at the blade of a sword was not the best way to win over the hearts and minds of the people. Nikolaos destroyed the temple of Artemis for political reasons. Pagan rituals were co-opted by both Christian leaders and government officials to win over the hearts and minds of people around the world, either by fact, fiction, fire, or the blade of a sword, as St. Lucy found out. Female contributors to Santa Claus were made to seem ugly and evil. Older white men were portrayed as Santas, and they were stereotyped to be both powerful and wise. St. Nicholas became the prototype for Santa Claus for political reasons even though there were plenty of other figures that were far more representative of the Santa we have come to know and love.

In order to ensure his market-share, St. Nicholas attacked the temple of Artemis, which was of huge importance and relevance in its day. He felt disdain about the frivolity, drinking, and sexual expressiveness of the people who went to the temple. Christian views of the day were strict and tended to forbid much of the free-spirit and joyful celebrations that were common among the non-Christians. The people who worshipped Artemis did not want to give up their enjoyable practices in exchange for Christian ones which they must have regarded as oppressive and restrictive. Essentially St. Nicholas was responsible for wiping them out. It should be no surprise if the locals found Nicolas the invader to be an awful person even if he was deemed a saint.

A more palpable method of getting people to believe what you want is co-optation, where the beliefs of the competing system are transformed and incorporated into part of a new ideological system. Over time, it was hoped that people would forget the origins of their faiths and views, and will come to embrace the new one if it is made to seem familiar. This cooptation of views must occur slowly and allow people to have continued links to the past, links that are incrementally diminished as alignments to the newer ideology are strengthened. Early Christian leaders figured out that they better allow people to keep their pagan traditions so they smartly incorporated them into new religious customs. Pope Gregory I, in the year 601 AD, argued in a letter to St. Augustine that conversions to the faith would be easier if people were allowed to keep their traditions and recast them to have Christian significance. So this is precisely what happened – a slow but steady cooptation of the traditions different cultures had embraced for generations. The war using Santa as a weapon went from being violent at the blade of the sword to one being smiling as people's traditions were whittled away.

As I did my research on Santa Claus, I was surprised by how extensively this socially-constructed figure had been used by adults to advance their own ideological, religious, economic, and political agendas. Earlier in the book, it was pointed out that the Puritans didn't celebrate Christmas. In fact, some of the leaders went out of their way to punish people who did. The impact of immigration on changing the way leaders viewed both Santa and the December holidays is another example of the social construction of reality as they brought forward competing perceptions of him and the holiday. As the nation was growing and industries began thriving, commercial industries began to see the utility of using Santa Claus to advance their agendas.

So did the US military. Economic, ideological, and powerful interests made it acceptable to use Santa Claus as a convenient tool to advance their causes. Using a commonly embraced figure such as Santa Claus to shift people psychologically so that agendas could be advanced was something I didn't expect to find, but did.

Santa and the Civil War

The decision to use Santa Claus to advance a political agenda in the United States became pronounced during the Civil War. By the mid-19th century, the American public had gotten accustomed to celebrating Christmas with gifts, decorations, songs, and the arrival of Santa Claus.

The Civil War was taking its toll on the nation. A sense of national melancholy pervaded both the North and the South. People were emotionally invested in the war, worried about the survival of the nation, their own survival, and the survival of their loved ones. It was common for people who lived in the North to have family members who were soldiers in the South, and vice versa. The Civil War posed great personal distress for people as each side tried to sway them to their positions. President Abraham Lincoln wanted to find some vehicle to turn the tide so the war would end. Who could the President call upon who would help? You guessed it – Santa Claus.

The image of Santa Claus being a larger than life kind of guy who knew everything and could fix anything was promoted when President Lincoln asked Thomas Nast to create a drawing of Santa with some Union soldiers fighting in the Civil War. Nast, who was a child when his family emigrated to the US from Germany, vehemently opposed slavery and became a fierce supporter of the Union cause. Lincoln knew he could count on Nast to share his views by using his drawings to break the spirit of the Confederacy. Nast drew upon his childhood images of St. Nicholas and created a now-famous picture of a white-bearded Santa in his reindeer-drawn sleigh visiting a Union army camp. He drew Santa wearing a star-spangled outfit, wearing red-and-white striped pants, and a blue jacket with white stars. Nast embellished a sense of patriotism by showing Union soldiers giving him artillery salute, in front of the American flag blowing in the breeze beside a sign that read, "Welcome Santa Claus." In the picture, Santa sits in his sleigh handing out gifts like pipes, stockings, and a jack-in-the-box to soldiers and young drummer boys.

But in Santa's hands is a dancing puppet of Confederate president Jefferson Davis, with a string tied around his neck. It doesn't take much imagination from looking at Nast's picture to assume that the Confederate president is being lynched by Santa Claus. Other *Harper's Weekly* pictures by Nast show his pictures of a lonely Union soldier sitting by a fire gazing at photographs of his family on Christmas Eve, while his wife kneels with her hands clasped in prayer wishing for her husband's safe return as moonlight illuminates their cherubic children asleep in bed, dreaming of Santa. Other pictures show Santa climbing down a chimney or traveling by reindeer as he delivers Union soldiers presents out of his sleigh. Together, Nast and Lincoln created newspaper drawings in which Santa joined forces with the North. This form of propaganda was designed to break the spirit of the Southern troops. If Santa Claus, who had become a beloved cultural character, sided with the North, the logic was that this would serve as a form of psychological warfare against the South. Santa was strategically drawn as someone bigger than life in Nast's pictures in order to be intimidating to the Confederate soldiers. Santa Claus, of course, never endorsed this action. This was one of the first forms of psychological warfare designed to end war.

The Civil War's economic impact on families made it hard for parents to buy their children Christmas gifts. Wartime shortages resulted in fewer gifts to buy. Christopher Klein (2019) found historical reports that Confederate parents explained to their children that the Union blockade had prevented Santa from traveling to the South. Sometimes Southern children were told that Santa Claus had been shot by the Yankees. This provided an explanation to them why there would be no gifts, but it also socialized them to resent people from the North, who had been constructed into being their enemies. In Virginia's newspaper, the *Richmond Examiner,* there was a column that stated there wasn't really a Santa Claus, and instead demonized

Santa as "a Dutch toy-monger" and "an immigrant from England" who had nothing to do "with genuine Virginia hospitality and Christmas merry-makings." This fed an anti-immigrant sentiment. Images of Santa supporting the North did indeed have a demoralizing influence on the Confederate army, and also on American society as a whole.

It was mind-boggling to imagine that the beloved Abe Lincoln strategically figured out that if he could get the public to see that Santa Claus was on the side of the Yankees that it could break the back of the South. Nast's drawings of Santa supporting the North and ostensibly not caring about Confederate children shocked me. They took a beloved figure who was to bring gifts to all children around the world and manipulated his image to strategically alienate children who just happened to live in the southern part of the country. Those children were in no way responsible for the war or what their parents or government leaders chose to do. To indicate that Santa wasn't going to bring gifts to Confederate children seemed just plain wrong.

The notion that nothing was sacred, not even the altruism of Santa Claus, to government leaders who wanted to promote a political agenda is worth considering. Using a universally beloved icon for one's personal benefit has become commonplace. Religious leaders did it back in the day of St. Nicholas. And here is Honest Abe exploiting Santa Claus too. Whether you were for the North or South in the Civil War is irrelevant – that's not the issue. The issue is anytime a political leader uses someone like Santa Claus for political agenda-staking, it should at least make us raise our eyebrows.

Santa Claus in World War I, WWII, and the Korean War

Sometimes setting forth a political agenda can be positive as well as negative. What appears to have happened is that the Civil War set the stage for Santa Claus to be enlisted for future war efforts. During World War I, Santa Claus was transformed into a patriotic figure, akin to Uncle Sam. The U.S. government produced countless advertisements and artwork that showed Santa with the troops. He was also seen as a viable candidate to promote the public buying bonds to support the war effort. The National World War I Museum and Memorial in Missouri contain photos of Santa Claus visiting children and soldiers during the war.

In a story I had never heard before, in 1914 during WWI, the struggles of families whose men were off at war gained the attention of philanthropists who decided that children deserved gifts and joy at Christmastime. A humanitarian drive started in Chicago to collect gifts for British orphans. Soon donations began pouring in from around the country. A national appeal went out, asking the children of America to be Santa Claus for little boys and girls whose daddies died fighting for their country. The appeal encouraged them to "stretch out your hands across the sea bearing messages of love and hope and sympathy to children of a war-ridden Continent, messages from fortunate America to unfortunate Europe" (Corocoran 2014).

In New York, a ship made to carry coal, the USS Jason, was packed full of donated toys, sweets, nuts, petticoats, gloves, and other items for those in need. Navy crew members loaded the boat with 5 million toys and treats weighing over 12,000 tons. It became known as The Santa Claus Ship, as it traveled across the ocean to deliver its gifts.

When it arrived in England, charities and the Soldiers and Sailors Families Association helped distribute gifts first to children who had lost their fathers in WWI battles, then to children whose fathers who were considered missing, and then to refugee families. The ship then traveled to Belgium and other parts of Europe to deliver presents to children.

News of this well-appreciated act spread across the nation. The McKinley Music Company created a song about it that highlighted how President Woodrow Wilson and his Secretary of the Navy had allowed a navy ship to become the Santa Claus Ship. The fact that the president of the United States considered it so important to help the suffering children across the ocean that he would allow one of the navy's great warships to be turned into a Christmas boat full of garments and toys was universally deemed as a wonderful gesture of humanity. But this act of international philanthropy was short-lived, as this was the only time the Santa Claus ship sailed to deliver gifts to war-torn children. In the following year, no donations or deliveries occurred; the Santa Claus Ship was thus a lovely blip in time.

World War II began in 1941, two weeks before Christmas with the bombing of Pearl Harbor. Santa Claus was again deployed to help with the war effort, according to Klein (2019). The Santa character was used to urged Americans to buy war bonds, conserve resources, and maintain silence to prevent leaks to the enemy. He was also used to promise that he would deliver weapons to soldiers to fight Hitler, Tojo, and Mussolini. The War Production Board produced posters of Santa wearing olive-colored army uniforms with a helmet on his head as he carried a rifle slung over his shoulder, with words that announced: "Santa Claus Has Gone to War!". Another War Production Board propaganda poster showed Santa along with airplanes and munitions with the tidings: "Merry Christmas to All and to All a Good Fight." Soldiers like my dad found Santa to be used by Western Union on the holiday telegrams soldiers would send to their loved ones. In subtle ways, Santa was portrayed to be behind "our boys" who were bravely fighting against our WWII enemies.

Using Santa to support good against evil was akin to his tradition of dividing children into categories of naughty or nice, where good children were given gifts while naughty children were given switches.

Supposedly President Franklin Roosevelt loved Santa Claus. In an attempt to keep inflation from spiraling during World War II, FDR used Executive Order 9250 to establish the Office of Economic Stabilization to freeze wages for everyone across the nation. However, he allowed a Bonafide Santa Clause that allowed for department store Santas, who met standards appropriate to honor the role of Santa, to be excluded from the wage-freezing order.

During WWII in particular, it was common for someone in a battalion or unit to be designated as their Santa Claus. This person may dress is Santa attire, be the one to distribute gifts to soldiers, and coordinate festive activities to lighten the spirit of military personnel. In memory of the Santa Claus Ship of WWI, some soldier-Santas took the lead on creating gifting or celebratory activities for local children. This is how Jim Yellig, mentioned in the first chapter of this book, got his start being Santa Claus. Trying to create moments of joy in otherwise brutal and hard circumstances is part of the Santa Claus legacy, and certainly observed in these wartime stories.

Santa Claus kept showing up in subsequent wars. For instance, in the Korean War, Operation Santa Claus was created as a combat cargo effort to send some of the airmen in Japan home by Christmas. Soldiers like Dale Parish dressed up as Santa Claus to arrive with soldier-elves to deliver an orange, candy, and trinkets to children in their mud-hut school, which he recalled as one of the highlights of his life. Sailors like Ben Bower did the same, and he, like Jim Yellig, became a Santa for the rest of his life. Being a Santa and giving to grateful children around the world became a life-changing event for countless wartime military personnel.

Susan Kee writes in a 2019 Facebook post that an Australian Santa Claus soldier came to gift Korean children during the war and that Santa Claus became much more than a gift-bringer to the children. Korean children did not know what Santa Claus was but they appreciated foreigners who were kind enough to give them gifts. She states that "What these kids may not have known is that these soldiers came to give us something far greater than Christmas presents. These brave young men from 21 United Nations countries, came to fight for and die, to give the most precious gift of freedom to Koreans. Today, South Korea is a prosperous and free nation due to the courageous service and sacrifice of countless young men who came to defend South Korea against communist tyranny during the Korean War". Hence, the growth of Santa Claus was profoundly impacted by war. And as I learned, the Cold War in many ways really launched him into the children's psyche on December 24 when he supposedly leaves the North Pole to make his journey delivering presents.

The Militarization of Santa's Christmas Eve Trip From The North Pole

As a child, my parents turned on the television set every Christmas Eve so we could track Santa's journey from the North Pole. The meteorologists would periodically interrupt programs to give viewers a NORAD update on where Santa was at different moments in time. They put up a visual flight path similar to the one I see when I fly in airplanes that shows where I am and how close I am to my destination. When I became a parent, I too turned on the TV or internet so my own children could enjoy the excitement of seeing where Santa was – and how we'd all better get to bed before he got close to where we lived! Little did I know until I did the research for this project how political NORAD's innocent-sounding activity was!

In an article by Matt Novak (2014), the history of how NORAD's annual coverage of Santa Claus's journey began is detailed and excerpted below. The common story is that on Christmas Eve in 1955 a little boy thought he was dialing a phone number sponsored by Sears that let children talk with Santa Claus but he accidentally called CONAD, the name for NORAD back then, the military command center that patrolled skies for Soviet nuclear missiles. The guy who answered the phone, Col. Harry Shoup, supposedly played along and pretended to be Santa. As the story goes, this was the beginning of NORAD's annual coverage of announcing where Santa Claus is as he crosses the skies making his journey around the world.

This sweet and sentimental tale is reportedly untrue – a propaganda manipulation by the government with the goal of achieving an entirely different purpose. Novak found the wrong-phone-story is a myth. Reportedly a child did dial CONAD by mistake, but it wasn't on Christmas Eve, and he wasn't calling Santa. But it planted a seed that Col. Shoup and military leaders identified as useful in its campaign to woo the American public into acceptance of its new military initiative.

Some background information on what was going on at the time militarily is needed first to understand the creation of NORAD's Santa Claus calculator. During WWII, the US and Canada were concerned that there may be a German or Japanese incursion into Alaska or the Maritime Provinces so they began developing a strategic alliance for their mutual protection. In an American Federation of Science history of NORAD, I learned that in the late 1940s the Soviet Union had developed an atomic bomb and long-range aviation that enabled them to make a direct hit on Canada and the United States. Canada built a series of Doppler radar detection units along its west coast, but there were gaps that would have allowed Soviet missiles to sneak in. Canada and the US worked together to construct a multi-tiered attack notification system in which attacks from either the Pacific or Atlantic oceans would be identified and intercepted. They established a combined air defense organization called Continental Air Defense Command (CONAD), that over time became called the North American Air Defense Command (NORAD). By the 1960s, a quarter of a million US and Canadian military personnel operated a complex system that would enable them to identify and intercept surface-to-air missiles. As the space race escalated between the US and the Soviet Union, so did networks to protect the US from nuclear attack. NORAD's name chanted from Air Defense Command to Aerospace Defense

Command. But when the Cold War ended, there were growing concerns about funding and longevity for NORAD. This has resulted in a reconfiguration of its mission over time.

The 1950s military officials commissioned to protect the US from Soviet missile attack realized that they were having a difficult time selling the creation of their expensive nuclear defense system to the American public, who was just recovering from the horrors of WWII. They had developed sets of public relations campaigns and films in the mid-1950s aimed to justify their existence and create a sense of urgency to protect citizens from Cold War threats. These included veteran Jimmy Stewart in the movie, Strategic Air Command, which was made to show the public that they needed to be prepared for war since enemies can strike with air power at virtually no notice. Dragnet star Jack Webb starred in the film 24 Hour Alert that promoted the importance of America's fighting fleet, strategically based on Col. Shoup's experiences. The military had been aggressive in advancing its interests by imploring Americans to see the importance of this defense system. It was working so-so.

Now back to Santa Claus and NORAD. The child's accidental call to CONAD inspired military officials to enlist their most beloved good-guy - Santa Claus – to come to their rescue. As Novak points out, "who better than Ol' St. Nick to join the fight against the godless commies in the Soviet Union?" Thus Santa became drafted and enlisted as a character that would help fight the good fight against nonbelievers.

On Christmas Eve 1955 the Associated Press published a story about Santa Claus being granted safe passage by CONAD as he made his journey from the North Pole.

CONAD's resources were highlighted, announcing that Santa was traveling at 45 knots at an altitude of 35,000 feet to arrive in time to deliver his gifts to children across America. He would be protected by US and Canadian defense units to steer him into the jet stream that should double his speed and steer him around stormy weather. The message conveyed that "the Soviets were so evil that they'd even attack Santa if given the chance. But the US military wasn't going to let that happen".

This endeavor proved to be a spectacularly effective public relations success. Over 30 years later, NORAD's coverage of Santa's journey is an annual occurrence. In the 1960s NORAD sent out vinyl records to radio stations across the country that they could play to alert people on Santa's progress between Christmas music played by the NORAD Commanders Orchestra that you can still hear today on YouTube. NORAD promoted the idea that Santa was a Cold Warrior, protected by the brave military representatives of NORAD. These images could be found in print, magazines, newspapers, on television, and later on the internet. Commercials indicating that NORAD saw "nine unknown objects" entering US air space that it zoomed to protect us from turned out to be Santa and his reindeer, reinforcing the idea that the military was always there to protect citizens – and Santa.

Even after the Cold War was over, NORAD had an incentive to keep Santa Claus alive. He was essential for perpetuating NORAD's positive public image. Funding for NORAD's traditional mission was in question after the end of the Cold War and military officials had to figure out how to redesign its mission to keep it alive. Computer technology opened up the opportunity to create a Santa Tracker that children could visit online. NORAD partnered with America Online and Analytical Graphics to obtain images that fascinated and delighted. In the 2000s NORAD partnered with Google Earth, and Google purchased CIA-funded mapping software company Keyhole. NORAD stopped partnering with Google and works with Microsoft. In response, Google launched a competing Santa Tracker program, and its program does not provide military escorts to Santa. But NORAD continues to promote fighter jets escorting Santa, even though child advocacy organizations such as the Campaign for A Commercial-Free Childhood reported they were uncomfortable with the militaristic, violent underpinnings of this new marketing strategy.

It appears that NORAD's use of Santa is transforming where he goes and how he travels is continuing into the 21st century. I still like Santa tracking on Christmas Eve. But I have to say, that I'm going to be looking at it a lot differently than I did when I was a child.

Santa, Presidents, and Christmas

Believing in Santa has become such a political hot-potato that it has reached the presidential level. If presidents say they believe in Santa, or don't, it influences what people will think of them. The tension between believers and non-believers in Santa Claus has resulted in a Santa Claus war of sorts, as people align on either side of the issue. Politicians, religious leaders, academics, parents, and the media have all waded in to give their two-cents on the issue. What has resulted is nothing less than a war on the holiday. This contributes to the parent's confusion about whether or not they should encourage their children to believe in him or not.

Something as simple as a decorated holiday tree has even been controversial. Historical accounts vary with disagreement over whether it was President Franklin Pierce, Benjamin Harrison, or William Taft putting up the first White House Christmas tree. Theodore Roosevelt opposed cutting trees down for decorations and decided to instead celebrate the season by inviting 500 children for a party there. Cutting down trees for the holiday was castigated as being a form of arboreal infanticide, a forestry fad, or pro-German. Even the types of decorations put on the tree can be controversial, as outlined in a Note at the end of this chapter. The colors selected, the types of ornaments, the tree-topper, the lights, the number of decorated trees all end up having symbolic meaning or agenda statements to different groups. It seems curious that something as simple as a decorated tree can have such huge political ramifications.

Near as I can tell, presidents may have their picture taken with Santa, but none has officially donned a Santa Claus costume. There was, however, an official Santa contender for president. During 2012, Santa Claus ran as a candidate for president of the United States in 15 states. Actually. Nevada resident Santa Claus, formerly known as Thomas O'Connor, was an advocate for vulnerable children and ran on a child rights platform. He announced that none of the candidates were talking about anything with respect to children, and he was running to promote their health, education, safety, and welfare by restoring America's heart and soul, and stop perpetuating the nation's war machine. He visited every governor's office in the nation in his

Santa's Bless the Children Tour, and he found that all were receptive except Arkansas governor Mike Huckabee (Holpuch 2012). O'Connor claimed to be a monk, one who did not approve of the war against children and wanted to fight for the nation's leaders to better protect children's rights. He obviously didn't win the election, and I would guess that the important things his platform advocated went discounted because Santa (and by association, children) are often discounted. But the fact that Santa Claus wasn't considered to have a message worth considering as a viable leadership direction for the country is thought-provoking.

President Lincoln identified that Santa Claus was a powerful tool that could be mobilized to sway public opinion towards his agendas. Most every US president has had their picture taken with Santa Claus. The pictures convey that even presidents believe in Santa. There are pictures of First Ladies shown kissing Santa, their children talking with Santa, Santa shaking hands or hugging presidents, or presidents like Lyndon Johnson even dressing up their dogs to look like Santa. The Bush presidents, Ronald Reagan, Jimmy Carter, Clintons, and Obamas showcase many photos of their families with Santa Claus. Robert George, a Southern Californian, was dubbed by the Associated Press as the Santa Claus to six Presidents., starting with Eisenhower. George reportedly had a fondness for disadvantaged and disabled children (Montanaro 2016). The lighting of the annual Christmas tree is a social media event for enthusiastic crowds.

Santa is a sticky-wicket for presidents. If he is made to represent a religious character, this may be seen to violate the separation of church and state. But if he doesn't make an appearance in some form, even if portrayed as a totally secular being, presidents may be viewed analogously to Scrooge. Whatever they do sends a message. If presidents show they believe in Santa Claus, it sends messages. One message is that believing in Santa is endorsed at the highest national level. The implication is that presidents and Santa are sharing secrets to help and protect the public. Their relationship conveys that Santas are there to help the president and the country when needed. If a president announced that they didn't believe in Santa, the fall-out could be extensive. If Santa likes the president, then perhaps voters should like him too. If presidents don't believe in Santa, what does that say about him?

Certainly President Lincoln, President Eisenhower, and most presidents over the last hundred years have found a partnership with Santa to be advantageous. But in recent days, the tension between Santa and politics has become apparent. As a current example, President Trump ran on a campaign promise to make December 25 not a secular winter holiday that could include people of all persuasions but implied he would make it a Christian focused holiday that put the Christ back in Christmas. He promised that people would be saying "Merry Christmas" instead of the more politically inclusive "Happy Holidays". So where does Santa fit in - is he a representative of a Christian holiday or a representative of a variety of secular celebrations? During a December 2018 government shutdown, NORAD still took children's calls that were patched to the White House so the president and first lady could answer a few. President Trump took a few calls; instead of following the protocol that NORAD provides its volunteers who answer phones to say as they pretend to be Santa, Trump went off-script. A seven-year-old was asked if she still believed in Santa because, as he told her, "At 7, (believing in Santa) is marginal, right?" Data shows that many children of that age still believe in Santa, and concern was raised about what it could mean to a child for the president to disavow belief in him. More recently, First Lady Melania Trump was recorded as saying "Who gives a fuck about Christmas stuff and decorations?" (Stieb 2020). Evidently, the pressure of how to decorate was extensive for her. Are such views in keeping with the Santa Spirit? Whether these are examples of how leader's "front-stage behavior", like what they say, may be at stark contrast with what their "back-stage behavior", like what they really believe, is something thought-provoking (Goffman 1959). Just as Lincoln manipulated Santa to influence the direction of the Civil War, Trump threatened that if his presidential opponent, Joe Biden, is elected that Biden will "cancel Christmas" (Reuters 2020). Using a figure or festival to promote one's political agenda seems alive and well a century later.

As December 2020 approaches, one can look at the international impact of the coronavirus on the population and wonder what the holiday season will hold. Will people be encouraged to get together with family, even if there is the likelihood of catching the virus? Will people stay apart and rely on technology to celebrate physically distant but socially close holidays? Many people have lost their jobs or homes due to the economic impact of the pandemic. What will be the political spin of the virus and the holiday season be? Will Santa show up or not? I guess we will have to wait and see...

What I Concluded

Until doing this research, I never knew that Santa Claus was used as a form of political psychological warfare. I learned that Santa Claus, in his various forms, has long been used as a political tool. Who knew?

Santa Claus has been transformed, manipulated and co-opted by governments, the corporate industry, religious groups, and ideological zealots. While Santa Claus is not being used to advance wartime at this moment in time, it doesn't mean that he's not being used for political purposes or to promote someone's agenda. We continue to witness the ongoing debate about whether the December holiday is secular or spiritual, and whether the government should have any say in Santa, and if people want to interject him into the debate over his role in the separation of church and state.

The history of Santa Claus is rife with conflict as he is used by one side or the other to promote their agendas. We've seen it with religion, with politics, and with consumerism. What is seldom discussed is the war over the mind of children. At stake is the way children understand spiritual and social relationships. President Lincoln used Santa Claus as a vehicle to make Northern children feel superior and Southern children abandoned in order to break the back of the Civil War. Advertisers use Santa to get parents to spend, and sending has gotten tied to children's perceptions of personal worth as beloved human beings. If children don't get presents they think they should have, they may feel rejected – so we hurry out to buy them more things so they feel special, as if their specialness was tied to their material objects. People who are religious, from all different types of religious persuasions –use Santa to show why he is wrong-headed. Picking on a fantasy character to shoulder the blame is ridiculous.

We are seeing psychological warfare waged on different fronts as well. Cooptation of Santa Claus has been so extensive and pervasive it makes me better understand why some people hate Santa. But Santa could be coopted for positive reasons too. This leaves me pondering - how should I explain Santa Claus to my children?

Notes on White House, presidents, Christmas and Santa: https://www.npr.org/2016/12/25/506420373/i-saw-first-ladies-kissing-santa-claus-and-a-first-dog-dressed-as-him;

https://www.whitehousehistory.org/press-room/press-backgrounders/white-house-christmas-traditions; https://en.wikipedia.org/wiki/White_House_Christmas_tree; https://washington.org/visit-dc/holidays-white-house-first-family-traditions#:~:text=1909%2C%20A%20'Blue'%20Christmas%3A&text=Taft%20was%20the%20first%20president,portion%20of%20the%20White%20House.; https://www.history.com/news/white-house-christmas-tree-decorations-photos; https://nymag.com/intelligencer/2020/10/melania-trump-who-gives-a-f-k-about-christmas-stuff.html; https://www.npr.org/2018/12/25/680077240/president-trump-to-7-year-old-are-you-still-a-believer-in-santa; https://www.reuters.com/video/watch/idOVD0STZHB

Jill Jackson Miller & Sy Miller quote

Let there be
Peace on earth
And let it begin
With me

Jill Jackson Miller & Sy Miller

Created in 1955 for the International Children's Choir

Chapter 8

Big Biz & Santa

The Dilemma

Santa Claus has become a very attractive figure for advertising, not just joy and altruism, but also for selling objects ranging from candy to cigarettes to cars. The name of Santa Claus has become synonymous with materialism for many folks. For many people, when they hear the word "Santa" they automatically think "things". When I ask children to "tell me about Santa" the first thing most of the pipe up with is "presents". Some children (and adults) get quite specific about what the present should be, including color, brand, and model. Children could tell me about how he's nice, fun, or kind – but the "thing" answer is most common.

One reason some parents don't want their children to believe in Santa Claus because it would make them greedy. This is curious to me since Santa as a mythical character could not possibly make a child greedy. There are clearly other dynamics going on. So how did the commercial industry take over Santa Claus? I wanted to find out.

What I Discovered

The commercialization of Santa has a long and varied history. There were many festivals occurring around the world that focused on joy, feasting, altruism, and gift-giving that existed long before Santa or the holiday we call Christmas. There were many key figures who morphed into the character we have come to know as Santa Claus who shared the central attribute of gifting others. Giving people presents to let them know they were cared about permeates all traditions and figures. The story of the Three Wise Men bringing culturally appropriate gifts of the day, gold, frankincense, and myrrh, to honor the birth of a baby who they thought was special, incorporated the gift-giving tradition.

It makes sense that given the history that one of Santa's key traits would be gifting. While he is associated with the gift of joy, laughter, and altruism, he is also associated with giving material objects that were desired across the world by people in different cultures. These included delicious or coveted things to eat (like sweets or fancy cakes), objects to bring delight (like toys or musical instruments), money (to make life easier), clothes (like socks, gloves, or other attire), or coal (to keep people in cold climates warm). The fact that Santa Claus got associated with bringing presents seems like a normal and natural transformation of celebrations and figures.

It also became fuel to fire-up the incomes of growing businesses. As I learned, Santa was viewed as a very suitable candidate for exploitation to green the palms of entrepreneurs in the development of capitalism. His loveable, altruistic portrayal was valuable to incorporate the transformation of the public's psyche to view consumerism and materialism as positive attributes.

Artistic and Literary Contributions

As pointed out in the chapter on Santa comes to America, a small but effective group of artists and authors converged to shape how the public saw Santa Claus. They inadvertently laid the foundation for the creation of big-Santa-money by corporations.

Quick recap - while Charles Dicken's didn't exactly have Santa Claus in his *Christmas Carol*, he did have spirits – which were essentially the same thing, of wise characters to show us how to do what is good and right for others. Santa was made kindly and shown to be friends with cute little reindeer, introduced in 1821 in New York printer William Gilley's 16-page book, *A New Years' Present to the Little Ones*. Thomas Nast's drawings starting in the 1860s painted pictures in people's minds of what Santa Claus looked like and how he was a good patriot who was there to help protect us and our country. Clement Moore's poem on The Night Before Christmas became the standard for not just what jolly Santa looked like, but how generously he behaved. The newspaper editorial on, "Yes, Virginia there is a Santa Claus" inspired the public's desire to believe in him. By the 1920s, Norman Rockwell's *Saturday Evening Post's* portraits of Santa Claus embedded in our brains an image of a wise, kindly, and fun gentleman whose raison d'etre was to bring joy to others – especially children. Annually from 1931 to the mid-1960s, Haddon Sundblom created a new Santa picture for each Christmas for Coca-Cola advertisements that were disseminated around the world. Santa Claus became cast as a vehicle for bringing families and the community the opportunity to bond together. Other advertisers seized upon this attractive image of Santa Claus to promote their own products. Within a few generations, the image of Father Christmas and other European or pagan images had been forgotten. So had their simplicity and focus on joy and community-building, especially as big-business began to thrive.

The Emerging Paradox of Gifts and Wealth

From an anthropological view of cultural transformation, the shift from the US being an agricultural society to an industrial one had huge impacts. Reliance upon the family, growing one's own food, counting on the community to help, and making your own furniture, clothes and buildings shifted to a more externally-derived, money-driven world where individual advancement became the focus more so than community solidarity. Working in factories had a two-fold benefit – one to the workers who gained a stable, predicable income and one to businesses, who were able to grow exponentially. The industrial revolution triggered the arrival of buying, not making, what you needed, as a variety of new merchandise came became available. The old celebrations and values slowly changed as societies developed.

This is also observed in the relationship between religion and business. The gift-giving component of traditional societies and festivals became something both religion and business rallied around. In what has become referred to as the Paradox of Christmas, there is a tension around whether gifts are good or not. It is clear that giving to others was deemed to be a good and honorable thing in most religious traditions. But especially as businesses grew, the gift-giving tradition shifted in form and content. What was considered a "good gift" shifted as well.

Philosopher David King (2017) observes that in the three Abrahamic faiths of Christianity, Islam, and Judaism, giving is an important aspect of being a follower of faith. Tzedakah in Judaism means justice, and giving to others, especially the poor, is a commandment and a moral obligation to be followed. The notion of gemilut chasadim refers to the importance of giving loving-kindness to others and using one's opportunity to give can create tikkun olam, or the healing of the world. Giving to others is one of the five pillars of Islam. Many Muslims hold that a religious obligation of zakat, or giving away at least 2.5% of one's assets is central to their faith. Giving additional gifts, especially to the poor, is referred to as sadaqa, the same root word as the Jewish word for justice, tzedakah. Some Christian faiths hold that God commands people to tithe or give away one-tenth of your income to the church or people in need. The Gospel of Matthew has a story where Jesus tells a rich man to sell all his possessions. Malachi 3:10-12 tells us to open our floodgates to pour out our blessings to others. Acts 20:35 reminds us that it is more blessed to give than to receive.

But it's not just Abrahamic faiths that focus on generosity. It seems to be an underlying premise of all faiths. For instance, in Hinduism, the Bhagavadgita encourages giving to others, or dana, as an important part of one's religious duty, or dharma. The Isa Upanishad text holds that true joy and peace come from detaching from wealth and materialism. Wealth need not be bad - it is the clinging attitude that people have toward possessions that interferes with seeing ourselves as responsible for the welfare of all.

Buddhism defines generosity as one of its three central practices. Generosity is one of the six paramita in Mahayana Buddhism and is considered crucial for the attainment of enlightenment. Giving to others benefits them; building a hospital, providing a meal, or showing kindness helps alleviates the suffering of others from sickness, hunger, or worry. If one has positive intentions, giving serves as a way to eliminate attachment to things or greed. By using possessions to benefit others, we develop altruism and helps us to remember that we are all interconnected. Everyone who is alive and all we have comes thanks to the generosity of others.

As stewards of the natural world, Native American or First Nations peoples prioritized gifting as a way to honor others, including clan members and future generations. Unlike European based values, wealth in many Native American cultures is measured not by possessions but by wisdom, generosity, sharing, and caring for the community. Many Native American celebrations incorporated the notion of potlatch, a Chinook adaptation of the Nootka word pat-shatl, which means giving to others. During ceremonies, give-aways of one's wealth or possessions to others honor them and may also represent a transfer of power between generations. Making objects to give to others held importance, for it conveyed time, thought, and effort that someone put into making it for someone special.

Monks from a variety of religious traditions take vows of poverty to give themselves to the work of their faith and to shun greed or the accumulation of material objects. The idea in most of these faiths wasn't that material objects were bad – in fact, having enough was good and enabled people to give to others. For instance, the Buddha Siddhartha was born a prince and had extensive wealth that enabled him to chuck it all and go in pursuit of the meaning of life. Being able to give tzedakah or sadaqa to help others and achieve social justice for the poor was possible because people had been enough wealth and opportunity that they could do so. In indigenous cultures, having enough wealth that one could give to others was good, but it also enabled them to elevate their status in the community. So wealth wasn't necessarily bad in any of these faiths. It was the obsession with wealth and materialism that got in the way. Turning a blind eye to the suffering of others was the problem. If people gave gifts, they should be gifts of the heart, well-intended, joyful, and meant to improve the wellbeing of others. Giving gifts just to give them, without meaning, was not designed to grow one's spirituality.

In a historical review of Christmas, Melissa Leone reports that Americans were still continuing the tradition of simple, thoughtful gifting to others by 1745. Reports of giving clothes and apples were common. Emphasis was on bringing cheer to the poor and giving charitable gifts that people in need could use. Gifts tended to be home-made and useful.

Santa Claus became associated with crass materialism, seemingly around the late 1800s. Supposedly the first known reported advertisement for Christmas gifts occurred at a bookstore in 1806 in Salem, Massachusetts. Instead of focusing on the spiritual and communal benefits associated with giving to others, the emphasis shifted to the material and financial importance of the gift. This shift fits perfectly with the rise of industrialization, factory-growth, and the influx of new material items that people could purchase.

Sociologist Max Weber in the 1930s saw the intersecting relationship between capitalism and Protestantism in early America. Essentially, in life, one doesn't know whether we are going to be saved by God or not. Therefore, we look for tangible signs. If people are poor, sick, without family, hungry and homeless, they must be cursed by God, but if they are healthy, rich, with big families and large estates, God must be smiling on them. The rise of capitalism provided a convenient vehicle for people to gravitate towards. As capitalism provided them the chance to get lots of money, hence big homes, lots of property, businesses, animals, good health, wealth, and large families, it became a visible way for people to believe that they were better than others. People who didn't buy into the capitalistic dream remained without extensive material resources, which became used as justification that they weren't good people or blessed by God. If people were fortunate to have lots of money, they could have more to spend, give away, and grow the religious or political organizations they liked, as well as their businesses.

Just as the government and military saw Santa Claus as a convenient figure to promote their causes, the growing world of business did too.

Enter the Santa-Advertisers

It was the 1900s when advertisers really took hold of Santa Claus to advance the purposes and purchases. The prevailing sentiment of the day was that the business of America **WAS** business, and the nation's retailers quickly saw Christmas's potential for profit. Historian Lisa Jacobson found companies identified that holidays created the opportunity for spending seasons, and all businesses had to do was develop merchandise and market them in accordance with Christmas, Easter, Valentine's Day, Halloween, and the like. But it all began with the merchandising of Christmas. But how were merchants going to sway parents to start indulging their children by purchasing them lots of toys, sweets, and presents?

The tradition of gift-giving permeated most cultures and the figure of Santa Claus became a perfect promoter of presents. Companies started developing all kinds of product lines to sell. All of the previous configurations of the Santa character that had been different in size, attire, attitude, and companions became homogenized into a chubby, jolly, white-haired, white-skinned older man who was always kind. He was no longer accompanied by Krampus or frightening-figures but cute little elves. His welcoming, abundant persona made him the ideal symbol for consumer abundance. Retailers identified this and put into place plans to mobilize financial success in Santa's sleigh.

Around that time there was a demographic shift that also impacted parents' desire to gift their children. As Viviana Zelizer noted in her book, *Pricing the Priceless Child,* throughout much of history children had high mortality rates or were regarded as expendable burdens. The emotional investment in children was therefore low. But a cultural shift occurred in how children were valued when children valued as "priceless". Emotional, social, and financial investments in children grew at home and in the community. This change in how children were viewed fit perfectly with the creation and marketing of toys, games, clothes, and other child-directed items. Jacobson observed that one reason why parents quickly embraced Santa Claus is that he gave them a way of disguising the commercialization of toys and having Santa bring them would assuage any parental guilt over spoiling their children with frivolous gifts. Parents could still give utilitarian or educational presents, but Santa could be the one to bring "spectacular gifts with lots of bells and whistles."

Consider the dynamics - increased money in the home for purchasing the plethora of new items being marketed, holidays being promoted as festive family gift-giving opportunities, children becoming increasingly sentimentalized, and increased parental financial investment in their young offspring - these all converged to transform Christmas into the major commercial holiday of the year. Tying commercialism with religion with family bonding around precious children made for a perfect corporate endeavor.

Santa's association with conspicuous consumption, especially in the marketing world of the merchant, has been an effective ploy, relying upon a concept psychologists call 'cognitive dissonance.' Merchants take a beloved icon (Santa) and connect it to a product (toy, clothing item, etc.), to create a subtle linking of the two items in the head of the potential consumer. If Santa is good, and Santa is selling that item, then the item also must be good. Plug sentimental music and pretty backdrops into advertisement and people feel a positive relationship with the thing they're considering buying.

Gift-giving around Santa's arrival became a way to create fun for everyone and solidify family ties, bonds, and affection. Just as religions from different traditions all viewed gifting as a way to help the vulnerable, marketers also tapped into commonalities in religions that made us, the giver, feel better about ourselves, and viewing ourselves as better people because we were able to give. The commercialization of holidays tapped into these core values and symbolically attached love to giving material presents.

Traditionally, some of the Santa figures delivered their gifts when children didn't see, sneaking down the chimney and tucking them into their stockings or putting presents at the foot of a tree while children were asleep. But marketers decided to make Santa Claus visible and put him front-and-center in stores, advertisements, and anywhere the public may see. His presence in stores, parades, television, and print embedded the notion that when children saw the picture of Santa, their brains would immediately go to the question of "what can he bring me" materialism.

Using Santa to sell extra-ordinary merchandise that wasn't usually available, or was expensive, became a lucrative way to increase corporate revenue. Soon in the advertising world, Santa wasn't bringing just baby-dolls and harmonicas, but today can be seen hawking automobiles, jewelry, trips to exotic destinations. The not-so-subtle message conveyed that the bigger and more expensive the object, the more Santa must love us. Advertising and merchants have been quite effective in this shift in his persona.

Melissa Leone's 2011 review of the commercialization of Christmas and Santa Claus in the United States found that by the late 1800s, the *New York Evening Post* had an advertisement for "four hundred and fifty kinds of Christmas presents and New Year's gifts, consisting of toys, children's [sic] and school books, Christmas pieces, Drawing books, Paint, Lead Pencils, Conversations, and Toy cards, Pocket

Books, Penknives". She notes that holiday ads started coming earlier and earlier in the calendar year as the years went by, and by the late nineteenth-century holiday shopping was big business.

I found it very hard to document how many toys are being sold these days, or how much money corporations are making from Christmas sales. What was clear is that Americans spent Over one trillion dollars on Christmas in 2019, with 7% of people refusing to spend anything for the holiday because of religious or political reasons. Online Christmas purchases in 2019 were over $723 million. By the time you add in electronic devices, educational gifts, clothes, sweets, toys, bikes, and heaven-knows-what-else, the amount spent by families and the amount earned by corporations is in the unknown but no-doubt-huge trillions of dollars.

Coca-Cola's Contribution to Santa's Fame

The advertising company most associated with the rise of Santa Claus as a corporate icon is Coca-Cola. Their ads featuring Santa Claus have become the picture of Santa that comes to most people's minds, thanks to Coke's effective marketing campaign. But its contribution to our understanding of Santa has a history that seldom gets told.

While Coca-Cola gets credit for being "the" company that shaped our image of Santa, the White Rock Beverage Company had been using Santa for advertising since 1915. Their ads had Santa driving a truck, not a sleigh, filled with White Rock water and carbonated drinks. White Rock had gained 90% of the carbonated drink market by the 1930s. Coca-Cola executives identified that carbonated drinks had lucrative potential; if Santa Claus had helped White Rock to be so successful gaining market-share, then perhaps Santa could do the same for Coke.

Coca-Cola began advertising in the 1920s with promotional ads in magazines like *The Saturday Evening Post*. Their first ads with Santa had him looking stern, similar to the style of Thomas Nast. But White Rock's Santa looked pleasant, not strict. So for its December 1930 ad, artist Fred Mizen painted Santa Claus in a department-store drinking a bottle of Coke. The transformation of Santa being a guy that the public could relate to inspired Coca-Cola executives to pursue a more aggressive Santa-ad campaign. Archie Lee at the D'Arcy Advertising Agency helped company executives to create a new Santa. They commissioned illustrator Haddon Sundblom to develop images that made Santa into his own entity, not merely a man dressed up as Santa Claus. Sundblom asked his friend, Lou Prentiss, a retired salesman, to be his model for Santa. He used the neighbor's two daughters to be the child-models in his original picture, painting one as a girl and one as a boy. His 1931 picture debuted in the *Post*, and later in magazines designed to touch diverse audiences, such as in *The New Yorker, Ladies Home Journal,* and *National Geographic*.

The campaign was so successful that Sundblom developed other figures to join Santa. He created Sprite Boy, a little sprite or elf to join Santa. About twenty years later, the Coca-Cola company introduced the drink, Sprite, to its repertoire. By 1964 the Coke Santa became plastered on store displays, magazine and newspaper ads, billboards, and about everywhere possible. Santa was depicted in various situations, homes, doing different things with different people – but always with a Coca-Cola in his hand. Coke, not milk, has become regarded as Santa's favorite drink. The Coca-Cola Santa Claus remains the primary visual associated with him.

Department Store Contributions

Department stores turned out to be a fantastic vehicle for the dissemination of Santa, the gift-giver. The creation of department stores was a gigantic development from the corner general store that had often served communities. Prior to the 1800s people made their gifts, but department stores changed this. "Good" gifts were often regarded to be store-bought, not hand-made. Mass production increased the number and availability of goods at affordable (to some) prices. Department stores had everything, from shoes to clothes to kitchen goods to toys and countless other objects that people never knew they needed or wanted until they were put out in front of them to buy. Stores displayed certain products as Christmas merchandise. They worked with people like Louis Prang, a German immigrant who developed color technology, to mass-produce holiday cards to be sold.

To understand how Santa came to be in department stores means stepping back in time to consider what life was like for their founders. Macy's Department Store reports being the first to bring Santa. R.H. Macy, son of a shopkeeper in Massachusetts, opened the store bearing his name in New York City in 1858. It sold dry-goods. The store's logo, a red star, came from his days on a whaling boat when the star guided his vessel home. Mr. Macy was an innovative businessman. Instead of having customers barter what they would pay, he instituted a one-price policy where a specific item would sell to every customer at the same rice. He offered money-back guarantees, introduced the Idaho baked potato and tea bags, sold towels that were different colors, as well as custom-made clothes, and was the first store in New York City to obtain a liquor license.

Macy identified that Santa Claus was a good marketer for his store, and invited him to be present in the store during the 1862 holiday. Two years later he installed elaborately decorated and illuminated store window displays at Christmas to promote certain products. Decorations were key to attracting consumers and led to the phenomenon of window-shopping. There were lots of decoration themes that could be co-opted from other cultures, and were, like wreaths, stockings, decorated trees, lights, music, porcelain dolls, and ornaments.

However, Edgar's Department Store in Brockton, Massachusetts also claims to have had the first department store Santa, but theirs is in 1890. It makes that claim because they allege their Santa looked more authentic than the one at Macy's. The back-story is that James Edgar, known as Colonel Jim, promoted his Santa and children arrived by train from the surrounding cities to catch a glimpse of the man they couldn't catch when he came down their chimneys. In the decade that followed, department stores around the country had their own Santa Claus available to meet, greet, and listen to children.

That store also has an interesting philanthropic history. Edgar had once said of Santa Claus, "I have never been able to understand why the great gentleman lives at the North Pole. He is so far away...only able to see the children one day a year. He should live closer to them." His attitude permeated the legacy of the store. In 1920 the store manager heard that children weren't going to school because their children could not afford to buy them shoes or repair their worn-out ones. Brockton was once a shoe-making town so he closed the top floor of the store, bought a shoe-repairing machine, and hired a half-dozen cobblers who repaired 5000 pairs of shoes for children and the needy. In this way, Col. Jim has helped to keep Santa Claus alive.

F. W. Woolworth opened his "five and dime" department store in Lancaster, Pennsylvania in 1879. It proved to be a smart business move because his inexpensive prices under-cut those of his competitors, and he displayed merchandise that customers could handle before they bought things. Children could see and touch toys that they longed for. Many stores had counters where they could get a drink or a snack. Legend has it that a salesman selling glass German ornaments visited Woolworth in 1880, and Woolworth agreed to see if they would sell – and the case of 144 ornaments sold in a day. Supposedly between 1880 and 1939 Woolworth's sold over 500 million ornaments.

The John Wanamaker department store in Philadelphia made Christmas displays to lure in customers. Once inside, he staged store sing-alongs and passed out songbooks that featured religious carols, thereby linking commercialism, the solstice December festival that had become known as Christmas, the presence of Santa Claus listening to children's wishes, and Christianity. The subliminal message of the Santa=commercialism=Christmas=Christianity was not to be missed. A shrewd early marketer, Wanamaker knew the importance of linking sentimentalism with commercialism. But Leone notes that the holiday's secular appeal was taking hold, and traditional folk symbols like reindeer, snow people, and candy canes became desirable marketing tools

– but nothing was as good as Santa. By 1940 she notes that Santa was credited with annual sales of over $500 million.

The Chicago department store, Montgomery Ward, commissioned Robert May in 1939 to create a coloring book they could use as a holiday giveaway in the store. The book was titled Rudolph the Red-Nosed Reindeer. Johnny Marks, May's brother in law, wrote the song by the same name. Ward's also joined the Santa department store brigade.

Until today, Santas could be found in almost any type of store around the world during the holiday season. However, with the arrival of the COVID-19 virus and the international concern over the spread of communicable disease, mall Santas will likely be a thing of the past. It is not safe for children to visit with Santa for fear of spreading the virus. Many parents are economically devastated by the pandemic and cannot afford to have a Santa who is expected to bring gifts. Fred Selinksky, known as Santa Fred and is the Chairman of the Board at the International Brotherhood of Real Bearded Santas, reports that Christmas is going to continue to come, but whether Santa is going to be a part of it is up to parents (Hendricks 2020). Other holiday events, celebrations, and Santa-focused events have been canceled around the world due to the fear of spreading the virus (BBC 2020).

The presence of Santa Claus was capitalized by the Salvation Army, who hoped to tap into people's philanthropic tendency to help others. Gifting the poor was always a part of traditional winter festivals, as well as in most religious traditions. By the 1890s the Salvation Army had instituted their practice of sending Santas into the streets of New York to solicit donations so they could help feed and help those in need. And while they no longer wear red Santa suits, volunteers ringing bells to solicit donations for the poor can still be found across America today. It is likely that this year, volunteers will be wearing masks to limit the spread of the virus, along with the traditional Santa hats.

Santa Claus Parades

The old song, "I love a parade" reflected a sentiment in my household. My dad was a parade-aholic and marched or road in every parade in town for any occasion. Fourth of July, Memorial Day, high school Homecoming parades, you name it. I grew up watching the Macy's Thanksgiving Day Parade as a pseudo-sacred event, and it remains a ritual in my household.

Parades are a community bonding experience. The military usually starts the parade, wearing their uniforms and marching as they carry national, state, and local flags down the street. Teens and adolescents have an opportunity to play their musical instruments in public together in unison down the street. There are fancy-decorated floats with beauty queens, sports teams, church groups, and other organizations. Politicians ride in convertibles, waving at the crowd, doing friendly shout-outs to motivate voters. Every civic-minded group is there en masse, walking behind their banner, with gymnasts doing cartwheels, moms pushing babies in strollers, and folks showcasing their dogs on leashes. There's music, color, smiles, waves, and often candy being tossed out as children scramble to pick up the pieces. At Macy's Christmas parade, the heart-thumping highlight comes at the end with the arrival of a very dapper Santa Claus in a magnificently decorated float as he waves and wishes everyone good cheer.

It never occurred to me to consider the historical backstory of Santa Claus parades until doing this research. What I learned is that the Santa Claus parades hail from pagan processions at times of celebration, as well as the ancient Roman Triumphs. Stick with me while I explain the fascinating correlation between paganism, the Roman triumph, the church, and big business in the construction of the Santa Claus parade.

Historical reports indicate that parades have been common throughout the world. When bountiful harvests came in, members of the community would celebrate by joyously joining together and showcasing some of their products, or showing gratitude to the gods for providing the yield. They may sing, dance, make music, feast, play games, and happily share with others. There are parade reports from the time of different pagan groups, the Egyptian pharaohs, Babylonians, Sumerians, as well as of processions to honor Athenae, goddess of Athens, celebrations of Eleusinian mysteries, and the Roman triumph.

The Roman triumph is regarded as key to the Santa parade in the following ways. The Roman triumph was a political-showcasing of a military commander or ruler to honor their success defeating an enemy. The honored-one would wear regalia that made him (they were almost always males) look kingly or even divine. Crowns made of green laurels would surround their heads. Some painted their faces red, wore red boots and capes while riding in four-horse drawn chariots through the streets of Rome (get the Santa similarity?) accompanied by people in the military, or those who were captured. These victory parades were huge publicity opportunities for the leader to announce how great they were and for the public to bow down in awe.

The longer the procession, the more important the leader must be. There were standard processional orders of who came first in the line, and what types of people should come afterward. The honored-one came last, the person everyone waited alongside the parade route to finally see in his fancy horse-drawn chariot. We see this today in Santa parades, with the military flag-bearers coming first, and then bands, officials, floats, marching civic groups, and ultimately Santa Claus, who arrives in a modern form of the triumphal entry. Thus it makes the Santa today a manifestation of the Roman triumph, or accolades leaders or the gods of ancient days received.

In Peoria, Illinois in 1888, the Frederick Block of the Schipper and Block Department Store held a December parade that featured Santa Claus. This supposedly laid the foundation for the idea that department stores could benefit from holding holiday parades. Department stores figured out that parades were magnificent ways to pull lots of people together at the same time to witness an onslaught display of merchandise wrapped in holiday cheer. In 1905 the Mr. and Mrs. Timothy Eaton of Toronto met Santa Claus when he arrived by train and they all walked to the Eaton Department Store where he greeted customers. This led to what became the Toronto Santa Claus parade, which in 1908 had one truck with a band to escort Santa to the store. In 1915 Eaton's brought in reindeer from Labrador to pull Santa's sleigh. In 1919, Santa arrived by plane. They created a book with a character called Punkinhead around 1947, and Punkinhead became an annual parade figure.

Gimbel Brothers Department Store in Philadelphia had their first Santa Claus parade in 1920, with 50 people, 15 cars, and a firefighter who was dressed up as Santa. In 1924, both Macy's in New York and the Hudson's Department Store in Detroit held Santa Claus parades. Macy's parade drew 10,000 observers who saw floats, marchers, bands, and store employees dressed up in costumes (an homage to the Roman triumph processions), along with living animals from the Central Park Zoo, according to History.com. The first big helium balloon, for which the Macy's parade has become famous, first appeared in 1927 with Felix the Cat. Hudson's parade showcased large paper-mâché heads that the store's display director saw on a trip to Italy.

The Santa Claus parades have gotten bigger and more elaborate as the years have gone by. The parade was first televised in 1958. The first African-American parade Santa made his debut in 1971 in Grand Rapids, Michigan's Art Van Santa Parade. Santa Claus parades can now be found all over the country, indeed all over the world. Each one is designed to capture the local culture, kick off the holiday celebrations – and announce the beginning of the shopping season.

Hawking Santa to Sell Products

During the 1800s as businesses started to realize the potential buying-power associated with Santa Claus, new merchandise was created and linked directly or indirectly to him. Toymakers seized the enthusiasm to create and market new merchandise to stores. For instance, in 1902 after President Theodore Roosevelt freed a bear that was to be shot, his kindness generated the sale of Teddy Bears, which remains a hot-selling item over a hundred years later. Gender-specific toys were marketed in the 1950s so children would know their role expectations, with Kenner Easy-

Bake ovens, irons, vacuums, and baby dolls for girls while boys received Tonka trucks, guns, Lincoln logs, and construction sets. Marketers created a demand for toys and parents rushed to the stores to buy them, including Chatty Cathy, Cabbage Patch Kids dolls, Tickle Me Elmo, Furbys, Star Wars, Transformers, and countless others.

Carley Stec's blogpost contains 24 advertisements over the last 100 years that highlight how Santa Claus has been used to sell products. The visuals are fascinating. A jolly Santa was shown in 1915 driving a motorized sleigh full of White Rock water, but by the 1950s he was hawking Coca-Cola. In 1983 he was shown enjoying Seagram's Crown Royale alcohol. Pepsi converted him in 2011 to be in their ads too.

Santa is shown supporting the tobacco industry starting in 1919 when he is shown smoking a Murad Turkish cigarette, with the ad reading "When I asked grown-ups to judge for themselves what Xmas present they wanted, they all chose Murad Turkish cigarettes". By 1949 he was pushing Camel and Prince Albert cigarettes.

The kinds of products promoted by Santa ads were wide and varied. For instance, in 1935 he was encouraging people to help him by purchasing Whitman's chocolate candy as gifts, in 1959 he was wanting people to buy Jell-O, and in 1977 it was Quaker Oats to make him cookies and in 1996 it was M & Ms. In 1938 Santa was encouraging people to buy Esso oil for your car; in 1940 Bell Telephone used him to "ring in the new year", and in 1948 Time Magazine was using him to sell subscriptions. He has been used to sell cars of many different brands. By 1969 Santa was moving into high tech, selling Hoover vacuum cleaners, 1972 it was Kodak Instamatic cameras, in 1977 it was Smith Corona typewriters, 1997 Hewlett Packard products, 2007 Niko motion detectors, 2011 I-Phones. In 2019, it was Baby Shark.

Like in any marketing enterprise, the consumer target keeps shifting. Since the 1960s when the Coca-Cola Santa became pervasive, there have been new images of Santa introduced, and increasing amounts of Santa imagery. According to a search on Amazon.com, there are over 900 books and 60 videos about Santa, not counting other items. A Google search for "Santa Claus merchandise" yielded over 9 million products. Whereas stores began putting out Santa merchandise after Thanksgiving, now it is commonplace to see Christmas displays up before Halloween. There are Christmas in July promotions as well.

What I Concluded

Santa Claus has indeed been commercialized and exploited for profit. The only Western country that doesn't seem to have commercialized him is reported to be Cyprus, where gifting and celebrations seem more true to moderation, food, and the fellowship of one another. Advertisers have been very effective in using Santa Claus by using psychology. The term cognitive dissonance applied. It means that if I like Santa and Santa likes Coke, then maybe I should like it too. If Santa smokes certain brands of cigarettes, that's the type that I should choose. If Santa frowns and shakes his head in disapproval about a certain brand of candy or car, I better not like them either. Marketers know this logic stream and they have used Santa Claus to capitalize on this basic human cognitive trait.

I think about religious folks I know who want their children to appreciate Christmas for religious, not material, reasons. Santa was created from all the different forms to be a secular figure, not a religious one. Dictionaries define secularization as taking the religion out of something. Curiously in the construction of Santa there has been a systematic attempt to attribute conspicuous consumption of material goods with Santa as a good thing. So in this way, using Santa Claus to promote political, religious, or material agendas permeate the historical construction of his character. Whether Roman rulers, military leaders, or department store entrepreneurs, people who want the public to think in certain ways call upon traditional beloved attributes, customs and values to coopt him.

So is Santa responsible for the rise of materialism and consumer greed? No. He is an imaginary figure who could not possibly do that. He has been used by advertisers who want to link a positive association with his goodness to the goodness of their products. Take Santa Claus away and undoubtedly consumerism will continue to prevail. What's curious though, is if there is a movement to paint Santa as a negative character, will the things that he has been associated with also be maligned? Time will tell.

Glen MacDonough and Victor Herbert quote

Toyland, toyland
Little girl and boy land
While you dwell within it
You are ever happy then.
Childhood's joyland,
Mystic merry toyland
Once you pass its borders
You can ne'er return again.

Glen MacDonough and Victor Herbert

"Toyland" (1903). M. Witmrk & Sons.

Chapter 9

The War Between Santa and Jesus

The Dilemma

I have met plenty of parents who don't want their children to believe in Santa Claus because they want their children to see "Jesus as the reason for the season". I know lots of other parents who love for Santa Claus to be the gift-bringer because they don't want to have a religious-oriented holiday but still want them to experience the fun of the December festivities. There are folks on the religious right who view Santa as Public Enemy #1 during Christmas, while there are folks on the left who feel Santa should be forbidden because he is Christian and therefore doesn't come to Muslim, Jewish, Buddhist, or children from other faiths. The religious battle of Santa is so great to make the television show, South Park, do an episode on The Spirit of Christmas: Jesus vs Santa, in the wrestling world at a fight between Jesus and Santa (plus disciplines vs elves) at a Freak Show Wrestling competition, or in a Santa vs Jesus rap battle.

One of my favorite songs is "All God's Critters Got a Place in the Choir" which finds that no one is better than another, and there is room for everyone in life. I was a religion minor in college and learned that the fundamental values in all faiths are essentially the same – it's just the details and rituals that vary. So I honestly don't understand why adults have constructed what seems to be a war between Santa and God, and Jesus in particular. So I set out to find out.

What I Discovered

In your mind, are Santa and Jesus enemies or competitors? Could Santa and Jesus be friends? There is a classic Christmas ornament that shows Santa Claus, with his hat off, kneeling over the baby in the manger. Each December it is easy to witness the conflict that well-meaning adults create between Santa and Jesus. Churches hold discussion groups, there are editorials in the newspapers, and parents find themselves wondering if they are "bad parents" if they "do Santa". When they can't fight their desire to invite Santa to be a part of their holiday celebrations, some adults report feeling guilty, and they create a mixed set of messages for their children about the meaning of both secular Santa and a Christian oriented Christmas. They merge them together when they are not the same. Both Santa and Jesus can show up at the same time on the calendar and both can be important; one does not have to distract from the other. Jesus wouldn't want to cut in on Santa's time any more than Santa would think it appropriate to move in on Jesus. Like it or not, Santa has been forced into being regarded as a competitor of Jesus during the Christmas season. In some circles, while the St. Nicholas is accepted, Santa is not and might be maligned as something evil.

The jingle of Jesus Is the Reason for The Season is a direct attack on Santa Claus. Many parents are concerned that their children will not learn the religious foundations of Christmas while others are more enamored with presents from a Santa-secularized Christmas than they are worshipping the baby Jesus. There is a real subcultural backlash against Santa. Santaphobes have been very vocal about his flaws, which have been strong enough to make any parent sit up and take notice as they evaluate such claims. He has been deemed a health pariah because he is chubby, eats cookies, and drinks Cokes. Pictures used to have him smoking a pipe, but no more! He has been called a stalker who "sees you when you're sleeping and he knows when you're awake". Some anti-Santa groups have gone so far as to allege that SANTA is really SATAN (just jumble up the letters in his name), and that if you let your child enjoy Santa Claus, you are really participating in a form of child abuse. Wow.

Viewing it from a different perspective, Santa has perhaps done more good to convert children into believing in a higher power than any other individual of our time. He encourages good behavior, hope, faith, concern for others, joy, and love. What in heaven's name is wrong with that? Why on earth would Jesus disapprove of these messages? Santa is a secular character that embodies attributes that fit each and every religion. Santa is no more Christian today than any other religion, since his origins come from many different ideologies and histories, and the values of generosity and concern for others are universal. Ironically for the anti-Santaists, his creation was undoubtedly influenced by religious figures. In particular, was the influence of St. Nicholas, Father Christmas, St. Basil the Great in Greece, and Chriskenchild, or the Christ Child himself. There are also descriptions of how angels help to deliver gifts. The Santa story has also incorporated aspects of other religious heritages, such as Greek mythology and Nordic paganism. The bishop and martyr, St. Nicholas, is viewed as the patron saint of children, the poor, and sailors and he performed most of his miracles in southern Europe. He was sometimes pictured in his bishop attire riding a flying steed as he dropped sweets, fruits, and nuts down chimneys of good children and punished bad children. This portrayal of St. Nicholas was more common among Protestant denominations than Catholic cultures, who maintained more of a religious than the secular portrayal of his character. Overtime in the United States, he became pictured as a jolly, old, fat elf man riding in a sleigh pulled by eight tiny reindeer, largely at a time in which the United States was undergoing migration, industrialization, and the growth of economic systems. Religious figures and cultural characters such as Santa appear to be interwoven because of social forces.

Having its citizens being good and following orders is an important thing for any society, and it is important to socialize children to follow instructions. Getting a gift for being good is reinforced in many religious tenets as well. The notion that goodness is associated with reward is present in Old Testament stories such as that told in the book of

Job, who bears his suffering to ultimately receive rewards. New Testament stories tell of gifts – expensive and rare gifts of gold, frankincense, and myrrh, that the Magi gave to the baby Jesus. Muslims share gifts each Eid al-Fitr, Ramadan's gift-giving festival. Hindus in India celebrate and give gifts during their religious celebration of Diwali, or festival of lights. While Santa goes by many names over time, so does the character whose behavior underlies Diwali, showing how religious events often integrate many different people and stories into their traditions. Zoroastrians of Iran, who believe that happiness is important, have integrated the sharing of special foods during monthly celebrations. At the Jewish holiday of Hanukah, gift-giving is common for eight days in a row. While some people view Kwanzaa as an African American substitute for Christmas, it is neither political nor religious. It does, however, encourage the giving of gifts, usually of an affordable, educational, or artistic nature on January 1st, the last day of Kwanzaa. In China, gift-giving, often in terms of money in red envelopes, assures good luck for those you care about. Therefore, from as far back as history records, there have been instances of gift-giving rituals that are keenly associated with religion. Inherent in this unity is the notion that religion has loving, caring, joyful tenets for human interaction.

    Santa Claus encourages not just the social benefits of teaching children how to be good neighbors and citizens in their communities. Santa Claus can be used to help children to believe in God. Teaching children to believe in Santa at a time when they believe everything their parents tell them prepares their minds to accept a notion of God when they are older. Faith in Santa Claus serves as a springboard for religious belief., which may be comforting if you want your child to believe in God, or discomforting if you don't, according to journalist Gary Grassl (nd). Religion is based upon things that you believe in but cannot see or prove except with the knowledge of the heart, according to Boyer (2002). God is too heavy a topic to introduce to small children; they need simpler ways of understanding themselves. Their world is one of imagination, and psychologically, belief in Santa and God are produced by the same processes. Both require children to suspend disbelief in order to believe. Folk religions made this connection long ago and capitalized on the creation of shared imaginal experiences through the use of childhood myths like Santa. All imaginal experiences depend upon faith.

> "Children experience the world in ways that differ from adults, but their experience has just as much validity and their faith just as much truth and sacredness as the faith and experience of adults. Children's sacred beliefs should hardly be belittled as untrue or as cute fantasy. Youthful beliefs form the developmental foundation for imaginal experience and for awe-inspired faith. What a pity if adults have forgotten so much along the way that we can envision childhood make believe only with condescension and no longer with any measure of awe and appreciation." (Boyer 2002:4).

When children keep alive a fantasy figure like Santa alive in their minds, especially when they do so in a playful, accepting way, it helps lay the foundation of faith. When children are introduced to awe, learn certain values thru ritual practices, and later impact practices thru their own actions, which helps to modify or preserve the existing ritual practices.

One of the most effective wars against Santa has been lodged by the Christian community. As far back as 1927, Rev. C.E. Wagner warned his congregation that "Santa Claus will crowd out Christ" and admonished parents for being more concerned with teaching their children about Santa Claus than about Jesus. Another reverend stated, according to Barnett (1976) that "Santa Claus is a modern representation of the heathen god Nimrod who is a defiant hater of God and Satan's earliest effort to produce Anti-Christ." Fearing that children will come to love Santa more than "Jesus, the reason for the season", the strategy used has been to "put Christ back in Christmas" and make children and adults feel bad about believing in Santa. Guilt is part of many religious traditions and is used as a motivator to inspire people to do the correct things. However, guilt is often unnecessary and interferes with joyful experiences.

Interviews I made with parents indicate that many secretly feel like they are bad parents because they spend more time talking to your kids about "Santa Claus is coming to town" instead of the arrival of Baby Jesus. They enjoy singing "Rudolph the Red-Nosed Reindeer" with more gusto and emotion than "Away in the Manger" or "Oh Little Town of Bethlehem". If you are reading this and find that you have too, you are not alone. This guilt complex that parents feel at Christmas time is at the crux of adult frustration over how to handle the holidays. Many feel as if they are too pro-Santa they aren't teaching their children good religious values. On the other hand, if they are solely religious in focus, they worry they will alienate their children from a whopping good time when it comes to celebrating Christmas the Santa way. Religious guilt over whichever way you choose seems pervasive.

Religion is very serious, heavy stuff for anyone to contemplate, but it is especially overwhelming for children. This is one reason why psychologists like Jean Piaget indicate that children can't really grasp the magnitude and nature of God until they are approximately twelve years old. Children need to develop a conceptual framework that will allow them to really understand and appreciate the complexities of that which is divine. Believing in Santa Claus means one thing to a very young child, but as children mature there is the natural progression into a belief of the impossible, the magical, and that which is most wonderful. Inherent in this progression of thought is the child's slow but steady progress toward understanding God.

Some religious authors have asserted that one of the "problems" with Santa is that he is made to seem so Godlike. There are some obvious links between commonly held descriptions of Santa Claus and God. Some Santa critics are concerned that children will be confused when they observe the similarities made between them, and they are worried that children's allegiances will go with Santa instead of God. This is a simultaneously curious argument. On one hand, they don't want Santa to be a replacement for God or Jesus. They want Christmas to be regarded as a religious holiday in which Jesus is the sole focus of the soul. On the other hand, as religious people, they want children to learn how to follow in the footsteps of Jesus and other religious leaders. It could be that Santa is the perfect figure to show children that people can become Godlike in their behaviors. In this way, belief in God and belief in Santa could be seen as totally consistent, congruent partners in shaping children's belief that they can be good and loving to others, for whom they share a spiritual connection and responsibility.

In what way is Santa perceived to be a synonym for God? According to several web sites that explore this relationship, the following lists have been constructed. Santa, like God, is omnipresent, because he can visit hundreds of millions of homes in one night. He is seen as omniscient, all-seeing, and all-knowing because he knows if each and every child has been bad or good. He is just and good because he rewards children who have shown good behavior with rewards and he punishes naughty children lumps of coal as reminders that they need to do better. Although Santa is not omnipotent, he is powerful because he can make gifts for millions of children and deliver them in one night to the right child. Santa, like God, is thought to be eternal and can never die (see *The Theology of Santa*). Other religious authors have gone to great detail to find exact biblical passage comparison to compare Santa with God. Christmas reinforces the universally held religious values of people being dependent upon each other, as well as the importance of nurturing children. Children are passive in the Santa Claus ritual the same way people are regarded to be part of the "flock" of "the good shepherd." They are tucked into bed with special care on Christmas Eve after hanging up empty stockings, which is analogous to a dependent baby Jesus being wrapped in swaddling clothes and laid in a manger.

Santa is the main symbol of the holiday because he evokes a sense of tradition that stretches across both the religious and secular dimensions of human life. St. Nicholas had significant religious symbolism because of his generosity but he also became a functional substitute for the folk deities or pagan gods. Below is a list of other comparisons:

Comparisons of God and Santa

JESUS CHRIST		SANTA CLAUS
Has white hair like wool.	Rev. 1:14 Dan. 7:9	Has white hair like wool
Beard - curly and white.	Isa. 50:6 Rev. 1:14	Beard curly and white.
Throne is in north of the temple.	Ezek. 1:4 Ex. 26:35 Psa. 48:2 Isa. 14:13	Comes from the North Pole.
Omniscient - all seeing, all knowing.	Rev. 10:6	Omniscient - knows about all.
Ageless, eternal.	Rev. 1:8 Rev. 21:6 Heb. 13:8	Ageless, eternal.
Judgments from book of life death.	Rev.20:12 14:7; 21:27 2 Cor. 5:10	Makes lists of judgments.
Investigative judgment.	Dan. 8:14 Ecc. 12:1 Matt. 10:26 1 Cor. 4:5	Checks list twice.
Salvation by faith that works by love to all in book of life.	Matt. 24:21 Rev. 21:27 Rev. 22:14	Gifts given on basis of a list. (Gifts by works along).
Day of Atonement and forgiveness once yearly.	Lev. 23:26-32	Christmas rewards once yearly.
Confess sins to Jesus.	1 John 2:1 1 Tim. 2:5 Ezra 10:11	Confess wrongs to Santa.

Keep law in Christ's strength.	Jn. 14:15,21 Jn. 15:10 Psa. 119:60 1 Jn. 2:3 1 Jn. 5:2	Promise to be better next year.
Obey your parents in the Lord.	Eph. 6:1 Prov. 6:20 Col. 3:20 Ex. 20:12	Asks children to obey parents to please him.
Takes eyes from man to Jesus.	Heb. 12:2 2 Cor. 4:18 Ps. 141:8	Comes on Christ's Birthday, taking eyes from Jesus to man.
Hour of His coming a mystery.	Lk. 12:40 Mk. 13:33 Matt. 24.36 Acts 1:7	Hour of his coming a mystery.
Christ is the giver of good gifts.	Lk. 11:13 Matt. 7:11 Jas. 1:16-17	Gives good gifts to children.
Called children to His knee.	Matt. 19:14 Mk. 10:14... Lk. 18:16	Calls all children to his knee.
Sits on royal eternal throne.	Matt. 19:28 Matt. 25:31 Heb. 1:8-9 Ps. 45:6	Sits on royal, eternal throne.
Judgments come like a thief in the night.	1Thess 5:2.. Lk. 21:34 2 Pet. 3:10	Visits late at night.
Judgments come in "one day".	2 Pet. 3:8 Rev. 18:8 Isa. 47:9 Jer. 50:27	Swift visitation to whole world in one day.

Omnipresent - desires to be in all!	Ps. 139:7... Prov. 15:3 Jn. 15 Gal. 2:20	Omnipresent - in every shopping mall.
Only God is good and can impart obedience.	Matt. 19:17 Psa. 25:8 Col. 1:29	Be good for goodness sake.
Eyes likes flames of fire.	Rev. 1:14 Rev. 2:18	Has a twinkle in his eye.
Wore red robe stained with blood.	Matt. 28:38 Rev. 19:13	Wears a red suit.
Comes in clouds of heaven.	Acts. 1:9-11 Rev. 1:7	Comes in cloudy winter sky.
Throne moved by powerful angels.	Ezek. 1 Rev. 4:2-10 Ps. 104:3-4	Sleigh powered by mystical powerful reindeer.
Lives in sparkling, clear city.	Rev. 21:18..	Lives in sparkling ice palace.
Served by millions of angels.	Rev. 5:11 Dan. 7:10 Heb. 12:22	Served by many alien elves; origins unknown.
Only giver of righteousness.	Rom. 3:10 Rom. 5:19 Rom. 10:4 1 Cor. 1:30	St. Nick - Name implies he has righteousness of himself.

From The Santa Files: A Counterfeit Jesus Christ by Dave Ruffino

Clearly, there are some real, if not massaged, comparisons between our contemporary understanding of Santa and statements about God/Jesus. Parents are, by intent or default, engaged in the symbolic interpretation, or labeling, of Santa Claus as either a good guy or bad one. The "facts" are such that one can interpret the relationship between God and Santa in a variety of ways. One can make a defense either way.

Then there are the Santaphobes who argue that it's blasphemous for people to give Santa Claus attributes that are clearly divine. Some people have argued that it is sinful to make an association between Santa and Jesus and that the only way to give children a true indication of what Christmas is all about is to eliminate the presence (and presents) of Santa. Jehovah's Witnesses have long sought to extinguish the role of Santa from the Christmas holiday. "Throughout the year parents punish children for telling falsehoods. Yet parents abet the Santa Claus lie. Is it any wonder that many children, when they grow up and learn the truth, begin to believe that God is a myth too? ....Christmas is dangerously deceptive. It undermines Christianity and obscures the principles of true worship" (Awake, Dec. 22, 1955).

Other people have gone so far as to allege that letting one's children believe in Santa is actually a form of child abuse. Consider the quote from one website:

> "I beg you! *"Stop child abuse. Tell your children the truth."* Jesus is the "Reason for the Season", not Santa. Most children start out having confidence in their parents to tell them the truth. It is often a tremendous shock to children to find out that their parents have been lying to them. Often it is the children at school who have been laughing at your child as your child holds his ground in his belief in Santa

while defending his parents -- only later to find out that the "Laughing Kids" were "telling the truth," - not mom and dad. No wonder kids don't want to accept Jesus as they get older. Perhaps they're afraid that if they put their trust in Jesus, He'll turn out to be a hoax as well. A lie is still a lie! Stop it. Turn to Jesus and repent." (http://www.free-gifts.com/Santa_Claus.htm)

But there are those who try to reconcile that Santa and Jesus are compatible, as found in this poem found on websites like Desk Top Angel http://www.desktopangel.com/christmas/lord_and_santa_claus.htm or Liberty Land http://www.members.tripod.com/joart515/id33.htm:

When Santa Claus met Jesus Chris so the story goes
He bowed his head and then he said, "Dear Lord, I need to know.
Every year I fill my sleigh with lots and lots of toys
And I fly high across the sky delivering them with joy.
I get letters from the children, they ask for many things
And so hard I try to satisfy with each toy that I bring.
It is my mission every year to reach each child I can
To leave love and joy with every toy as I fly throughout the land.
But lately, Lord, I'm wondering – Am I doing wrong
To drive my sleigh on your birthday and hear cute Santa songs?
I'm troubled, for there is no way I would invade your territory
I'd feel very bad if I made you sad, I do not seek such glory".

So then the Lord, who's very wise spoke to Santa's heart direct,

"You're a necessary emissary, you are one of my elect.

I'm pleased to see your jolly self make so many children smile.

I too rejoice for girls and boys and feel you're most worthwhile.

On my birthday years ago in the manger where I lay

You bowed to me on bended knee, you too were born that day.

Dear Santa Claus I've chosen you my first Ambassador of Cheer

Please celebrate on my birth date and do this every year.

You're a blessed fantasy and dream, and you're essential on this earth,

You're a needed part in all men's hearts of everlasting childlike mirth."

And then there are pro-Santa Christians who think that believing in Santa is good for children. As Whitesell (2013) alleges, Santa-phobia is the result of the atrophy of the Evangelical imagination. He alleges that people should believe in Santa even if he doesn't really exist. Fundamentalists, he argues, tend to be so narrowly biblical that information not directly mentioned in Scriptures is off-limits, or in the case of Santa, a lie. While people wish to be as wise or enlightened, these higher-level faculties must be exercised, practiced, applied, and cultivated. Santa provides a springboard for developing a mind that will actually enable one to embrace the effervescent beauty of Santa, and later God.

Another key argument against teaching children to enjoy Santa Claus is that Santa is really Satan. Consider the words found on a web site no longer available called "The Devil Is In Your Chimney: Is Santa Claus Satan?" In the following article from Freehold, Iowa, the position is taken that every time a so-called Christian child asks Santa for something, he is praying to Satan. With each request fulfilled, parents are unwittingly making a pact with the Devil. The Santa = Satan followers allege that the red suit that Santa wears is really Lucifer's favorite color and that his last name, Claus, is Olde English for "hoof-claws". The devil, according to their view, decided to turn the holiest of days for Christians and twist it into an anti-Christ coup. Why? They allege that Satan once was God's favorite angel, but fell out of grace when he tried to seize power. Their story holds that God gave Satan his own place to rule – Hell, and his own holiday to celebrate – Halloween (Remember the earlier section on Krampus? Any of this seem familiar?). Despite his ability to tempt people, Christmas continues to overshadow Satan's own holiday. So Satan scrambled up the letters of his name and pretended to be jolly in order to tempt children to give up their souls for presents.

> "When your little boys and girls have grown up and no longer believe that Santa is real, they will find out just how real Satan is when he comes to collect their souls in exchange for all those presents! And God will turn a deaf ear to their pathetic wails of desperation. God will say, "You were more interested in that fat demon who was giving you presents than my Son who was giving you salvation, so you can all rot in Hell for all I care. So talk to your children before

it is too late! Tell them that Santa is no kindly old man; he is an evil demon. And next time your family sees some propped up gin-soaked vagrant in a Mall wearing a red suit with white furry cuffs, set a good example and witness for the other deluded people waiting in line. Loudly, rebuke him! Announce to all the children in the store "Not only is Santa a lie, he will ravage you sexually, drink your blood and drag your palpating carcasses down to Hell with him! It is only through setting a good example that we can put the Christ back in Christmas."

Other anti-Santa followers have gone through the Bible and come up with passages to "prove" that Santa is really Satan. They assert that Satan has dressed himself up to look god-like, but he is actually the phony-baloney anti-Christ. For instance, they liken Santa's red suit to the clothes dripped in blood mentioned in Revelation 19:13; Satan wears a prophetic white beard (Revelation 1:14); and that there really is no elves or workshop, indeed there is nothing at the North Pole (Job 26:7). Some authors have taken this task of comparing the biblical relationship of Santa, Satan, and God more seriously.

Another website I found that has disappeared asserts that:

"Millions of children all over the world are taught that Santa is Real and are deceived just as easily as the serpent deceived Eve in the garden. And they will deceive everyone his neighbor, and will not speak the truth: they have taught their tongue to speak lies, and weary themselves to commit iniquity." (Jer.9:5) "For many deceivers are entered into the world, who confess not that Jesus Christ is come in the flesh. This is a deceiver and an antichrist." (2John.1:7) "and all liars, shall have their part in the lake which burneth with fire and brimstone: which is the second Death.... Parents put their children in Santa's arms and the children look at Santa with awe and tell him their prayers and wishes for toys or whatever, and he smiles and lays hands upon them and says "Ho Ho" and sends them on their merry way to... hell?"

What I Concluded

While people have a right to their opinion, it just doesn't make sense to me that a rational person would pit Santa Claus against Jesus, God, or other abstract beings of goodness. It seems as caring adults we would want to do everything possible to nurture children's psyches and widen their hearts. I am sure that on the surface the anti-Santa folks may truly believe they are doing the right thing, but I find their logic is "over the top." Clearly, there are correlations between Santa and God, but I cannot think of anyone who really believes that Santa is God. They are not in the same ballpark. The child developmental literature clearly indicates that children are unable to perceive God until they lay the cognitive framework down that will enable them to grasp this kind of sophisticated concept. The work by Piaget, Bruner, Erikson, and others, who we will be discussing in the next section of this book, all indicate that magical thought is normal, natural, and essential for children's brain development. The feigned competition between Jesus and Santa may well be advanced by low-level thinkers who are themselves stuck conceptually and are unable to move forward in highly abstract thought.

Every society has many different systems of beliefs, symbols, and practices, and conflict may occur particularly between those of religious and non-religious orientations. Religious systems appeal to an absolute, sacred, transcendental authority while nonreligious systems, such as those which endorse Santa Claus, appeal to traditions and social relations. There has always been an attempt by religions to be seen as the official religion of the people. Folk traditions such as Santa are kept alive by informal groups of people through daily lives, beliefs, and practices. Santa may threaten religious members who fear the folk practices will take over the role of religion. In order to keep down competition, discrediting competitors, and finding fault with their ideology and practices are commonplace. Some aspects of folk tradition get ignored or tolerated by religions, but when ideas get too close to being competitive, like Santa, such notions must be attacked in hopes of eliminating them as a threat.

I've concluded that Santa is no more a threat to Christianity than Luke Skywalker or Sponge Bob Square Pants; to view him as a competitor is misplaced energy. As Clark (1995) asks,

> "Does believing in Santa Claus undermine faith, or in some paradoxical way does it serve to support faith? .... Without a doubt, children have much to teach adults about matters of faith. Those of tender years are apt to reach out to eternity in passionate ways, as Robert Cole's book, *Spiritual Life of Children* documents. When adults want to reach out spiritu-

ally, some find themselves wishing for childlike trust to replace their cynicism and skepticism. Those in the midst of the youthful wonder years occupy a life stage when awe and suspended disbelief are tolerated, even valued, in our culture."

So is Santa a religious icon to be worshipped, one that takes the place of a higher deity? Nope. Santa may have been partly influenced by religious roots, but these roots are multi-faith, and even then none were entirely responsible for how he was shaped. Santa as we know him evolved over time. He has utility for spreading the word about how people are supposed to treat one another. Santa is NOT a competitor to Jesus; to cast these characters against each other creates a division that benefits no one. Children can grasp the concept of Santa Claus much more easily than they can comprehend God. At a young age, they can understand a quasi-deity who can make presents, and deliver them under magical circumstances to all of the children of the world. Once children understand how Santa works, it is a relatively simple step to accept an omnipotent, omniscient, all-loving, and all-just God that cares for all children everywhere, irrespective of how they look, what they believe, or where they live. Believing in Santa allows children to feel that somewhere there is a person who is all good, all giving, who loves them unconditionally and accepts them just the way they are.

V. V. Deloria quote

The future of mankind lies
waiting for those who will come
to understand their lives
and take up their responsibilities
to all living things

V. V. Deloria

God is Red: A Native view of religion. 1994. Fulcrum Pub.

Chapter 10

Science & Santa

The Dilemma

What does science have to say about Santa Claus? As a scientist and researcher myself, I want to know. But how does someone research a make-believe character? The data substantiates that Santa Claus is a socially constructed character who was never a flesh-and-bones, breathing human being. In doing research on him, I have contributed to the science of studying Santa Claus's transformation.

Santa Claus hasn't been a hot-button topic for many researchers, even though he is a perfect topic to study attitudes, practices, culture, politics, business and economics, family, psycho-social development, creativity, and imagination, and other very important and relevant topics. When I tell people I am doing Santa Claus research, the general view is polite rolling-of-the-eyes as people fail to understand that I am not talking about a children's character, but one in which thousands of organizations, millions of lives, and billions of dollars have been influenced.

So why is it that people think that researching Santa Claus is dumb, or "just" a children's topic? What I am finding is that Santa Claus is an awesome sociological, anthropological, psychological topic that is particularly relevant not just for the study of children but for the study of how cultures transform. I am learning so much about how governments, businesses, religious organizations, and others impact the lives of parents, who then influence the lives of children. This is a study of the sociology of knowledge, and I am wicked psyched the more I delve into the topic. So why aren't others interested, I ask myself. So I decided to see what little is written on the topic from scientists, and here is what I found (in addition to what I have in the other parts of this book).

What I Discovered

Researchers tend to study tangible things like what people think or believe, what they say and do, or what they are in some way. They can use surveys or interviews to get an idea about what people think or do, we can observe their behavior, we can use secondary data sets like what consumer reports say they buy, or we can look at case studies or historical documents. Researchers can focus on macro social forces, like the institutional impact of Santa Claus, or micro factors, like how parents, teachers, and children interact with each other to shape our conception of him. As a research topic, I am finding studying Santa Claus to be utterly fascinating because of all these multi-level factors and forces.

There are facts-based people who think children shouldn't believe in Santa because Santa Claus, as a man, doesn't actually exist and the stories about him are either lies or myths. These types of people point out that there is no way that Santa can visit 2 billion children in 31 hours (counting time zone changes) to make over 98.1 billion stops over 75.5 million miles with a sleigh that must weigh around 321,300 tons, carried by reindeer that usually can run only 15 miles per hour since no known species of reindeer can fly like that. People coming from this position have a good point to make – it would be difficult to actually do everything the Santa story would indicate.

Normal people can't fly to the moon, go to the deepest depths of the sea, or travel faster than the speed of light. Yet they do. Sometimes logic interferes with understanding what is real. Official United States government agencies publically support Santa. The US Postal Service has been celebrating its Letters to Santa program for over a hundred years, with millions of children writing to Santa. It even has a dedicated Santa website. NORAD, the North American Aerospace Defense Command's Santa tracking program, found that over 20 million different visitors annually go to its website on Christmas Eve to see where Santa is on his journeys. A website dedicated to proving that Santa Claus exists provides more documentation than I can cover here – take a look at the following website, and make sure to scroll through to the end, where there are a variety of articles and documentation from Santaologists. At the end of the extensive proofs that Santa exists, the website poses the question – [The History Channel, the Discovery Channel, six official government agencies and a mainstream Aerospace Engineering University] "all tell you that Santa is real and millions of people around the world agree. What's it gonna take for you (to believe)?"

Below I've divided this chapter into sections that include research on Santa's reindeer, college student views of Santa Claus as based on their experiences, and Santa Claus organizations. I am saving researchers by social psychologists, family scholars, and community investigators for discussion in chapters in Part II of this book.

Santa Claus, Elves, and Reindeer

Scientists have entered into the debate on whether Santa exists. There has been a set of investigations on whether Santa really exists and whether reindeer can fly, which has yielded some fascinating findings. In the book, *Flight of the Reindeer,* Robert Sullivan offers "proof positive" that there is a Santa Claus and that reindeer really do know how to fly. Sullivan, a senior editor at *Life* magazine, diligently gathered documentation from respected scientists, historians, zoologists, and Arctic explorers to prove once and for all that Santa is not just a myth. I will synthesize some of the findings in Sullivan's lovely book now.

Sullivan observes that there are anthropological records that prove that for over 2000 there have been people acting as Santas all around the world. "There are records of children in northern Africa getting mysterious presents as long as that. There are stories of strange midwinter visitations made to Native Americans that long ago. There are aboriginal traditions in Australia that speak of a flying man from the north. There are reports of a curious Arctic city of eves that date that far back. There is eve firm support for the claim of those Inuit of Kuujjaq that Santa Claus did pass through their land a thousand years ago." (page 20).

Phillip Cronenwett was the former librarian of Arctic studies at Dartmouth University and his work led him to believe in the existence of Santa, as described in Sullivan's book. I attempted to reach out to Phillip to interview him for this book, but sadly found he had passed away in 2018. So I will recap what he and Sullivan reported in Sullivan's book. Cronenwett reported that "Santa Claus is two things indisputably – he is an elf and he is a good man." He discovered that Santa came from a village in south-central Greenland near the town of Holsteinborg. There are artifacts archeologists have collected in that area that confirm the presence of what could be called elfin communities. Elves, he proposes, probably originated in Iceland and spread to Greenland, Ireland, and northern Europe. Angelic beings were said to dwell on the Hamarinn Cliff and around Mount Asfjall, where twenty different types of elves lived. Locals around the manufacturing town of Hafnarfjordur are convinced that elves lived in hidden worlds but were fond of the local humans. The elves had traditions of having good community relations, were serene, generous, and industrious – qualities associated with Santa himself.

Sullivan refers to the work of the adventurer Will Steger, who reported that he met Santa who said that the elves fled Greenland after Viking Eric the Red attempted to colonize the area. The community that Santa and the elven people lived heard of the invasion and felt they would be doomed, so they packed up their belongings into sleds that the reindeer pulled and moved out before the Viking invasion. Santa reportedly was a wise navigator and moved his community to safety. Some went across in boats to Ireland, while others headed westward and across into Labrador and eventually set up a new community in Goose Bay, Canada. The story goes on to say that Eric the Red's son was also the sailor, Leif Ericsson, who navigated ships across to North America. Santa (or the person we have come to associate as Santa Claus) recognized the danger this posed and moved his community to the Arctic, where he felt his community would be safe. Sullivan regards them as the original homeless people who kept having to move in order to find a place where they could live safely.

Craig Heinselman also investigated whether the Santa and reindeer legends could possibly be true, with the same conclusion – that Santa could be real and that some reindeer can, in fact, fly. These authors provide convincing photos and evidence from people like Sir Edmund Hillary, who explored the North Pole, that make nonbelievers believe, as well as those who long ago gave up hope. The (Benjamin) Franklin Institute in Philadelphia studied whether the Santa Claus story has truth or lies embedded into it in an article posted on their website entitled The Science of Santa's Reindeer. Here is a synopsis of what they concluded. Small reindeer are known as Peary caribou, or rangifer tarandus. They live in northern parts of Europe, Asia, Russia, and North America, and are not found at the North Pole. Reindeer prefer to live in herds, sometimes small and sometimes up to a million deer. The Peary are smaller than other reindeer and seem well-suited to live in the extreme northern climates. Some grow an antler rack that has a complex configuration that creates a vortex of wind at high speeds. This rack acts as a big mainsail that can lift the deer upwards. Only the Peary caribou seem to have the ability to do what could be called flying. Reportedly some have cleared rivers with a jump and a glide that for all intent and purposes resembles flying. They cannot fly like birds, in that they have no wings. But they can float and are buoyant. Their coat is made of two layers of hair, one of which consists of hollow hairs that trap air to hold in body heat. This accounts for why they are buoyant.

Another main characteristic of Santa's reindeer is that they have red noses. This is made famous in the song, Rudolph the Red-Nosed Reindeer. Interestingly, scientists have found that it is entirely possible that reindeer can have red noses. Professors in the Netherland's Erasmus Medical Center and Academic Medical Center and the Department of Arctic and Marine Biology at the University of Tromso in Norway found that some reindeer noses have a red tinge because of the presence of a highly dense and rich nasal microcirculation, which means they have many blood vessels packed into their small nasal area, which helps them to regulate their body temperature in the frigid cold environments where they live. In the Elsevier journal, *Parasitology Today*, scientist Halvorsen hypothesized that reindeer have red noses because parasites have invaded their nose area, which has turned the membranes the color red.

I find it pretty fascinating to think that there is scientific proof that there were little people who could be called elves, that there are small deer that can maneuver themselves in such a way that they look like they could be flying, and that there have been seasoned explorers back in the day who knew where to move their communities when they were being encroached by invaders. All of that seems totally reasonable from an anthropological perspective. It seems as though actual facts could be embellished with one's imagination – but that the embellishment didn't negate the reality of the initial observations.

Thus anthropologists, historians, and biological scientists have dedicated their professional lives to studying the Santa Claus story and to discern what parts of it may be scientifically plausible. But data is not always sufficient for shifting people's perspective. People tend to believe what they want, whether they are correct or not. Let's now take a closer look at what some college students had to say about their experience with Santa Claus so you can compare it with your own.

Student Research on Santa Claus

As human beings, we do research all the time by asking people what they think about something, or about things that they do. I started by asking the question "Do you believe in Santa? Why or why not?" to the foremost experts on Santa – children. These were children I knew from my own informal network. Young children are honest when adults ask them questions that they think are stupid. They looked like me as if I was daft for even questioning the existence of Santa. They would blink their eyes and shake their heads in amazement that I would ask such a ridiculous question. Of course, they believed in Santa! It seemed to be a normal, natural, and obvious thing to do. They took his existence for granted the same way they take breathing for granted.

They had ready explanations of where Santa lives, how he is able to fly around the world to see all the children in a single night, what kinds of cookies are his favorite, and how he makes all the toys in time. Their answers were complex and convincing. No adult could create such vivid stories -

they were generated from their own internal creativity. No television show script or media hype comes remotely close to the imaginative stories children concoct in their own brains about Santa Claus. If you don't believe this, just go talk with young children about Santa and see for yourself. Conclusion: little kids believe in Santa and have excellent explanations of who he is and justifications for everything he does. They don't have an issue with him. They have a different perception of reality than adults.

But when we ask people we know, we likely have a skewed audience who likely think and act a lot like we do. Trying to get funding to conduct a national random sample of people's attitudes and actions around Santa Claus simply isn't the country's priority. I wanted to ask diverse groups of people I could access but didn't know well about their Santa experience in hopes of getting a larger frame of reference.

College students were a perfect group for me to study. They were close enough to their childhoods that they could remember and feel the emotions associated with their Santa experiences, but they were old enough to have some objective distance from them. Many were of the age to contemplate having children, and if they did – would Santa be a part of their lives?

The college student study went through two phases. The first was a set of focus groups with students in four Sociology of Children courses at a New England university to see if students were interested in the Santa Claus issue. They were. Three questions were posed – did they believe in Santa when they were little, would they want their own children to believe in him, and was Santa a positive or negative figure for children to believe in. These questions generated lively discussions that helped craft the second phase of the research.

Phase two consisted of a voluntary, anonymous online survey about their experiences with Santa Claus when they were children. Child-studies students (which included primarily psychology, sociology, social work, and education students with a smattering of others) were provided a Survey Monkey link to take the Santa survey. The project was approved by the university Institutional Review Board. Over a year period time, students in five classes were asked to complete the survey. One hundred and forty-six students responded to this survey. Most of the respondents were female (92.5%) and 75% were between 18 and 25 years of age.

When asked if they believed in Santa Claus, 93.1% indicated that they believed in Santa when they were young. Only 8 (5.5%) of the 146 reported that they never believed in Santa Claus. Do college students say they still believe in Santa? Over 1 in 4 confirmed that they still do (27.6%), and 91.1% of all respondents saying that they were very glad they had grown up believing in Santa.

Besides documenting the fact that most of them believed in Santa when they were young and a quarter of them still did, there were other fascinating conclusions generated in the study. When parents believe in Santa, their children are more likely to as well. Most parents encouraged their children to believe in Santa - 89.7% of the students said their parents encouraged them to believe in him. When asked if they would encourage their own children to believe in Santa, over half (57.6%) of them said they definitely would and another quarter (25.7%) said they would encourage their children to believe in Santa but they would try to provide a context for them to do so. Thus 83.3% of students said they planned to have their own children believe in Santa in one form or another.

When asked about what they appreciated about Santa Claus, it wasn't about getting material gifts. What students remembered most fondly was an emotion, feelings of love, appreciation of time spent with family, the thrill of anticipation, and a sense of togetherness and community. It wasn't about the gifts – it was the emotional connectedness and family bonding that was important to them. For most of the students, Santa didn't bring big or expensive gifts. Stockings appeared to be where the action was – as one student gushed, "I love my stocking the most!" Over 82% of the students reported that Santa left small items in their stockings; toys were common gifts (86%) and candy and sweets were received by 58% of them. Clothes or needed items were received by 67%, showing that Santa had a practical side. Only about a third (37%) reported that Santa gave them expensive presents, indicating that parents used moderation in creating the Santa Claus gifting experience. It was the small, fun things that seemed to matter most to the respondents. Seventy-two percent never saw Santa associated with religion. For almost everyone (91%), Santa was about fun.

And who was it that made Santa fun? It is often an entire family operation. Mothers and fathers were usually co-conspirators in creating Santa, as were grandparents, uncles, aunts, and older siblings and cousins. Families watched movies together about him (88%), read stories (86%), and children were encouraged to use their imaginations to think Santa about how Santa would harness his flying reindeer at the North Pole (85%) to visit their homes. Three out of four left Santa cookies and his reindeer carrots on Christmas Eve, and two of three wrote him a letter. Santa Claus was a form of bonding with their peers, as over 84% indicated their friends believed in him too.

Table 1
Childhood Experiences Of Santa Claus

Activity	Definitely	Sometimes	Did not do
I wrote letter to Santa	63.7% (93)	23.3% (34)	13.0% (19)
I left cookies or snack for Santa	75.2% (109)	15.9% (23)	9.0% (13)
I believed he would visit my home	84.2% (123)	11.6% (17)	4.1% (6)
He left me small things or stocking gifts	81.5% (119)	6.8% (10)	11.6% (17)
He left me toys	85.6% (125)	8.2% (12)	6.2% (9)
He left me candy or sweet	58.2% (85)	19.2% (28)	22.6% (33)
He left me clothes or things I needed	66.9% (97)	18.6% (27)	14.5% (21)

He left me expensive gifts	37.2% (54)	44.1% (64)	18.6% (27)
Santa did not bring me presents	7.7% (11)	2.8% (4)	89.5% (128)
I watched movies about Santa	88.3% (128)	9.0% (13)	2.8% (4)
We read stories about Santa	85.6% (125)	10.3% (15)	4.1% (6)
I believed reindeer could fly	84.2% (123)	10.3% (15)	5.5% (8)
I believed the North Pole was Santa home	85.6% (125)	9.6% (14)	4.8% (7)
My friends believed in Santa	84.2% (123)	12.3% (18)	3.4% (5)
I thought Santa was fun	89.0% (130)	6.2% (9)	4.8% (7)
I thought Santa was scary or frightening	0.0% (0)	9.0% (13)	91.0% (131)
I believed Santa was created by businesses to earn $	4.1% (6)	11.7% (17)	84.1% (122)

I believed that Santa was a religious figure	6.2% (9)	21.9% (32)	71.9% (105)

If parents didn't believe in Santa, they didn't encourage their kids to either. Only 5.5% of the students said they were glad they didn't grow up believing in Santa, and these were the same people who also said that their parents didn't believe in him. Parental encouragement, yea or nay, as well as ambivalence towards Santa, is transferred from generation to generation. This finding points to the important role that parents play in shaping their children's belief systems. If parents can see Santa as a source for interpersonal bonding instead of fragmentation, this would likely go a far distance helping children see that others are more similar to them than different.

So what were examples of family traditions that endeared Santa to these young adults? Here are some of their quotes:

My mom had this little "Christmas Countdown" calendar that we counted down every day until Santa came, on Christmas. I got to move the counter. On Christmas Eve, my mom and me would bake cookies for Santa, and we'd leave them on the counter with a note for him. My mom also gave me a few carrots and had me leave them on the porch so the reindeer would have a snack too. Santa didn't wrap my presents, he would set them up all around the living room. On Christmas morning I would wake up really early, like 5am, anxious to get my presents, and my mom would want to sleep longer, so she told me that I could go downstairs, and see the toys

Santa left, and that I could play with those. Santa also filled my stocking with lots of smaller little presents. Even my extended family incorporated Santa into our rituals. Every year on Christmas Eve all of my aunts, uncles, and cousins would go to my grandparents house. My grandfather had all of the kids go out on the porch, and would tell us to look up at the sky, and see if we could see Santa fly by on his sleigh.

We always had the traditional Christmas tree and stockings that Santa would put presents in. Starting right after Thanksgiving we would start to read books about Santa every night at bedtime and listen to x-mas music. We would also attend the Santa parade every year and I would give my Christmas wish list to the Santa there. We always made cookies together, wore matching family pajamas on xmas eve and sprinkled reindeer food on the lawn.

My family rituals regarding Santa were that we were to be good and especially around Christmas. Santa was watching so to behave extra good. We would read stories about the North Pole and Santa and his elves throughout December. In early December my sister and I would look through toy catalogs and ask Santa for specific items. On Christmas Eve there would be a huge family party on my mom and dads sides of the family. We would go to bed early so he could come.

The entire month of December was based around Santa. On Christmas Eve my uncle would point out at dinner a flashing red light in the sky and have us believe it was Rudolf. We also used the North Pole Radar to find out where he was at this point of time. We would make cookies for Santa, carrots for the reindeer. It was fun to see on Christmas day, broken carrots on the front lawn.

Santa brought the family together, and I loved the mystery on how he knew what I wanted. Christmas is about bringing joy to the holidays and spending time with the ones you cherish most.

Giving to those less fortunate and finding the meaning of giving to those in need. It's not about the gifts, but about family getting together and enjoying each others company. Everybody lights up when we see someone dressed in a Santa costume.

Believing in Santa Claus opened up my imagination.

On Christmas day my parents would leave a letter out addressed to my siblings and I praising us for our hard work throughout the year. Santa Claus was an incentive for us to do better.

Santa Claus was a positive figure in my childhood. And now that I am older I like that my parents didn't use him as a bargaining chip to make me behave.

Christmas was just so much more magical and wonderful than other times of the year. Life is hard and I think everyone needs a little magic at some point in their lives :)

I remember thinking that he was real at one time but didn't have enough time to get to all the children in the world and that's why our parents took over to help him out.

I always associate Santa with happy and fond childhood memories. He brought so much joy when I would think about him and anything associated with him. He was a magical man and I loved looking for the sleigh led by eight reindeer on Christmas Eve. Some of my favorite childhood memories I have Santa to thank.

I'm glad my parents wanted me to have a special Christmas season every year by encouraging me to keep on my best behavior so I could receive a lot of gifts. The magic of it all stands out in my head and always will forever.

As a child, I was raised appreciating Santa because he was a magical, imaginative, and intuitive character that provided satisfaction and pleasure on the holiday of Christmas. Santa never held a religious or important value in my life as a young child. It was simply the social norm in my community.

My favorite memory throughout elementary school was going to the Christmas Shop which was a store set up in the school and everything was around $1. Our parents would give us $5-$10 to buy family presents. I thought this was the best thing in the world at 6 years old. I got to be Santa too.

Generosity is a good thing. It's fun to give. I learned that every child deserves presents on Christmas, that giving is better than receiving, and giving is really a gift that you give yourself and it can make you cheerful.

I loved his contagious joy, his unconditional love for all living things.

Kindness is the most important thing.

With all of the negativity in the world, Santa represents something positive for people to focus on.

Students reported the same positive memories with Santa time after time. They talked about Santa being associated with gifts but also with magic, love, imagination, innocence, kindness, generosity, love, joy, toys, happiness, laughter, love, anticipation, wonder, cheer, laughter, giving, receiving, family, Christmas spirit, wonder, hope, "that fun mystical feeling", playing games, food, spending time with family, charity, faith, generosity, amazement, and encouragement to be good. When they were asked about negative experiences with Santa, there generally weren't any. Common statements were like these:

I don't really associate any negative feelings with Santa. As a young child I believed that Santa was a hard-working man who made and delivered gifts on a holy day to children who 'deserved' them. I was relatively young when I realized that Santa was not in fact real, and never harbored any negative feelings before or after recognizing Santa's lack of existence. He just was a figure that represented the magic of giving, a story that had lots to teach me.

While Santa is really one giant lie that gets told to children, I don't think it's mentally damaging or detrimental. People lie all the time. You gotta figure it out.

It's adults that make Santa seem bad. Kids like him.

Be careful on that naughty-nice stuff. As a child you believe that if you are good Santa will come bring you toys, therefor if he didn't does it mean you were a bad kid? So if poor kids didn't get much, did this mean they were bad? Of course not.

I'm sad that I never got to really believe in him as a child. I feel a little cheated.

Students were asked if they had anything they wanted me to know about Santa Claus. Almost all of them wanted to add extra information about the importance of Santa Claus in their lives. Here are a few of their responses:

I think I still believe Santa. I know he doesn't exist but I hope he does. Hope could be the essence of existence, don't you think?

Santa coming was fun and exciting and gave us something to look forward to.

Santa Claus was a man who brought happiness, not just because he brought my siblings and I everything we wanted, but because he allowed my family to get together and be merry.

He taught me to believe in the good and simple things in the world.

Growing up was hard because my parents were divorced and not financially well-off, so Santa was something special and created a lot of happy memories. When Santa came, we could forget about the other junk, even if just for awhile. He gave us an opportunity to have fun and to show we appreciated each other.

He was greatest part of my childhood memories. I wouldn't trade believing in him at some point over anything.

Santa Claus and God were never the same thing.

I think it was mostly the anticipation of getting something. However I do realize now that the reason I didn't get some gifts now, isn't because the elves didn't make them in time, but instead my mom wasn't able to afford them all. But it didn't matter to me. She made the holiday special; she made me feel special. I just love Christmas.

I wish I was still a kid and had Santa to come on Christmas Day. It was so magical and he gave me hope in something to look forward to. No matter what present I got even the littlest ones were the best.

Santa Clause brought much joy and magic and wonder and all positive things to my childhood. I think that it is important to have magic as a child because it's a way to utilize the imagination. Children of any era need to be able to let the imagination run wild, but especially children today who are hooked on technology and don't have to lean on their imaginations as much to keep them busy.

When I was a young child my parents struggled financially so they really worked hard instilling what they believed was more important and was the importance of family. So even though my parents couldn't afford a lot of "Santa" gifts, I grew up a pleasant memory. I loved that my family went out of their way to create such a magical time for me.

Believing in Santa kept me young. If I stop believing, then I am old.

Santa Claus was a consistent positive figure in my life, someone I could always depend on who made me believe magic and miracles were possible.

The meaning of Santa to me has changed over the years. When young, I viewed him as a person. Now, I still believe, but in a different sense. I look at him more as a concept and way of uniting people in a loving and giving spirited way. Just as important, but in a different way

And simply put, in the words of one student, "I just love Santa Claus. I loved him back when. I love him still."

Student observations indicated that Santa Claus had been a positive experience for them, even when they didn't believe he was a breathing, flesh-and-bones person. The thing that was most vital was the family togetherness that having Santa visit evoked, along with the reinforcements they had to engage their imaginations. Santa was never linked with religion in their minds. He was a separate entity entirely. And they found their lives improved because they had the experience to believe in him, and saw his presence in their futures as they became parents to be something they'd like to replicate.

Research on Pictures of Santa Claus

In the process of putting together this book, I went to websites to look at the different ways Santa Claus is presented. Historical and cross-cultural pictures of Santa were somewhat diverse, with ethnic representations, different physiques, and costumes that were brown, green, and not necessarily red with white fur trim. The thing that most of the historical pictures had in common was that the Santas were all elderly men. Women were not regarded to be Santa candidates then – or now.

I reviewed websites of contemporary photographs of Santa Claus, such as Shutterstock, Adobe Stock, StockSnap.io, Pexels, Unsplash, Burst, Pixbay, and others. These websites rely upon photographers to submit their pictures so their content reflects what photographers take. I expected to see and did see, pictures of old, bearded white men in red suits being portrayed as Santa Claus. That made sense to me. But I was overwhelmed to see almost no pictures of nonwhite Santa Clauses. Photo after photo of old white men giving presents to children, who were largely depicted to be white, reflecting a time when old white men were deemed to be those with wisdom, those who had the power to give gifts to others, those who were the ones in charge of driving the sleigh of life. It wasn't that having old white men portrayed as Santa as a problem for me, since that is how the story has been told for generations. It was the lack of anyone else of any type being portrayed as Santas that troubled me.

There were almost no pictures of black or brown men photographed to be Santas, sending the message that they weren't. Moreover, there were no female Santas. Women were sometimes included in the Santa pictures, but they were often sex-symbols, scantily dressed, and sending the message that Santa was a lusty old dude. The only other option was for women to be either mommies or Mrs. Claus types. There were no images of women as Santas. The biggest competing set of photos of "alternative" Santas were men driving motorcycles or other vehicles, or those with six-pack abs and muscles galore. The message: Santa is a "real man" in stereotyped ways.

For people who want to allege white supremacy in the Santa story, the photos painted an overwhelming depiction that it was true. For people who resented old white men being in charge, well, that was the image I observed after looking at thousands of Santa pictures. The lack of a female presence, unless one was flaunting sexual availability, was impossible to miss. Photographers ostensibly were merely shooting what they saw. The question is, how can we start to see Santas through a more diverse lens? Will that door be opened so that there is more diversity in the Santa image? That seems to be vitally important as we go forward to reconsidering who Santa Claus should be for a diverse population globally in the future.

Research on Santa Claus Organizations

Not just anyone is "supposed" to be a Santa. Like any profession, not just anybody can be a doctor, technician, teacher, astronaut, or accountant. Credentialing organizations exist to provide oversight to ensure that people who purport to be a certain kind of professional actually has the qualifications to do so. There are a variety of Santa training schools and credentialing organizations that attempt to self-monitor who gets to be a Santa and to set standards for their behavior. While all need to take The Santa Claus Oath created by my personal Santa, Jim Yellig, there seems to be a lot of pressure to conform to traditional standards in an ever-changing world.

In a study by Farah Stockman (2019), she studied Santa societies and found there were quite a few. These organizations are both gate-keepers who decide who to let in and who to keep out, and they attempt to institute measures to ensure quality control. Stockman found that internally there were a lot of political dynamics in them. For instance, there are debates about whether people who serve as Santa Clauses should grow their own beards or whether fake beards (some of which cost thousands of dollars) are acceptable. There are standards set for how they should dress and act. There are things that Santa should say and do – and things they should not. Issues of privilege and inclusion have become hot topics. What if women want to be members of Santa societies and serve as Santas in the public eye? There are some Mrs. Claus societies – but what if women want to be Santa Clauses themselves? It did not appear that the societies welcomed, or would allow, women to be Santas despite the fact that during World War II they were hired to be department store Santas. There was also apparent organizational controversy about whether membership should be open to elves, Grinches, reindeer-handlers, or other secondary Santa figures.

There is reportedly in-fighting between liberal and conservative Santa Clauses within these Santa Claus credentialing organizations, between those who welcome inclusivity and those who want Santa societies to be exclusive clubs of only men with real beards. Some cite the reason being pressures from parents, supposedly mostly from mothers, who demand that Santas that interact with their children look and act in traditional ways, such as having elegant, expensive suits, professionally coiffed beards, and who can speak multiple languages, including sign language. Santas have to look and act the part.

The first official Santa society seems to be the Amalgamated Brotherhood of Real Bearded Santas. It splintered due to interest and geographic conflicts into other organizations such as the IBRBS, or International Brotherhood of Real Bearded Santas, which has morphed into groups like FORBS (Fraternal Order of Real Bearded Santas), the Lone Star Santas in Texas, Buckeye Santas in Ohio, Palm Tree Santas in Florida, the Illinois Professional Santas or the New England Santa Society. These are membership-driven organizations that do philanthropic service, provide scholarships, make sure children get gifts, do training, networking, and a variety of other benefits.

There are also schools that are designed specifically to train people on how to be a good Santa Claus. Some of them include the Charles Howard Santa School, Legendary Santa University, Northern Lights Santa Academy, Santa Claus Conservatory, and of course, the Saint Nicholas Institute. There are others designed to help Santas be performers or good business people. But showing the trend towards greater gender inclusivity, there is Santa Nana's Holiday University, which trains female Santa wannabees how to showcase Santa Claus from a feminine perspective. They all have a curriculum on how to behave, act, and what to anticipate as they go into the world as Santa Claus.

From my research on the different Santa organizations and schools, there is a lot of tension over who should be considered a Santa. Issues of inclusion and exclusion are front and center in these debates. For instance, many require that only men can be Santas. If women want to be involved, they are typically shuffled off to the Mrs. Claus categories. This is pretty sexist, fellas. And to assume that a woman is married reinforces an old-school approach that doesn't fit scads of females today. The "real men grow beards" thing also seems to cause challenges for these organizations. Not all men can grow abundant body hair or beards. It's not in their genetic make-up. While some guys like to sport beards, others don't for all kinds of personal or professional reasons. The requirement that men have real beards excludes a lot of men, and by default excludes men of a variety of racial and ethnic groups in which beards aren't characteristic. Some of these organizations look down upon people who buy beards. Some won't allow them, even though some are professionally coiffed and cost over $3000. There is an ageist factor as well, with most Santas being over age 62. Wisdom is associated with age, but there is no logical reason why people who are younger (or very young) can't be a Santa.

There isn't a race requirement, but these exclusive Santa clubs do seem to recruit a very white group of older guys. While there are some Santas that are encouraged to be multilingual, such as speaking Spanish or using American Sign Language, there isn't an apparent presence of people who represent a wide array of ethnic, racial, gender, ability, or linguistic characteristics. If they exist, they aren't being well-publicized. And then there is the issue of Santa being a symbol of white privilege. The notion that only older white men are wise, good leaders, powerful, who are in charge of gifting others (especially children), and can do magically amazing things by default excludes the presence of wisdom, altruism, leadership, and magic in other types of people. If the Santa power-figures are primarily old white men who are macho enough to grow their own beards, they would appear to be a cohort that is representative of traditional power structures. In a diverse world where it seems there should be room for everyone to have the opportunity to be role-models of altruism, joy, and loving-kindness, shouldn't there be room for more Santa diversification?

Add into the discussion the trend that when Santas traditionally talk with children, what is the topic of their conversation? Presents. "What do you want for Christmas?" is the standard Santa question. But what if instead of material items, what if the Santa conversation was shifted to discuss non-material things of value that children could relate, and aspire to? The traditional materially-based questions Santas are groomed to ask may be more attainable for children who are upper and middle class. How can Santas become more relevant for children whose families have suffered economic hardships and can't deliver them many or expensive items? It seems that the discourse and conversations Santas have may need to be reconsidered in order for him to be relevant today.

It was interesting to realize that even Santa Claus recognizes the need to change. If the current-day Santa's don't, I would guess that they will contribute to Santa being a character that had meaning in the past who has little relevant meaning in the present. If they help Santa Claus wannabees to incorporate the best of Santa's qualities in a more racially, gendered, ethnic, cultural, religious, and inclusive ways, then Santa Claus may transform to be relevant for tomorrow. The reported in-fighting among leaders in these Santa organizations reflect the larger tension around him in society.

What I Concluded

Scientists could do a better job investigating the relevance of Santa Claus in today's world. Their conceptual bias to view him as a children's topic demonstrates the lack of importance that children's lives have had. Santa embodies political, economic, psychological, cultural, power, race, gender, ageist, business, governmental, and sociological issues worthy of examination. As a pediatric sociologist, I know the field of child studies has not become important until recent years. Even so, most colleges don't have courses on the psycho-social factors that impact children's lives. Child topics are relegated to departments of education, psychology, and child development. They seldom can be found in business, political science, religion, or sociology.

The intersection of Santa and science is most apparent in two places. One is the anthropological and historical understanding of what happened in the past. There are bits and pieces of information that we can put together like a mosaic to make sense of the character we have come to know as Santa Claus. The other is to assess people's attitudes and behaviors around the Santa issue. This latter form of data tells us much more about the people we are studying than about Santa Claus him/herself. Years ago the sciences supposedly divided topics and the psychologists took children and the sociologists took the family. This is likely one reason why there isn't much research on Santa Claus as a social phenomenon of inquiry. Another is that the lives of children simply haven't been regarded as that important. If they were, I daresay we would be approaching their care and wellbeing in drastically different ways. I think that this leaves parents in a lurch not knowing exactly what to do as it pertains to Santa Claus and how to handle him with their children.

The science that is available seems to lean heavily towards Santa Claus bringing positive things to children that far exceed toys. Throughout this research project, I have reviewed hundreds of studies and reports, many of which can be found in the bibliography of this book. Benefits of a Santa state of mind include cognitive, psychological, social, community, and family benefits. The creation of hope, dreams and how to make them come true is a huge thing for children to acquire.

It appears that one big reason that Santa Claus has come under attack is that he remains to be a bastion of traditional power structures that reinforce white supremacy and male privilege. I wouldn't be at all surprised if Santa Claus becomes under greater attack in the coming years for these reasons. The question arises whether we are going to be pro-active and create Santa Claus to be a symbol who embraces diversity as "he" delivers altruism, joy, and lovingkindness, or whether we as a society are going to be reactive and try to defend or re-conceptualize after there is a full assault on his character. I suspect that if we proactively transition him to be inclusive and diverse as he delivers his gifts that his transformation will be smooth and easy; if we wait until he is under attack then our ability to use Santa to be a universal bringer of goodness to all children will be much harder. As a sociologist who studies social change, we need to remember the old Bob Dylan song – "The times they are a'changing". It's time to get with it, for children's sake.

John Greenleaf Whittier quote

For somehow, not only at Christmas,
but all the long year through
The joy that you give to others
Is the joy that comes back to you

John Greenleaf Whittier
A Christmas Carmen 1900

Part 2 Santas of Today

Chapter 11

Questions about You

The Dilemma

Most parents muddle into the Santa Claus issue without fully thinking about how they want to address it. How we handle him is actually a lot more complicated than most people think. What did we experience around the Santa figure, what did we like about him, what were we afraid of? How does the co-parent feel about Santa? And what, individually and together, do we want to do about how we handle Santa Claus with our children? These are great questions for us all to consider as we grow forward.

What I Discovered

In my investigation on whether or not to encourage my children to believe in Santa, I have figured out who he was in the past. I've looked at all the festivals and the cast of characters contributing to our understanding of who Santa Claus is, what he looks like, what he does, and why he arrives around December 25. I've shared with you what I learned how government, religion, and big business all concocted different personas of Santa Claus. Before I can determine who I want Santa to be in the future lives of my children, I needed to get a grip on the social and psychological, community, and family factors as well. In this chapter, I'd like to share with you the questions that I had to pose to myself – and for you to answer them for yourself.

Who do you think Santa Claus Is? Who do you want him to be – and why?

Not so long ago it seemed normal and natural for children in the United States to believe in Santa Claus. But this is no longer the case. In these days of ideological and cultural diversification, many parents are uncertain whether they should "let" their children believe in him or not. They may wonder if it appropriate to encourage their children to think that fantasy characters could be real. They worry about whether they will be lying to their kids if they tell them Santa lives at the North Pole overseeing elf toymakers and travels by reindeer-pulled sleigh across the night sky before he will arrive at their house with gifts. But it's interesting – parents generally don't have the same anxiety or concerns about letting their children believe in Spiderman, Baby Yoda, or Mickey Mouse. They are fantasy characters too, but Santa seems different to them for some reason. I suspect that it's because Santa is really a figure designed by, and for, adults. The political and ideological associations with Santa are much closer to home for them. Their emotional investment in Santa is much different than their investment in Spiderman.

Some parents are legitimately concerned about letting their children trust older men in dress-up who they don't know. Should they let their children confide personal wishes while sitting on their laps? A host of older men in trusted positions, like Boy Scout leaders or priests, have been accused of child sexual abuse, so how can parents know if the men who promote themselves to be Santa are safe? While sitting on Santa's lap may have been OK years ago, it simply isn't today.

Concerns that some Santas could have ill-intent, may be alcoholics, stalkers who "see you when you're sleeping and know when you're awake" can make parents feel edgy about perpetuating the traditional Santa story. Just because someone dons a Santa suit doesn't make them safe. This is why the Santa screening and credentialing organizations mentioned in the previous chapter are so important.

I realize that Santa is oft associated with Christianity, but I find it fascinating that he's come under attack by both the religious left and right. The religious right sees Santa as a competitor with Jesus for children's affections. Some religious zealots have gone so far as to view S-A-N-T-A as the alter-ego of S-A-T-A-N. The religious left may fault Santa for not being inclusive enough of all faiths and for being a wedge that separates believers of one view from believers of alternative perspectives. Wishing to demonstrate cross-cultural sensitivity, "Happy Holidays" has replaced the "Merry Christmas" greeting, which really annoys some folks. Communities seem not to know what to do about holding winter community festivals anymore, and some have gone so far as to ban the presence of all December holiday religious symbols, including Santa Claus himself, at public events and school functions. Some people feel that Santa is used to discriminate against non-Christian children, poor children, or nonbelievers. Others believe Santa Claus is not good for children because he embodies crass materialism and encourages children to become greedy, gimmie consumers.

Yet many believe that Santa Claus's messages and values are true and good, and important for children to embrace. Santa teaches the art of giving and receiving, of planning, of hope, of patience, and trust that miracles can happen. They may see Santa as a representation of democracy, who delivers gifts to all children irrespective of who they are, what they (or their parents) believe. Others view Santa as a tool in which capitalist societies try to impose their materialistic agenda on societies that are not democratic, Christian, or capitalistic. They may view Santa as an international indoctrinator of Western ideology.

Wow. That's a lot of weight to for a fictional character to carry.

Who do YOU think the person we have come to call Santa Claus (SC) really is? What is your perception of him, experience with him, and feeling about him? Figuring out your answers to fundamental questions are useful to get out of the way first, because how we plan to address him in our homes and communities in the future stems from our understanding of him in the past.

Who we think Santa Claus is may be influenced by our childhood understandings of him. Understanding who Santa is at any particular point in time is an example of how people engage in the social construction of reality. What we think about Santa Claus is quite personal, therefore it is important for us as individuals to think about our relationship with Santa. Since children's understanding of Santa is influenced by the significant others in our lives, such as parents and teachers, it is important that adults have a clear understanding of the mental processes that combine when they tell children what Santa is, and what he is not.

Take a moment to answer a few questions. Your answers will help prepare you for the material presented in the following section of the book.

Look back into your own childhood and reflect upon the following:

>Did you believe in Santa Claus?
>Do you believe in Santa now?
>What were the characteristics of YOUR Santa?
>What did your parents say about Santa? Did they give you the same message about Santa, or did your mother present Santa differently to you than your father?
>What did you learn from your grandparents, siblings, and other significant others about Santa?
>Did you like Santa?
>What made Santa fun?
>What parts of Santa didn't you like?
>Did you think he was scary?
>How did you find out that Santa wasn't a real person?
>How did you feel about that realization?
>Do you still believe in Santa Claus, in one form or another? Why or why not?
>How do you wish the Santa issue had been handled differently for you?

Now, **reflect upon your children and what you want for them** regarding Santa Claus:

Do you want your children to believe in Santa? Why or why not?

What do you want them to get out of their experience with Santa?

How do you want to handle Santa for your children that are similar to what you experienced as a child?

In what ways do you want to handle Santa Claus for your children that are different from what you experienced?

How important do you think it is for kids to believe in fantasy?

Are you excited about making Santa for your family, or do you dread it?

How do you feel about telling children that the gifts under the tree on Christmas morning didn't come from Santa via the North Pole? Do you have a good answer ready?

If you told your children there was a Santa when they were little, are you unsure how you should change the story now that they're older?

Are you nervous that after you "spill the beans" that your children may think that you have been misleading them for years? Are you afraid they may think you lie to them?

Is there a point at which you think children should quit believing in Santa?

Do you know a good way how to tell them that there isn't a Santa Claus, or at least a Santa that flies by reindeer to deliver gifts to all the children around the world in a single night?

What do you think they will do once they learn "the truth"?

What IS the truth, anyway?

What do you think are the benefits of knowing "the truth", and what do you think are the benefits of believing there might be a Santa Claus?

Are you aware of different ways to explain Santa to children, ways in which some may be better than others for you, your child, and other children?

If you find yourself a little confused about what to say or do about the Santa issue, you have lots of company. Perhaps as you went through the list of questions, you were able to identify what Santa meant to you when you were a child and what you would like for him to mean to your children. You may have remembered Santa as a wonderful experience, or you may have associated Santa with upset, trauma, or fear. You may want to gift your child with the same wonderful experiences you had, or you may seek to protect them from being hurt and let down like you were. What you choose for your children is keenly associated with the emotions you experienced as a child. You do not come to the Santa issue being neutral. You have emotions, perhaps positive or perhaps negative ones that impact how you feel about Santa Claus that have nothing to do with what Santa actually is. Identify them and own them. You do not have to blindly dump them onto your child. Your experience does not have to become your child's experience. Your reality is not necessarily their reality. You have the power of choice; as a mature adult, you can choose what you think is the best way for you to handle the Santa Claus question for yourself, and for your child.

What kind of relationship did you have with Santa? Let's compare the possible personal experience with Santa and how it impacts what we want for children to experience about him:

- You had a positive experience with Santa as a child and you now go out of your way to make sure your children have one too.
- You had a negative experience with Santa when you were a child so you want to protect your child and downplay their Santa experience.
- You had a so-so experience with Santa when you were a kid and you are willing to play along with the Santa thing, but only so far.
- You had a positive experience with Santa but reject doing Santa with your own children. You may do so if you have married someone who is anti-Santa, or you have had an experience that has made you change your position about your upbringing. You may reject Santa to your kids, but deep down inside you may feel uncomfortable about "sizing down" your children's exposure to Santa Claus.
- You had a negative experience with Santa when you were a child but you became a Santa enthusiast with your kids. You may have experienced a Santa epiphany in which you come to appreciate the meaning of Christmas with Santa, or you want to re-do your own history by making sure your kids have a positive Santa experience.

- You had a negative Santa experience when you were little but co-parent with someone who likes Santa. You struggle to pretend liking Santa, but your heart is never really in it. You do the bare minimum as a result.
- You liked Santa until someone spoiled Christmas and now you have problems disassociating the joyfulness of Santa with the negativity that someone dumped onto you or your experience of the holiday.
- You come from cultures in which Santa was not a priority and aren't particularly invested in pursuing the Santa experience for their children. People in this group are more likely to institute boundaries around what Santa is and does, and they do not feel emotionally caught by the Santa issue.
- You come from a religious framework that rejects Santa, and you feel as though you are doing your children a service by having them reject Santa too.
- Why do you want your child to "know the truth" about Santa, anyway? What is the purpose of your telling children that Santa may not be exactly like the Coca Cola depicted jolly old elf in the red suit? Parents really need to think about this question.

Reason 1: Parents are tired of the charade: Are you telling the child that Santa isn't real because they have a problem with it, or because you are? Many times, parents secretly want their children to know that there isn't a real Santa out there because they are tired of all the time and effort to "be" Santa. The arrival of Santa Claus requires a significant amount of sheer physical labor: hours shopping for the right presents, wrapping them just-so, assembling complex toys and bikes, hiding the gifts until Christmas Eve, trying to get the kids into bed and asleep at a reasonable hour, and then staying up late putting the gifts out only to be awakened at the crack of dawn to watch them rip into them. It costs more to be Santa than it would just to give someone a wad of cash or a single gift. It's not just the cost of the gift, but all the costs associated with making the holiday perfect that ups the ante. And then there is the emotional expenditure associated with saying and doing the right things. Parents may find themselves wondering, "What would Santa do?" Making sure to wrap the Santa gifts in different papers, being consistent in what you tell who, and not to "let the cat out of the bag" all take emotional effort. It is not unusual to find that some parents just want to be able to go to the store, buy the gift, stick it under the tree, sleep in, and not worry about acting like Santa. If their kids know the truth, they feel they're "off the hook".

Reason 2: Parents want their children to know what is real and what is not: The question of reality is one that parents routinely have to address when they raise kids, in a zillion different contexts and ways. "Are unicorns real?" "Are there really witches?" What about mermaids, pirates, or the tooth fairy? Ultimately comes the big question is, "Is God real?" But what is real? How can you prove to a child that black holes, oxygen or germs exist? Why is the first group regarded differently than the scientific examples? Each parent has his or her own understanding of what is real and what is not. Inevitably, parents shape their own children's sense of reality in accordance with their own views. In this way, children grow to become parents, who then shape their own children's views. So goes the replication of society.

The question of what is real becomes more controversial as one looks at the different conceptual frameworks from which to choose. If a parent relies upon a scientific point of view, then they may feel comfortable teaching their children that it is unlikely that reindeer can fly high in the sky pulling a chubby guy driving a sleigh loaded with enough toys to deliver to every child on the planet in one night. Similarly, in the traditional Christmas story, could Mary really have had a baby if she was a virgin; the immaculate conception is thought to be impossible for those who believe that sperms and eggs must unite in order to create a child. There must be a tangible, observable cause-and-effect from this point of view. If you can't prove it, it doesn't exist. However, it is useful to note that what scientists thought didn't exist at one point in time may shift as their scientific methodologies improve. For instance, it now appears that black holes are real, that time travel may be possible, and that extraterrestrial, alien life forms could exist. Splitting something as tiny as the atom was thought impossible, and who could fathom that so much information could be contained on a microchip the size of the head of a pin! According to researchers who believe a type of reindeer exists that moves in such a way as to resemble flying, they argue that flying reindeer could in fact be real. A competing view holds that supernatural forces routinely interact between nature and humans. It is possible for things to exist that are hard to see, catch, or prove. Fairies were thought to be real, as were creatures like unicorns and centaurs. Pookas and boggarts are still thought to exist and interfere in the lives of regular people. Leprechauns are thought to exist, especially around St. Patrick's Day, and some people feel as though their homes are haunted by ghosts. Millions of dollars have been spent trying to prove the existence of the Loch Ness Monster, and some people are confident that the Yeti exists in hiding. There are those people who believe in ghosts and the spirit world, who are convinced that when people die their souls linger on earth for a while afterward. Harry Houdini, the famous magician, was confident that he could contact his deceased mother and that she could communicate with him from the grave. While characters like the Tooth Fairy or the Easter Bunny are understood not to be real as presented, the fact remains that people throughout the world adhere to belief systems that embrace the existence of beings that are very hard to prove or disprove. Antoione de Saint Exupery is credited with saying, "It is only with the heart that one can see rightly; what is essential is invisible to the eye." This view is an important one, according to Clark (p 1) who noted that "Once upon a time in Western history, when adults and children both believed in fairies, there was no question but that the most essential realities were invisible to the eye. Spiritual beings, from leprechauns to angels, were an accepted part of the plane of existence, even to grown-ups. No more. In today's skeptical era, the hallmark of "mature reasoning" is to able to distinguish "fantasy" from "reality". Yet, perhaps the realm of angels and fairies is just as real -it all depends on how you look at the world and what you see in it. "Nobody sees Santa Claus, but that is not a sign there is no Santa Claus. The most real things in the world are those that neither children nor men can see. Did you ever see fairies dancing on the law? Of course not, but that's no proof they are not there. Nobody can conceive or imagine all the wonders there are unseen an unseeable in the world."

Reason 3: Parents want their children to focus on the religious aspects of Christmas, not materialistic ones: This is a common reason for turning children away from believing in Santa, even among people who are not particularly religious. There is cultural pressure to downplay crass materialism while looking for the more spiritual meanings of life. This is not necessarily a bad thing. Parents, who remember the joy of sneaking downstairs to see if Santa had come when they were little on Christmas morning, may sheepishly feel that they aren't doing a good job parenting if they let their children view Christmas as Santa time instead of Jesus time. They may like Santa themselves, but feel it is better parenting if they encourage children to view Christmas as a holy time. What parents don't often realize is that they have inadvertently gotten sucked into a debate that is centuries-long that stems from a conflict between the church and those who aren't strong adherents of the faith. Historically, paganism was the dominant religious system, and most people relied upon their relationship with the supernatural forces to intervene on their behalf and to help them during times of trouble. Christianity, as a new and competing belief system back in those days, found it useful to discredit the competition. By promoting their views as the best, they were able to retain the market share, if you will excuse a more contemporary use of terminology. As a result, Santa is regarded as a big threat by people who profess to be very religious. Even those who are very religious may not realize they've gotten pulled into this long-standing conflict. If a parent adheres to a more fundamental religious point of view, they may view Santa Claus as a threat to the underlying premise of Christmas. They may want their children to view Christmas as a religious holiday. They encourage their children to "put the Christ back into Christmas" instead of focusing on Santa Claus, toyland, and flying reindeer. More zealot advocates of this view allege that Santa may actually be Satan. Santa distracts good little girls and boys from worshiping Jesus, the same way as Satan tantalizes them with worshipping things of the flesh and material world instead of the godly. As will be shown in this book, Santa isn't a threat to the spiritual underpinnings of Christmas. In fact, Santa may actually be a vehicle to increase children's belief in God – and should therefore be embraced by the religious community, not discredited.

Reason 4: Parents want to discourage materialism, and believe that telling children that Santa isn't real is a convenient way to get across the message that being greedy isn't good It is, of course, offensive to see children being greedy and materialistic. But Santa is not to blame for parents going out and getting themselves in debt by buying too many things they can't afford at Christmastime. Santa is not to blame because companies that exist to sell things find Christmas to be a convenient holiday to hawk their merchandise to willing patrons. There are two issues here that need to be separated. The first is greedy materialism, and the second is Santa as a gift-giver. Most children are perfectly happy with getting modest gifts that are fun and meaningful. As children learn cultural messages and see their parents distribute fountains of gifts, they learn to expect over the years that such behavior is normative and they can logically expect lots of presents during the holiday. They may get sucked into a belief system that links Santa and materialism. However, this need not be the case.

As will be explained in this book, Santa may actually be a wonderful vehicle for teaching children altruistic behavior and the importance of giving to others.

Reason 5: Parents figure that other children may tell their kids about Santa not being real, so they'd rather beat them to the punch and provide their children with their own explanations and interpretations. Knowledge is power, whether you're four or sixty-four years old. Having access to information that no one else in your peer group has enables you to have leverage over them. Being left out of the loop isn't a comfortable place to be no matter how old you are. Often, when one child learns that there is no Santa, he can't wait to spill the beans to his friends. Usually, this is done with enthusiasm, and quickly the "nonbelievers" ban to make fun of those children who still believe. It is not the truth, but the peer group pressure of exclusion and ridicule is what causes the greatest problem for children when they learn that Santa isn't real from classmates. Parents don't expect their kids to get off the school bus with questions about the reality of Santa. Older kids may take gleeful pride when they shatter the picture of other children who still believe in Santa. When children are told that Santa isn't real and don't learn it by accident, parents may feel they have lots of latitude with how to handle the way they divulge the information and the way they handle their children's reactions. Parents can tell them in ways that are sweet, uplifting, and loving that make them feel good about Santa and themselves; they can tell children in a matter-of-fact, nuts-and-bolts fashion with little emotion, or parents can tell them "the truth" in ways that can be described as mean spirited. Some adults almost gleefully shatter children's illusions of Santa and Christmas because it gives them a perverted source of power over them. Maybe these adults actually have the children's best interests at heart, but the disclosure of the information is handled so inappropriately that children get upset. The important thing to remember here is that if parents are trying to buffer their children from the harshness of reality, then they should protect children from it by supporting them, not disintegrating them.

Reason 6: Knowing the "truth" about Santa is a rite of passage. One of the jobs of a parent is to teach a child how to become a responsible adult. Parents introduce adult roles to children slowly and incrementally over time so that when they reach maturity, they are able to function successfully. Children are given holiday tasks to accomplish so they may learn how to carry on the family's celebratory traditions. They may begin by making special holiday cookies or helping to decorate the tree; these simple tasks teach a child how to do these things when they are on their own, and they have no parent there instructing them how to do it. Learning to "be" Santa is an important role transition from childhood to adulthood. When parents ask the older children to help them to be Santa for their younger brothers and sisters, it may evoke two simultaneously distinct sets of emotions. It may make the child feel momentarily sad to officially know the truth in which they are told to leave part of their childhood behind, but it is quickly offset by the new role of the adult elf who operates behind the scenes making the holiday special for others. Older siblings may be asked to make footprints in the snow, put out presents, make "ho ho ho" sounds, jingle bells, or the like.

In a reflection of this transition, Maurice Reidy recalls how his parents officially broke the news to him, but not in the manner that he had expected. He had already put together hints that indicated Santa wasn't real, but he had expected that his parents would handle this rite of passage in a manner that was reflective of the importance of the situation. Instead, "It was Christmas Eve and my father asked me to stay downstairs while my seven younger siblings went to bed. He cornered me by the Christmas tree, and said, ..."could you help your mother put the presents out tonight? That was it. He turned away and headed toward the kitchen. Puzzled by my father's elusiveness, I followed my mother into the garage, where to my amazement--she uncovered dozens of wrapped presents from behind our Chevy station wagon. She handed them to me casually, asking me to bring them to the living room. Then we went to the basement, where she produced twice as many gifts, hidden beneath boxes of old sweaters. If my mother approached her job rather methodically (judging by her demeanor, we could have been taking out the garbage), then I carried out her orders in a state of awe--amazed not so much by the number of presents as by the fact that she had successfully hidden them from so many prying eyes."

Figuring your position out

So, in sum, are you telling children there isn't a Santa because you want them to:

- Acquire a more religious perspective about Santa and Christmas

- Acquire a more scientific approach to a phenomenon like Santa
- Avoid being made fun of by other children for being a believer
- Understand what Santa is from your point of view instead of being influenced first by what other people think Santa is
- Empower your child to be the first in his peer group to know that Santa isn't real
- Avoid a materialistic view of Christmas
- Learn that while some parents may mislead their children or lie to them, you do not.
- Have a greater grip on what is real and what is not

All of these reasons are commonly cited by parents as justifications for why they want for their children to know that there isn't really a Santa Claus. Undoubtedly, there are plenty of other unique reasons as well. Parents usually have good intentions when they want their children to reject the validity of Santa. Perhaps you don't want your child to know that there isn't really a Santa. Maybe you believe there really is a Santa if you use a broad interpretation of him.

Conversely, what are the most common reasons why parents do want their children to believe in Santa?

- Parents want their children to appreciate the magic and hope that Santa brings.
- Parents don't want their children to grow up; disclosing the truth about Santa is a sign they are no longer little.

- Parents want to continue a cherished family ritual that includes the joyful presence of Santa.
- Parents genuinely like playing Santa and don't want to lose that opportunity.
- Santa is fun and the Christmas holiday would be less pleasant without him; it would be just a day of eating and materialistic exchanges.
- Santa is a convenient way to gift children or reward them.
- They enjoy the theatre of the entire Santa experience.
- Parents don't want older children to know because they're afraid they will spoil the holiday for younger ones who still believe in Santa.
- Parents continue the belief in Santa because they want their children to be open to the possibility of alternative explanations of reality.
- Parents genuinely believe that a form of Santa does exist, whether in symbolic or spiritual form, and this belief is of fundamental importance to the child's later healthy personal and social development.
- Parents believe that Santa is real (in one way or another) and to deny his existence would be a lie.

Perhaps you find yourself agreeing with several different reasons for why you believe it is not a good idea to tell children the "truth" about Santa, and why you think you should. It is possible that adults will have conflicting feelings and positions on the Santa issue. Your children will too. This is not an either-or situation; you do not have to choose one position or another. Rather, realize that Santa

Claus evokes a myriad of emotions for both parent and child. Children will inevitably be influenced by the views and experiences of their parents, teachers, and other people whose opinions matter to them. Therefore, it is of particular importance that adults be clear about their position on Santa before they mold the minds and emotions of innocent children on this issue.

Thus, our understanding of who we think Santa is and what we want our children to know about him is important to have figured out in our minds. Santa Claus is a product of social construction in which we are architects for our children. And our parents, and society as a whole, have been designers and builders of our own sense of reality about this guy.

What I Concluded

The questions posed in this chapter are the ones I've had to ask myself. They have helped me to zero in on my past experiences, what I think and feel about Santa Claus, and why. In answering the questions, I found that my answers weren't really about Santa at all. They are reflections of my mind, my emotions, the things that made me happy, the things that scared me or made me sad. In hindsight, my answers to myself reflected ways I wanted to increase the chances that my children would experience joy and feel loved. They were also ways I wanted to protect them from sadness, ridicule, or disappointment. My answers were more about me than about them – and certainly had very little to do with Santa, when it came down to it. Maybe you found that too.

It is clearer now to me how parents are driving the sleigh when it comes to Santa Claus being a product of social construction. Parents who had a positive experience with him as children want to replicate that magic for their own; parents who had a negative experience with Santa (or Christmas) may find they want to spare their own children's heartache. We have a lot of choices when it comes to how we want to present Santa. But before we start acting, we need to reflect upon what we think about him and why. This is what I hope this chapter gave to you.

Washington Irving quote

Christmas is here
Merry old Christmas
Gift-bearing,
heart-touching
Joy-bringing Christmas
Day of grand memories
King of the year

Washington Irving
Manfords Magazine 1893, vol 37:591

Chapter 12

Santa and the Inner Life of Children

The Dilemma

All parents I know want their children to grow up happy and healthy. They do not want to scar their children psychologically. They go out of their way to do the right thing for them. Parenting is wicked hard. There isn't a blueprint for how to do it right. We all just do the best we can and hope it is good enough.

A fundamental question for parents to grapple with is this - Is Santa Claus good or bad for children to believe in? Every December I watch the news and media get inundated with blogs and articles from parents and professionals who weigh in with their opinions on both sides of the debate. As a mother and a scientist, I want better information than mere opinion. I want to see the research.

What I Discovered

As a mom and as a professor, I straddle many different worlds in trying to figure out what is best for my children. My go-to is to head for research and literature from experts who study a topic I'm interested in so I can learn best-practices. The problem is when it comes to Santa Claus, academics haven't done a ton of research on him, as I pointed out earlier. So I have done the best I can to pull together bits and pieces of information for you that I have found useful. I have included a list of reference material in the back of this book that I have used for those of you who are curious, doubt, or want to learn more.

Santa's Influence on Imagination

Child development experts unanimously concur that helping children to build an active imagination is good for their mental and cognitive development. Creativity is learned when imagination is nurtured. For instance, we know that young children love to play dress-up. When they don a firefighter's helmet or fairy-princess dress, they assume behaviors that they associate with the characters they are playing. When playing with Legos, Barbie, or Matchbox cars, children use their imagination to create complex scenarios and stories. One of the best gifts we can give children is the opportunity to use their imagination, to be creative, and to find the gifts that are uniquely theirs. Fantasy is creative imagination, unrestrained fancy, or engaging in thought that is apart from normal reality. While fantasy is associated today with video games, movies, or a way for children to escape from reality, it is far more than that.

There was once an assumption that when children reached a certain age they would push fantasy aside and deal rationally with the real world. But increasingly, child-development experts recognize the importance of imagination and the role it plays in understanding reality and making contributions to the world. Imagination is necessary for learning about people and events we don't directly experience, such as history or events on the other side of the world. It allows us to ponder unknown places, what people feel, how things work, the future, or what they want to do when they grow up.

Whether we are trying to understand how a computer can hold vast amounts of information, if there is a Heaven, what climbing a mountain, or living through a tsunami could be like, or how the lives of people living in China or Costa Rica are different from our own, it requires imagination. To create the telephone, train-tracks, spaceships, or Facebook, it required imagination. Musicians, actors, and artists need to use their imagination; so do architects, engineers, and construction workers. Whether contemplating history, our lives, or the nature of reality, we have to use our imagination. Fantasy characters are not mere entertainment for children but they embody the opportunity for children to internally process information that can lead to creativity, imagination, and problem-solving. These are important skill-sets to acquire. It is also influenced by their significant others like what their parents tell them, their culture and traditions, and their geography. A child living in rural Africa would logically have a very different experience of Santa than would a same-aged child living in Santa Claus, Indiana.

Looking at the phenomenon from different points of view is important in solving problems, designing cars, or developing new products. Making the impossible possible has been a driving force for humankind forever. Whether we are trying to figure out how to start a fire with stones and twigs or working with a team to send people to the moon, everything starts with imagination. This required that I get familiar with what psychologists teach us about imagination. Here's a bit of what I learned from them.

One of the most well-known scholars on the topic of fantasy was Bruno Bettelheim, in his 1976 book on *The Uses of Enchantment: The Meaning and Importance of Fairy Tales*. He alleges that fairy tales and characters such as Santa give children the opportunity to grapple with their fears and notions of reality in a safe, symbolic manner. When exposed to imaginary characters and socially evolved stories, children are forced to interpret them in their own way. While using imaginative play they wrestle with ideas, explore meanings, and grow emotionally in ways that ultimately prepare them for their own futures.

Professor Jackie Wooley researches how young children make distinctions between fantasy and reality at the Imagination and Cognition Lab at the University of Texas Austin. She finds that children have a much greater ability to discern fantasy from reality than many adults assume. They can appreciate fantasy characters like Santa and "believe" in him while understanding that he isn't real. They do the same thing with Mickey Mouse, Willy Wonka, Harry Potter, and a host of other characters. Two things can be real simultaneously; children can thus both believe in a figure like Santa Claus and not believe he is real, all at the same time without it posing conflict or contradiction for them. Children can comprehend pretense and pretend in play and they are able to enjoy it even while understanding its limits in reality (Harris and Kavanaugh 1993).

Jean Claude Piaget analyzed children's development and found that their abilities to comprehend information varied according to their age and development. Piaget believed that children interpret, organize, and use information from the environment so they can construct conceptions of their physical and social worlds. Their intellectual development is not simply an accumulation of facts, but a progression of thought through a series of distinct stages of intellectual ability. Piaget's work inspired the thought that children perceive and organize their worlds quite differently than adults. Young children do not conceptualize information in the same way as when they are older. Direct experience is important to this model. His theory found that mental representations or schematas are created in the minds of children who are attempting to organize information and apply them to new situations. Children develop the ability to think in abstract ways over time and experiences that mean one thing at one point in time may mean something different later on. As this pertains to Santa, young children don't understand or care about his reality status; when they are toddler and early elementary school-aged the mystery of Santa is paramount. As children move into adolescence they derive more sophisticated reasons for why believing in Santa is "for babies"; in the teen years when their understanding of Santa takes on a more abstract, rather than concrete, meaning. Their comprehension of Santa changes as they mature.

Imagination, as a developmental process, evolves through interaction with others. Lev Vygotsky's Sociocultural Theory (1978) is similar to Piaget's in that both feel children's development builds upon previous experience, but Vygotsky felt their learning was due to social and cultural experiences rather than abstract means or maturation. Through self-talk, thinking out loud, and discussing with others, children develop their understanding of themselves and reality. As this pertains to a child's comprehension of Santa Claus, children need to talk with other children (and adults) about who he is. Parental, peer, and media influences become vital influences in shaping how they view characters like Santa. Thus it is entirely possible that a very young child may not believe in Santa and an older child may. Vygotsky sees that the development of imagination parallels a child's development of speech. In social conversation, children take concepts and engage them in an internal conversation. This inner speech is associated with a child's self-consciousness and self-regulation (Berk 2008).

Howard Gardner's work on multiple intelligences is a more contemporary model of child development. He alleges that heredity, environment, and experience intersect to create different "intelligence" strengths within children. These include kinetic or body intelligence, musical/rhythmic intelligence, logic intelligence, verbal intelligence, interpersonal and intrapersonal intelligence, and naturalistic intelligence, to name a few. When children have certain intelligence nurtured they are more likely to develop while other attributes aren't because they aren't as well supported. The introduction of Santa Claus can reinforce many of these different types of intelligence. These include the nurturing of fantasy and imagination, the use of logic, spacial and naturalistic intelligence through exploring issues of the possibility of flying reindeer, Santa getting down a skinny chimney, or how it could be possible to visit all the children of the world in a single night. He can encourage mental and skill attributes through making crafts, singing songs, baking cookies. Social and interpersonal intelligence can be gained through learning how to gift and how to receive presents. Through the singular character of Santa Claus, a child is able to develop a variety of essential "intelligences."

Imaginative play provides children with the opportunity to act in different roles and consider what other's thoughts and behaviors might be. Ossorio's (2006) dramaturgical model finds imaginative of play to contribute to children's development of judgment. Play, especially in young children, is for fun, not problem-solving per se. Children are not necessarily concerned with enforcing rules; imaginative play gives them opportunities to create variations on a theme, new versions of a particular social practice, or create totally new practices. A child pretending is incorporating social practices and expanding on their possibilities while at the same time learning to act authentically. Santa brings opportunities to think about far-off places, elves, flying reindeer, how toys are made for and then delivered to the right persons, or how it could be possible to slide down a chimney. Children can develop their own ideas about science, transport, production, and propose hypotheses about how seemingly impossible things could be possible.

Children are inherently creators (Roberts 1991). They construct worlds and characters that increase their own mental potential. When children play they invent ideas, and it is in those cognitive inventions that they construct an inner world that may flow into their adult lives and into the larger community as a whole. An example of this is how a 12-year-old built a functional, inexpensive Braille printer – out of Legos! (Thomas 2014). The world is an ever-changing place and children need to develop cognitive skills so they can take an idea and adapt it to have meaning in different ways and contexts. Some developmental psychologists are concerned that technology and media influences may be reducing children's opportunities for developing imagination and internally creative play (Kantor 20xx).

The Campaign for a Commercial-Free Childhood (2013) found that many of today's toys provide fewer opportunities for imaginative play and may be socializing children into restricted roles and perceptions of the world, not enhanced ones. This is ironic since the use of imagination seems more important than ever as children enter an increasingly diverse world. We don't live in a homogenous society anymore. People come from different places, worship different faiths, like different foods, and have different customs and lifestyles. The ability to see things from other perspectives is a useful skill-set for children to acquire. Learning to see reality from different angles can lead to tolerance, the embracing of diversity, and the openness to possibilities. To deny children the appreciation of fantasy figures can cheat them of childhood pleasures, but also make it harder for them to solve a host of problems in their adult lives.

Parents and Imagination

In their everyday lives, adults have little reinforcement for engaging in imaginal activities. Adults pride themselves on being reality-based, and scorn others who are "out of touch with reality." I was seriously chastised by my daughter's first-grade teacher for suggesting to her that unicorns might exist. She wore a unicorn sweater, played with toy unicorns, loved the movie, The Last Unicorn, and enjoyed reading stories about princesses and unicorns. I let her believe in fairies. I thought her teacher might turn me in for child abuse because she felt I was not grounding my child in scientific reality.

There is a place for fact, but there is also a place for fantasy. Myth exists because people find it to be soul-soothing. Parents live vicariously through the experiences of their children so they can once again enter the realms of wonder and awe. Parents read their children scary fairy tales; they hide money under pillows after they swipe the kid's teeth, and they encourage pretend play through dolls and action figures. Childless adults are a large percentage of Disney World attendees, whose eyes are just as starry as those of children in strollers. The resurgence of retro everything, from television, movies, clothes, foods, and cars, enables people to travel into another place and time; adults love retro because it reminds them of the way things used to be, while their children and grandchildren love it because it is the opposite of science fiction, helping them to imagine the way things were "back when" as compared to the future.

The anticipation of something wonderful happening is part of the human spirit. At night adults as well as children look up at the stars and chime, "Starlight, star bright, first star I see tonight, I wish I may, I wish I might, have the wish I wish tonight." People in rural areas may make a wish when they see a load of hay pass by. Conversely, people may try to ward off bad luck by not stepping on a crack, not letting an object divide them when they are walking with another person, or throwing salt over the shoulder if some is spilled. Adults often rely upon intervention from spirits, gods, or people they've never seen. Believing that they matter, and that someone, somewhere sees and knows that they matter, provides us with a source of emotional comfort.

Adults use imagination differently than do children but imagine nonetheless. They fantasize about getting the perfect job or big promotion or finding the soul mate who must be waiting for them somewhere - but how many people actually realize those fantasies as realities? As adults plunk down cash at the register to purchase that lottery ticket, don't most of us fantasize about how we will spend the big bucks we might win? People may imagine themselves to look like sports figures or beauty queens; males of all ages can be seen wearing jerseys with the number of their favorite basketball, football, or hockey star as they spew forth stats and facts about games played and performance averages. With bulging bellies pressing against those jerseys, fans rage at players, as if they could do better if they were on the field playing. Fantasy =\= reality.

Adults need to believe they are going to find that perfect lover, get that big job, or win that lottery ticket. Why? Doing so gives us hope. It helps us to endure the difficult days, even if there's only a fraction of likelihood they will come true. Many people become obsessed with celebrities and entertainers, and they spend considerable amounts of time thinking about them instead of the real, everyday people in their lives. People, USA Today and Parade Magazine editors all know this, as they give us stories and images so we can spy on their lives and imagine what life would be like living with them. Robert Redford, Brad Pitt, and other men have been voted one of the most attractive men alive, which speaks to the vast number of women who fantasize about being with them. A woman I know is sure that this one actor will be her husband one day if she can just get a chance to meet him; my secretary was ga-ga over her favorite singer and sent him flowers at his concert, hoping he'd invite her backstage afterward to be with him. Men are no different. Larry traveled thousands of miles many times to see Shakira in concert. Nicole Kidman, Catherine Zeta-Jones, and Angelina Jolie are all rated as some of today's most attractive women by men who fantasize about being with them, just as men did Marilyn Monroe and Audrey Hepburn years ago. As testified through the presence of girlie calendars and the use of explicit magazines, many men fantasize about relationships of all sorts with women. The use of steroids, an increase of anorexia, and obsession with fitness and low-carbohydrate diets all are tangible indicators that people have fantasies of themselves looking differently. If we just buy that piece of fitness equipment, diet book, or color our hair, we're sure we have a chance of being attractive. Embracing myths helps keep us alive. So is believing in Santa really all that different?

Santa, Empathy, and Altruism

Children benefit when they learn to care about others. They cannot learn it without our assistance. So how do we do it? Parents, teachers, and anyone who is in the position of being a role model to children help children see themselves as certain kinds of people. The Santa figure helps role model the kind of person who is responsible and caring. From this shift in self-concept will come lasting behavior and values that are not contingent on the presence of someone to dispense threats or bribes, according to experts like Kohn and Cotton. Cooperation is key to this outcome because working together creates a humanizing experience that helps children to take a benevolent view of others. It allows them to transcend their own egos; it helps make people real and not objects; and cooperation encourages trust, sensitivity, open communication, and what is known as a pro-social activity.

Other benefits for children include more accepting and respectful attitudes toward people who are different from themselves. This includes sociodemographic factors such as race, religion, ethnicity, gender, sexual preference, ability level, socioeconomic status, nationality, and the like. When children learn how to share and cooperate, they are more likely to understand other people's points of view, and they can relate to them in a more positive, constructive manner as a result. Children who have learned empathetic and altruistic behavior have been found to do better in school, have more friends, have higher self-esteem, and view themselves to have more positive connections with others. Success cannot occur in isolation; it can only come through our ability to communicate with others. By talking with others, we are better able to understand their needs, beliefs, motivations, and lifestyles. In doing so, we are able to examine how similar they are to ourselves. When we communicate with others, we are also able to view ourselves through the eyes of others. This is akin to what Cooley called "the looking glass self." It is useful for children to realize how other people view them so they can modify their behavior and become more of who they would like to be.

Learning the foundations for cross-cultural empathy is enhanced if children can first focus on the similarities between themselves and others, according to Hahn. Later, when differences are explored, they don't seem so great, and the distance between "us and them" seems more manageable. The more empathy we can feel, the greater the emotional connectedness that occurs between people. Some scientists feel that the bonds we create with others aren't just emotional, but they exist as real energy systems that have essences and that can be measured. Positive relationships or energy feels very different from negative ones, and both result in very different outcomes. Liking and respecting each other helps to create a world in which we can seek mutually acceptable problem solving and beneficial developments. Rejection and hostility lead to hatred and wars. It's as simple as that, scholars tell us.

Learning how to not just get along, but to actually like people who are different from us, is of utmost importance in human relationships. Children are less likely to accept discriminatory stereotypes when they realize the commonalities that exist between people, and more likely to build constructive relationships in which problems can be overcome. But all this is much harder to do than to say. Role models provide children with opportunities to directly observe the behaviors of problem solving, generosity, and benevolence, but watching isn't enough. Children need direct involvement in learning how to do this. Experts point out that children need ongoing practice in imagining how other people view the world and themselves. They need people who can listen to their feelings and help them to overcome barriers that will snag human relations. Parents who encourage altruistic behavior and good communication skills on a regular basis are more likely to have children who can "own" them as they incorporate such behaviors into their own sense of self. It is the repetition and reinforcement that makes children accept them as part of their own customary behavior. It is difficult for children to obtain true feelings of empathy and altruism if they only observe such behaviors in one-shot or intermittent episodes. The old saw, "show, don't tell," aptly describes how children learn by watching, not by being told what to do. How else can children know how to care about others?

The Santa Claus figure allows children to imagine another world, another perspective, and other people's dreams and needs. The ability to engage in such complex conceptual tasks helps them to develop both affective and cognitive empathy as well as pro-social behavior. A standard message is that Santa goes all around the world just to make children happy – even when he's never personally talked with them. There is a message that the Santa character believes all children are important just because they exist. The altruistic, empathic message conveys that children are special and deserve to be acknowledged for just being the best of who they can be. This is an extraordinarily important lesson for children to learn. Santa models empathetic behavior for the entire world. Who else does that which all children universally can identify with and relate to?

When children implement Santa spirit-like behaviors by thinking about what others need and want, and they go out of their way to make gifts happen, it provides adults an opportunity to give them positive reinforcement for the development of these attributes of generosity and concern. Positive trait attribution, or "dispositional praise," as it is sometimes called, refers to the practice of emphasizing to children that the reason they exhibit pro-social behavior is that it is in their nature to do so. Positive trait attribution has been shown to be a powerful means of enhancing empathetic understanding and behavior. Empathy is an important skill for children to acquire.

Santa as a Buffer to Life's Challenges

Children can learn early on that life isn't always easy or fun. Many confront abuse, tragedy, death, and heartbreak at very young years. "Might it be the case that the harshness of real life requires the creation of something better, something to believe in, something to hope for in the future or to return to a long-lost childhood a long time ago in a galaxy far away" (Boyle and McKay 2016). Fantasy, either in cartoon figures, toys, movies, or video-games, is a huge commercial product, demonstrating people's need to experience a momentary buffer to life's challenges. Drugs and alcohol could be seen as a diversion to them as well. Thus Santa and his elves can be seen as providing a bit of blissful respite and hope in a world that is harsh and cold.

Around the world, there is an attempt for individuals, communities, and philanthropic organizations to make sure that needy children receive gifts from Santa. Thinking back to World War I and the Santa Ship that sailed across the Atlantic to give orphans Christmas presents, or the WWII soldiers who dressed up as Santa to give local children a moment of fun during the holiday reinforces the notion that people can relieve the suffering of others. Toys For Tots is a program found across many communities where people and stores collect and deliver gifts, food, and clothes to children to help them forget about their poverty and struggle for a little while. These gifts cannot transform their lives long-term, but they provide a moment of respite, of hope that tomorrow may be better and that there are caring people out there who could be mobilized to help them.

What I Concluded

Imagination. Creativity. Play, Empathy. Altruism. Problem-solving. Bonding with others. These are internal benefits that Santa has been used to deliver to children. In none of my research did I find Santa being mean, exclusionary, or punitive. Adults may have used him to pursue their own negative agendas, but in reviewing what the Santa figure can bring, there are very positive psychological benefits that children can gain. From a cost-benefit analysis, it seems children have a lot they could gain from a positive Santa character that they may not get through ordinary means.

Charles Dickens quote

Happy, happy Christmas,
that can win us back
to the delusions of
our childhood days,
recall to the old man
the pleasures of his youth,
and transport the traveler back
to his own fireside and quiet home.

Charles Dickens
A Christmas Carol 1843

Chapter 13

Santa, Peers, and Play

The Dilemma

People who know how to play, and how to play well with others, tend to have lots of friends. Yet a lot of people don't play, period, and they certainly don't play well with others. In the adultified world of work, it seems like many people work all the time and grouse at others. Complaining seems to be a national past-time from people who are half-empty Eeyore's, needing to be filled up. I can't help but wonder – didn't they get to play as a child? When my head turns to Santa, I wonder if these negativity-wielding adults didn't get to enjoy childhood or have a fun Santa. Now, I know that is a stretch of the imagination. But I think a lot that I learned about how to play, and to play well with others, from my early experiences with Santa. While I started out looking at how much fun it was to play with each other, I had to examine the fact that some children don't get to play. Their lives are filled with struggle because of their demographic characteristics or merely because their parents are poor. If Santa Claus is really supposed to be there for all children, no matter who you are – is he really? Thus I went out to discover - how does Santa Claus impact play and peer relationships?

What I Discovered

The version I learned about Santa Claus evokes the importance of play in a variety of ways, like getting ready for his arrival, decorating the house, writing him letters, cooking festive foods, singing songs, and listening to hear if reindeer hoofs are dancing on the rooftop. He may bring presents fun to play with, but often the seeds for play are planted in the advent month before his arrival. Such activities may focus on "doing", not "getting". Indeed, my mama role-modeled how to "make" Santa. She also taught me that Santa had to bring things that were just for fun. She gave us socks and underwear, but Santa gave us Mr. Potato Head, Chutes and Ladders, tinker toys, dolls, fire trucks, and the Game of Life. She liked to play. She giggled with delight when she made us happy. She always made sure that we received gifts designed for joy, gifts that would encourage group interaction, and facilitate play. Laughter was her key ingredient in the recipe for a happy holiday.

Some critics of Santa allege that Christmas should be a time for spiritual reflection, not toys and play. I learned that Colonial-era children often got no gifts and were expected to spend the holiday, or holy-day, in prayer. Adults, in their work-obsessed way, may devalue the profoundly important role that play has in our lives. So I took a closer look at the relationship between Santa and how his role facilitates children's play.

Experts abound with the conclusion that play is essential for the human spirit. The American Academy of Pediatrics set forth a set of guidelines for pediatricians to prescribe play as essential to children's health and development (Ginsburg 2007 Yogman et al 2018). Their journal article in *Pediatrics* states:

"Play allows children to use their creativity while developing their imagination, dexterity, and physical, cognitive, and emotional strength. Play is important to healthy brain development. It is through play that children at a very early age engage and interact in the world around them. Play allows children to create and explore a world they can master, conquering their fears while practicing adult roles, sometimes in conjunction with other children or adult caregivers. As they master their world, play helps children develop new competencies that lead to enhanced confidence and the resiliency they will need to face future challenges. Undirected play allows children to learn how to work in groups, to share, to negotiate, to resolve conflicts, and to learn self-advocacy skills. When play is allowed to be child-driven, children practice decision-making skills, move at their own pace, discover their own areas of interest, and ultimately engage fully in the passions they wish to pursue. Ideally, much of play involves adults, but when play is controlled by adults, children acquiesce to adult rules and concerns and lose some of the benefits play offers them, particularly in developing creativity, leadership, and group skills. In contrast to passive entertainment, play builds active, healthy bodies. In fact, it has been suggested that encouraging unstructured play may be an exceptional way to increase physical activity levels in children, which is one important strategy in the resolution of the obesity epidemic. Perhaps above all, play is a simple joy that is a cherished part of childhood." (Ginsburg 2007).

Children naturally engage in play; it is both recreational and instructional. Play is one of the most important learning tools that young children have. Play is so essential to children's health and wellbeing that the United Nation lists it in their Convention on the Rights of the Child (which is the most ratified human rights document in the world) as a right that should be guaranteed to all children (Office of the High Commissioner for Human Rights 2020).

The long-term benefits of play are well documented. The UN has taken the stance that play is vitally important for children because of the plethora of outcome-data that has been produced by researchers around the world for decades (Barnett 1990; Berk, Mann, Ogan 2006; Bornstein et al 1997; Fein 1981; Garvey 1991; Hughes 2009; Hurwitz 2002; Isenberg 1988; Kelly and Hammond 2011; Lego Foundation 2020; Lillard et al 2012; Pellegrini 2009; Saracho 2009; Singer, Golinkoff, & Erikson 1985; Vygotsky 1967).

Play has been called "brain food" because it helps brains develop in ways that are vital to academic success. It provides the foundation for learning including language, reading, thinking, and reasoning skills. Play arouses curiosity, which leads to discovery and creativity. Play develops skills such as adaptability and flexibility, which are fundamental to getting along with others, problem-solving, and positive, proactive behavior. Play helps children to become more responsible people as they sort through values of cheating and fairness. Playing brings inquisitiveness and joy, which helps to provide meaning in life. There are a variety of emotions generated from play that include empathy, compassion, and humor. According to the Institute of Play, the thing that most Nobel Laureates, innovative entrepreneurs, artists and performers, well-adjusted children, happy couples, and families, and the most successfully adapted mammals have in common is that they play enthusiastically throughout their lives. Conversely, a common denominator shared by mass murderers, abused children, burnt-out employees, depressed mothers, caged animals, and chronically worried teens is that play was rarely a part of their lives.

Plato is thought to have said, "It is the essential nature of man to play." Today, experts have found through observation, research, and knowledge that Plato was correct. They have been able to document the importance of play and why it is so necessary for healthy child development. Play appears to be hardwired into our genetic code. Adults, like children, want to play because it is instinctive and fundamental to basic human nature. Practical experience leads us to know what researchers say is true – that humans seem biologically designed to play throughout our entire life cycle, starting in infancy. Children delight in play, and teens may be scolded because they prefer to "goof off" instead of doing their work. What adult doesn't like to play? Their play may be more sophisticated, their toys more expensive, but adults also like play-days. Play has been found to teach us how to manage and transform our negative emotions and experiences. It supercharges learning and is a foundational factor in good mental and physical health. People who laugh and play, according to researchers like Norman Cousins, live longer and happier lives.

The National Association for the Education of Young Children (Bongiorno 2020) and play expert David Elkind (2007) synthesizes why play is important for children. **Play helps children grow strong and healthy. Play reduces stress.** Play helps children grow emotionally and find joy and entertainment. Play is intellectually stimulating, as it can be both simple and complex and include symbolic play, sociodramatic play, reading, interpreting, and learning games with rules, all of which give children different benefits. In short, play is the child's laboratory, **a child's context for learning.**

Through Santa-oriented play children learn and develop cognitive skills – like math and problem solving such as when Santa might arrive; physical abilities – like how to get the tree to stay up in the stand or running around playing reindeer; new vocabulary – like the words they need to play with toys; social skills – like playing together with toys or making cookies in the kitchen; and literacy skills – like writing a letter to Santa. They engage in problem-solving (how does he get all those presents in the sleigh that reindeer pull across the sky in a single night?), altruism (what would sister like as a present?), empathy (but we better make sure to leave carrots out for the reindeer because they'll be hungry too). The singular character of Santa is jam-packed with multiple learning opportunities.

Dr. Edgar Klugman, one of the foremost experts in play, has found that through pretend play, children transform themselves, others, and objects from real into make-believe. Pretend play can be both a solitary act (like when children flip through a book about Santa or play with a toy), or it can be a group activity (like singing carols or playing Monopoly together). He notes that play reaches its highest level at preschool and kindergarten age and becomes less important as a child grows older – which is exactly the time when belief in Santa is most pronounced. Pretend play helps children process emotions and events in their lives, practice social skills, learn values, develop language skills, and create a rich imagination – which is shown elsewhere in this book to lead children toward success.

Parent-child play is especially important for healthy child development; it also facilitates the creation of positive parent-child bonding (Ginsburg 2007; Henry 1990; Lillard 2011; MacDonald 1993). Play helps children gain relationships and social skills, as well as the opportunity to process the world around them. As parents and other family members play with the children at the holiday time, many opportunities for parent-child bonding are created. Santa creates a regular routine each year for structured and spontaneous fun. Francine Ferland (2009), a professor at the University of Montreal and a leading researcher on play and its impact on a child's development, finds that during play parents and children together can forget our troubles and be creative and original with each other. We can teach one another how to make even mundane experiences fun – for instance, in this current day of COVID-19 hand washing instruction, rather than being told to wash their hands all the time, think about how they would feel if their parents said they should try the magic bar that will erase all the germs on their hands?

Research indicates that if there is no play, trust and skill in communicating mutual pleasure just doesn't develop. Openness of one's heart to others is enhanced through the joy of play. If play is minimal or contains conflicting signals, social skills are not integrated or refined. Aggression, anxiety, mixed signals, or indifference from parents, caretakers, and teachers stops the development of optimism, hope, and playfulness. Depression, fearfulness, and cynicism grow in their place. Play-deprived kids have been found to be more vulnerable to impulsive behavior and more prone to violent behavior. Through play children learn the long-lasting benefits of belief and trying to be good; perseverance is necessary to the development of well-adjusted children and adults.

There is a significant concern among child advocates that play is being eroded from the lives of children or even becoming endangered as children are pushed out of childhood and into living lives that resemble those of adults (Flaxman 1990; Ginsburg 2007). Play experts like Diane Levin (2019) of Defending the Early Years and actor Matt Damon's mother, scholar Nancy Carlsson-Paige (2008), have fought to protect young children and their right to have a developmentally appropriate, happy, healthy childhood. Play is a big part of that. Young children are given toy computers and cellphones instead of blocks and stuffed animals; even dolls are designed to do things rather than to just be. The pressure for even young children to focus on success is more embedded in their toys and activities. They are expected to work, to produce, and not to fritter away their time. Yet play is as important to a child's development as food, water, love, care, and hope and through it children experience fun and joy. Moreover, play to a child is essential to learning. Play is to a child as school is for the adolescent or work is to the parent; it is a form of cognitive stimulation.

Through the Santa experience, children learn to play as they go through family and social rituals in preparation of his visit. Through the before-and-after Christmas interactions, they get opportunities for playing to become learning. To children, play is not a distraction or a waste of time; it is the time in which they are learning how to engage in life. Toys, as manufacturers and educators quickly remind us, are just as important for children as books and computers. According to physician George Sheehan (1993), play is life lived. Without play – without nurturing the child that still lives in all of us – we will always feel incomplete. This incompleteness is not just physically, but also creatively, intellectually, and spiritually as well. No matter what our age, he recommended that we add life to our years.

The annual visit from Santa oozes playtime possibilities. Child development experts agree that play is very important in the learning and emotional development of all children. Through play, children develop their personalities and a gain a positive sense of self as they realize their potential through the experience of success. As children tinker with their Christmas toys, their creativity and imagination are unleashed. Thinking about the nature of Santa and his reindeer helps them to gain important problem-solving skills.

Play enhances everyone's quality of life by making it more interesting and enjoyable Adults often recall some of their happiest holiday moments being those spent playing games or acting silly with those they love. I daresay that my own children happily recall their favorite Christmas mornings as those when they unwrapped the coveted teddy bear, the silly rubber alligator, the surprise box full of doll heads, or the kitty backpack that they initially mistook for their own orange marmalade cat. Electronic devices cost more but ultimately mean less to them. It is laughter and play they remember.

Santa and Peer Relationships

Play is important for peer bonding and interaction. When kids play together, they make important transitions toward independent thought and responsible behavior. As children share Santa experiences and insights, they do more than play; they are processing information and coming collectively with ideas about the nature of goodness and myth in the world. According to sociologist William Corsoro (2018), a child's development is embedded in peer interactions that result in new interpretations and contributions to the messages they previously learned from the wider adult society. Practices that we share collectively with others help children to organize and understand their experiences. In turn, they help construct new meanings and behaviors.

Peers are enormously important in shaping a child's picture of the world and their place in it. Everyone needs friends, no matter what age we are. Friends help us in a multitude of ways. We do things together and have fun; we share information and learn from one another; we bounce ideas off each other; we exchange hopes and dreams as well as or fears and disappointments. They help us to figure out how to overcome challenges. Our peer groups help define reality. Research has found overwhelming evidence for even young children to have a need for connection with others their own age (Bengtsson and Johnson 1992; Coolahan et al 1990; Howes 1989; 1992; Kurdek and Krile 1982; Ladd 1990; Parten 1932).

Peers can be a positive or negative influence on children. What I learned that I want to focus on here is that peers can serve to engage children in their own problem-solving about Santa Claus. There is power in children putting their heads together to explore who he is and how he does things on their own terms without outside, adult intervention. So often adults wade in and give unsolicited advice or perspectives that disempower children to figure things out for themselves.

Santa Claus is known by almost every child in every part of the world. He may go by different names, arrive by means other than flying reindeer, and wear costumes that aren't red and white fur, but children understand that he is the same basic character. He gives children an opportunity for a singular character that they can all talk about together as they explore. Santa is a vehicle for juvenile collective debate on whether or not he is real, and why or why not.

Think about universal figures that children can bond together over. Disney has done a great job exporting Mickey Mouse throughout the world; media promotes figures like Sponge Bob Square Pants or Poke'mon have become universal - but are those characters who promote positive values commonly associated with Santa Claus? Santa, at the heart of children's conversations, allows dialogue about altruism, dreams, mystery, and magic. When children share different experiences with Santa, they are discussing their families, traditions, experiences, and things that are of importance to them. Their conversation stems from internally driven ideas and real experiences, unlike externally-focused scenarios associated with media characters. This is a more real and engaged type of interaction than pattering back what they saw on television or in a video-game.

Santa allows for children to have an important type of collective conversation with one another. It is useful to remember that developmentally, children do not look at Santa in the same complicated way as adults. The idea that Santa knows what children need and want is not something children usually spend much time thinking about. They simply accept what he does to be natural and true. Unlike adults, children take a more relaxed, integrative approach to belief and faith.

Santa helps children to work together and draw the line between what is plausible and what is not. Young children may believe there are actually skeletons in the closet or monsters under the bed; by adventuring forth to confront those fears, they are able to develop greater independence and responsibility for their own actions and emotions. Often, adventure-type play in which children are confronted with the forces of good or evil will help to solidify the selection of values and decisions. Parents can help them by not telling them what to think about Santa but allowing children the opportunity to figure things out for themselves. Using imagination and make-believe activities of what Santa can, and cannot do, can be fun as well as conceptually exhilarating.

Santa Claus and Peer Exclusion

Though my interviews with children from different cultures indicate that they view Santa Claus in a positive fashion, we need to dig deeper. As a white, European-based ethnic person who grew up in a Christian household in a pretty homogenous community of people "like me", my peers had the same basic Santa experience as I did.

But not all children do. The US, indeed the world, is more diverse than ever before. A 2019 Pew research study about diversity changes around the world found that countries were more diverse in the past and that in general people thought this was a positive thing.[i] In the United States, like elsewhere, children are at the forefront of racial and ethnic diversity transformation.[ii] The population of white Americans is declining as the number of mixed-race and non-white children will be the majority. This fact alone means that having an old, white guy representing Santa Claus has to change if Santa Claus is going to be used as an enduring, positive figure in children's lives.

So I think about how Santa Claus is perceived by children, and these questions come to mind. How do children who live in geographically hot areas or in the Global South relate to a Global North snow-bound Santa character? How do children who have skin that is not white relate to him? Is there inherent white supremacy perceived (even if not intended) because it is a white guy giving out the presents? What if it was someone with brown or black skin – would he be perceived differently, and if so how and by who? While the older I get the more I appreciate the presence and value of wisdom earned with age, why does Santa always have to be old? Some children are quite wise, and many are very generous. These are not necessarily age-related attributes. And then there is the other question – why are Santas always male? Why can't females be Santas – especially since in the homes that I know, it's almost always women who are putting in the time, effort, and money-making Santa real?

I know I'm not the only one who thinks that for the sake of all children, it's time to give Santa Claus a face-lift that would make him more inclusive. When Aisha Harris (2013), an editor at the New York Times was a little girl, she observed the many different ways Santa Claus could appear and asked her father if he was brown like her or if he was a white man. Her father astutely "replied that Santa was every color. Whatever house he visited, jolly old St. Nicholas magically turned into the likeness of the family that lived there". That explanation served her well for years, but she observes that "Two decades later, America is less and less white, but a melanin-deficient Santa remains the default in commercials, mall casting calls, and movies. Isn't it time that our image of Santa better serves *all* the children he delights each Christmas?" Harris concluded that "America abandon Santa-as-fat-old-white-man and create a new symbol of Christmas cheer. From here on out, Santa Claus should be a penguin". She selected a penguin to be the new image of Santa Claus for some good reasons:

"For one thing, making Santa Claus an animal rather than an old white male could spare millions of nonwhite kids the insecurity and shame that I remember from childhood. Whether you celebrate the holiday or not, Santa is one of the first iconic figures foisted upon you: He exists as an incredibly powerful image in the imaginations of children across the [world]... That this genial, jolly man can only be seen as white—and consequently, that a Santa of any other hue is merely a "joke" or a chance to trudge out racist stereotypes—helps perpetuate the whole "white-as-default" notion... Plus, people *love* penguins. There are blogs dedicated entirely to their cuteness. They're box office gold. Most importantly, they're never scary (in contrast to, say, polar bears and reindeer). Most kids love Santa—because he brings them presents. But human Santa can be terrifying—or at least unsettling. And, with a penguin Santa, much Christmas folklore can remain unchanged. Being a penguin, Santa Claus can still reside in a snowy homeland—though for scientific accuracy we'll need to move him from the North Pole to the South.... Will kids have a harder time believing in Santa the Penguin—aka Penguin Claus—than in the fat white guy he's replacing? I don't think so. Kids are used to walking, talking bears, and gigantic friendly birds...since *we* created Santa, we can certainly change him however we'd like—and we have, many times over. Like the holiday itself, Santa has long since been extracted from his religious roots, even if the name St. Nicholas still gets thrown around. Our current design takes inspiration from multiple sources, including Washington Irving's 1809 description of St. Nick ...[and] Clement Clarke Moore.... Since then, Santa has been redesigned and re-appropriated to push everything from soda to war. So let's ditch Santa the old white man altogether, and embrace Penguin Claus.... It's time to hand over the reins to those deer and let the universally beloved waddling bird warm the hearts of children everywhere, regardless of the color of their skin" (Harris 2013).

Also, not to be missed, is the issue of social class. Race and gender exclusion are one thing, but economic disparity and Santa Claus also has to be looked at squarely in the eye. Poverty and homelessness are at epidemic proportions too during the COVID-19 pandemic. Brenden O'Flahtery, a professor of Economics at Columbia University, projects that with unemployment rates that are equating that of

The Great Depression, that there could be a 45% increase in homelessness in the US with over 800,000 people being homeless by the end of summer 2020.[iii] This predicts that Santa Claus isn't going to be coming to a bunch of homes this Christmas.

I work on national policy issues for homeless children and must say that the mandated gift-givingness pushed by advertisers each December makes me so sad. These are wonderful children who did nothing wrong except have parents who had economic trouble in a terrible economy that seems to be awful for people who are poor but super good times for the ultra-wealthy.[iv] They are just as entitled to hope and joy and the opportunity to play like any other child. Good-hearted citizens around the community step up year to donate gifts so children will receive something from Santa, and that's wonderful. I know people who don't have much but spend hundreds even thousands of dollars out of their own pocket trying to be an elf who delivers presents to needy children. Santa issue is troublesome when the message that good children get gifts but naughty ones don't. Focusing on the spirit of loving-kindness and non-material gifts Santa can bring seems like a better direction to go to make him inclusive for everyone.

What I Concluded

Child developmental scholars indicate that having friends is essential for children's wellbeing. So is play. Both teach them skills on how to interact with others, work as a team, problem-solve, and do so in a world without parental intervention. Santa Claus isn't the only vehicle to facilitate that. But he is a universal figure that all children can relate to. He is full of mystery, science, history, and perplexing things for peers to discuss and figure out on their own terms.

It still seems to me that there are more benefits to what a Santa Claus figure can give children socially than eliminating him from their lives. But it does seem clear that the "play" forms associated with Santa should be framed in a peaceful, fun, educational and collaborative format – not violence, aggression, mean-spiritedness, or exclusion. It also seems clear that children have different experiences of Santa Claus, holiday celebrations, and gift-giving. Foisting upon them a racist, ageist, materialistic character will not be as helpful for children to learn values of altruism as would a more culturally-inclusive character. Despite the fun that Santa brings, I think that maybe he might be able to bring more fun to more children if he had a face-lift. But what that looks like, I don't yet know. So maybe it's not just the presentation of Santa that we need to attend to - perhaps it is how we present him to be that is the bigger issue of concern.

Notes:

[i] Poushter, Jacob and Fetterolf, Janelle. 2019. How people around the world view diversity. https://www.pewresearch.org/global/2019/04/22/how-people-around-the-world-view-diversity-in-their-countries/

[ii] Maher, Matt. 2020. Children are at the forefront of change. PRB.org. https://www.prb.org/children-are-at-the-forefront-of-u-s-racial-and-ethnic-change/

[iii] Community Solutions. 2020. https://community.solutions/analysis-on-unemployment-projects-40-45-increase-in-homelessness-this-year/

[iv] Kristof, Nicolas. 2020. Crumbs for the hungry but windfalls for the rich. New York Times. https://www.nytimes.com/2020/05/23/opinion/sunday/coronavirus-economic-response.html?smid=em-share

David Grayson quote

I sometimes think we expect too much of
Christmas Day.
We try to crowd into it the long arrears
of kindliness and humanity
of the whole year.

As for me, I like to
take my Christmas a little at a time,
all through the year.
And thus I drift along into the holidays
— let them overtake me unexpectedly —
waking up some fine morning
and suddenly saying to myself,
why this is Christmas Day.

David Grayson

A Day of Pleasant Bread. 1926. Doubleday

Chapter 14

Santa Over the Child's Lifespan

The Dilemma

Answers to questions about "who is Santa Claus?" or "is Santa Claus real?" seem to be very fluid. What you get depends on who you ask and when you ask it. I know that I have perceived him differently over the span of my life. There have been times Santa has been a driving force in my life, and time that he has been irrelevant. Is my experience similar to, or different from, that of others? I wanted to find out.

What I Discovered

Santa Claus has different meanings from the time children are infants until they become young adults. He means different things to us at different points across our lifespan. Scholars like Piaget, Bruner and Vygotsky note that belief systems change over time through the processes of adaptation, particularly assimilation and accommodation.

Assimilation involves children's interpretation of events in terms of existing cognitive structures. They cannot understand an event beyond what they are capable of mentally. It would be ridiculous to expect a four-year-old to understand the basis of nuclear physics. They can't. It is not because they are dumb or stupid; they simply haven't yet laid the conceptual train tracks that will allow for the successful delivery of that information.

Laying the foundations for higher-level thought takes time, and each new piece of information builds upon previous ones. Therefore, introducing a concept like Santa Claus gives children the foundation on which to make inferences about abstract concepts like faith later on. Accommodation refers to changing the cognitive structure to make sense of the environment. Children, with respect to Santa, may play along with parents and act as though they still believe in him when they actually don't. It could be that they don't want to risk the chance of losing the opportunity to get gifts, or it could be that they don't want to shatter their parent's needs to be Santa. Older children enjoy laughing about themselves when they were younger because they learn that they are now able to think differently about something they had interpreted in another way before. It is possible, and natural, for children to accept that some people believe in Santa while others do not, and they can learn to appreciate that both have reasons for being correct in their view. Children, as Taylor (1999; 1997) points out in her work, are often able to find ways to accept several different conceptual frameworks for something at the same time because they mentally construct a way for themselves to manage contradictory thought. Two entirely different and seemingly contradictory things can be absolutely true or exist at the same time.

Early in a child's life, when intelligence develops through the undertaking of motor actions, such as crawling, walking, or grasping items, Santa is not a big deal to children. They may be much more entertained with unwrapping a present than the present itself. They do not really care who the present is from or how it got there. They like the box, the paper, the ribbon. It is parents and grandparents who are invested in the experience of teaching their children to believe in Santa. Teaching children about Santa is fun for adults. It helps them to kindle the fires of their own happy memories. When families encourage children to believe in Santa, they are creating hope that their children's future will be happy.

Sometimes parents forget that small children have no emotional or cognitive investment in Santa. However, children do have an investment in pleasing their parents and evoking a positive response from them. Many parents have gotten their feelings hurt when a child doesn't understand the expense or effort they went through to get them a particular gift. But this is not their job at this point in time. This is why children are much more entertained by items that they can manipulate with their hands, the boxes the gift comes in, or "do something" toys. Also, young children can be frightened by Santa; they do not know this man, he is wearing clothes to which they are not accustomed, he may be loud with his "ho ho's" and parents may try to foist them to sit on this stranger's lap. It takes time for them to acquire a framework that lets them know that Santa could be a positive figure.

Can a young child know if something is real or not? The study of pretense requires the differentiation of knowing that the world is presented one way when it is in fact another. Experts have found that children have this skill by the time children are 18 months, they can identify pretense in others by 28 months of age, and by the age of 4 most can understand the role fantasy plays in everyday life (Sobel 2006; Wooley 2009). Children enter the world not know what is real and they spend the early years of their lives looking for cues to try to figure it out. Living with ambiguity becomes normal for them. They figure out that there may be multiple dimensions of reality. Consider the popularity of Mickey Mouse. Most children are introduced to Mickey at a young age. They know that he isn't a real mouse that hides in the walls of houses. The magic of Mickey is that he allows children to imagine; children do not infer that Mickey is the same as the mouse their parents caught in a trap. They imagine that Mickey is real; he sleeps in a bed in a real house, wears shorts, has a girlfriend named Minnie and nephews, and he can be Tugboat Willie or the Sorcerer's Apprentice. It's totally normal that they use fantasy to pretend. They understand complex reality in a simple way. Children probably understand that Santa isn't like regular people and his presence provides them with an opportunity to figure out what he's like.

As children become toddlers and grow into early elementary school, Santa is more important than when they were babies. They are more likely to believe in him during this stage and parents become more invested in engaging in the play of making Santa. They frost cookies, cut snowflakes, sing Rudolf the Red Nose Reindeer, write letters to Santa, and enjoy making simple presents to give to others. Children need concrete physical examples for them to be able to relate to larger, more abstract things like the value of giving to others. They are not yet into making major cause-and-effect associations; it is entirely plausible to them that Santa and his reindeer could be at their house one moment, at in Australia with a sleigh drawn by kangaroos the next. They aren't bothered by the details that snag adults conceptually.

One of the main characteristics of children around age 2 to 7 is that they are egoistic, in that everything is about them, or at least everything should be about them in their opinion. They have difficulty understanding life from any other perspective than their own. They are "me, myself, and I" oriented and building of a self is of utmost importance. When children develop a sense of themselves as deserving and competent, it has lifelong benefits. It does not mean that children are selfish and greedy because they are me-oriented. This egoism helps bind children to others, in that they believe that everyone thinks as they do, shares their feelings and desires what they want. Children at this age tend to have a sense that their perception of the world is absolute and objective, and it is difficult for them to understand that others may want something different. The character of Santa Claus is particularly useful because he helps teach children that every child is important and that every child has unique needs and desires. "I got a doll. Tom got a truck. Lucy got a ball." This is useful for children to learn.

Santa is portrayed as a likable guy that they can easily relate to, but learn that while they may get what they want from him for Christmas, other kids may want, and get different things.

During this stage of development, children are very interested in how nature and people come to be. Their interest in magic is absolutely developmentally appropriate and fulfills an important intellectual function. Think about the fascination of magic from a child's point of view; things routinely appear and can disappear at a whim. They wonder where the sun has gone when it passes behind a cloud; they may get distressed when a parent leaves the room, and then are surprised when they look up to see them standing there again. Things can also increase or decrease with dramatic effects, like air in a balloon. Or, take water, for example; one minute it is liquid, the next it could be ice, or it could disappear entirely as it turns to steam. Life is magical, a mystery to be unfolded. Reality is not firm for children in this age group. It seems to shift at will. It is hard for children to comprehend what is "real" without a clear understanding of what is not. Therefore, while Santa starts out being portrayed as real for young children, over time he can be portrayed to be unreal so that children can get their hands around a tangible example of relativistic thinking. Having children go through the intellectual process of weighing information to determine if Santa is real or not has absolute cognitive benefits for them. It is much easier for them to engage in this process relating to a lovable character like Santa than it is for them to do it with less familiar, abstract concepts.

As children get bigger they acquire skills to understand symbols in their play instead of relying upon simple motor play, like stacking blocks. Legos are enjoyed because they incorporate both mechanical skills and symbolic representations. Symbolic play requires that children use their imaginations to see one thing, like a purple plastic piece, as representing something else, like themselves when they play the game, Candy Land. They learn that one thing can represent another, different, and less visible thing.

The development of transductive thought is important because it assists children to think about something as being real without the object being present. Children may pretend to be monsters, knowing that they are not really monsters but thinking that monsters may actually exist somewhere. They are able to manipulate the symbol of the monster to have several different meanings. As this pertains to Santa, he may start out representing the red-suited jolly elf-man but later may symbolically refer to the spirit of giving. It would be difficult for a child to comprehend the spirit of giving without having something tangible that they could link the concept to, such as Santa. Children try to understand the difference between reality and fantasy, but this can only occur slowly over time. The more concrete examples they have, the greater the opportunity children have to develop transductive thought and symbolic interpretation.

Young children, especially those in this 3–8-year-old category are heavily invested with moral and ethical considerations. People may be either good or bad; they see things in black or white dimensions. If Santa is good, he should not do anything bad. They want to know the rules of a game and get annoyed when people don't follow instructions. This is the time children learn that their behavior has ramifications to how they will be treated (enter the "naughty and nice" dogma). Children willingly follow the instructions from legitimate authorities, like their parents.

When Santa rewards good behavior and fails to bring presents to children with bad behavior, this is a tangible way for children to identify exactly what it means to be good or bad. Otherwise, it is hard for them to figure out the principles underlying how people are supposed to act, especially when they are exposed to conflicting information. This is why the naughty and nice list became part of the Santa story. The notion of "being on your best behavior" may be confusing for children, and they need concrete examples, like Santa Claus, to show them how to act appropriately. However, as I have conducted my research, I find a few of the initial Santa figures were out to punish children. They focused on generosity and kindness. The punitive Krampus and Knecht Rupert figures were developed along the way as ancillary characters, undoubtedly created by adults to keep children in line. It makes me reflect upon how religious leaders, political leaders, and business people have exploited the image of Santa Claus to fulfill their own agendas. These other-oriented agendas were not designed to support the traditional Santa messages but to exploit it for their own purposes. Therefore, it seems like traditional reliance on the naughty-nice dichotomy needs to be eliminated or at least re-cast as we consider transforming Santa into the future.

Around age 7 children no longer need external supports since they will have integrated a mental framework they learned through social interactions. This means that talking with others about Santa Claus is an important thing for children to do, as it benefits them to struggle with the ideas of "is Santa real?" on their own, without adult pronouncements of their own perceptions of reality. Vygotskian theory holds that imagination may serve personal wish-fulfillment or advance creative problem solving, particularly in art and science. During adolescence, there is a convergence and collaboration between imaginative and thinking concepts. Thus, older children will come to view fantasy characters differently than they did when they were younger. Their early exposure to fantasy empowers them with the skills that they will find useful later on. Their understanding of reality varies according to the social and interpersonal contexts in which they live (Smolucha and Smolucha 1986; Vygotsky 1978).

Most children question whether Santa exists. By the time they are seven years old, most have concluded that Santa probably isn't real, whether they have been specifically told or not. Intellectually, children between eight and eleven years of age are in Piaget's concrete operational stage, in which intelligence is gained through logical and concrete sources of information. Kids at this age are proud that they have figured out why reindeer cannot fly or how it is impossible for Santa to come down your chimney on Christmas Eve, especially if you don't have a chimney. They want to flaunt this newly acquired way of viewing the world to show they are able to think more maturely than they were a few years before. The rejection of Santa is in many ways indicative of a mental revolution that is going on internally about the way they think about the world and their role in it. Santa isn't just a guy who delivers gifts at this point in life; in their minds at this point in time, Santa is an untruth. Their desire to know and show their intellectual development requires that they reject lower-level thought. They may feel "silly" that they ever believed in Santa. Children who feel they have been "lied to" about Santa almost always are in this developmental stage. They are not yet able to comprehend that Santa may represent something other than a whiskered man from the North Pole who delivers either gifts or coal. But they will. Some children do this at earlier stages than others. It largely depends upon who they interact with and the norms around Santa that are presented to them.

Russian psychologist Vygotsky stresses that children's social and psychological development is always the result of their collective actions; it is essential they have the opportunity to work through issues like Santa with others (especially their peers). In this way, they are able to reproduce a culture that contains the knowledge of generations. As children grapple with everyday problems such as "does Santa exist?" they are able to develop collective strategies through interactions with others to give them a model for addressing other kinds of problems as they mature into adulthood. In this way, dealing with whether Santa actually exists is a very important social process.

The internalization of strategies to deal with uncertainty is a useful process for children. Vygotsky alleges that every function of the child's development occurs twice, first on the social level and then on the individual level; first between people (interpsychological) and then inside the child (intrapsychological). He implies that all our psychological and social skills (cognitive, communicative, and emotional) are always acquired from our interactions with others. Rogoff (2003) adds that human development is always a process of people's changing participation in socio-cultural activities of their communities, implying that the collective sharing of Santa information has significant long-term benefits. Children must develop and use such skills at the interpersonal level first before internalizing them at the individual level. Children's ability to think abstractly grows tremendously during this time period, and the development of abstract thought is one of their single most important developmental tasks until they hit the next stage, adolescence.

Children become increasingly competent at adult-style thinking as they mature. They use logical conceptual operations, often in the abstract rather than the concrete in a process called hypothetical thinking. Children will put together inconsistencies in the Santa story as they attempt analytical skills. Most children come to the conclusion that Santa isn't real long before their parents actually get around to telling them that fact. Children are perceptive and actively sort through information to decide what is real from what is not, and Santa just becomes a part of that larger conceptual process. The Santa figure provides children with an important social opportunity for them to share collective peer behavior. Parents view and portray Santa in one way; children view him quite differently. There are few social phenomena that children experience in a way that allows them to exchange information and share perspectives. Children's questions to each other such as "How did he get into your house if you don't have a chimney?", "Do you think reindeer really fly?", and "If you didn't write him a letter, how did he know you wanted that (toy)?" allow them a collective experience to interpret what is real and what is not. While adults may wish to meddle in this type of conversation by putting in their own two-cents about the real nature of Santa, frankly, this may do children a disservice. It is far more valuable for children to work together to figure out this social puzzle. They will talk with peers, process the Santa situation, and collectively come up with reasonable answers.

By the time they are age ten or twelve, most children have come to the conclusion that Santa isn't real, at least not in the way they originally thought. Even the child who most believes in Santa soon learns that they will be made fun of and excluded if they don't change their view. Rejection of Santa is, simultaneously, an acceptance of a peer-based and more worldly view of themselves. Peer camaraderie is important as children seek to live their lives outside the confines of the family. Making a successful transition from the world of the home into the world of peers is vital as children develop a self-identity of themselves as competent individuals.

This peer interaction is a very important part of what William Corsaro (2018) calls interpretive reproduction of culture, meaning that children bring their own ideas to the table and share them with other children, who come up with new interpretations about the things that have previously been taught to them. For parents to definitively state that Santa is real, or conversely that there is no such thing as Santa, denies children with the opportunity to sort out the answers to this question for themselves.

By the time children become adolescents, the Santa issue will have been momentarily resolved. Around age 12 children are more comfortable with abstract thought. It is assumed that this is a transition time from being a child to becoming more adult, when they are more responsible to make sophisticated choices or to understand a complex phenomenon, such as comprehending the true nature of God. This is developmentally why many religions wait to have children declare their commitment to the faith. Christian confirmations, Jewish bar or bat mitzvahs, and partake in rites of passage that occur around this age.

As they grow into teenagers, it is no surprise that Santa would cease to be important. They are far too concerned with other developmental issues, such as developing their own unique sense of identity and dealing with role confusion of who they should be. Children in their teens are torn between deciding who they should be, since their family has one agenda, their peers another, and they themselves have their own ideas of who they should become. Peer influence becomes increasingly important during this stage of life and being ridiculed is to be avoided. By this time, children have come to understand that Santa could not possibly slide down chimneys, travel by reindeer pulled sleigh. They understand that their parents made him available to them. Rejecting or even making fun of Santa becomes important for them to redefine themselves as more mature and sophisticated than they were.

During the teen years and children and able to think abstractly, parents may engage them to become involved in the Santa charade. They may be asked to help put presents under the tree, make deer-hoof prints in the snow, or to create surprises. They can better appreciate what Santa is about, why he is important, and why younger children need him. They are able to comprehend that parents aren't lying to children when they teach their children about Santa, but they are teaching children higher-level values and the basis for symbolic thought.

What I Concluded

Examining how children at different developmental times in life understand and relate to Santa Claus helps me to appreciate why there is so much variability in how Santa Claus is perceived. A developmental approach is quite utilitarian when understanding why there are times when children accept or reject Santa Claus. Families also go through developmental evolution when it comes to Santa. While it was tempting to put it here, there was so much to it that I will elaborate upon that in the next chapter.

Mary Ellen Chase quote

Christmas, children,
is not a date.
It is a state of mind.

Mary Ellen Chase

Windswept. 1941. Islandport Press

Chapter 15

Santa, Symbols and Families

The Dilemma

Who is Santa Claus really for anyway – children or adults? It could be that Santa is really designed more to entertain the parents than the children. Some families have huge parties with lots of decorations, festive foods, music, laughter, and presents galore, while others exchange few and modest gifts with Santa's role being virtually nonexistent. Some incorporate elaborate rituals, with certain cookies, letters, and signs that Santa had come, while others play things by ear with no traditions at all. A lot of the families have joyful festive non-religious holidays where there's a lot of music, laughter, decorations, and generosity of spirit and resources. Others are just glum and it's as though it's a struggle for everyone to just get through enduring the day. While some parents spend thousands of dollars on making the holiday special, while others dread shopping and all the time, cost, and effort and can be found at the store at 10 pm on Christmas Eve doing their first shopping for the holiday.

I came from the type of home where parents worked with us children to write letters to Santa, decorate the house, sing songs, bake cookies, and prepare for family get-togethers to celebrate Santa's arrival and the moment when gifts are exchanged. Santa's visit was a family event. I loved running back and forth to see what relatives and neighbors got. I grew up expecting that I should, and would, do exactly the same thing to make Santa special. It never occurred to me that I didn't have to – I never really considered that there was a wide array of choices I could make around if and how I wanted Santa Claus to be a part of our family life. So what's up with the variability around Santa Claus, and what are the fun-loving families doing that make their holidays so special? So I had to ask myself, exactly what are the parents and the rest of the family getting out of it? A lot, I found out.

What I Discovered

Most adults report that holidays are more fun when there are little children around because youngsters share their own exciting interpretations of Santa and the delivery of the gifts. Through children's ability to play and be imaginative, everyone benefits. The arrival of Santa Claus is the highlight of many people's holiday, whether they celebrate Christmas or not. Families, mothers, in particular, seem to play a huge role in the construction of what Santa Claus means to children. In doing my research, I discovered how many parents live to make Santa and start shopping for their family's gifts in March as they keep their eyes peeled for just the right thing for certain people as they go through the months leading up to his arrival. Why it is so important for parents and grandparents to build the perfect Santa experience needed unpacking.

Believing in Santa Means Different Things at Different Points of Life

Santa doesn't mean the same things to people at each stage of life. The giggling small child, the doubting adolescent, the ponderous young adult, the excited new parents, middle-aged parents who strive to keep hope alive, and the grandparents who are reliving their lives through the eyes of little ones – all of them can have a beneficial relationship from believing in Santa that helps them grow. "As children, in the brief years of belief, we take Santa for granted, in the same way, we rely on our parents' love. It is only afterward that he is truly cherished. When you're a child he brings you presents. When you're older, he brings much more. Like other legendary, mythological creatures, or the saints of old, he is simply who we need him to be, evolving with us and filling our need for magic, amazement, and surprise. The magic dust comes down the chimney, and jolly as ever and covered with soot, he takes shape before our very eyes." (Mary Haley in Clark, p. 37).

Psychologist Erik Erikson, who was a student of Anna Freud, asserted that human personality develops in accordance with how they meet specific life challenges at particular and predictable points in time. Erikson was fascinated by how people come to believe and act the way they do. He felt that people cannot go through life's challenges alone;

rather, they need social relationships and interactions in order to know what to think and how to act. When children talk with family and friends they come to understand Santa, the world, and themselves. It is important to remember that childhood is not just chronological age, but it is also a time during which children's lives are being constructed, both literally and figuratively. What children take in – whether food, media, love, or attention – may influence them for the rest of their lives. Thus, it is a serious business being a child, since physical, psychological, social, cognitive, and developmental factors all hang in the balance.

The socialization of children is one of the main functions of the family. This is the process of teaching norms, values, customs, traditions, and what people expect from one another. Making sure that children's physical, cognitive, social, and emotional needs are met is part of the role requisites for good parenting. Families regularly incorporate rituals to instill values and normative behavior in children. These rituals can be as simple as brushing teeth in the morning or taking a bath and reading a story before bedtime. They include more elaborate and complex rituals surrounding major events, such as birthdays and holidays. The annual arrival of Santa Claus is accompanied in many families by a predictable set of behaviors and occurrences, activities designed to instill values, and promote family bonding.

Erikson alleged that people go through eight critically important developmental stages of life as they journey from birth toward death. Children experience a challenge during each stage that must be overcome. At each stage, the individual is confronted with a life lesson to be learned. If learned well, people can move forward into healthy development; otherwise, people will play out unresolved issues through the whole of their adult lives. A basic premise of his work is that people cannot understand certain concepts or emotions until they are ready, and how we deal with the present influences our future. By believing in Santa Claus, children learn values, skills, and information that would be difficult for them to achieve in other ways.

Developing trust is the most fundamental challenge children experience. Lucky children in the first year of life learn that there are people who love them, who will consistently care for them, and that the world is a safe and good place. This gives them a firm foundation of trust by the time they become toddlers. As Erikson's stages pertain to Santa, infants are so absorbed with a plethora of physical and motor tasks that Santa is a non-issue. What is an issue, though, is to develop a secure attachment to their parents. As they learn to develop a trusting relationship with their parents, they are hopefully able to generalize that feeling to others as well. When parents act excited about Santa, they create a bond with their child; they laugh and interact in special ways that are designed to entertain the child. Children learn that Santa is fun because their parents are having fun creating him. Through this interaction with parents, children are able to generalize the love their parents show them around the Santa issue to others. As a trust issue, parents worry about whether they will be seen as trustworthy figures if they tell their children Santa is real and then later they learn he is not. They are concerned that children may doubt what they tell them in the future if they "lie" to them about Santa. In this way, the concern isn't on Santa's reality status but on how children may perceive the parent's trustworthiness over time.

As children become toddlers their next key developmental task is to learn autonomy. Parents are encouraged to help their children develop the use of initiative. They are also to help give children the confidence to cope with future situations that require choice, control, and independence. Sitting on Santa's lap with mom and dad close by is more than a photo opportunity; it helps little ones to see that it might be safe to trust others. Engaging children to believe in Santa helps them to use their imaginations as they contemplate the existence that there are good people from other places that may do something nice for you. This builds upon their previous developmental stage and allows children to carry forth their imaginations into concrete reality, such as making a gift or card as a gift for someone they care about. This is the kind of action that Piaget called assimilation, referring specifically to the child's ability to assimilate some new idea or action from a previously familiar one.

Toddlers and those just past the toddler stage can comprehend tangible things such as sleigh, reindeer, and elves. Santa Claus may be perceived as a real person, psychologist Douglas Kramer of the University of Wisconsin, explains. Children of this age cannot yet grasp abstract concepts, such as the presence of a divine being that encourages goodness in people. While children may talk about divine beings such as God, they actually lack the cognitive ability to really understand what God may be. When they engage in religious talk as they fold their hands and bow their heads, they typically do so in order to evoke a positive reaction from their parents. They may be able to patter back certain prayers, but they lack a real understanding of what those words actually mean until they become older. Santa, in many ways, provides children with a tangible buffer that gives them their first opportunity to explore what is concrete and what is abstract. Children can read stories and sing songs about him. They can draw pictures of Santa. They can write Santa letters because he is real, and sometimes he answers them. They can talk with Santa (or people dressed up to look like him). They can leave him cookies that are usually eaten. Santa may visit their houses, even though they may never actually see him. One can argue that they could do the same kind of things with God, but the intangibility and the lack of an identifiable physical presence make it a lot harder to relate to a deity. Trying to define God is a challenge even for most adults. Santa can be pretty straightforward and simple, all things considered. The image of Santa works well for children as they begin the process of this kind of complex thought.

As children leave the toddler stage and proceed into the world of young childhood, they are ready to tackle their next life challenge. They have to learn how to achieve a balance between their eagerness for adventure, the learning of the sciences, and the demand for more responsibility. This is shown through their learning to control impulses and fantasies. It is important that children have active imaginations during this stage of life since it is the basis for curiosity in other realms as they mature. They must learn to handle emotions such as fear, anger, and confusion. Imaginative play, learning about mythical characters, engaging in role-plays, and make-believe activities are helpful to them in achieving this task. Santa's images and details are so rich and diverse that they inspire imagination.

Erikson's developmental challenge of dealing with shame and doubt arrive in the Santa debate when children believe in Santa and their peers make fun of them for it. Parents don't want their children to be the butt of ridicule, as it can feel devastating to a young child. In order to avoid their children being ashamed of believing something that is not true, parents may either decide to say Santa isn't real from the start, or they may have ready an explanation of why the other children aren't correct in their assertion. Sometimes children who love Santa don't want to let go of the positive associations they feel with him, so they act as though they don't believe but internally feel guilty about it. The guilt feelings may be about rejecting Santa (because they don't have 100% proof he doesn't exist) or guilt for believing when his or her friends do not. These pose internal issues for the child to resolve. According to Erikson's model, these challenges aren't necessarily a bad thing. Sooner or later kids are going to have to confront issues of trust, shame, and guilt. Learning how to manage them successfully in a safe context around a tangible character such as Santa can lay a foundation for positive growth around such feelings later on. Other psychologists agree that the discovery that Santa isn't real doesn't have to be seen as a life-crisis, but more of a learning opportunity of life that can serve them well later on.

As children grow older, they learn more about history, science, and cause-and-effect relationships. They naturally will come to question the reality of Santa during this time. They will wonder why he has been so beloved for generations if he doesn't exist. Pondering the nature of reality is a logical process as we mature. In order to prove their knowledge of science, some will announce to younger children that there is no such thing as Santa. This emboldens their sense of maturity but may crush the spirit of little ones.

Wise adolescents will learn to let young children discover Santa in their own way and time, while arrogant ones may sometimes be cruel in the pronouncements.

During young adulthood, Santa is less of an issue because people are absorbed with finding their own self-identity and grapple with the universal question of "Who am I?" Issues of friendship become increasingly important as they struggle with how to incorporate significant others into their lives. As this pertains to Santa, most young adults don't actually care about him outside of an advertising or cultural iconic way. If their friends want to pretend that Santa exists, they are likely to hop on that bandwagon; if their friends make light of him or ridicule his existence, young adults are likely to do so as well. If they associate with people who don't believe in Santa, they may resent parents' indoctrination of him into childhood; conversely, if they are with people who appreciate Santa, they may feel exhilarated at the thought of incorporating him into their own holidays.

One of the most important developmental challenges for young adults is the issue of the intimacy versus isolation challenges of starting important, long-lasting, loving relationships. It is entirely possible that people will link up with partners who do not have the same understanding of Santa as they do. When people explore their different meanings of Santa, they may find value in each other's perspectives. In the early stages of relationship building, it is common for partners to bend their positions on Santa; people who have not been accustomed to a particularly beloved view of Santa may be willing to become more enthusiastic about him if their partner adores a Santa Christmas. People who believe in Santa may try to convert the other partner, or tone down their celebrations out of respect. Those who grew up with tense experiences around the Santa figure may seek to reduce their more enthusiastic partner's participation in Santa traditions. Couples usually work out an accommodation of how they can deal with holidays in a mutually comfortable way.

But when people become parents, Santa re-emerges as an issue. Parents contemplate what parts of their own childhood they should pass on to their own children, and what parts should be re-invented or eliminated. If two people who had positive Santa experiences have children, they may naturally incorporate traditions from their past into the new family unit. If new parents did not grow up with a Santa legacy, it is likely that it won't be important for them to integrate into their family. If one parent is excited about having Santa and the other parent doesn't care one way or the other, usually the enthused parent takes the lead in building a Santa presence into their present. The Santa issue becomes tenser for people who have a mixed view of him. People who have had a real fondness for Santa may be pressed to downplay or eliminate him when with partners who don't believe in Santa. To do so means that they would surgically cut their past from their future; if they liked what they gained from their past, it may be difficult for them to justify eliminating Santa for their children. People who grew up in anti-Santa households will almost always find it challenging to incorporate a holiday season that includes an active role by Mr. Claus. Couples may find themselves unexpectedly squabbling over the holiday season as a result. They aren't really fighting about Santa, but they are fighting over the symbolic representations of what Santa means. Santa becomes an easy scapegoat in these cases, as people misalign the target to be the man in the red suit instead of the underlying, more sensitive issues. Frequently a seasonal attack on Santa is either due to him being a symbol for religious, economic, or political issues. If adults remember a Christmas filled with conflict or tragedy, they may come not to like Santa – not because of what he is, but because of the way they feel when they recollect that time. Given that Santa is not real, when couples are having a real fight about him it is important that they look at the actual causes of the conflict.

Middle-aged parents developmentally have a different view of Santa. If they are working several jobs and money is scarce, they may try to downplay Santa and gifting to children who are still small. The pressure on parents may just be too much for them to create magical, extensive holiday festivities. If there are no longer little ones at home to entertain by tantalizing them with the expectation of Santa's arrival, the holidays may become boring. Parents may find that they have to work harder to make the holiday meaningful. They may find alternative celebrations to replace the excitement that Santa once held. Some families go away on exotic vacations over the holidays; some may decide to forgo the purchase of many small gifts in favor of one large and expensive one, while others may incorporate new traditions or activities. There may be less emphasis on putting gifts out on Christmas Eve when the children are in bed, fewer presents (or more gift cards) in the stockings of adult children, and less excitement on getting up early on Christmas morning to see if Santa arrived.

When people become grandparents, their orientations toward Santa may shift yet again. Babies bring new enthusiasm to adults, who again get to relive not just their childhoods but their children's childhoods as they prepare to celebrate Christmas. Grandparents carry forth the potential of the legacy for carrying on Christmas traditions. They may excitedly encourage grandchildren to help them make cookies or crafts they made with their own parents many decades before. They will tell tales of long ago to children whose eyes glisten with amazement. Magic again becomes real as the potential for what could be possible gets reborn in their grandchildren as they prepare for Santa's arrival. Grandparents may have the discretionary time and income to help make Christmas magical if they are so inclined to do so. But this relationship is not one-sided; children enable older people to reassess the scope of their life. They help adults to remember the past and heal old scars as they help new little ones to learn how to wait for Santa. This is why having young children around during the holidays may feel so much more rewarding to adults.

This use of Erikson's theory is just a hypothetical example that helps explain why so many parents are invested in having their children, and grandchildren, believe in Santa Claus. I have modified this one and incorporated key principles of others, such as the importance and influence of culture, social interactions, maturity, religion, economics, and feelings of political correctness to show why Santa's meanings change. It helps explain why parents get nostalgic when their children quit believing, how belief resurfaces in adulthood, and its renewed importance during the grandparent's years. Certainly, there are other theories and hypotheses that help us to understand the longitudinal transformation of Santa's meaning.

Parenting Styles and Children's Joy of Santa

There is concern that parents are part of children's play and Santa problems. Some long to be **Super-Parents** and do everything so "right" for their children that they tend to control everything and leave nothing to chance. They can take different forms. Super-parents can be way too excessive with their gifting and need to make their holiday "the best". Putting thousands of lights onto the house (homage to Chevy Chase/Clark Griswall in Lampoon's movie, Christmas Vacation), giving too many gifts that are too expensive in nature, spending heavily on food, decorations, going to exotic or expensive destinations, are symbols of their need to excel. They set a standard that no normal human can live up to. It sets up unreal expectations for how their children are supposed to create festivities.

Embarrassingly, I fell into that category at some points. I was married to a man who wasn't into Christmas or the Santa thing, so I became determined to show him, as well as my children, how wonderful Santa Claus could be. While I didn't have much money to spend on holiday, I started preparing in July so I'd be ready. I found special snow-glitter that I threw into the bottom of the fireplace so it looked like Santa left it when he came down the chimney. The feed-store sold cow-hoofs for dogs to chew, and I bought a bunch and put them into the snow, two-by-two, for eight tiny reindeer and make sleigh-tracks with my boots. I wrapped each child's gifts in their own wrapping paper design. All the presents were hidden well before the holiday with no chance they could find them. I would be up all night putting toys together and laying out the gifts in the perfect locations so when they came downstairs the next morning they would have an "ah-hah" moment. Their stockings were filled with the cutest things ever. I chomped the carrots that the children left for the deer, left a few cookie crumbs from Santa's plate of goodies, had friends write letters from Santa to the children, and even had Grandpa dress up as Santa to deliver the gifts as he shook bells I sewed on one of my mom's old belts. Everything had to be just so.

It was excessive, now that I look back on it. In retrospect, I was creating for my children the kind of Santa visit I always wanted but never got. Their pediatrician, Theodore Miller, told me that by having children we are able to re-live experiences and re-do parts of our lives in the way we wished them to be. Right on, doc. He was correct. I could quit the Super-Parent thing and know that my children were going to be fine.

There is the **Tiger-Mom** (Chua 2011) approach to parenting, with its focus on setting up one's child for success. Their emphasis on the academic approach to life, very high expectations for success, and an authoritarian parenting style may interfere with just letting a kid be a kid. Time for play, fantasy, and being silly is not regarded as a high priority – so Santa may be regarded as a frivolous non-essential figure to be in a child's life. This could mean not empowering children to have fun with their own imaginations and relationships as they play and explore the magic of Santa. These kinds of parents mean well, but they are the types that always told their children that Santa wasn't real, and they instructed them with scientific logic about why he couldn't possibly exist.

Helicopter parents (Cline and Fay 1990) are those who tend to hover and smother over everything a child does.

Their intent is to keep their children safe, but in assessing potential risks to their children they limit a child's ability to be autonomous in what they think or do. These kinds of parents try to keep in tune with the trends of what other children are doing around Santa so that they make sure their child is in the know and not left out. If they think that other children are going to "spill the beans" about Santa, these types of parents may try to be a step-ahead and intervene. They may interrupt what an adult or another child if they think they're going to say something that could scar their child's psyche. When disclosure becomes inevitable, they may say something like, "Honey, there's something I need to tell you about Santa....", and they try as kindly as they can to knife Santa in the heart. Helicopter Santa parents mean well, but they have real boundary issues.

Helicopter parents are a stone's throw away from **Lawnmower, Snowplow, or Bulldozer parents** (Haller 2018; Romero 2019). Whereas helicopter parents are hovering and smothering a child, lawnmower parents are trying to cut a path for their children to walk that will be obstacle-free so they don't get stuck in the weeds. Snowplow parents are trying to clear the way of momentary impediments, like deep snow - things that would eventually melt away and take care of themselves if the parent didn't do anything. The bulldozer parent is at a whole other level, moving away rocks, boulders, digging up roots and stumps, and making sure there are no obstacles.

These three parent types are just different levels or dimensions of the same basic phenomenon. As this pertains to Santa Claus, the lawnmower parent is trying to lay an easy, clear path for their children to walk so they don't have to confront challenges that snag them up. For instance, they don't want their children to be left out of getting the prized present of the season.

OK, I'll admit it - for a while I was also a lawnmower parent. When I was little, Chatty Cathy was THE present to get. I didn't get one at Christmas because my mom told me they were all sold out. Thus when my daughter was young, Chatty Cathy II, retroversion, came on the market. My daughter succumbed to peer pressure and pleaded for one. Moms like me went flocking to the store to get them. Like my mom's experiences, the stores were all sold out of them. In desperation, I called a no-name store and by golly, they said they had some. I skedaddled straight to the store and went to the toy counter. The clerk said they were all out of them. I was devastated. But I looked behind the counter and saw one. "I called and they said you had one," I told the clerk. "Is your name Nancy?" he asked. "Yep," I lied. I pulled out cash so there was no way they could track my name on a check or credit card and I beat it out the door to the car as fast as I could. I wasn't going to let my little girl experience the same Chatty Cathy heartache that still felt thirty years later. OMG. What was I doing???

Maybe I had escalated to being a snowplow parent. I am sure she would have survived if she had never gotten Chatty Cathy. I didn't give her the opportunity to figure Santa out for herself, and I felt it would break her heart if she didn't get the doll, and if she stopped believing in him. Secretly, she probably had a pretty good idea he wasn't "real" by then anyway, but as my children told me years later, they all knew but were too polite to spoil my good times by telling me that. They saw that there were more benefits for them if I thought they continued to believe. I am confident that my daughter would not have been scarred for life if I hadn't basically stolen the coveted doll that another little girl somewhere was expecting Santa to deliver. My apologies to her and her mama, whoever she was.

Bulldozer parents are an entirely different breed. They are the "Don't F**k with my kid" type of parent who is going to go through hell and high water to make sure their child gets what they want. They wouldn't have felt bad about Chatty Cathy – they would have felt they were entitled to get her. They are the type who may announce to a crowd of children that "Come on you guys, you know there's no such thing as Santa, right?" If other parents weren't ready for their child to know that, tough luck. They would work hard to set the standard for their child to get the biggest and best present. These are the types of parents that other parents hate.

Let us not forget **Guilt-Tripper parents**. Parents I know have dampened children's holiday joy by making them feel bad that they got presents and other children didn't. They are the ones to make children who still feel bad when they remind them that it's scientifically impossible for a real person to do all the things attributed to Santa Claus. These are the parents who make a child feel bad if they didn't jump for joy about receiving a particular gift. I know parents who want their parents to give away their gifts so others can get them – which is fine to teach altruism to children, all children want to receive at least a little gift that conveys to them that they are special.

Symbolism of Santa

For many families, Santa is a cultural expression of our life's journey; he is a symbolic representation of the marking of time and events. We can remember our past by mentally zeroing in on what happened at a particular Christmas. Unlike rudimentary day-to-day events, Christmas carries a significant emotional weight that makes it is easier to recall the past by referencing that single day.

Santa's message inspires us to see the goodness in others and acknowledge that they matter to us. Playing Santa encourages children to recreate these values. Gift-giving and gift-getting allow them to consider - What do people we care about want or need? How could we get it for them? What would it take from us to make the gift possible? This requires thinking about others. It demands creativity on our part to make the gift, to earn what it may cost to get the gift, and our emotional investment in delivering it. In making others happy, we learn we too can become happy. In giving of ourselves, we learn that we get much back in return.

The creation of Santa and the accompanying story of reindeer, elves, and the like provide children with a tangible way of dealing with bigger issues. The story about Santa Claus isn't really about Santa at all; it is a story that uses fantasy to reinforce longstanding social values about love, kindness, and generosity. In general, stories and the creation of fantasy characters have a purpose that far exceeds the surface issues, according to scholars in this area. American writer Flannery O'Connor indicates that a story is a way to say something that can't be said any other way. A caveat in writing is "show don't tell"; a story like Santa is told to children because simply making statements about what Santa stands for are often quite inadequate, especially to the mind of a child. Telling children that it is important to be good and that it's nice to give other people gifts may seem obvious to adults but not to children. The Santa story makes real a kind old man who takes the time and effort to find out what each child truly desires, and then he goes about working hard to find ways of making their dreams come true. Stories like those told of Santa supply children with the opportunity for imagination. Philosopher Alasdair MacIntyre alleges that through hearing such stories children learn true moral behavior as they observe the character's challenges and behaviors. Philosopher Martin Buber states that it is insufficient to tell children how to behave; they must intuitively experience the values.

Commonly shared stories about Santa Claus help children to identify with him. From the yearly yearning of his arrival, children learn how to become altruistic, hard-working, patient, hopeful, and joyful. Stories such as the Santa tales can also help children to emotionally relate to a positive role model as they integrate the benefits of being good and doing for others. Parents cannot force a child to be truly good or nice because it is the right thing to do; if they use too much force, such attempts may backfire entirely. Children must integrate these positive behaviors and values into their own psyche and adopt them as their own if they are to grow into adulthood with goodness, kindness, and joy etched into their hearts.

Santa is ostensibly a real person as he is presented to children. He is not a God, nor was he ever intended to be a replacement for baby Jesus. Santa, as an adult, has all the finest attributes of adults, but he is also mortal; he is overweight, gets tired, and he needs help from others even though he works very hard to get the job done. He is a leader. He takes care of others, be they reindeer, elves, or little children around the world. The essence of a good fantasy story is to create a character that has both virtues and flaws, who struggles to overcome obstacles or make difficult choices between right and wrong. Santa does this as he attempts to deliver toys to all the children in the world in a single night, as he wonders whether he should reward all children or only those who are nice, not naughty.

Santa helps children to decide what kind of people they want to be. Will they be good or bad? Will they help others or will they be greedy and self-serving? As children evaluate how they want to be treated by Santa, it helps them to decide how they should treat other people. Santa is the Gold Rule in action, but the Santa story makes the tale more palpable to little folks. Santa helps children to subtly understand that a person's decisions in life will define what kind of person he becomes. This, according to Santa scholars, is a very important message to give to children – that we can control our own destinies by what we believe and how we act.

The story of Santa is full of symbols. For instance, Santa's sleigh is small and his pack can only hold so many things inside it; Santa cannot possibly bring any particular child many gifts and he certainly cannot bring them a pony or big or expensive gifts. This is a message that seems to have gotten corrupted. Where does Santa put his gifts? In stockings! Stockings can't hold very many things so there is a built-in limit to what he should be expected to bring. Tradition holds that Santa brings candy, a toy to play with, and a little something of value to us, whether money, a trinket, or something we long for. They are symbolic of wishes for a sweet life, for delight to be found around us, and to be given something that makes our future a little bit easier. The presentation of Santa hand-carrying gifts to everyone is important to remember, as it can liberate parents from the pressure of his pack being seen as a never-ending supply of elaborate gifts that they themselves could never afford to purchase.

Most of Santa's gifts are home-made; they are made by elves in the North Pole. It can take them all year to make the gifts they deliver. The types of gifts typically given by Santa represent thought of what each person needs and wants. The uniqueness of the person is in the forethought of the person making the gift. Santa doesn't just go to the store and grab things off the shelf and shove it into the stockings of children with little consideration. The whole gifting process is infused with thought-filled concern.

Santa reinforces the values of community, perspective, and engagement. He teaches us that we have to be motivated and engaged to make things happen. If children don't write a note to Santa, he may not necessarily know what they want. He reinforces the importance of being able to consider what you want, prioritize them, and then have the skills to appropriately ask for them. Just because you ask for something, it doesn't mean that you will get it. If what they are asking for is beyond the boundaries of what Santa could do, children can learn that they may need to creatively engage others to help them. This may mean parents, brothers, and sisters, or people from within the community. It may mean working for what you want. It could also mean that we have to adjust our ideas. Santa teaches that you have to work to make things happen; gifts don't just magically appear.

Santa doesn't act alone; he has elves, reindeer, and a host of others to help him achieve his goal. The gift-giving season becomes a pleasure for the entire community, who find delight as he sails off into the sky with his package-adorned sleigh. Sometimes Santa is accompanied by helpers who could appear as grandparents, firefighters, soldiers, community leaders, or mischief-makers. Santa's arrival for gift-giving is a community-wide event, unlike when children receive a present at home for their birthday. His entourage helps teach children that we need others to achieve success and make our dreams come true.

We anticipate Santa's arrival with excitement and preparation. He reminds us that all good things take time and effort. His arrival is designed for the pleasure of a single moment when something special is delivered. And what is that one thing? Joy. Absolute unmitigated delight, ear-to-ear smiles, with laughter and gratitude that all come from the sense of being loved. The swelling of bliss and gratitude that bursts alive when we feel happy and loved must be cultivated and grown inside; it cannot be purchased or inserted. Years from now the candy will be eaten, the toys will be discarded, the socks will be outgrown, but the memories – they will stay alive in us forever.

Santa means different things to different people. He has meant different things across time and place. He also means different things at different points throughout our individual lives. This book will comfort parents who still believe in Santa and want children to appreciate his role in holiday celebrations. It will serve as a guide to adults and professionals who aren't sure how to steer the Santa Claus conversation through treacherous snowfalls. It will help people who do not believe in Santa to place him into a context that appreciates his contributions across time. And it will be a guide for community leaders, teachers, and others who are trying to straddle the line between giving respect and acceptance to diverse views while living in a communal world.

Santa Claus is a symbol that enables children to learn values, behaviors, and develop abstract thought. He is a timeless psychological and sociological template of how society is to function. We can see how changes in Santa and society have intermeshed over time. Exploring him and his changes reflect the transformation in social values and how societies value themselves. How we choose to represent him today will impact the future directions and values that we as people will uphold.

Santa can be conceived as a symbol of goodness, caring, and generosity that creates a tangible framework that children can use to identify these characteristics in others. Moreover, Santa Claus can be a vehicle that can help children to explore and understand the nature of human relationships, perhaps even explore the nature of the concept of God itself. Child development scholars indicate that children need the ability to dream and imagine alternative realities in order to be successful in life. This book provides a child-centered view of Santa that argues it is appropriate to allow him to be a continued presence in the lives of children so they can continue to share in the long legacy of delight and joy that Santa can bring.

"The childhood cult of Santa Claus is a reservoir for the human capacity to suspend rational disbelief and to experience wonder at the unknowable, the transcendent. As such, Santa is not solely a childhood cult at all, but a ritual by which both adults and children are touched through expressive symbolism." (Clark 1995:44)

The advent season, or four weeks before December 25, is a time of anticipation for the arrival of Santa Claus (or

Christmas, if that is your tradition). The idea that once a year the child in all of us will receive gifts is a symbol that we are acknowledged just for being. We longingly await the moment when we peek around the corner to see if our hopes and dreams have come true – that a Santa leaves a tangible sign that we matter, or if someone representing the Santa Spirit cared about us enough to leave us a little something. The character of Santa gives children the opportunity to wonder, and to find magic.

As children, we learn that we can play Santa too, and we find pleasure by using our talents to make someone a gift or saving our hard-earned money to get others something that may make them happy. Growing from being toddlers with wide eyes to being grandparents with wide hearts, the importance and meaning of Santa Claus keep evolving inside of us. It is this advent that develops inside of us over time that helps to provide us with the sweet meaning of Christmas. So it isn't Santa that matters – it is the symbolic representation of what could be possible that does.

Santa Claus has been constructed to deliver delight to families for generations. Conscientious parents today wonder if they should allow him into their homes and if they do how they should present him to their children. The truth is that many adults like Santa as much as children and they really don't want to get rid of him either.

Yet new parents are trying to be responsible adults and worry about whether they are doing the right thing to let their kids believe in Santa. There are several key thorny issues for parents around the issue of Santa. These include the multidimensionality of respect, culture, and the complexity of money. Respecting each other's faith, needs and histories are essential to creating happy holidays. Families have traditions, rituals, and legacies they wish to carry on. If we intermarry or have a family member whose background does not embrace Santa Claus, there will be natural issues to be discussed and overcome. We grow up in different religious, ethnic, national, and social class backgrounds. We are not the same; we have unique responses to events even when they may appear similar on the surface. The more cultural differences we have, the more challenging it may be for parents.

Money is one of the prickliest considerations that parents face when thinking about how to incorporate Santa Claus. If people have discretionary income they have more choices than people who have a hard time affording food, heat, and rent. When children see that some children get a large number of expensive gifts "from Santa", they may feel cheated or unloved when they don't. It may be easier for parents to deny the existence of Santa instead of explaining why some kids get a lot and other children don't get anything. But as the students interviewed for this project reported, money didn't create a happy holiday. It was the emotional bonds, spending time, laughing, and loving each other that mattered. It is entirely possible to create a positive Santa Claus experience spending little or no money at all.

Why do people look forward to seeing Santa? Often it has nothing to do with religion or the celebration of the birth of baby Jesus. It may not necessarily be Santa they are looking forward to seeing. Rather, the thrill is to get together with the people who love them love us, to spend time reconnecting, and to build the basis of a future together. Families travel from far and wide to be at home for the holidays. The arrival of Santa and the subsequent opening of gifts is typically the highlight for most families as they celebrate the holiday. A festive meal could be planned before Santa is due to come, and people from far and wide may go out of their way to be together for the moment when he comes or when it's time to exchange gifts. Arriving after the time when "Santa came" is an emotional let-down for most of us. Sharing the moment when collectively the family announces that "It's time!" is exciting and heart-warming. Santa may bring gifts, but he brings us an opportunity to let others know that they are dear to us; he allows us the chance to laugh and create new bonds. Old rifts can heal during this time as people go out of their way to use this moment to focus on the importance of our relationships. Santa is a symbol, an excuse to let people show we love each other that is embodied through the sharing of gifts. It is not the gift that really matters – it is the manner of the giving.

While the arrival of Santa is the main holiday event, he motivates dreams and generosity for weeks before. People of all ages make gifts, from potholders to knitted sweaters to music playlists that take hours to make. Folks take extra jobs to earn more money so they can buy things that will make their loved ones happy. Hours are spent shopping for exactly the right gifts. Surrounding all of these events is a conversation between and amongst family members about how to make others happy "when Santa comes". Santa becomes two-fold – he brings the opportunity to receive gifts, but he also creates the opportunity to gift others. In this way, Santa is external as he brings presents, but he is also internal as people of all ages get to "be" Santa.

Santa cannot exist without the love of families. He embodies good values of love, caring, sharing, and putting the needs of other people first. People remember the holidays when they sat around at home, eating too much of festive foods that only get cooked once a year, and catching up on each other's news as they play with the kids. Most families have their own sense of humor and ways they affectionately tease each other. Children often love this time of year because they feel this is a time of plenty – plenty of food, plenty of people, plenty of gifts, but most importantly plenty of love, with aunts and uncles and cousins and grandparents milling around together, laughing, sharing, and caring. The excitement increases and intensified as everyone awaits Santa's arrival; their joyous reactions help make the thrill of Santa contagious. "Children's excitement at Christmas is made possible by the unique juvenile capacity to see beyond the world as it is and to suspend disbelief so as to allow for magic and fantasy.... The capacity for fantasy and wonder is expected to be short-lived, restricted to the early years of life, when mystical events are still thought possible... When families encourage this stage for their children through the rituals of Christmas, they symbolically validate for themselves the importance of wonder and transcendent reality" (Clark 41).

The arrival of Santa is a secular holiday and is essentially a celebration and commemoration of family life. Love for family, the importance of giving to children, self-sacrifice, sweets to eat, and a sense of plenty even when things the rest of the year are sparse, are central themes of the holiday. Common rituals symbolize the love of family and nurturing of children, and link the members with a sense of their history. Santa helps us to share positive family values of love, generosity, sharing, and laughter. Family life holiday rituals are designed to create opportunities for older members to imprint upon younger ones the motivations, strategies, and skills for carrying on things that have been of importance according to family and cultural traditions. This is why people who are busy all year long suddenly take time during the holiday seasons to visit with one another, cook familiar foods, exchange gifts, but most importantly spend time together. It is important to have rituals that enable children to simply have fun. The shared interactions, the sense of familial community, and the delight that people take in one another and doing small things with each other, for each other, are those that matter most to children. These are the things that shape children's desire to carry on traditions, just as their parents thrilled to pass them on to their children.

A Santa focused holiday is designed to put children first. The sayings that "Christmas is for children," or "Christmas isn't fun without children" illustrate the central place that children play in this holiday. In a Santa based holiday, adult social positions are of lesser importance relative to those of children. Grandparents, parents, aunties, and older siblings may be involved behind the scenes as they do their work to create a good holiday for the kids, but it is assumed that their actions should be quiet and invisible to children. In this regard, the family conspires together to give children a day of joy. Some create reindeer hoof prints or sleigh tracks in the snow, other parents nibble off the ends of carrots left for reindeer, or jingle bells in the middle of the night. Most secretly enjoy eating that 2 am special Santa cookie left on the table, and pride themselves by making sure those bulging stockings are beautifully displayed before they tuck themselves into bed. They may spend too much money, work endless hours, and invest all kinds of energy into making sure their children get to experience hope, awe, wonder, faith, the importance of family, and the opportunity to believe in magical things that you can't see or prove, except by the spirit of the heart.

Santa as Legacy

Why do adults invest so heavily in all these things? They get something marvelous back in return; like Peter Pan, they get to revisit Neverland for an evening where hopes and dreams can become real. Therefore, while Santa has the trappings and trimmings of frivolity, at the core he has very serious meanings and implications for everyone, of every age.

Parents hope their children will carry with them fond memories of these cherished days. Children's participation in cultural routines and rituals is very important for their socialization. The routines of celebration, food, and events associated with the preparation for Santa and Christmas provide them with the security and shared understanding of belonging to a social group. The predictability of year-after-year holiday rituals gives them a framework within which a wide range of socio-cultural knowledge can be produced, displayed, interpreted, and preserved. Cultural routines and rituals serve as anchors that enable children to deal with ambiguities, the unexpected issues of life. These can include going shopping together – which entails looking at decorations, feeling the holiday air, and discussing whether certain people will like potential gifts. Family members may make crafts and cook special foods; they may wrap gifts in fancy ways to please the recipients. Singing songs, watching movies like The Santa Claus, or The Grinch, or Santa Claus: The Movie, or the Polar Express, which all help to build bonds among family members. Learning all the words to the Chipmunk's Christmas song was imperative in our household, and to this day I can recite every word and verse.

Parents enjoy introducing Santa Claus family rituals to children and probably enjoy them more than their children. When parents introduce Santa or other mythical characters to children, they are given the opportunity to re-live their childhoods and interweave them into the lives of their children. I love baking the same kinds of Christmas sugar cookies and springleys that my mother baked with me when I was small – which are the same kinds of cookies that she baked with her mother when she was a girl. We string cranberries and popcorn and make construction paper chains for the tree, just as families have done for generations. Joining in with countless other households across the nation, we read The Night Before Christmas in what can only be regarded as a deeply cherished ritual.

The meanings of these family rituals are enhanced by these routines that reinforce the message of the myth. For instance, writing Santa a letter, or leaving cookies and milk out for Santa and carrots for his reindeer, are important activities that the entire family may participate in. In Sweden, they leave cinnamon sugared porridge for Santa so he can have a hearty, healthy, warm breakfast on his journey around the world. In my family, my mother always had a holiday jigsaw puzzle out of the table for us to work. People would spontaneously sit down to put in a few pieces, and find themselves surrounded by other members of the family, chatting away about all kinds of meaningful and nonsense topics. My cousin and I both put out puzzles for our children to work, hoping they will capture some of the same warm, loving moments like we did long ago with our mothers and siblings. These simple acts help children to find collective support, joy, and they, in turn, seek to share these delightful moments with others both now and in the future.

By repeating a behavior, the present recalls the past and brings unity as the family re-enacts traditions each year. For instance, at my house, the children all decided, on their own, that they would listen to one particular Christmas song. Before they all walked down the stairs to see what Santa brought. They created the ritual that no one could come downstairs to even sneak a peek to see if Santa had come without the other. Therefore, they say they tiptoe down the stairs one at a time together, and turn the corner arm in arm to see the lit tree and tinseled gifts waiting. Then they open their stockings together in a "no parents allowed" moment and share the glory of the children's hour that is exclusively theirs. They make the decision when to invite the adults to share in their experience. It is understood that the adults are to stay in their beds until invited.

My mentor, Ray Helfer, MD, a pediatrician at Michigan State University, was convinced that in order for parents to become good at their job, they had to overcome their own pasts. This means that for parents who had negative Christmas experiences, they could overcome them by making sure their children had good ones. In this way, the parents not only make sure their children don't have the same kinds of problems that they do, but they end up healing themselves in the process. Empathy is strongly correlated with altruistic behavior in children and adults according to Eisenberg (1983) in her study of children's prosocial responsibility and altruistic behavior. She found that when parents model the behavior they want their children to follow, the results are much more effective than moral exhortations or preachings about what to do and what not to do. Children imitate their parent's behavior, for both good and for ill. Children who have seen their parents be generous are more likely to be generous also, in both their youth and in their adult lives. As a personal example, having watched my parents give so generously to others, I felt an absolute moral obligation to make sure I give generously to others, especially the people who are nearest and dearest to me. I am inadvertently replicating my own history in a new generation.

I know that I have been the ringleader in the encouragement of my children's magical belief in Santa Claus. But I am not alone. Child development experts have found that adults, especially mothers, actively cultivate children's belief in the magical, as a way to keep children young and extend their belief in fantasy. I go out of my way to cultivate the presence of Santa. I start my Santa planning about a day after Christmas; I often have 80% of my shopping done in July, since I like to pick up gifts that I know my dear ones will like when I find them. If you wait too long and expect that special gift to still be there, sometimes it's not, so it's better, in my opinion, to buy things you want when you see them. I casually peruse catalogs, websites, and stores keeping my eyes open for those special holiday gifts that will make the day special. My children fret about exactly what to get the other since no regular present will do; it has to be symbolic and significant – and under $20. They find or make gifts that will make each other laugh, gifts that will remind them of the other 364 days of the year that they are loved.

The importance of finding meaningful experiences through holiday traditions are expressed in the children's classic by Chris Van Allsburg's book, The Polar Express: "On Christmas morning my little sister Sarah and I opened our presents. When it looked as if everything had been unwrapped, Sarah found one last small box behind the tree... Inside was the silver bell!....Though I've grown old, the bell still rings for me as it does for all who truly believe." Children, at Christmas, have the upper hand because they have not yet lost the ability to believe. Their parents, however, often have. A Polar Express train ride rolls through the north woods of New Hampshire, captivating adult imagination because it reminds them that once they did believe, that they had magic and that anything was possible. I took my own children on this actual train ride on The Polar Express and can say with absolute delight that I liked wearing my nightclothes and robe in public, along with a train full of boys and girls, moms and dads, and grandparents who drank chocolate that tasted like melted chocolate bars. The train engineers with jolly faces looked just like those in the book. When we arrived at "the north pole", we were greeted by hordes of smiling, waving elves who led us to the room where we together would see the old man character in the book transform into a child again, for a few brief moments, a transformation that would allow for Santa to come. As we sat there, everyone in the room again became children and we too could see Santa. As he passed by us, some reindeer hay fell from his boots, and to this day, we put this hay out every Christmas Eve. My children introduced me to The Polar Express book, I introduced them to the train rides, and together, we have woven a bond that I hope will hold us close our whole lives long.

Frances Chaput Waksler poses the question, what if adults never told children Santa Claus was real but were instead invited by their parents to participate in a game of "Let's Pretend Santa Claus is Real"? Would children have just as much fun? Waksler thinks they might. It might be a way to liberate children who are pretending to believe in Santa in order to protect their parents' feelings, preserve their own chances for getting presents, and allow for a more egalitarian relationship between parents and children as they create a special, magical world together. This is one way that parents who don't want their children to believe in Santa could still introduce Santa into their lives in a positive way and allow them the joy of playful imagination. It also would enable them to develop a form of Santa that both parents and children, could create that would be appreciated without tension at home, or in their community.

It's a whole lot more fun to believe in Santa than not to. Maurice Reidy (1999) talks about how he has made the transition from being a recipient of Santa to being Santa himself. "These days, I am quite a scrupulous Santa Claus. When my youngest brothers go to bed on Christmas Eve, my mother and I go foraging through the house, retrieving presents. I routinely make sure that Santa's wrapping paper differs from Mom's wrapping paper. (I will not tolerate mistakes like those that shook my faith.) I also always make sure to eat half of the cookies and drink some of the milk left on the dining room table and, when no one is looking, I toss half-eaten carrots in the driveway, and slyly point to them on the way to church on Christmas morning. I suppose I am like that man I heard about somewhere who shovels deer-dung onto his roof every Christmas Eve. Some may think that such childish pranks are beyond an educated man such as myself. But I find solace in such trickery."

Santa rituals help create a sense of wonder and awe, which is reassuring to parents who would prefer that their children not grow up too fast. But children will grow and lose their belief in Santa as they mature. Santa is what British Psychiatrist D. W. Winnicott (1965; 1971) would call a "transition object." Santa provides a buffer between the world of childhood and the world of adulthood. Children naturally invest blind faith and trust in what their parents tell them. Instead of viewing Santa as a "lie", the way some Santaphobes state, Winnicott would regard in children's discovery that Santa and parents have a united relationship. He alleges that as children sort through what part of Santa is real and what part of Santa may be their parents, children come to know that their belief in Santa has been an expression of their faith in the unconditional love of their parents. They also discover that the seeds of this faith can be passed on through the participation in the same cultural rituals with their own children.

Parents may continue to play Santa long after their children are grown, and it is a ritualized behavior that both parents and children enjoy. Children know that Santa isn't real, at least in the way they thought when they were small. In their world of peers, they may actively dissect Santa and the mythology built around him. But this is peer behavior; it is an expression of their maturity, their independent thought, and their striving to no longer be a child. This is a healthy step in their development toward adulthood. But they may never utter a word of non-belief to their parents. There is a stark division between the world of peers and the world of home, and events such as Santa and Christmas can codify key family values. My children, who are grown now, have never told me they don't believe in Santa. To do so would shatter one of the most wonderful times of the year for all time. Once a year, we can all anticipate a period of joyful fantasy that honors the love we feel for each other. The world of "home" and family can, at these critical moments each year, be re-established. Sharing traditions and expressions of joy are reminders that a home is a place where hope can be nurtured, where dreams can come true, where faith and trust are rewarded, and love is present.

We know that children don't necessarily take all of the traditions learned at home into their adult lives. They may keep key rituals that have positive emotional meaning for them, such as leaving cookies and a note out for Santa each year. Like Santa, we transform and modify our traditions and create unique rituals as part of our holiday season. This behavior, known as interpretative reproduction, shows how we are all key players in the development of culture. Cindy Dell Clark gives a lovely discussion of this point with this example:

"When Kay was three years old, her father held her on his lap and read to her on Christmas Eve Clement Moore's well-known poem, "A Visit from St. Nicholas." Each Christmas Eve since, this has been repeated. When Kay was five years old her sister Jane was born, and during the succeeding years, the reading of this poem on Christmas Eve became more and more of a ceremonial event. As the two daughters became older, they would sit on either side of the father on the family sofa and mother and other relatives would be present. After the reading, refreshments came to be served, and talk would follow about Christmas celebrations of former years. As time went on, the ceremony became more and more elaborate. Candles were lit while other lights were extinguished, and the conversational aftermath lengthened. Nothing ever deterred Kay and Jane from being at home on Christmas Eve; dates with boys, even after their engagements had been announced, were not made; once Kay did not accept an invitation to a much-desired trip so that she might be at home for the reading. After Kay's marriage, she and her husband came to her parents' home on Christmas Eve in order to be present for the event. This practice has been continued down to the present time, but by Kay and her husband and by Jane and her husband. Last year the father read to both daughters, their husbands, three grandchildren, and the grandmother." (p 31).

What I Concluded

Exploring family relationships with Santa helped me to better understand my own. One of the best outcomes of family rituals and shared holiday experiences is that people make time to remember those they love. Often during the year, we rush about and may forget to let people know we care. As humans with frailties as well as strengths, we may sometimes be neglectful to do things that mean a lot to children. We make mistakes. We let people down. Sometimes we are wrong or wrong others. The holiday season provides a structured opportunity to remind those we love that we really do care about them.

There are points when families are falling apart and need something to bind them together. There are moments when we are sick, in despair, and need some lightness to lift us up. All families have moments of tension, and sometimes family members may not be particularly fond of each other. Santa is a vehicle to help us have a mutually agreed upon time to "bury the hatchet", to "forgive and forget", and to let love reign, even if only for a day. Gift-giving allows family members to try to make amends by showing others that we genuinely care; gifts are a symbolic representation of transformation from being callous and hard, to being generous and soft-hearted. Intergenerational connections are created through the shared belief in Santa Claus. Certainly celebrating the arrival of Santa is a form of family entertainment, but he also evokes values like respect for elders, generosity for others, and to remember even the meek and mild among us. Ultimately, the cycle of life takes over, and parents become grandparents who watch their own children taking care of passing on important holiday rituals to their own children who may pass them on to their own babies. These reciprocal extensions of holiday family rituals are examples of exchange theory, which basically holds that children actively take the lessons learned by their families and re-create them in relationships of their own.

I've concluded that children's experiences in the family prepare them for entry into their world as peers, adults, and parents. Early family rituals and interactive experiences provide them with emotional support and interpersonal skills and attitudes that will last them their whole life long. There is a wonderful sense of family belongingness when children are teaching their little ones to celebrate in ways that are similar to that of generations before them. Best of all, joyful, loving family holiday rituals help remind children of the importance of home, and the beauty of love.

Rachel Field quote

Now not a window small
or big
But wears a wreath or
holly spring
Nor any shop too poor to show
Its spray of pine or mistletoe
Now city airs are spicy sweet
With Christmas trees along each street
Green spruce and fir whose boughs will hold
Their tinseled balls and fruits of gold
Now postmen pass in threes and fours
Like bent, blue-coated Santa Claus
Now people hurry to and from
With little girls and boys in tow
And not a child but keep some trace
Of (Santa) secrets in his face.

Rachel Field

For Christmas. Poems. 1957. Simon and Schuster.

Chapter 16

Santa and the Community

The Dilemma

Why has Santa Claus become a symbol of community divisiveness? From everything I learned, all the winter festivals were designed to bring community members together. All the key figures who have morphed into the character we have come to know as Santa Claus had an altruistic, well-being to others approach. Why then has Santa become a polarizing figure?

One December guests sat at my table over dinner and said in front of my children how they were glad someone in town cut down the community holiday tree. They saw the tree as a Christian, religious symbol and they came from a different religious persuasion. The things they said to justify this aggressive act stunned me. I was raising my children to be respectful of all faiths, and here were supposedly religious people of another faith who were intolerant, favoring divisiveness, and were anything but faithful warriors of inclusion of all God's critters. They felt haughtily empowered by their hate-filled words. My children sat there respectfully, mouths open, having never heard such talk. I too said nothing, for which I am now ashamed. I just had never heard people talk like that before and I didn't know what to do, since "being nice" was part of my upbringing, and I thought being rude to my dinner guests was inappropriate even though they were the ones being rude.

That town decided against having any holiday symbols of any faith as a result. Like other communities across the nation, leaders don't know what to do. They want to not offend anyone, want to include everyone, and they just don't know how to do it. I thought it was important to take a closer look at this.

What I Discovered

Communities around the country are having a hard time figuring out what to do about the December holidays and Santa Claus. This is apparent from their conflict about what kinds of decorations to put up to what kinds of celebrations they should have, or forbid, during the season. My father was the mayor of a city and I witnessed many heated discussions around the kitchen table as community leaders tried to persuade him to do this and not that. The conflict over what cities and towns should do about the December holidays has increased since then, and for community leaders, it's serious stuff. How to be inclusive and not divisive is a thin rope to walk successfully. Leaders want to make sure they show respect for everyone, don't alienate anyone, and get votes at the next election.

Back to ground zero - winter solstice festivals were always community events. They were designed to bring people together. They were supposed to be fun. There were decorations, delicious foods to share, music, dancing, theatre, laughter, sharing of information, and cherishing children. There were usually representatives of the community (often elders) who gave gifts or said words of wisdom to inspire members of the town to feel connected and altruistic. Children were encouraged to attend and dance with glee. People of all ages came to pursue relationships with others. Leaders worked to create kind, joyful, altruistic, respectful events. They were people who knew how to listen to others, how to laugh, solve problems, and had the ability to make people feel good about themselves and the future.

Somewhere along the line, these attributes were morphed into the character of Santa Claus as we have come to recognize him. And somewhere along the line, Santa Claus got connected with Christmas, who was connected with Jesus, who was connected to Christianity, and so it goes. As a result, Santa Claus became erroneously the poster-child of Christianity, which pissed-off a good number of religious people. By the time the business people and advertisers got hold of him, Santa became equated with mass commercialism and materialism. Add in politicians and religious leaders using him to advocate for certain ideological or political positions, and no wonder people started to question the legitimacy of Santa Claus at community gatherings.

But what I have discovered in doing this research is that Santa Claus was none of those things. He is a socially constructed figure that could be constructed in any way that a community wishes. So my question is – what do we, as communities who care about one another, want him to be?

Individuals choose how, or whether, they are going to incorporate Santa Claus into their lives. Families decide if, and how, they are going to involve Santa in their traditions. Community leaders also have a choice about whether they are going to let Santa Claus be an ongoing part of their winter celebrations or whether they are going to force him out. However, members of the community have little control over their leaders' decisions. What is in the best interests of one may not be in the best interests of another. Good intentions of one group may not be perceived as goodwill by another. In a diverse, collective society, we have to be sensitive to the needs of others. This is why have to communicate and work together. It is entirely possible that communities have much to gain from assuming an inclusionary position on Santa.

Communities, like families, have traditions, histories, and legacies that they create through the socialization of children. Every society has an organized set of social norms and practices which constitute how community members should behave. If a community teaches tolerance and appreciation for diversity, children come to see that as the appropriate way to interact. If they learn to polarize and compartmentalize people, and to believe that they are somehow superior from watching the behavior of their community leaders that is precisely what they will learn.

Community Variation of Santa Claus

While Santa has historically been a vehicle to pull people together, it appears that now people are using him to pull them apart. Let's consider ways communities can respond to the December holidays. The arrival of Santa Claus could become a community-wide event that brings joy. In Brazil, Santa arrives by helicopter and lands in the middle of at Rio de Janeiro's Maracanã stadium that is packed with thousands of people of all ages who cheer with delight. In Australia, Santa is thought to come by a sled pulled by kangaroos, in Belgium he comes on a big boat with a white horse that he then rides through the town, and in Chile Viejo Pascuero, or Old Man Christmas, visits homes at night carrying a lantern in his hand to light his way, with a sack filled with gifts for children in the other. In Denmark, businesses and organizations incorporate Jultraefests, or Christmas tree parties, into their December annual events so people can celebrate together. Some Chinese communities encourage citizens to decorate homes with lights and paper lanterns where children await a visit from Lam Khoong-Khoong, or "nice old father," Dun Che Lao Ren, which translated means Christmas Old Man. In Guatemala, people have mixed their old and new traditions and cultures including indigenous people, Spanish and German influences where local men dress up in costumes and entertain giggling children, while in Nigeria adults may dress up in costumes, play music, sing, drum, and dance for children at Christmastime. All around the world, communities have decided to have fun with the arrival of Santa and they have transformed him into a recreational and bonding experience for the people.

People in the US seem to be going through angst about how to appropriately handle Santa. Some communities have decided to incorporate all winter holiday celebrations and in front of city hall, you may find their visibly desperate attempt to not offend anyone by having every holiday icon imaginable, including Christmas trees, nativity scenes, menorahs, Kwanza candelabras, snow people, reindeer, elves, and a plethora of other religious-holiday artifacts. Other communities have responded at the other end of the continuum by not allowing any holiday decorations or artifacts in public places. Both choices end up annoying someone.

Look at the responses of two communities as it pertains to Santa Claus. In Community A, community leaders are terrified about offending others. Santa is forbidden. His icons are not allowed at parties, in schools, in parades, or at the mall. Santa songs are not played. Decorations are sparse. Parents pick up the message that if they are caring people then they should downplay Santa. His absence could be associated with Christianity and in a decision to have no religious iconography, he has been tossed to the wayside. It could be that Santa is seen as a bad role model, an unhealthy fat man who encourages conspicuous consumption and forces parents to get themselves into debt delivering items that will soon break. He may be presented as someone who will exclude certain children. Or he may be presented as a bum or potentially scary guy. Whatever he is, he is unwelcome. Part of the community is angry over this decision and feels it is discriminatory; the others feel unsatisfied with this "victory" because nothing was truly accomplished by his absence anyway. The result: no one wins.

Community B embraces Santa. Cheerful decorations adorn the town. The post office has a North Pole box where children can mail their letters to Santa Claus. Special post-elves compose hand-written letters to each and every child on behalf of Santa. The town library has created its own "Polar Express" ride for children and their families, where mom and dad join the kiddies dressed in their pajamas as they drink hot chocolate and take a ride to the North Pole. Every December 24, Santa arrives with a police escort as he rides on a Christmas lighted fire engine that goes down each and every street in town as he shouts Ho Ho Ho and waves to each house. This occurred a week after the town breakfast with Santa and the festive house-decorating competition. Santa came to the school to gift every child. The local church has made sure everyone in need received a food basket. The toy drive ensured that every child could have appropriate and happily wrapped gifts. It doesn't matter what one's religious or political persuasion is – everyone works together to make this a special time of year for children. People young and old from all walks of life come together to work as neighbors as they build bonds around a common purpose – to bring children joy. Community B is my hometown.

Where would YOU rather live?

Anticipating the arrival of Santa can create a time when our families and community work together to create a single period when giving to each other and making one another happy is at the forefront of our minds. Working together in this way isn't a burden but a joy. What a marvelous thing it is for a child to see his or her parents, grandparents, brothers, and sisters, aunts and uncles, cousins, and neighbors all bustling around working to make sure others have a happy holiday experience. Making merry doesn't just happen – we have to work and cultivate it.

Problems Facing Communities

One of the biggest struggles facing a community is how to become cohesive but respectful and attentive to the needs of all its individual members. This is the classic tension Tonnies described in his designation of Gemeinschaft and Gesellschaft. Communities have undergone significant changes over recent years (Macionis 2012). Homogeneous small towns have grown in size and diversity in their population composition. When people live in villages where everyone knows each other, works together, attends the same church, same school, and shares the same recreation, it's easier to be in agreement on what's important and how to do things. But as cities have become more heterogeneous, we don't necessarily know what other people think, need, or want. We may not know our neighbors. Their language, culture, traditions, faith, and way of life may be unfamiliar to us. It's natural to think that people feel and want the same thing as you – but this can be an erroneous assumption.

Leaders in a community must take into account the spread of differences. Former Boston mayor Tom Menino stated that he was mayor of all of the people in the city, not just part of the people. This required any decision that he made to take into account the needs of everyone, not just some. Essentially, people in leadership positions have the mandate of leading –whatever they decide will have rippled-out implications that may be widespread. So if they advocate for the presence of Santa or his absence, there will always be ramifications. Leaders have to figure out how best to meet the needs of all the people, and this task may be challenging indeed.

How to manage issues of diversity are tougher for once homogeneous communities that are undergoing change. A varied population composition requires more than acceptance of dissimilar racial, ethnic, religious, or socioeconomic groups; as community members mix and mingle, their differences provide opportunities for teaching tolerance. Therefore, the decisions that the town council, school board, or CEO make set a trend for others. The tone set on how we, as a community, are going to address issues of diversity is no small thing.

There is no escape from the December dilemma. Sidestepping it will only result in trip-ups. Considering how to forthrightly deal with Santa is important, not so much for Santa per se, but because leaders need to be clear-headed about the underlying tensions that make Santa Claus an issue to begin with. Decisions on how to handle issues of diversity ought not to be a popularity contest. In a democratic society where everyone is equally important to the life of the community, it is useful for leaders to think through how they are going to put democracy into practice.

Bringing People Together -Leaving People Out

Santa can be found on television, sitting in the mall, his photo pasted to windows, in newspaper advertisements, and on objects from chocolates to trash-bags. He is impossible to miss and impossible to avoid. Santa has become a great sales representative for stores and products of all sorts. For people who don't buy into the Santa thing, surviving the holiday can be pretty challenging. Even for people for whom Christmas is their favorite holiday, the merchandising of Santa can be over-the-top. Many people simply plow ahead full steam through the season without thinking seriously about whether Santa should be quite so visible.

As a child, I never contemplated the fact that others might not like Santa. When I was in elementary school back in Indiana, Santa Claus came to visit each classroom (along with a host of Rotary Club elf helpers), and he gave every child a small box full of sweet treats, an orange, and a silver dollar. I never even thought about his visit not being fun for everyone. I just assumed that everyone felt the same way I did. The other children, including the non-Christian ones, seemed to be having a good time. All of us children were treated the same, even though some of us had blonde hair, snowy skin, and blue eyes while others of us had black skin, dark hair, and brown eyes. The fact that some children had different religions or came from other places and cultures didn't enter my consciousness; kids were kids and we had lots more in common than our differences would indicate. This was during a time and place when we looked to integrate, not to separate, with each other. We sought to find common themes among us, minute things like skin color or gender didn't faze us back then. Recall that children are developmentally very ego-centered at elementary school ages. I had not yet learned to "take the role of the other" or view the situation from another person's point of view. I just assumed we all thought the same and wanted identical things. It was easy to assume that when no one said otherwise.

This childlike assumption of sameness can be a problem for those who unknowingly walk into public functions that end up having more of a religious flavor than they anticipated. When I moved to a New England town, I took my children and an eclectic crowd of friends to the local Thanksgiving Day Parade. The street was filled with marching bands and colorful floats – my favorites were lobster boats with Santa hatted fishermen pulling in their tinseled, rubberized "catch." The parade was loads of fun and ended at the local park where there was a seasonal community sing-a-long. I was expecting fun holiday tunes like Frosty The Snowman and sentimental tunes like Silver Bells. Being Christian myself, I was prepared to sing a few carols like Joy To the World. I knew my eclectic crowd would not be offended at the presence of a few carols so long as there was a balance in the evening's selections. But after the fourth song, the community singalong felt like a religious service. The tunes were all standard – if you used only a hymnal. The focus on baby Jesus was awkward for many of the large numbers of people assembled. The people who ran the event forgot to make room for diversity. There were no Hanukah or dreidel songs. There was no Rudolph the Red-Nosed Reindeer, no Winter Wonderland, no Frosty. There were only holy Christian songs. The evening's master of the ceremony had an obvious, palpable religious agenda. The people around me became visibly edgy. I too felt uncomfortable, embarrassed that I had dragged diverse friends to what was becoming essential a pseudo-revival. They had consented to the parade; they had not consented to religious indoctrination. They weren't the only ones; the jovial mood of the entire crowd of parade-goers quickly dissipated, and people began drifting away. The people who ran this community event seemed shocked by the mass exodus.

If the singalong was a private party, it wouldn't have been an issue. The problem is that a small group of people with a religious ideology were promoting it in the public forum when others weren't aware that this was going to be the evening's agenda. The well-meaningness, but insensitivity, of the organizers, contributed, spoiled the evening. Insensitivity is not usually due to malicious intent, but by not taking the time to think about how it would feel if others who don't share the same point of view.

The result? This "only my way" kind of attitude and behavior has resulted in some communities feeling that they can have no holiday public displays of any religious icons or symbols that could possibly be perceived as offensive. This, in turn, makes the Santa supporters downright mad and resentful of those who are curbing their expression of free speech. Conversely, when I visited a different faith community whose sermon was on "the December dilemma," the almost hostile view of anything Christian (including Santa) left me feeling alienated with my own beliefs demeaned. It was instructive to be on the other side of the argument. The people who were running the program were just as intolerant of a pro-Santa set of beliefs as they were alleging Christian insensitivity to their religious rituals and celebrations. The old saw that "one person's rights end where other people's rights are violated" may sound reasonable, but putting that into practice is very challenging.

People who want an unrestrained Santa Claus should logically anticipate negative reactions from other people who feel their toes have been stepped upon. Such reactions are logical outcomes where there isn't a sense of community between all the residents. When one group is running the show and anyone who is different finds their needs pushed aside, ultimately no one wins. The disenfranchised group wants equal time, and an equally loud voice and visible presence, which is reasonable in a nation that touts itself as a supporter of equality and justice for all. If you've never been left out, it's hard to imagine what all the fuss is about when people complain. But if your views have been denied or ridiculed, even small, symbolic acts like the arrival of Santa Claus can evoke upset reactions. The reactions, both for and against Santa, are filled with symbolic meanings that may have nothing to do with fact. Interpersonal tensions will inevitably continue, both on an individual and a community level, if people don't weigh where the correct place for Santa is and isn't.

If Santa Claus is presented as a secular figure that cares for all children, irrespective of their background, he can be a bridge for building a sense of belongingness. If, on the other hand, he is presented as a Christian representative who deals out preferential treatment as he remembers some children well and ignores others entirely, it is understandable that he would become a wedge for community collaboration. For instance, in Community A, Santa only comes to certain children; some children get gifts from him and others don't. In Community B, every child receives gifts from Santa that are of equal importance. If he comes to school, every child is gifted the same. If he is in the parade, he greets each child enthusiastically, whether they are shy or eager. By reaching out to the children who are a bit uncertain whether they should like him or not, he helps to build a foundation that teaches them he can be trusted to care.

I am not sure how a community can teach children to appreciate the differences in others if they homogenize holidays to the point that different groups have to hide their unique attributes. When faced with a diverse population, some communities have chosen to force others to assimilate to make everyone seem pretty much the same. Except in today's world, we're not. Accommodation is where we force people to tone down their unique ways to be more like ours. This is what communities have largely done with respect to the celebration of Christmas. It is the attitude that Christmas may not be your way, but it's mine, so you play along in order to get along. This has been the holiday formula used for years, and as Harris (2013) notes, it doesn't work for large segments of the population. A pluralistic approach allows for each group to keep their uniqueness and live together with others. Some people liken it to a salad that contains carrots, tomatoes, cucumber, cheese, sprouts, and a variety of other different and delicious foods. It is more interesting, even though we like certain foods in mixed salad more than others. Compare that salad to one that is a quarter head of iceberg lettuce. It's all the same, there's nothing appealing about it. Diversity, whether in communities or salads, makes for a more interesting experience.

Learning to live harmoniously together isn't something that comes easily for some people. We have to learn how. Engaging in deliberative dialogue about how to bring people together over the holiday season could be an instructive process for communities. Providing an open community forum for people to talk about how to celebrate each other's traditions in educational, joyful, and non-offensive ways could open the door to a variety of creative options.

Words Say a Lot

What we call the Santa related holiday ends up raising hackles among certain groups of people. Strategically selecting words that fragment the community is unwise; a better choice is to choose words that are more inclusive. I don't call him St. Nicholas, Kris Kringle, or any of the associated names for Santa Claus. They carry too much baggage. Frankly, I just prefer to call him Santa. No Claus.

There is a historical tradition of wishing others Merry Christmas. Christians and non-Christians extend this greeting to each other without having a religious overlay; the greeting may simply be a wish for a happy time of the year. When I sent a Merry Christmas card to my Jewish camp counselor when I was in high school and he got offended, I didn't understand why – I was just trying to tell him I liked him and wanted to wish him happiness. To me, the greeting was secular but to him it was religious.

Extending happy wishes to others is a kind behavior. When it comes to community gatherings, especially those that use taxpayer dollars in a country built on religious freedom, it is more appropriate to use inclusive greetings like Happy Holidays or Seasons Greetings. They are more inclusive and less tainted. We have to remember that not everyone is Christian. Not everyone celebrates Christmas. Yet as we saw earlier in this book, most traditions embrace some sort of winter holiday celebration that includes key components of family togetherness, eating, drinking, enjoying each other's company, and the exchange of gifts.

People use the default, secularized "Merry Christmas" because it conveys a wish of joy during this time of year. The secularized "Merry Christmas" may be met with chagrin to those who want to "Christ to be put back into Christmas". The greeting need not have a religious connotation at all. That said, it still carries a lot of baggage for many people. Happy Holidays and Seasons Greetings have become customary greetings that honor a variety of December celebrations without the taint of any particular religious preference. Less commonly used greetings are Happy Winter Solstice, Winter Festivals, Season of Gratitude, Have a Joyous Celebration, Best wishes for a happy new year, Season of Peace, and Have a Wonderful Season. Franklin, Michigan renamed their annual Holly Day celebration the Winter Festival because its sponsors decided that Holly Day sounded too Christmassy. It seems as though no name we pick is going to please everyone. But we could at least try to pick words that wouldn't alienate anyone.

Similarly, what do we call the decorated tree? A Christmas tree? A Hanukkah bush? A holiday tree? Many people who have no religious ties to Christianity put up a variation of a Christmas tree; they enjoy the lights, the ornaments, and the smell of pine or spruce. Going back into history, the tree was not originally a Christian symbol at all. Many winter festivals promoted decorations of greenery as a reminder that spring and new growth would soon follow. The use of a winter tree with lights and decorations has long traditions among many different cultures. Refusing to have a decorated tree present for the community is not in keeping with age-old traditions by many different groups.

Having a brightly adorned fir tree is part of a long multicultural history of winter celebrations. No alternative term has risen that has become culturally embraced. The term Christmas tree has become secularized as well and doesn't need to refer to a religious orientation at all. But if one wants to play it safe and call it a holiday tree, why not? A tree is a tree – it's adults that hang political overlays on it.

Music

Music effuses our soul and inspires thoughts. Ideally, it is uplifting and helps us to find our higher selves. When music is shared together in song, the merging of voices is like a tapestry where we all combine ourselves to create a larger, more beautiful whole. But music is like food – we all have different tastes. When trying to bring a community together, the safest course of action is to select songs that everyone can enjoy. It is wise to avoid songs that polarize members of the audience. For instance, songs that have religious themes should be avoided in community forums. This is especially the case for publicly funded events, such as parades, sing-alongs in the park, school functions, and the like. If a private group or religious group wants to have religious songs, they have every right to do so. But people attending community events expect songs that are secular, as religion tends to be a personal choice.

Here are my recommendations for songs that have a higher probability of being accepted by a diverse community[i].

Good Community Holiday Music Choices

Jingle Bells
Silver Bells

Frosty The Snowman
Winter Wonderland
Sleigh Ride
Must Be Santa
Deck the Halls
Rudolph the Red-Nosed Reindeer
Jingle Bell Rock
Here We Go a Wassiling
Holly and the Ivy
My Favorite Things
Suzy Snowflake
Let It Snow
Sleigh Ride
No Place Like Home for the Holidays
The Most Wonderful Time of the Year
Must be Santa

Christmas carols or songs that have a decidedly religious focus of any sort may need to be omitted. Songs that are questionably acceptable for community forums that aren't religious include Santa Baby, Grandma Got Run Over By a Reindeer and songs that have to do with substance use, sex, or other illegal or illicit behaviors. But even the secular type Santa or winter holiday songs or their instrumental versions may not be satisfactory for some people. Thoughtful consideration of music at community events is important.

Taking Care of All Children

Let's play a game called "What If?". What if all communities decided that children were the most precious thing they had? What if communities were determined to make sure that every child got everything it needed to ensure a happy life? What if we made certain that every child felt he or she was special? What if we were resolute to help them understand what their unique gifts and talents were, and then give them all an opportunity to use them? With unwavering position, what if we made sure they all had enough to eat, safe homes, decent clothes and shoes, physical health care, dental care, mental health care, social support, education, recreation, citizenship training, and meaningful life and career training? What if we made sure their parents had good jobs so they could take care of them, that the parents had been trained so they knew how to be good parents, and they had enough discretionary time so they could read to them and actually play with them?

What if children's needs were met 365 days a year, and not just at Christmas? What if the well-being standards for children set forth in the UN Convention on the Rights of the Child were actually implemented? I bet that would be the best present of all to give them if we really and truly were committed to the statement that children were the most precious things in our lives...

The caring community message s is beautifully captured in a children's book by Patricia Polacco (1996). She describes a story of days gone by in Michigan when a Jewish child realized that her best friend and Christian neighbor's family were so sick with scarlet fever that they were unable to prepare for Christmas. The girl talked with her family and they decided the best Hanukah gift they could give was to create a Christmas for the ill family. They cut down a tree and decorated it with Grandfather's hand-carved animals, the cook latkes, and they took these holiday items to their neighbors so they could celebrate their most cherished holiday. The Christian family recovered and, in turn, made them a menorah. Together, they celebrated Hanukah. By helping each other to celebrate the holidays that meant the most to them, in the ways they regarded as most meaningful, it cost them nothing but gave them the most wonderful gifts in return.

This is not just a wonderful story of how two religions can get together and have a great holiday season; there are real-life examples of similar acts. Feeling joy because someone else celebrates Christmas is nicely described by Jeff Jacoby (2004), a Jewish columnist who writes for the Boston Globe, who states,

"I enjoy Christmas decorations – and Christmas music and the upbeat Christmastime mood – and I say that as a practicing Jew for whom Dec. 25 has no theological significance at all. I have never celebrated Christmas, but I like seeing my Christian neighbors celebrate it. I like living in a society that makes a big deal out of religious holidays. Far from feeling threatened when the sights and sounds of Christmas surround me each December, I find them reassuring. They reaffirm the importance of the Judeo-Christian culture that has made America so exceptional – and such a safe and tolerant haven for a religious minority like mine."

In Jakarta, Indonesia's capital, the largest and oldest Catholic Cathedral in the country is located back to back with the largest Mosque. They share a unique tradition during the Christmas season when the Muslim community helps prepare for their Christmas celebration by preparing some parking space in the surrounding area that belongs to the mosque. At the other time, during the Muslim 'Hari Raya', the people from the Christian church help prepare parking spaces for the Muslim celebration. In Jakarta, parking space is something in constant demand and not simply affordable. They may not feel entirely comfortable going into each other's houses of worship, but they know that as a community, it is important to help each other to celebrate the holidays that mean so much to them. By doing so, they have affirmed the spirit of a caring community, and the adults are teaching their children the valuable skills of empathy and cooperation.

What I Concluded

It is entirely possible for us to acknowledge other people's holidays and celebrate with them without it compromising our own personal beliefs. Holidays don't have to be an either-or choice but could be one of inclusion, not exclusion, in which we share in other people's joys and traditions.

In my analysis of this problem, the Santa issue really isn't about Santa at all. The problem is the lack of community that we feel with those with whom we live, work, and interact. Santa Claus is being used as a scapegoat because we're unwilling to look at the real source of the issue. If we genuinely cared about others, we would be very happy to help celebrate holidays and events that mattered to them. If we genuinely cared about others, we would not knowingly and strategically do things that alienated, isolated, ridiculed, or hurt them. If we did so accidentally, we would find ways to make things right and ensure they knew we respected them. And if other people genuinely cared about us, they would do likewise. When we both actually, genuinely, sincerely care about each other and experience a sense of community with each other, we would find ways to work together so that we both got what we needed. One person's joy wouldn't diminish our own, any more than our joy should sadden or anger others. Santa wouldn't be a threatening issue, because the real issues that underlie the tension surrounding Santa Claus would have already been resolved.

Psychologists call this process "cognitive dissonance" – when we care about someone, we are more willing to like what they care about; when we don't like particular groups of people, it is convenient to disassociate ourselves from things they care about – it is easy to dislike other people's holiday celebrations because we dislike them. Holiday symbols like Santa don't represent that which they truly are, but they take on entirely different meanings as people attribute their own emotions to these symbols. Look at it objectively - it makes no sense to be angry at an elderly, overweight man who smiles a lot, is devoted to bringing children presents and joy, and asks for nothing in return except for children to do their best to be nice to others. If people are angry at Santa, chances are good that they're really angry about a whole bunch of other things that they simply dump onto him. He is not responsible for people not liking him. We are responsible for the tensions that we feel when we look at the Santa symbol. That is the issue we need to explore.

When people like each other, they engage in a reciprocal relationship where they are willing, even happy, to celebrate each other's holiday events. They are not threatened by sharing in such a cultural exchange; they learn something new, they get to share in the other person's excitement, and they themselves may find pleasure in doing so. But if people don't like or trust each other; when we're suspicious of their intentions and we have a history of not getting along well, it's often easy for us to be opposed not only to celebrating their holidays with them but to dislike the holidays themselves, just because we don't like the people for whom the holiday is important.

Children learn altruism when the entire community comes together giving of scarce time and resources to create parades, make music, hang twinkling lights, and decorate trees in the town square where they may select a star that holds the request of a needy boy or girl that they have the power to fulfill. Having neighbors help neighbors feels nice inside. Watching adults and community leaders going out of their way to make others happy, even for those they don't know, is a lovely lesson for children to learn.

[i] http://gilmichelini.com/acceptable-list-songs-public-school-winter-concerts/

Bob Hope quote

My idea of Christmas,
whether old-fashioned or modern,
is very simple: loving others.
Come to think of it,
why do we have to wait for Christmas to do that?

Bob Hope

https://www.searchquotes.com/search/Gay_Christ-
mas/#ixzz6Z4tk63s9

Chapter 17

Santa in Contemporary Events

The Dilemma

Is Santa just for little children and older adults? What about young adults and the young in spirit? What is happening in social media, in movies, videos, and music to make Santa Claus dead or alive? I wanted to find out.

What I Discovered

It's clear that Santa Claus has brought decades of joy to millions of people. People are already taking into their own hands the transformation of Santa Claus. This is especially obvious when we look at the fun that young people are creating around him. To them, Santa is no longer a fat old white man but a symbol of fun and engagement with life. As we look at his transformation, consider some of the most obvious examples of his contagious attraction. These include Santa Con, Santa races, Santa conferences, and how Santa Claus is portrayed in films, video games, and music.

Santa Con

Santa Con is officially described as a charitable, non-political, nonsensical Santa Claus convention that happens once a year to spread absurdist joy.[i] It is also known as a pub crawl that occurs in cities all across the world where people dress up in some sort of Santa attire like elves, reindeer, Father Christmas, St. Lucy, Snegurochka or dress in some representation that embodies the joyful Santa Spirit. It started in 1994 and is so popular that it is now an annual event. Santa Con New York is reported to be the largest with thousands attending, but there are over 300 Santa Con events in more than 40 countries.

Santa Con is an attempt to build a sense of community at the local level, as the organizers work with police officers, bars and restaurants, business and government leaders to construct a charitable event in the name of Santa Claus where everyone who signs up to attend is committed to fun, generosity, and appropriate behavior. But it builds community beyond geographic boundaries through crafty websites, apps, videos, photo galleries, and even a Santa Con Songbook. Their events can be occurring all around the world, but members attending Santa Con can communicate with other Santas everywhere. This collective bonding in the spirit of charity for children and fun for adults has attracted thousands of Santa Clauses.

The recommended Santa Code is for people to wear a full head to toe Santa suit or other appropriately themed Santa type costume – not just a Santa hat. Santa Clauses must donate to the Santa Con charity, or other suitable charities that seek to promote the Santa Spirit. They are to be kind to children and make them laugh and go out of their way to be thoughtful to them. People who attend Santa Con are to spread joy and peace - not terror, vomit, trash, or illegal behavior. They are not to fight with others and are to be respectful to the police, who are asked to be good partners in Santa Con. Santas must be of legal drinking age and are encouraged to tip bar staff generously. Organizers for Santa Con have tried to set standards to ensure that this event will generate donations to charities to help children, to be generous to wait-staff, to be respectful to policies and communities, while they are having fun. For instance, in Figure 1 there is a tongue-in-cheek admonishment for everyone to behave.

There are mixed reviews of Santa Con. Some of the Santas at Santa Con have on occasion tipped too much holiday cheer. There are reports that some of them have misbehaved.[ii] The majority of reports on social media indicate that it is a very fun time and the heavy charitable theme should not be discounted because a few people don't act in the Santa spirit. It is important to remember that such individuals are Santa posers who are not acting in good faith with carrying out the Santa Spirit. It is therefore not Santa that is responsible for the problem, but individuals. The fact that there is an international movement of young people who give to charities that will support children's well-being in the name of Santa, while they are having fun, seems to have many positive attributes to consider.

Santa Claus Races

Fun and fitness go together today. Holiday road races have become common, such as Turkey Trots at Thanksgiving, a 6.66 mile run at Halloween in Salem, Massachusetts (home of the famous witch trials), Krampus runs, and Santa Claus races. At Santa races, runners are encouraged to wear Santa attire, and their registration fees and sponsor donations are usually donated to charity to help the needy during the December holidays.

Races can be of different lengths to accommodate runners of different ages and abilities. For instance, there is a Lil' Elf Run of 100 yards all the way to Santa marathons and half-marathons. Most races tend to be 5K or 10K distances. One of the best known is the Santa Claus half-marathon at the North Pole, Alaska which goes past places like the Santa Claus House, St. Nicholas Drive, Kris Kringle Drive, and Snowman Lane. Honoring that the Santa spirit can exist at any time, their run occurs not in December but August. The Santa Hustle [iii] is another well-advertised race that is promoted as a race series, but there are also courses known as the Santa Shuffle, Santa Run, Santa Stampede, Santa Dashes, Run for a Claus, or the Great Santa Run. There are Santa races occurring around the world, with some famous ones occurring in Rovaniemi, Finland; Newry, Maine; Santa Run Tasmania; Tokyo, Japan; or Madrid, Spain. These races are not to be confused with the computer game app, the Santa Claus Race, or the Tehachapi, Santa Claus Grand Prix bicycle race.

There are also other Santa or winter-festival themed events found around the world. Some people dressed up as

Santa Claus can be found doing Penguin or Polar Plunges and going into frigid waters for a cause. These community-wide events where people join together dressed in holiday garb can be found in California, Kentucky, New York, New England, and in cities like Zurich or Berlin. The number of Santa-inspire community events found around the world are countless and focused on sharing joy, fun, and charity – which are foundational to carrying on the spirit of Santa in his original form.

Santa Claus Conferences

There are hundreds of conferences dedicated to the spirit of Santa Claus that occur around the world. The largest and most famous is the World Santa Claus Conference (WSCC) that has been held annually since 1957 in Denmark's Dyrehavsbakken or Bakken amusement park, outside of Copenhagen. Thousands of Santas converge there in July to do trainings, conduct business, network, enjoy the amusement park and have a jolly good time.

Other major conferences in the US are sponsored by FORBES, or the Fraternal Order of Real Bearded Santas, IBRBS, or the International Brotherhood of Real Bearded Santas, or the Santa Family Reunion. These organizations have thousands of members each, and they focus on networking, training, and having fun. The Discover Santa conference held in Branson, Missouri, boasts that it is the world's largest Santa Claus convention. It lasts for five days and draws around 750 Santas and is a networking and trade show, and designed to be a good time for those who attend and those who watch.

Films and the Construction of Santa Claus's Image

Social media guru John Herman of New Hampshire notes that a legend is someone who's dead but can live on through the stories we tell about them. Books, poems, music, and film have all helped Santa to live across generations. Movies create images that burn in our memories for generations. Perhaps the most important classic film promoting the spirit of Santa (and Macy's Department Store) was the 1947 Miracle on 34th Street, starring child-actress Natalie Wood. The film highlights how a hard-hearted little girl comes to soften and believe in magic, hope, love, and Santa Claus. It has been remade, but the 1947 classic has an untouchable charm. Likewise, Bing Crosby's movie, White Christmas, never fails to bring a tear to the eye as a cast of characters goes out of their way to be secret Santas to make a retired general happy. And of course, by bringing joy to others, the main characters discover love and joy for themselves.

There have been many animated films promoting Santa Claus, like Burl Ives's Rudolph the Red-Nosed Reindeer, where Santa comes to befriend a poor little reindeer who is different and belittled by the other reindeer. The spirit of Santa is present in A Charlie Brown Christmas, and the joy and altruism of Christmas is present in a Sesame Street Christmas. The Grinch reminds us that even cold, rotten people can find goodness when their hearts grow when invaded by the Santa spirit that children naturally carry within themselves. The less known Emmet Otter's Jug-Band Christmas has puppets sharing their Santa spirit. And don't forget Fred Astaire in Santa Claus is Coming to Town.

Dicken's Christmas Carol keeps getting remade as filmmakers try to find new and different ways to promote the same message. Mr. Magoo's Christmas Carol is quite charming, as is A Muppet Christmas Carol. Bill Murray takes a different spin with it as Scrooged as does Jim Carrey in Robert Zemeckis' A Christmas Carol. George C. Scott plays a rather dark version of the film - but then there is Mickey (Mouse's) Christmas Carol for the Disney that's in all of us. There are other versions of the Dicken's carol as well, and no doubt we can anticipate more in the future.

My personal favorite Santa movie has always been Santa Claus: The Movie. Dudley Moore plays a well-intended elf trying to please the kindly Santa (David Huddleston) as Jon Lithgow plays the evil spirit of materialism and corporate exploitation of Santa. I also adore Love Actually, which only remotely has a Santa reference, but certainly sends forward a lovely message in a contemporary style.

The Polar Express takes us to the magical North Pole to meet a kindly Santa. Then there are sentimental Santa movies like Prancer in which a reindeer is a leading character. Home Alone I is a classic, with an adorable Macaulay Culkin in the lead, who shows that family is the most important gift. A Christmas Story is now older but we all still remember not to ask Santa for a BB gun for fear a child could shoot their eye out with it. Elf, starring Will Farrell has created an image of a kindly Santa that we try hard to impress with our goodness. Tim Allen's The Santa Clause has done for countless more. Allen's depiction of Santa is curious because he epitomizes how an average person can become a real and true Santa Claus. In the film, Ernest Saves Christmas (1988), a total dolt is able to help Santa, meaning we all could too. National Lampoon's Christmas

Vacation reminds us how someone as bumbling as Clarke Griswold can also be a Santa if you have a good heart and try very hard to make others happy.

Santa's association with unsavory characters has also become part of the Santa film genre, in an apparent fight between good and evil. One of the first major examples was Mel Blanc's 1979 film, The Fright Before Christmas, in which the Tasmanian Devil dons Santa Claus' garb and hops into his sleigh. Meanwhile, Bugs Bunny is reading to his nephew, Twas the Night Before Christmas, when the Devil "Santa" shows up. Saving or helping Santa has been something that all kinds of mythical characters do, such as Yogi Bear, the Family Circus, Inspector Gadget, and in films like Santa and the Ice Cream Bunny (1972), which is complete with fantasy figures like Thumbelina. In Elmo Saves Christmas (1996), a red furry puppet is engaged in a complicated plot to help Santa, along with the help of the Easter Bunny. The classic 1964 film, "Santa Claus Conquers the Martians, shows that Santa can be mobilized to fight even extraterrestrial enemies.

There is an entirely different picture of Santa being depicted in recent years. That picture of his attributes to be self-serving, cruel, a drunkard, a pedophile, a liar, poser, fake, and embracing most values that parents do not want their children to adopt. There are "scary" films in which Santa is either the main character or makes a token appearance, like Tim Burton's Nightmare Before Christmas, Gremlins, Jack Frost, or Black Santa. There are off-beat Santa depictions like in A Very Harold and Kumar Christmas, and Arnold Schwarzenegger Santa in Jingle All The Way, Vince Vaughn as Santa's brother in Fred Claus, and you'll surely want to watch Santa Claus Conquers the Martians. Santa is sometimes shown as corrupt and evil, like in horror and slasher films, such as Satan Claws (1996) or Tales from The Crypt (1972), in which a woman is terrorized by a maniac in a Santa Claus suit on Christmas Eve. There is a Bad Santa, and a murdering Santa in Silent Night, Deadly Night or you can watch a heavily-muscled anti-Santa who was cursed into being nice and delivering presents for 1000 years in Santa's Slay. There are drunk Santas, stealing Santas, criminal Santas, dirty-ole-men Santas, Santas who are lusty around women and potential pedophiles around children. Then there are films like The Lobo Paramilitary Christmas Special (2002), in which the Easter Bunny hires Lobo to kill Santa Claus.

The plots of some of these films are so far-fetched that while they are fun, they are difficult for even the smallest child to take seriously. Yet all of these films keep alive in our minds what Santa looks like and what he is about. So one can't help but wonder - what is the bigger purpose behind these shifts?

Santa Video Games

The video game industry has also sought to capitalize on the like-ability and lucrative-ability of Santa Claus. There are many games directed at children as a large consumer group. Some for younger children include Santa Claus Little Helpers, Crazy Santa Adventure Games, Santa Claus Mania Games, or Santa Mission.

Older adolescents, teens, young adults, and older adults find Santa Claus is marketed to them in adventure, often violent games. The website WIRED finds popular games that feature Santa include: *Santa Claus Saves Earth*, where he is trapped by an evil fairy who wants to keep Christmas from coming; *Clay Fighter 63 1/3* in which Santa Claus cameos as Sumo Santa in a Mortal Kombat type game. In *Christmas Nights*, there is a Santa-esque figure in a red suit, in *Sam & Max* there's a creepy, gun-wielding Santa trying to slip into houses at night, and in *ToeJam & Earl* the game focuses on Santa's gift-bringing ability.

Santa can be found in other games like *Dead Rising 4* where he becomes an ax-wielding Sadistic Claus; in Secret of Mana, Santa is turned into a mean boss called Frost Gigas because kids no longer believe in him anymore while in Rockstar's *Bully: Scholarship Edition*, when players are asked to destroy a more traditional Santa's Castle found in Bullworth Town, as well as setting up a back alley Santa's grotto. Santa is the star in Daze Before Christmas. In the game *Saints Row 4* DLC *How the Saints Save Christmas*, players are tasked with saving Santa Claus and have to contend with beheaded reindeer, an evil version of Santa Claus, and Matrix-like simulations. Not to be missed is *World of Warcraft's* Greatfather Winter, a gift-bringer who wears a red robe and has a white beard at the Feast of the Winter Veil celebration or *Gex3: Deep Cover Gecko* where players have to defeat an evil Santa.

What I Concluded

It is clear that people around the world find pleasure in playing Santa Claus. I would guess that most of them do not regard Santa to be a religious figure but a secular one designed to help lift people's spirits as they have fun. Whether going to a Santa Con event, doing a Santa-themed road race, Polar Plunge, or attending a conference, the uniting themes are twofold – building community and networking with others and increasing opportunities for joy. People are creating these events spontaneously on their own. They are not formed by governments or major institutions or organizations.

The film, music, and video game industries are actively engaged in using Santa Claus for financial growth. While many continue to support his altruistic, fun side, the juxtaposition of portraying Santa as evil, crazy, alcoholic, violent, or sex-obsessed have been money-makers for businesses. But they have also painted a new and different picture of Santa Claus, one that reinforces other social transformation trends, some of which are antithetical to promoting the Santa spirit.

Santa Claus speaks to us because he fulfills some universal human needs – connection, adventure, and joy. It is important that we see that the transformation of Santa Claus away from a singular person and that anyone can be a Santa is already underway. We also want to figure out what dominant message we want him to send.

Notes:

[i] https://santacon.nyc/ and https://www.cnn.com/2019/12/14/us/santacon-nyc-trnd/index.html

[ii] https://nymag.com/tags/santa-con and https://www.santacon.info/locations.html

[iii] https://santahustle.com/

Mary Engelbreit quote

For Christmas,
Give your heart.

Mary Engelbreit

Believe. 1997. Andrew McMeel Pub.

Chapter 18

Santa Around the World

The Dilemma

Is Santa Claus now a mostly United States character? To what degree has he been accepted as a positive figure around the world? I knew he had European roots, but where else? I was surprised by how far his beloved-ness had spread around the world.

What I Discovered

Santa Claus seems to exist everywhere. He goes by different names, arrives on different days, dresses differently, but everywhere he brings children small gifts and joy. The Santa character can appear independently as a secular figure and is often associated with selling items, as global commerce is a huge industry. Santa is also used by families and communities to bring presents and serve as a central figure around festivities and celebrations. Many cities build large events around the arrival of Santa Claus, with him coming by sleigh, boat, helicopter, train, being escorted by horses, reindeer, kangaroo, elves, dancers, singers, or theatrical performers.

How Santa came to countries that did not originally celebrate him seems to be an influence of several key factors. One is the global expansion of advertising and business, as companies are ever-seeking to develop new markets and consumers. For instance, pictures of Santa Claus drinking a Coca-Cola can be found all around the world. Another factor is the expansion of Christianity around the world. Missionaries have gone far and wide to introduce this religion to populations and as Christianity and Christmas became interlinked, the insertion of gift-giving and Santa occurred. Governments introduced Santa to new populations, like in World War I's Santa ship, World War II's soldiers like Jim Yellig who made Christmas parties for children around the world, or during the Korean War when Christmas was introduced to residents of South Korea. Immigration has always been a big factor in the dissemination of Santa Claus, as we have seen with the expansion of pagan traditions to new nations or how Santa Claus was brought to New York in the early construction of the USA. Intermarriage has spread Santa when people introduce his presence into new family traditions. Social media has made the world smaller as it is easy to share information that is common in one area with people in other places. Websites can be shared everywhere with a click, making it easy to transfer Santa related games, films, music, or events like Santa Con globally. There is, thus, no one single factor leading to how Santa got spread. One thing is for certain – Santa Claus has become a global icon that is here to stay.

It would have been fun if I had been able to travel around the world to see first-hand how Santa Claus is handled by countries, but that would have been very expensive and time-intensive to get to so many places all in a short period of time, as I do not have Santa's ability to travel the world in a single night. Also, with the pandemic in full-force, traveling is not recommended. Therefore, I was limited to what I knew first-hand from my previous travels, contacts with international friends and colleagues, or what I could find online or in libraries.

The bottom line is that Santa is always seen as a secular character. He does come around the winter solstice time, but that can range from early December through the first week of January. The common theme everywhere is that he is associated with happiness. He may bring presents, but this is not required. Santas can merely show up at community events, in stores, be found walking down the street with an entourage of helpers like elves or community friends, or he could emerge at family functions. It does not seem like he shows up at churches or at religious services. Santa is more likely to be found in developed nations rather than those that are developing. This is probably because developed nations have more embedded commercial enterprises to advertise and sell items, and residents may have more discretionary income to purchase gifts, decorations, and festive foods. There is, thus, a clear separation between the spiritual and the secular when it comes to Santa around the world.

Many countries regard Christmas as a religious time and do not engage in many of the secular practices, like gift-giving, decorations, or frivolity. As a religious time, it is regarded as a time of serious, spiritual contemplation. People acknowledge the holiday by going to church services and being with their loved ones. In some more traditional nations, Santa does not play a major part in holidays, and when he does he is seen as a separate entity rather than a religion-associated figure.

There hasn't been an intense or comprehensive study of the role of Santa Claus internationally. Almost always he is described in conjunction with how a country celebrates Christmas. For instance, the website Why Christmas (https://www.whychristmas.com/cultures/) has links to how the holiday is celebrated in many countries. I recommend that people go to websites like this or: https://www.whychristmas.com/cultures/http://www.factmonster.com/ipka/A0877748.html, http://www.myuniversalfacts.com/2006/11/
names-for-santa-claus-around-world.html,
http://en.wikipedia.org/wiki/List_of_Christmas_gift-bringers_by_country to learn how individual countries celebrate their holidays. There is too much variation to reasonably discuss here.

But one thing is for sure – all around the world countries have adapted their winter solstice celebrations to be in keeping with their culture, history, and traditions. They all have the theme of community benefit, emotional and social up-lift, generosity of spirit and resources, and family bonding. Foods, music, and how the ways holidays are acknowledged have great variability around the planet that seem so wonderful that I have a desire to visit them all.

The introduction of Santa Claus – or Santa Claus type characters – seems to be universal, according to multiple lists I found, such as http://robslink.com/SAS/democd96/christmas_gift_bringers.htm or https://en.wikipedia.org/wiki/List_of_Christmas_and_winter_gift-bringers_by_country. Look at all the places he's found, and all the names he goes by!

Afghanistan: *Papa Noël* (Arabic: ???? ???? *baba noel*); *Baba Chaghaloo*
Albania: Babadimri
Armenia: Gaghant Baba
Argentina: *Papá Noel, El Niño Dios*
Azerbaijan: *Șaxta Baba* ("Froze Dad")
Austria: *Christkind* ("Christ child")
Australia: Santa Claus, "Father Christmas" and "Saint Nick".
Belgium: "Santa Claus" is called *Père Noël* or Saint Nicholas by French speakers aor *Kerstman* ("Father Christmas") or Sinterklaas by Dutch speakers.
Bolivia: *Papá Noel, El Niño Dios*
Bosnia: *Djed Božićnjak* or *Božić Bata* for Christians, *Djed Mraz* for Muslims, and *Djed Mraz* or Deda Mraz brings gifts to children on New Year's Eve.
Brazil: *Papai Noel* ("Father Christmas"), *Bom Velhinho* ("Good Old Man")
Bulgaria: Дядо Коледа *(Dyado Koleda*, "Grandpa Christmas"), Russian-borrowed version of Дед Мороз *(Djed Moroz*, "Grandpa Frost")

Canada: Santa Claus (among English speakers), *Le Père Noël* ("Father Christmas") among French speakers

Chile: *Viejito Pascuero* ("Old Man Christmas")

China: *Shengdan laoren* (Traditional Chinese: ????, Simplified Chinese: ????, Cantonese: *sing daan lo jan*, pinyin: *shèngdànlǎorén* literally, "The Old Man of Christmas"), Dun Che Lao Ren ("Christmas Old Man")

Colombia: *El Niño Dios* ("God child"), Papa Noel

Costa Rica: *San Nicolás* or *Santa Clos*, *Colacho* (from "San Nicolás"), the *Niño dios* ("Child God," meaning Jesus)

Croatia: *Djed Božićnjak* ("Grandpa Christmas"), *Djed Mraz* ("Grandpa Frost"), *Mali Isus* ("Baby Jesus") for religious Christians, *Sveti Nikola* ("Saint Nichlaus") brings gifts on 6 December.

Czech Republic: *Ježíšek* ("Baby Jesus")

Denmark: *Julemanden* ("The Christmas Man")

Dominican Republic: *Santa Clos/Papá Noe*. Gifts are given by The Three Kings (*Los Tres Reyes Magos*) on Epiphany (6 January)

Ecuador: *El Niño Dios* ("God child"), *Papá Noel*

Egypt: *Papa Noël* (Arabic: ???? ???? *baba noel*)

Estonia: *Jõuluvana* ("Old Man of Christmas")

Finland: *Joulupukki* ("Yule Goat")

France: Le *Père Noël* ("Father Christmas")

Germany: *Weihnachtsmann* ("Christmas Man") or *Christkindle* ("Christ Child") (in southern Germany) brings the gifts on Christmas Eve. *Nikolaus* is celebrated on 6 December.

Greece: Άγιος Βασίλης ("Saint Basil")

Herzegovina: Deda Mraz

Hong Kong: ???? (jyutping: *sing3 daan3 lou5 jan4* (literally, "Christmas Old Man"), Santa Claus, Saint Nicholas, Father Christmas

Hungary: Angels bring Christmas gifts from baby Jesus (*"Jézuska"* or *"Kis Jézus"*). Mikulás ("Nicholas") is not a part of Christmas but on Dec. 6 puts candy in children's shoes which are to be polished and put in the window.

Iceland: *Jólasveinar.* In Icelandic folktales, there are 13 Santa Clauses.

India: Tamil: *Christmas Thatha* ("Christmas Grandpa"), ????? ?????? (in southern India) J*ingal Bell*, Santa Claus, Telugu: Thatha ("Christmas Old Man") Marathi: *Natal Bua* ("Christmas Elder Man")

Indonesia: Santa Claus or *Sinterklas*

Iran: *Papa Noël* (Arabic: ???? ???? *baba noel*)

Iraq: Vader Kersfees

Ireland: *Daidí na Nollag* ("Father Christmas")

Israel: ????? ???? (Santa Claus in Hebrew letters). Citizens may or may not recognize Santa.

Italy: *Babbo Natale* ("Father Christmas"), *Gesù bambino* ("Baby Jesus"), St. Nicholas; on Epiphany *La Befana* puts treats in socks the children have hung near the fireplace); *Saint Lucy* brings gifts to children on her feast day, December 13.

Jamaica: Santa Claus

Japan: ??????? (*Santa Kuroosu,* or *Santa-san*) or Hoteiosho (a god or priest who bears gifts)

Korea: ?? ??? (*Santa Harabeoji* or "Grandfather Santa"). South Korea celebrates Chuseok as a family Thanksgiving time, and Seollal as the lunar new year.

Latvia: *Ziemassvētku vecītis*

Liechtenstein: *Christkind*

Lithuania: *Kalėdų Senelis*
Luxembourg: *Kleeschen*
Macedonia: *Dedo Mraz*
Malta: San Niklaw
Mexico: *Santo Clós, El Niño Dios, Los Tres Reyes Magos*
Netherlands: *Kerstman* ("Christmas Man") or *Sinterklaas* (December 5).
New Zealand: Santa Claus, Father Christmas
Norway: *Julenissen*
Paraguay: *Papá Noel, El Niño Dios*
Peru: *Papá Noel*
Philippines: Santa Claus, *Los Tres Reyes Magos* ("The Three Kings")
Poland: *Święty Mikołaj* ("Saint Nicolas")
Portugal: *Pai Natal* ("Father Christmas")
Puerto Rico: *Jesús Christmas, Los Tres Reyes Magos* (The Three Kings Day), *Santa Clos*.
Romania: *Moş Crăciun* ("Old Man Christmas"), *Moş Gerilă* ("Old Man Frost," *Ded Moroz, Moş Nicolae* ("Old Man Nicholas")
Russia: Дед Мороз *(Ded Moroz*, "Grandpa Frost"), Чысхаан *(Chyskhaan*: "Lord of the Cold"), Sakha Republic (Yakutia), *Yamal Iri* ("Grandpa of Yamal"), and *Babushka*.
Scotland: *Bodach na Nollaig* (Scots Gaelic: "Old Man of Christmas"), Daidaín na Nollaig
Serbia: *Deda Mraz (*Деда Мраз*:* "Grandpa Frost"), *Božić Bata (*Божић Бата*:* "Christmas Brother")
Slovakia: *Dedo Mraz* ("Grandpa Frost") , *Ježiško* ("Baby Jesus")
Slovenia: *Bozicek*
South Africa: *Sinterklaas*, Father Christmas, Santa Claus, Vader Kersfees

Spain: *Papá Noel* ("Father Noel"), the *Tió de Nadal* in Catalonia, *Olentzero* in the Basque Country, *Apalpador* in some areas of Galicia, *Esteru* and *Anjanas* in Cantabria, and *Anguleru* in Asturias. More common and traditional Christmas present-giving figures in Spain are *"Los Reyes Magos"* ("The Three Kings", "Magi").

Sri Lanka: *Naththal Seeya*

Sweden: *Jultomten* ("The Yule/Christmas Gnome")

Switzerland: *Christkind*

Syria: *Papa Noël* (Arabic: ???? ???? *baba noel*)

Taiwan: ???? or ????? (both literally "The Old Man of Christmas")

Tatarstan: *Qış Babay/Кыш Бабай* ("Winter Grandfather")

Thailand: ซานตาคลอส (Santa Claus)

Turkey: *Noel Baba* ("Father Noel")

Turkmenistan: *Aýaz baba*

Ukraine: *Святий Миколай* (*Sviaty Mykolay*, "Saint Nicholas")

United Kingdom: Father Christmas did not originally bring gifts; Santa Claus does

United States: Santa Claus, Kris Kringle, Saint Nicholas, or Saint Nick. In Hawaii, he is known as Kanakaloka.

Uruguay: *Papá Noel, El Niño Dios*

Uzbekistan: *Ayoz Bobo* ("Frost Grandpa"), *Qor Bobo* ("Snow Grandfather")

Venezuela: *Niño Jesús* ("Child Jesus"), *San Nicolás* ("Santa"), depending upon the region

Vietnam: *Ông Già Nô-en* (literally, "The Old Man of Christmas")

Wales: *Siôn Corn* in Welsh

What I Concluded

Santa Claus has been transformed to fit into the culture and lives of people around the world. There are some common themes to his character that incorporate joy, altruism, and community-building. There are a lot of cultural variability factors, however, as parents around the world have figured out how to adapt his attributes into something meaningful for their children. He goes by different names and styles, but the fundamental characteristics remain the same.

It doesn't seem like children in many parts of the world deal with the "is Santa real?" question the way US parents seem obsessed. They have been taught to enjoy him without thinking that he is a singular real person. Parents appear to have been liberated from the "truth and lies" dilemma about Santa. It seems like we may have something to learn from them about this.

Antoine de Saint-Exupery quote

It is only with the heart that one can see rightly

what is essential is invisible to the eye.

Antoine de Saint-Exupery

The Little Prince. 1943. Reynal and Hitchcock

Part 3 Who Will Santa Become Tomorrow?

Chapter 19

Santa In Transformation

The Dilemma

Santa Claus has never been a static character – his entire history reflects one of social transformation. Starting back with the winter solstice festivals around the world, the influence of the Greeks and Romans, his cooptation by the church, to his distribution and dissemination around the world, he is constantly "under construction", even today. Given contemporary social unrest around issues of race, gender, nationality, and class, who Santa Claus has been in the past may not fit who Santa should be in the future. It's time for him to be re-imagined so that he continues to be relevant and useful in today's world.

I've observed that the debate about Santa isn't really about Santa at all; rather, it is an argument that is far greater, much more philosophic, and very political. He is the target of a misplaced debate about the role of religion, acceptance, materialism, politics, cultural diversity, and belief in contemporary society. The debate over Santa has little to do with the character himself and much more to do with the changing values of cultures in transition. Who was he in the past and what did he represent? Who is he today? And where do we want Santa to be headed?

What I Discovered

A rich and diverse history of Santa exists. Historical facts, as they can best be understood, will help us to decide how we want to answer the question of who is Santa Claus since he has been many things to many people. Beyond historical facts is our own personal experience with Santa Claus. How we came to view him when we were children has a lot to do with how we see him today. But so do major social forces. Let's take a look at them.

Reasons Why Santa's Gotta Go

There are reasons why some people think that Santa has outlived his usefulness and needs to go away. Major ones include:

Sexism and Misogyny. It doesn't take a genius to recognize that Santa Claus is always portrayed as male. He is a power-figure, wise, knows-all, can do anything, like fly around the world in a single night bringing toys for every child as he skinnies down chimneys. He is the one who makes decisions on who is naughty or nice. Mrs. Claus doesn't even have a first name; she has no life of her own except to make cookies or do things that Santa needs in order for him to be successful. Santa embodies the wide array of positive, strong-man attributes while the Mrs. embodies everything that women have come to detest about subservient females who give up their lives and identities for men.

When I investigated if I could become a member of Santa Claus credentialing societies, it was clear that I could not because I was female. I could join Mrs. Claus groups – but I am not a Mrs. nor do I want to fulfill the role that Mrs. Clauses are supposed to do. There is no reason why women can't be a Santa too.

The messages about men vs women's roles in contemporary society have changed drastically since the 1800s when Santa first gained his public persona. Do we want little boys and little girls to role-model the division of status predominant in the Claus household? I don't think so…

Racism. Santa Claus is almost always portrayed to be white. Much of the Santa history comes from northern Europe, where the skin color of people living there grew lighter as a form of environmental adaptation. Scientists have universally confirmed that race is a product of social construction since 99.9% of our DNA is the same no matter what skin color we have (Coates 2013; Gannon 2016; Genome News 2003; Jablonski 2018; Smithsonian 2020). Many of the origins of the Santa story came from other parts of the world where darker skin was common, as pointed out earlier in this book. There is therefore no legitimate reason why a Santa Claus can't have all skin hues. To keep him as white can be an example of the continuation of white supremacy. In a woke society, it is appropriate that Santa be of all racial groups.

Colonialism. While history indicates that altruistic, wise members existed in every part of the world, and while history also confirms that joyful winter solstice festivities were found in almost every community around the planet, the process by which Santa Claus has been exported to countries that never had him in what can be regarded as a form of colonialism (Shoemaker 2015). Santa colonialism in this context can be seen as advertisers strategically introducing him (and a variety of material products) into areas where Santa Claus never formally existed. This was a business model designed to attract new markets. It might also be seen as a haphazard by-product of Christian missionaries going into new areas to set up churches. Just as the Christian leaders went out to co-opt pagan and solstice festivals hundreds of years ago, it is possible that Santa Claus brought along a light-hearted, attractive appeal of Christmas, hence Christianity. I am not sure of this, but it seems that one can argue that Santa Claus has been used to promote a pseudo-colonialist consumeristic and ideological underpinnings into once Santa-free societies.

Classism and Materialism. Santa is more likely to deliver abundant material gifts to families with resources as compared to those who are financially less well-to-do. Parents who don't have available discretionary money may get into debt as they spend more than they have to make sure their children (and others) feel well-gifted at the holidays (Fields 2019; Paul 2018). Children who get little or nothing from Santa may feel penalized for not being good enough compared with wealthier peers who get lots of presents. Associating material gifting with personal value is quite troubling to me and something that socially responsible adults need to think carefully about perpetuating.

Health Messages. Some parents have reported that they think Santa sends unhealthy messages to children. The poem, The Night Before Christmas, has Santa smoking a pipe. He was used by advertisers in the past to sell a variety of cigarettes. There has been systematic action to make sure that Santa doesn't smoke anymore. The anti-smoking message seems to have taken hold in most contemporary depictions of Santa Claus. Advertisers have ensured that Coca-Cola has become the drink of choice for Santa. At one point in history, Santa's drink of choice was alcoholic. When he is given a glass of milk, proponents against the use of milk products complain. When he visits homes, he eats cookies – which means on Christmas Eve his belly must be full of sugary sweets. He is chubby, aka overweight, aka, obese. It seems that whatever Santa consumes is identified to be symbolic of a larger health concern for some group. Families seem to have a lot of discretion about whether to leave a thirsty Santa milk, a Coke, or a Guinness. As for the obesity claim, I think we need to be careful there. Many individuals have health conditions or are on medications that force them to pick up weight. The attitude that thin-is-in and fitness are good has great health benefits, no doubt. But stereotyping someone who is overweight as lazy, who eats poorly, is unfit, or doesn't care about their health is a form of discrimination.

In these days of the rise of eating disorders in children, we want to be careful about the food and health messages we send them.

Worker Exploitation. Santa's toys allegedly are elf-made in a North Pole factory. The elves live and work in the same place. It doesn't appear that they get paid or have vacation time. This is resembling of sweatshop factories throughout the world, historically and currently, where people work long and hard making objects that "the man" sells and reaps the profits from.

Ableism. Santa is never shown having an ability challenge. Yet one in four people has a disability, according to the Centers for Disease Control (2020). Children who have mobility, vision, or hearing challenges would likely be grateful to meet a Santa who did as well. Moving away from a "you must be perfect" image would be helpful for most people.

Antiquated Values. Not everyone may agree with the values that they think that Santa represents. Understanding the premise that reality is arbitrary, we know that not everyone perceives things the same way or values the same things. Depending on how one sees Santa, there may be dissent over whether values surrounding his character are appropriate ones for children today to hold. In the values argument, we must remember that adults are the ones who had Santa display certain values in the first place. Values change across time, so conscientious consideration about what values he should present would be a worthy discussion.

Reasons Why Santa's Gotta Stay

There are legitimate reasons why some people think that Santa should continue as-is or be transformed to exist in an updated way. While benefits of a Santa state of mind have been elucidated in this book, they briefly include:

Generosity. Giving to others has long been part of the winter solstice holidays. Gift-giving, sharing food, money, resources, and support are wrapped up in the Santa story. Presents are just one component of Santa's generosity theme.

Kindness. All of the Santa figures are depicted as being kind, thoughtful individuals. They are not violent in word or deed. Santa doesn't swear, yell, demean, or hurt others. His behavior is gentle, nonviolent, and well-being considered. While characters like Krampus may display aggression, Santas don't.

Joy. Being happy is a desirable human state of being. We all long to be happy. Santa and the things he brings, from toys, sweets, music, books, and creative opportunities, are designed to help bring us joy.

Equality. The traditional story is that Santa brings gifts to every child around the world. It doesn't matter where they live, how they live, or what they look like. All children are special and worthy just because they exist.

Gratitude. Santa's gift-giving teaches children not just to be altruistic to others but to also learn the attitude of gratitude. Learning to appreciate the time and effort that people put into doing nice things for others is an important thing for children to learn.

Imagination, Creativity, and Problem-Solving. The Santa story is rich with opportunities for fantasy, to use one's imagination, and be creative. The fact that one thing can have multiple meanings is an important thing for children to wrestle with. Questions like - How does he do that? – empower children to figure out the multidimensional facets of the Santa phenomenon.

Family and Community Bonding. Looking forward to the arrival of Santa Claus can bring families together by decorating, planning, and enjoying festivities. His arrival creates opportunities for working and playing together. This can also happen at the community level and facilitate the development of partnerships and collaborations as different groups of people work together for the benefit of others.

Imparting Universal Values. Santa Claus has existed for hundreds of years because he has brought something of value to people. This, I believe, is most apparent in the forms of altruism and joy. There are certain things that people around the world value of universal importance. Figuring out what they are and how to keep them alive seems vitally important for the wellbeing of children.

Symbolism in the Santa Story We Will Construct

What do we want children to learn from the Santa story? How we construct him in the future will spread not just a story about a guy who delivers toys but it will inevitably tell children a ton about what is important and how people are to treat others. It is with this intention that I believe that our transformation of the Santa story must be carefully constructed for the human rights benefit of all children.

Massachusetts English professor Dr. Melissa Juchniewicz (2007) argues that adults need to use a critical eye when considering what stories tell children. Stories create a set of social norms that children are to consider as right and appropriate. Sometimes they send hidden messages that we may not even be aware of. She asked me if the traditional Santa story subtly reinforced misogynist white supremacy in the minds of children. She pointed out how the famous Curious George stories that have been a popular-selling book for generations may send some dark messages to children:

"Take Curious George, for example, the "naughty little monkey.... The story tells the tale of a monkey who is captured and taken from his native Africa and transported to a strange world by a man defined only by a color (his yellow hat). The worst of the slavery propaganda is perpetuated by depicting the captive as childlike, troublesome, and dependent upon the man to resolve his problems. Ultimately, Curious George is grateful to this man who becomes his owner/master. Those who love the gentle, playful teaching stories might say, "Come on! There are children of color in the illustrations now. George isn't hurting anyone". But his world is a decidedly white world [while] his story plays out to avoid the obvious parallels." (2007:79)

Scholars have long analyzed not-so-hidden messages contained in fairy tales (Benediktsdottir 2014; Hodapp 2016; Todres and Higgenbotham 2016; Walansky 2020; Zipes). Stories like Sleeping Beauty, Snow White, Cinderella, and others reinforce stereotypes of women being submissive to men who will save them. Little Red Riding Hood and Hansel and Gretel's tale reeks of abuse. We thus need to be cognizant of the stories we tell children.

Critical to our determination of who Santa Claus will be in the future is our understanding of who he has been in the past. In this book, we have explored his different perceptions. If he is perceived as a person, a chubby old elf who skinnies down chimneys to bring presents on December 24/25 or is he a bearded guy in a fuzzy red suit at the mall that children can sit beside to get their picture taken? Is Santa like the jolly Coca Cola gentleman, or could he be seen in a different way? Is he a symbol of white supremacy? A drunken pedophile? Is he a mythological being who never actually existed? Was he created mostly for recreational purposes to be the highlight of parades or social gatherings? Is he a symbol of mass consumerism and materialism? Or a political symbol? Is he a symbol of Christianity, a replacement for the baby Jesus, or a representation of God himself? Could he be a secular figure who has nothing to do with religion, one who emanates from pagan or folk-traditions? The interesting thing is that we get to choose what he has been, is, and will be in the future.

Santa Claus is a symbol whose meaning has regularly changed across time, place, and culture. Santa has had different meanings in accordance with the political and ideological conditions of the day. The current discussion over Santa is no different. The Santa debate has always been a vigorous attempt by believers and nonbelievers alike to vie for their definition of reality.

When given a choice, my opinion is that we should choose what will be in the best interest of ALL children. The issue of how Santa Claus has been in the past is one thing – how Santa will be presented in the future is my big concern. If we are to take a human rights-respecting approach, it is of utmost importance that Santa is presented in a way that respects all people. This means broadening his horizons to be more inclusive to all since the message I hope Santa can deliver is one of peace, joy, respect, and generosity to all. There's room for all in the sleigh.

Sometimes he's portrayed in ways that make him seem like he's only coming to white, Western, Christian, middle-upper class children. But that's because someone made him to seem that way. He could just as easily be portrayed as coming to bring joy (and objects) to children whose characteristics were totally different. Santa could be made into a universal child-oriented character for all children of the world, irrespective of who they are, what they look like, where they live, or how rich or poor they may be. We can consider whether we want him constructed to socialize children to adhere to important social norms, such as being nice and not naughty, and to be good. But remember, we are the ones who define what is good, bad, naughty or nice – so we may want to think about what we want those universal behaviors to be. Santa can be a verb as well as a noun;

Santa can be defined as actions of kindness and generosity that are designed to make people feel joyful and loved. So Santa has been and could be, many different things including a behavior, an attitude, a person, or a thing.

According to Gittins (1997), everything, including Santa is a myth. Even

"the child is a myth, a fiction, an adult construction. So is childhood. Both, however, have become symbolically central to our culture and psychologically crucial to our sense of self. The child exists in imagery that pervades our conscious, and indeed our unconscious worlds; images of children are everywhere. They are not children we know but representations of the child designed and constructed by advertisers, television producers and photographers."

She argues that our minds are a crucial area where

"Memories of our own childhoods inform our ideas about who we think we are, who we think we once were, what we believe children are, and what we believe the child and childhood should be. ... We like to think that we are rational, logical beings who behavior consistently and coherently. Instead, we are fragmented, contradictory, complex beings. Each and every one of us consequently carries our own, usually well-hidden and frequently denied, emotional and irrational baggage relating to our own subjective experiences of having once been a child. What children mean is defined by adults who have enormous power over their perceptions of reality. ...Adult confusion between their own memories of their own lost childhood and the way in which they project myriad feelings of yearning, rage, and desire on to other children is fascinating. It is rarely acknowledged because it is seldom at a conscious level. Rather, adults tend to disguise their own needs as care or concern when their true feelings lurk in the shadows, invisible and powerful. The process is made more complex by the ways in which culture, particularly the advertising industry, represents children and make them appear simple."

Who owns the shaping of children's minds is a huge issue for contemplation. Parents greatly influence what their children believe and what they think is good and right, or bad and wrong. Adults can paint Santa as a kind and jolly wise man who cares for children and brings them presents. Their children would likely come to think that Santa is a good guy and innocently see only goodness resulting from believing in him. Parents can paint Santa as a punisher who will switch them, bring them coal, or reject them if they're not good. He can be presented as a discriminator who only cares for some children and not others. Adults can portray him as an extension of angels and baby Jesus or as Satan and an underminer of all things holy. Santa can be transformed into a view of a craftsman who helps children make things for others or as a source of commercialism who is a fountain of materialism. He can be seen as an extension of Christianity, a symbol of ecumenicalism, of secularism, or as a symbol of economic, religious, and political indoctrination that should be avoided. Santa can become anything we adults make him into. It is natural and normal that children would blindly claim their parents' views of reality (and Santa) as their own.

In this tug-of-war inside parents about whether it is OK for kids to be encouraged to believe in Santa or not, do we have the right to shape children's reality? We do this all the time. When it comes to highly emotionally-charged icons like Santa Claus, the issue is heightened. As sociologist W. I Thomas alleged, whatever we believe to be true will become real in its consequences. Parents impose their views upon their children, who in turn seek to impose upon other children. So when a non-believing child announces "there is no such thing as Santa" to children who believe there is, this may trigger an emotional response as the believing child wrestles with whether such a denial of his existence could be true. Like falling dominos, when someone shatters the Santa belief system of a child, it inevitably results in all children losing faith in the gift-bringing elf. It's pretty hard to believe in something that everyone else doesn't. As adults, we may wish to protect children's innocence and preserve their right to dream and believe in things they cannot see, but we may also want them to believe in fact and science and not to feel lied to because we told them Santa was real. We want them to have dreams but don't want them to be made fun of by their peers. Children do not live in a vacuum and they are not separate from other children, the views of adults, media, or the overarching beliefs of society. They cannot be insulated from others. We need to empower children by letting them speak for themselves, help them to have their own opinions, and shape their understanding of the world of Santa Claus as they see fit. If you ask children, they come up with their own unique, coherent ways of viewing him. Most experts feel that by age 2½ children are able to discern fantasy from reality (Wooley 2014; 2009; West 2014). Santa's reality status doesn't have to pose a problem for children since they naturally wrestle with multiple dimensions of reality on a regular basis. Santa can be seen to bring elements of joy, mystery, and excitement as children develop their thoughts in accordance with the more scientific views of reality. Allowing them the right to view Santa in their own ways has definite benefits.

We likely have different views of Santa Claus for all kinds of reasons that we have explored in this book. Santa is beloved or maligned not because of anything he inherently is because after all, he is a fantasy character. What we think about him we learned from our families, teachers, media, culture, political, and religious leaders. We all had different ones and differential exposures and experiences around the Santa figure, so it is logical that we would not perceive him in the same way. And as we see in this chapter, how Santa Claus is perceived today is different than who he has been in the past – and who he will become in the future.

What I am talking about is what sociologists call the social construction of reality (Berger and Luckman 1966). Reality is arbitrary. It's fascinating to me to see people get all riled up about Santa Claus because he is not an actual person. He only exists because we make him exist. Santa is a symbol that embodies a myriad of values, emotions, and expectations. In what is known as the Thomas Theorem, whatever we believe to be real will become real in its consequences (Thomas and Thomas 1928). If we think that Santa Claus symbolizes loving-kindness, that's what we see and will teach our children. And that is what they will believe and teach their children. If we see Santa as a tool to advance greed and consumerism, nonmaterialist parents may want their children to scoff at him. If people perceive that Jesus is Lord and think that Santa Claus is being foisted upon them as his replacement, people may resent and demean him. If we think that Santa represents Christianity and we have a negative association with that faith, it is understandable that children may be taught that he is bad. The list goes on, for generations and across time and space.

Whoever controls the mind of a child controls the future. This is a huge idea to understand. Children are socialized to view the world in particularized ways that they come to believe are natural, good, and right. Children then grow forward to protect and impose those beliefs upon others, and when they have their own children, they foist their views upon them. As a result, their children go forward to reconstruct the values they learned were important and the realities that they were taught were factual (James and Prout 2015). This is true in about every aspect of their lives. It is called the replication of society.

Maintaining order is important for families as well as societies. Having norms about how we are supposed to think and act creates a set of expectations so we know what to anticipate from one another. They increase our ability to function more smoothly. Many of the social rules to which we adhere are not written down; they are informal folkways. Social institutions, like families, schools, government, businesses or religion, develop customs and after a while, they are so ingrained that people automatically assume that they are normal, natural, and appropriate. Therefore, if Santa Claus always was present at a school or civic event and no longer was invited to participate, people may feel they were denied an experience to which they'd gotten accustomed. Likewise, if Santa was portrayed as a young, nonwhite female if she did wear a red suit and sport a fine fake beard, would people drag their feet or be outright resentful that their old traditions and expectations were being replaced by a new one? The conflict between maintaining traditional ways of doing things versus being open to the inevitability of social change is normal (Rabie 2013; Vissing 2011). Some of us are more open to personal and social transformation than others of us.

Santa Transformation Options

A common question asked when playing charades is - "Is it a person, place, or thing?" Santa is associated with all three – he is the morphing of different people, what he does is associated with different ancient festivals in a variety of places around the world, and he is associated with things like flying reindeer and stockings. He is also the embodiment of a spirit of altruism, joy, and goodness.

What we are observing with the changing nature of Santa Claus is part of a bigger social transformation. The debate over who Santa Claus was, is, and will be is a tangible, comprehensible example of the social transformation of society. The choices we have seem clear – we can kill Santa, we can keep Santa alive as is, we can give him a facelift (or more), or we can let him fade into history. More specifically:

1. We can encourage children to believe in Santa Claus and follow the traditions that have been mainstream in the homes and communities of believers for decades.
2. We can relegate Santa Claus to the fields of history, mythology, literature, art, and be seen merely as

a lovable fantasy character similar to the Easter Bunny, the Leprechaun, Valentine Cupid, Disney's Mickey Mouse, Star Wars' Obi-Wan Kenobi, or Albus Dumbledore in Harry Potter.
3. We can discourage children from believing in Santa Claus and justify this with the use of what he does being scientifically impossible or argue that he is an out-of-date figure that now is socially dangerous because he is associated with consumeristic greed, Christianity, pedophiles, machismo, or worker (elf) exploitation.
4. We can create sterile conceptions of childhood and community, where there is no place for anything seen as controversial, and where difference automatically fosters divisiveness. We can compartmentalize differences into distinct pots and handle them as such. We can handle holidays, their media coverage, decorations, and celebrations into a white-bread approach so as not to upset anyone or have individuals or institutions look as though they are biased of one group more than another. This may teach children that it's best to keep differences distinct.
5. We can create an entirely new persona or character to take the place of Santa Claus as a universal role-model of how to teach generosity, happiness, and positive values to all children everywhere. The use of media makes this entirely possible. But I am concerned that this new figure would be "owned" by some aspect of big business, some agenda-making and staking group that has its own values and ideas

that it wants to push forward. The potential for the controversy surrounding what this new character should look like is huge. Given the current-day heightened sensitivities about who or what is politically correct, I am not confident that developing a new character to replace Santa Claus will ultimately work as it pertains to promoting children's best interests as the primary and universal goal.

6. We can transform Santa to have a positive, meaningful role in the lives of all children by using him not as a person but as a symbol of altruistic spirit who teaches us to be joyful, generous, and attend to the wellbeing of others. He could be made into an inclusive, secular symbol of goodness and loving-kindness if we let him. This is what I refer to as the Santa Spirit. This is the option that I conclude is in the best interests of children – and society.

If children grow up having a positive experience of Santa, I hypothesize that they will be more likely to carry positive values and attributes forward to their children, who will pass them on to their children's children. Similarly, children who grow up having an ambivalent or negative view of what the Santa figure represents will likely replicate ambivalence or negativity to future generations. Contemplating how we come to feel the way we do about Santa Claus is a worthwhile intellectual and emotional endeavor for us because what we may discover is not just about Santa Claus, but it reflects a host of familiar, cultural, and value experiences as well that get codified around this mythical character who only really exists in our heads and maybe our hearts.

The future rests upon the ability of the children to become good stewards of the world. They need to learn about how to nurture each other, care about each other, and make sure others get what they need. Teaching tolerance is important. Role-modeling altruism and joy as families and communities come together around something delightful and loving is superb. Role-modeling intolerance, hostility, superiority, and exclusion will not create a happy world. Santa, if transformed in the ways I recommend, can provide children wonderful foundation skills that they can build on; he provides families with an annual time when they get together to create magical bonds with each other; he provides communities with the opportunity to teach tolerance and appreciation of diversity. Santa, in my opinion, should be kept alive but transformed for the children's best interests. He has the possibility of bonding individuals and cultures together around the thing that hopefully, they value most – the preciousness of children. But how should that be? Consider the following:

Tangible transformations. I've thought long and hard about what a Santa should look like. While anyone can act in the Santa Spirit at any time of year, a December holiday-bringing Santa should dress is a way that honorably acknowledges that the person is acting in that role. Santa credentialing organizations have emerged to set standards for "official" Santas, both in attire and action. They do a public service in that regard – but it seems that they may want to revise some of their appearance standards to be more inclusive. Let me explain in more detail.

How Should Santa Behave: If someone is promoting the Santa spirit, they should act in ways that glorify the best attributes and values of individuals. While it may be obvious, here is a list of Santa To Do and Don'ts that are wise for Santas to follow:

Things Santa Should Do

Be kind in word and deed
Ask questions and listen carefully
Have children sit in their own chair or stand
Smile, laugh, convey authentic joy
Use calm, soft language, patience
Respect children #1
Empower children
Don't lie
Tell the truth, but softly when necessary
Be sober and in control
Never curse or use bad language
Never refer to the child's gender or sex
Watch for parent signals
Convey fairness, equality in time
Know languages of key populations in area
Gentle interacting with children with challenges
Focus on the child's needs and sense of reality
Be sensitive to social class issues
Inspire gratitude and altruism

Things Santa Should NOT Do
Be mean, bossy or cruel
Ridicule children's words or actions

Hold children on lap, touch or kiss them
Frown, be grumpy, make faces
Use loud, aggressive language, say too much
Pay more attention to parents than children
Disempower children
Lie through your teeth if you feel you have to
Give misinformation if necessary
Drink, use drugs, be high, or be smoking
Swear or use inappropriate or sexual language
Call children by gendered or sexist terms
Pay no attention to parent signals
Spend more time with some children than others
Speak in English, disregard non-English speakers
Hurry along children with "challenges"
Talk about yourself, not the child or their needs
Promote getting lots of presents
Inspire greed and self-centeredness

The lists can go on and on, but I think the above creates an understanding that Santa Clauses today need to be mindful of being respectful to every child. The gender of children, even young ones, can be fluid, as can race or ability. It is impossible to tell by looking at what is going on in the body, head, or homes of children. Pushing no agenda and being a good listener is important. Inspiring and role-modeling how Santas are supposed to be is important. I saw a Santa in a wheel-chair who was so kind and loving to children that he was one of the best I'd ever seen. How empowering it was for children to recognize that Santas might have struggles too but they are able to overcome them and be happy as they give to others. Santa should never make children cry or be sad...

Clothing. There seems to be to me that a Santa "uniform" of sorts could be worn to distinguish those who are acting as Santa and those who are not. As I learned from looking at winter solstice celebrations and early gifters, the color red was commonly found. Red has the symbolism of passion, excitement, and importance. The official big red costume customarily portrayed in Coca-Cola type advertisements has an endearing history that doesn't need to be eliminated. But those big, fuzzy outfits are expensive (for the good ones) and not suitable for warm climates. The traditional Santa hat is the single-most required item of apparel and seems to me that should be maintained as a standard. There can be red outfits that appear suitable from swim trunks, running outfits, dresses, and other clothes. I'm sure the clothing industry will have an opportunity to help shape them, but so can we as individuals. People are creative and may come up with some fun and attractive designs for Santas to wear.

Beard. There is a clear distinction made in the minds of many people about the importance of growing one's own "real" Santa beard. This seems unnecessary as it excludes a great many people. As pointed out, many men cannot grow long beards or color them white. Fake beards vary in quality and design, but children don't seem to mind what they look like as much as parents. Beards are not necessary.

Gender. Despite a history of Santa being male, there is absolutely no reason why women can't be Santas. Relegating to be Mrs. Clauses is discriminatory, sexist, and out of touch with women's roles and contributions in today's society. Women are already acting in every aspect of being Santa except for being acknowledged as such. It's time to get with the times.

Race. Santas are found in every color shade of every race as we look around the world. And why not? To keep Santa white is no longer useful in an increasingly diverse society when there is a hearty history of the winter solstice and gift-bringers around the world. The concept of race itself is one of social construction, so let's construct the image in the minds of children that people of all races can be good. Santas should be symbols of inclusion, diversity, tolerance, and the best qualities of people – qualities found in every type of person.

Age. Traditional Santas are shown as elderly. Indigenous cultures honor elders for their wisdom and experience and that, in my opinion, is a lovely show of respect. Older people, especially in the US, are often pitied and ridiculed, as shown from the plethora of products on the market designed to keep people from looking "old. An elder Santa is a symbol of the benefits gained from being older. However, wisdom, kindness, and generosity are not the exclusive domain of elder people. These are attributes that can be found in people of every age. Therefore, there is no reason why younger people, even children, can't be Santas. There is plenty of room in the world for more and more people to act in the Santa spirit, so encouraging us all to act in that way could yield benefits. We all know people who are older who do not represent the altruistic, joyful, wise attributes of the traditional Santa. So give up on the age requirement. Let us all be Santas.

Helper-Companions. Historically, Santa could be accompanied by joyful elves that were nice or by scary furry figures that could hurt or eat you. Keep the scary companions away. Whoever is playing elves, reindeer, snowpeople, or other companions should adhere to the same do's and don'ts listed above.

What I Concluded

What I've learned through doing this research leads to the rational conclusion that the character of Santa Claus can help the child in all of us to believe in the potential of possibility. The arrival of Santa's visit allows us to have a moment each year when we can put aside the mundane to dream a bit, to imagine what could be, and to wonder if the impossible just maybe could be possible. Cultivating imagination, creative thinking, and problem-solving in childhood lays an essential psychological and cognitive foundation upon which these skills can be built upon as we go through life. Having a central secular character that everyone in the community or family can bond around can promote conversation, celebration, and contemplation of what's important and bring us together.

It's time for Santa to change. Change can be a good thing. Portraying him as exclusively an authentically-bearded old white man is out of touch with the changes occurring in the world. If we want Santa to be relevant for future generations, then we have to construct him as a positive, diverse figure who can take many forms so that all children can relate to goodness. Using Santa as a vehicle to enhance social divisions seems not to be in anyone's best interest, especially children. The Santa character's central attributes of trying to help people find joy and fun can lift one's spirit. The Santa character's attribute of teaching children how to give to others is important, especially in an economic-driven, individual-focused world where messages of me-me-me and gimmie-gimmie-gimmie are pushed down children's throats as normative expectations. The idea that there is someone who really listens to you, who understands what you need and want, watches out for you and has your back, and will help you to get them to the best of their ability is fundamental to the building of trust. Having hope, especially in these current days of pandemic health and economic challenge, is essential.

M. Kathleen Haley quote

I Believe in Santa
Having faith in Santa Claus
Is not for just the young,
I know I'll keep proclaiming him
As long as I've tongue.
And even though I see the gent
Unmasked before my eyes,
Reveling some familiar friend
Who's donned the quaint disguise

It doesn't change my mind a bit
I'll still believe, because
There's more than whiskers and a suit
To dear old Santa Claus.
Bright hopes there are
And dreams come true
Good cheer, unselfish sharing
Personified by gifts of love
Within the pack he's bearing
To call these angels Santa Claus
Is surely not deceiving
So I for one will never scoff
But go right on believing.

M. Kathleen Haley
In Believe by Mary Engelbreit, 1997. Andrew McMeel Pub.

Chapter 20

Rethinking Gifting

The Dilemma

Everyone I know likes getting presents. Near as I can tell, there's nothing wrong with giving or getting gifts that are honest and given with positive intentions. Symbolically, the exchange of gifts sends a message that someone has thought about what we may need or like and they wanted to help make our lives sweeter because they care about us. Presents mean that someone has gone out of their way to do for us because we are special. That's a wonderful message to deliver, irrespective of whatever the material object is.

It seems to me that the dilemma around the Santa and gifts is that parents are afraid that children will demand that Santa bring them lots and expensive gifts they can't afford. I think parents are also afraid that children's expectations for getting material objects will make them greedy, ungrateful, and thoughtless about what it took for someone to invest the time and resources necessary to giving it to them.

But Santa is a mythical character. He doesn't bring presents because he can't. He doesn't exist except in our minds. So it is our minds on which we have to zero-in on. What do we want our children to learn about gifts, and how can we use Santa or the gifting process to help them to learn positive attributes of altruism and empathy? That's what I needed to think more about.

What I Discovered

Christmas can be a wonderful time, not because of the gifts that people get but because of the gifting that occurs. Gifts are good. Seriously, everyone likes getting presents. Everyone likes getting surprised. Everyone likes to know that someone else cared enough about them to spend time, energy, and money on something that is designed just to please them. Gifting is part of every culture, and it is important for both the giver and the givee. Families like giving presents to each other; it is an expression of love, it is a desire to make those we care about happy, and it is a method of social bonding. Remember that old saying, "It is better to give than receive?" It's often true, and it is a good lesson for children to learn. Children don't know how to give, or how to graciously receive unless they are taught. Santa provides them a wonderful vehicle to learn these skills.

History of Gift-giving

In traveling back through history I found that even before the birth of Christ was officially determined by Pope

Julius in 350 AD, Europeans celebrated the Yuletide season by giving gifts and sharing food and drink. Remember the Three Wise Men? What was the mission that took them across the planet for months? To deliver gifts to the baby! The Celtic-Teutonic Druids used to make a gift of their holy plant mistletoe at the beginning of each year. In ancient Rome, gifts were exchanged during the New Year's celebrations, usually in the form of a simple, symbolic gift such as a branch from a favorite tree or gifts of foods from your garden. Among the Romans, such gifts were called 'strenae', a word said to be derived from the goddess of luck, Strenia. The idea was to share something that you had in abundance to bring good luck to the giver in the coming year. Remembering people who you care about during the winter holidays is a tradition that has long and cherished roots.

As Christianity gained popularity and began to spread, early church leaders believed that the custom of the gift was antithetical to its teachings, so they prohibited the custom, calling it "pagan." But gifting was such a major part of life for most people that the custom continued, even to the point of people resorting to gift-giving behind closed doors. Religious leaders grew to accept the custom and incorporate it into holiday rituals. Getting holiday gifts is now an engrained part of the Christmas tradition, and it seems linked with being good, in the Santa decision of whether to reward those who are "naughty or nice".

Early Puritans looked for signs that people were blessed by God, and they used the presence of material objects as a tangible indication. The notion was that if you were seen as good in the eyes of God, you would get rewarded. These rewards were having many children, lots of land, a successful business, and many lovely material objects, such as fine clothes, a luxurious carriage pulled by magnificent horses, or a nice home that was well furnished. If you were not blessed by God, the Puritans thought you may be punished with drought, infertility, death, disability, or bad luck. This is why the Puritan Ethic reinforces the notion of hard work; if you work hard you have a better chance of making money, which means that it will seem that God loves you better than people who don't (Weber 1958). This relationship between religion and the development of materialism (i.e.- capitalism) has been well documented by historians. Therefore, there is a long tradition that if you are seen as good, you will get money, land, big families, fancy houses, lots of clothes, things, hence gifts. Santa merely builds upon this pre-existing view. Just as adults strive, even today, to be rewarded for doing a good job, children are taught that if they do what they're supposed to, they may get rewards, prizes, or gifts.

Santa is the quintessential figure representing nurturing and generosity. He lives in the cold, bitter arctic world of the North Pole, yet he conveys warmth, jolliness, and cheerfulness, with his cookie-baking wife and hard-working elves seem happy. Despite his work-ethic, some people are opposed to Santa because they allege that he is the symbol of crass materialism and the cause of conspicuous consumption.

Some parents long for the beauty of simpler times and they convey a desire to shed the consumerism of today with a desire to return to 'the good ole days'. For instance, in Laura Ingalls Wilder's book, *Little House on the Prairie,* the children received a shiny tin cup, a peppermint stick, a heart-shaped cake and one new penny. They were thrilled with these treasures. But we don't live in Pioneer days anymore. Gifting adheres to social contexts and conventions. It is my belief that most parents attempt to instill moderation, benevolence, generosity, and gratitude into their children, and they do try to role-model these characteristics. But I also believe that sometimes parents get confused about how to balance the types of gifts they give to children, with some categories of gifts being forgotten, while other areas are over-gifted.

Parents often turn to books and media to help them out with this. This could be one reason why Dr. Seuss's famous book, *The Grinch that stole Christmas*, is so popular. It teaches that the meaning of the season is far more important than presents; when the Grinch takes all the gifts away, Christmas continues to come. The people of Whoville learn that love, sharing, and caring are what is important, even though gifts are fun to get. Parents, like Seuss, hope that children will get the message.

Theories on Gifting

Giving to others is encouraged in what social scientists call "exchange theory." When someone gives the child a gift, the child may feel they want to give something to them in return. This norm of reciprocity is thought to be a universal norm that is present in most societies. Santa Claus's gifts are a variation of the notion of paying goodness forward, in which you do something nice for someone and hope they will be nice to someone else in return, instead of only giving a gift if someone else gives you one first. Santa gives presents, parents give presents, and children learn that they are responsible for making sure to give other people presents as well. The issue is not the gift, but the gifting behavior.

The research is pretty clear about how to help children to learn empathetic, altruistic behavior. Work by Kathleen Cotton (1992) and Nancy Eisenberg (1983) have been especially instructive in helping parents to realize that their own behavior molds that of their children. The best way to help a child to become altruistic is to model that behavior. Talk is cheap; it is the action that counts. Showing children how to incorporate altruistic behavior into their lives is far more effective than merely telling them to do so. Santa Claus is a man of action; he practices what he preaches. And he makes giving to others so much fun that he encourages children to try gifting people at other points in time during the year. The Santa spirit is pervasive, saturating the child's sense of self as they internalize the norm of altruistic behavior.

Christmas gift-giving is essential to creating family bonds and solidarity. Parents devote a large part of their resources to educating, caring for, and entertaining their children. Some parents argue that materialism, greed, and selfishness is at the heart of Christmas, and Santa is the God of materialism and hedonism (Belk 19889; Caplow 1984). While there are certainly a lot of pressures on parents, it does not appear that Santa, a mythical character, is to blame for materialism. His social construction over time conveys that his character can be used to teach children to give and receive gifts, neither of which are bad things. Altruistic behavior, or the giving of oneself or one's things in order to benefit others even though they may not receive anything tangible in return, is a sophisticated behavior. Yet it is one that children must learn in order to be responsible members of society. People who have integrated a sense of altruism care more about others. When we genuinely care about others, we are more likely to "feel their pain" and find reasonable solutions when conflicts arise. This makes living in an altruistic family or society a pleasant and rewarding experience.

Altruistic behavior is termed "prosocial behavior." It is not done because the child will be rewarded for it, nor is it done because it has to be done. Altruistic giving is a voluntary, intentional act of helping others at some cost to oneself (time, effort, or money) with no expectation of any external reward. Altruistic behavior is thought to consist of several characteristics. Children perceive that their help is needed, or it will in some way make life better for someone else. They feel some social responsibility to help or give — that there is an emotional connection with the people they are considering gifting. Feelings of altruism are higher during the holiday season, when people of all ages feel more of social responsibility to help others, even when we know they are unable to reciprocate. They also must believe that they are capable of providing help or gifts. This notion of feeling empowered and competent is worthwhile to differentiate children who feel they can give from those who feel they cannot. It is a form of self-esteem, therefore providing children with the opportunities to gift others will help them to feel good about themselves, which will then flow out into other aspects of their lives.

Some child development experts indicate that children who learn giving behavior when they are very young are more likely to have altruism as a lifelong, integrated part of who they are. When young children don't learn how to give to others, it becomes harder for them to do so as they get older. Not impossible – but giving doesn't feel as comfortable or natural to them as it does to children who grew up engaging in routine altruistic behavior. Children will instill the lessons they learn when they are young about giving. Research reminds parents that the social norms encouraging responsibility and reciprocity are reinforced when children learn how to gift others. After seeing important people in their lives, like their parents, role-modeling giving behavior, altruistic behavior will be reinforced. Ultimately, with lots of occasions to witness altruistic acts and plenty of practice giving little presents to others, it is hoped that children will internalize it and make altruism a part of themselves. The old saw that "children are more likely to give what they live" is true. As children develop internal feelings of satisfaction and pride for giving, instead of for receiving, they will have made the transition into being altruistic people. Giving for the benefit of giving alone will be seen as enough – just as Santa does, and just as parents do.

Thinking about what other people may want for a gift helps children to think about who these people are as total human beings. As children mull over possible gifts, they may decide the person may not like this or that gift, but they may really appreciate something else. Social psychologist George Herbert Mead (1934) studied the necessity of teaching children to consider what life looks like from other people's points of view in a concept he called "taking the role of the other". The ability to see the world from other's perspectives is a critically important factor in social development. People do not live in isolation; they must interact and negotiate with each other about both important and minute things. If children learn that people naturally see things from different points of view and have unique histories, needs, and desires, this helps them to be less ego-centered, more altruistic, and more empathetic. If one feels empathetic, they may be better able to perceive the needs of others, and more willing to give up part of themselves in order to help them.

In order to do this, first, they have to engage in "role-playing;" in order for children to understand who they should become, they first have to try out many different roles, and consider options of motivations, needs, actions, and values. Playing Santa Claus for others is an important thing for them to do, for it teaches them to anticipate other people's needs and expectations. As children become older, they will move away from role-playing into "role-taking". They will no longer be acting out the way they think they are supposed to in order to keep true to a particular role; they will be acting out the new role-prescribed behavior because they now have adopted that behavior and role as their own. When children become parents, they will BE Santa Claus for their own children. They cannot be expected to do this successfully if they have not had experience learning how to do Santa-like things. Role-playing and role-taking are related to the development of astute thinking and have been found to help children have insight into different perspectives and it promotes genuine open-mindedness. Role taking discourages hasty and superficial problem examination and facilitates the construction of more fully elaborate and created problem-solving models. When children learn how to take the role of the other, cognitive benefits such as the discouragement of belief rigidity and the encouragement of cognitive and personal flexibility occur (Cotton 1992).

Santa and Christmas create opportunities for adults to model altruistic behavior. There are certainly many other times during the year that parents can do so, but holiday gifting is a collective social experience in which there is an expectation that all children will take time out to plan how they may gift those whom they love. When parents model altruistic behavior by helping others, children observe their actions. They may generalize from these observations and create their own ways to help others. When children receive positive reinforcement for engaging in altruistic behavior, they are more likely to keep it up in the long term and integrate it into themselves in the long run. For instance, my brother always fills holiday baskets for the needy in his community; his daughter watched him do this for years, and now, as an adult, she is part of the team that prepares and delivers these gifts.

When children gift others, they are acting as if they were Santa themselves. Pretending they are Santa is great fun for children who are the gifters. One of the children's favorite holiday gift-giving rituals is for them to play 'Secret Santas.' Children delight in trying to figure out what other children may like, and how, like St. Nicholas, to get them the gift without being caught doing so. Therefore, children are able to incorporate both the techniques and the emotional benefits of gifting from their observation of altruistic adults.

Children also benefit from the self-esteem and sense of belonging that comes with contributing to the wellbeing of others. Gift-giving during the holidays teaches children what it means to be altruistic. Concrete learning takes place when kids give up something, money or time, for the benefit of another person. As parents talk with them about why it is important to gift others, it reinforces key family, social, or religious values. Essentially, when parents teach children altruistic behavior, they lay a foundation for the establishment of good character.

Santa as Gifter

People like getting gifts but the commercialization of Christmas has gotten over-the-top. Some people are so adamantly against gifting that they have termed the holiday "Buy Nothing Day." Some religions, such as Jehovah's Witnesses, discourage their members from celebrating birthdays, or holidays such as Easter or Christmas, and they cannot accept gifts. By default, because Santa's character has been co-opted by advertisers, the cognitive dissonance reaction of "if Christmas is now commercialized and I don't like that, and since Santa is their messenger then Santa is the bringer of materialistic greed so I dislike him too" has occurred in the minds of many parents.

Christmas materialism can get offensive, to say the least. I personally avoid the malls from Nov 23 until after the first of the year. I can't find a parking space and I hate waiting in line. But I have to admit, there are often great sales right before Christmas. The decorations and music are wonderful. The selections are at their best. Mostly, people seem pretty nice and patient – both as consumers and as salespeople. Oh sure, sometimes you run into some who are grumpy but by and large, people seem pleasant as they juggle their bags full of hope that someone else will be happy. The emphasis on getting gifts, instead of giving gifts, is part of the problem. But let's face it – getting gifts is fun. Whoever said it isn't is a liar.

Let's get this clear once and for all – Santa is NOT the cause of Christmas materialism! If parents decide to go wild with their MasterCard's and buy all kinds of things they can't afford, and get things that kids actually don't need, why should Santa be blamed for their inability to control themselves? If parents focus more on the materialistic than the spiritual aspects of Christmas, is Santa to blame? Santa has become the ultimate scapegoat for adults' inability to control their spending. Santa has also become the victim for children who haven't been taught the boundaries of propriety when it comes to giving and receiving gifts. Neither Santa nor children are to blame for the crass materialism that so often gets associated with children. Do infants shake their rattles and demand new stuffed animals and pacifiers? I don't think so. Do three and four-year-olds throw tantrums when they don't get the latest "in" toy that they see on TV? Frankly, most of them are as happy with the wrapping paper and the box than what's in it. How many times have we seen children playing with the simplest and most inexpensive toys, while the complicated, expensive ones sit collecting dust? They are, literally and figuratively, too much. Adolescents and teens may ask for more expensive items, but this is part of their peer culture in which they are attempting to be acceptable and competitive in a society that glamorizes high tech, trendy, and all-too-often expensive items. But they aren't being materialistic just to "get stuff" and be greedy. This isn't it at all, usually. Most of the time when children are asking for things, it is because there is a social expectation that accompanies the gift; often the gift is the vehicle for children to achieve a much more important personal goal, like identity, respect, or importance.

When adults crab and nag at children for having a hefty list for Santa, who is the one that has bought them the gifts? Who has taught them over the years the set of expectations that they should have, and deserve, a holiday potlatch? Sorry, Mom and Dad. You can blame Fischer Price, Nike, and Sony if you like, but the reality is that companies are like cafeterias – they set forth a myriad of things from which to choose. The companies and stores have no expectation that you'll buy everything. In fact, you shouldn't. The person eating everything in sight at the cafeteria will find that soon obesity sets in, and the unhealthy side effects of consumption will ruin one's ability to function well. The same thing is with Christmas merchandise. Storekeepers expect you to pick and choose. If you can't exercise good judgment and financial control, that's not Santa's fault, it's not the store keeper's fault, and it is not the fault of your children. Look in the mirror; you know who is to blame.

But if one looks at the behavior of most families, it is clear that they do exert effort to avoid the materialism craze. This can be seen in large families when members draw names so they can limit their purchasing power. Often, an adult will draw the name of another adult who they will gift, but the adults may feel free to gift all the children since "Christmas is for kids." It is also common to see that people will set a price limit on how much people can spend on gifts for each other. It is embarrassing for all concerned when one person spends an exorbitant amount of a gift while the recipient/gifter spends little in comparison. Some families, or groups of linked people like those in clubs or social groups, may exchange gifts in a Yankee Swap routine, in which one person brings a gift without knowing who will end up with it; people swap around the collection of gifts until everyone gets something that they like. Children at school, and colleagues at work, may participate in Secret Santa activities, which both the giver and the getter enjoy. It is fun to play Secret Santas; we get to figure out what they'd like, sneak in to deliver a gift or do a little decorating when they're not around, and then spy on them as they get their gifts. Most people feel that there is nothing wrong with giving or getting gifts, so long as it's kept in check, and a little materialism keeps the economy moving.

Presenting Talk

Children look for logical connections and Santa gives us an obvious one that parents could use successfully when it comes to talking with their children about Santa bringing presents. Look at the original notions of Santa – he could put toys for all the children in the world in a single sleigh. Parents could appeal to a child's sense of logic about how many presents they should expect to get. Santa's sleigh could carry enough for every child to get a little something – but not a lot of things or big things. Children can visualize and accept that. This will reduce the list of things they hope he brings. Conversation with children around this can help them to prioritize what they really want.

Some parents fill an entire sleigh-full of "things" for one child alone! Historically, children did not expect the eternal fountain of gifts, like Harry Potter's despicable, greedy, corpulent cousin Dudley who threw tantrums when he didn't get "enough", even though what he had was already excessive by most standards. Rather, the gifting of Santa was to provide the child with a special thing that they longed for, needed, or could benefit from. Santa did not bring lots of toys to each child. The gifts were modest in nature; often they were sweet treats.

This gets us to the way people act when they receive a gift. Children benefit from learning the art of graceful acceptance. The most lovingly prepared gift can make the giver sad if it is not well received. It is important to keep things in perspective – the giver is giving the gift because he or she wants to do so. In that context, the gift actually belongs to the giver, not to the one who takes it home. Whether the person loves the gift or discards it is in some ways irrelevant; it is the process of the giving that ultimately matters. This has taken me a while to learn. When I give a gift, I'm giving it because I want to. It doesn't matter if someone enjoys it as much as I'd hoped or not, for once I give it away, it no longer belongs to me. If I buy concert tickets, I hope they will be used, but if a snowstorm or sickness precludes their use, or they decide not to use them, the person who got the tickets still knew that I cared. Caring is where the action is.

The content of the gifts is often less important than the symbolic meaning behind them. More gifts do not mean better. A few thoughtful, well-conceived gifts can mean more than many expensive but ill-conceived gifts that were purchased swiftly just to fulfill the obligation of giving someone a gift. When Kelsey was given only a pair of Wal-Mart slippers for Christmas, after purchasing lovely gifts for her husband, she was hurt and annoyed – not because of what the gift was or where it was purchased, but because her husband didn't put forth the time, energy, and perhaps financial commitment to show her at this special time of the year that he genuinely cared. When someone I cared about threw an expensive camera that I wanted at me in anger, it didn't feel good. Even though the camera was great, the spirit in which the gift was given was so horrid that I never cared for the gift at all. Instead of it being a source of delight, it was a source of upset every time I looked at it. I ended up giving it away because it made me so sad. What the gift is actually isn't as important as the message behind the giving. It is the symbolic meaning of the gift, and the relationship between the giver and gifted, that matter.

Most children today are grateful for the gifts they receive. Children originally have no expectations about the Christmas gift-giving thing, and they have to learn the desire, motivations, strategies, and reactions for dealing with the gift-giving process. On the morning of December 25, they are wildly excited to see so many beautifully wrapped gifts under the tree. Who wouldn't be? Most adults will admit that their hearts pitty-patter a little faster as they gaze at the glimmering lights shining on the beautifully adorned tree. Most adults also wonder if there is something wonderful waiting under the tree, just for them. By the time one counts several gifts for each family member, there' usually a significant pile of presents waiting to be opened. As children unwrap their own and watch others unwrap their gifts, they share in collective excitement and delight.

There comes, however, the inevitable moment when the gifts are all gone. It is natural for a child to ask, "Is that all?" or "Are there any more?" This innocent question has been known to drive parents into ballistic hysteria. "What do you mean, are there any more?! Haven't you had enough?? Why are you so greedy???" are common types of annoying parental response.

But wait. The question, "Is this all?" is a straightforward one. The child is asking for information. There has been such excitement in the ritualized opening of gifts that they want to know if the unwrapping moment is over. They want to know if they can now go play with their presents. They want to know if they can run into the bathroom or into the kitchen to grab a cookie and a glass of water. "Are there any more presents?" is not an indication of greed or dissatisfaction with what they have received. They may be totally content and grateful beyond belief. It isn't the children that have caused the upset. It is the parents who have overreacted to a simple question that begged closure to one moment of an exciting day so that another could begin.

The "are there any more?" question may also benignly mean "I've had a really good time opening presents. I don't want the good time to stop. Are there any more that I should anticipate because I don't know the rules of when this unwrapping presents thing is over?" My mother indicated that it was the unwrapping of presents that made things special, so parents had an obligation to make the gifts look attractive. After all, just putting the present, unwrapped, under the tree would be pretty anticlimactic. Wrapping them in newspaper or in a brown paper bag also isn't very exciting, compared to colorful reindeer paper, glittering ribbon, and shimmering bows. Thus, I learned to wrap separately every pair of socks and every pair of underwear. Even if the kids weren't totally enthralled by the gift itself, it was the anticipation, the expectation, and the unwrapping that made it fun.

This kind of misinterpretation is critical in the debate of Christmas materialism. There are two sets of reality going on; that of the parents who are weary, sleepy, hungry, and broke, and that of the children who are absolutely thrilled with their gifts. Occasionally kids get disappointed by not getting a particular object they wanted, or they received a gift that was (in their opinion) lame or tasteless. But these kinds of childhood reactions are by far the exception and not the rule. Most children are very grateful for what they receive. They understand that without the kind benevolence of their parents, they would have very little indeed. They appreciate the generosity of others. They understand the balance of power in the parent-child relationship. If children are greedy, it's because they have been socialized to believe in that entitlement. Greed, then, probably doesn't exist as much as adults think it does, and when it does occur it may not necessarily be their fault. To blame them for that wanting is, perhaps, unfair.

Sometimes over-gifting does occur, and there can be too much of a good thing even as it applies to gifts. If we wanted to give gifts that equaled how much we care for those we love, there would be a mountain of gifts that touched the sky. It is impossible to show people how much we love them through a mere gift – and yet, the gifts are symbolic gestures of how much care. When we are given so many things at once, it is sometimes difficult to appreciate all of them as much as we could if we had fewer of them, or if the gifting was better spaced apart. A major Santa rule is that Santa can't bring you everything you want or ask for. This is valuable for children to learn.

Rethinking The Types of Gifts We Give

Gifts can take many forms. They can be wrapped and expensive, unwrapped and meaningful, they can be gifts of experience, of song, of food, or simply gifts of time. At Christmastime, people may become more loving and unselfish. They take extra time to spend with their family and friends. There are unexpected presents that are received and given. It is especially meaningful when people give without expecting anything in return. Santa provides children with the opportunity to learn giving and getting behavior. Where else, in contemporary society, can children learn the benefits of giving to others, or how to graciously receive what others offer you?

We have a choice of what we want to consider as gifts. We have a choice about the types of gifts we want to give children or each other. We have a choice about whether we are going to succumb to the influence of advertisers. We have a choice about being wise and self-directed about what we want to give, spend, and go. Children's gifts, or gifts in general, can be classified into several categories.

There are **Gifts of Becoming**. These are gifts designed to help the child (or adult recipient) to explore new aspects of themselves, to develop some skill or trait, or to provide them with dreams that they may one day seek to make real. Examples of these could be sports equipment, music lessons, art supplies, a trip, or a camera. Another example is giving homeless children receive backpacks full of new school supplies. The calculators, crayons, binders, and dictionaries are given to children to help them do better in school, with an inherent expectation that they can be successful. Gifts of becoming, irrespective of type, don't mean much unless the recipient gets invested in them and transforms the gift into something greater.

There are **Gifts of Delight**. The emphasis of these gifts is to provide joy. Children are given these types of gifts with the hope that they will have fun. Examples of these gifts include candy and sweets to eat, toys to play with, books to read, music to listen to, or game to play. On the surface, Gifts of Delight could be seen as frivolous. But it is important to remember that these types of gifts, to children, can actually be learning tools. A computer game can teach hand-eye coordination, problem-solving skills, or create a sense of imagination and adventure. Gifts of Delight can also be gifts of humor. Laughter is a wonderful gift, so my mom always made sure there were silly presents under the tree, designed just to make us laugh. I have done the same thing with my children, and I dare say that the rubber alligator was a real favorite, along with the box of doll heads. We have some items that we recycle from one person to the other, year after year. And the horribly tasteless gifts a friend gives us each year has now become our favorite collective set of gifts to open, as we have a contest to see which of us "wins" by getting the most awful gift. The gifts don't necessarily cause the delight; it is what the gifts evoke in us, either individually or collectively, that makes them fun.

There are also **Gifts of Doing**, in which the child or recipient is given the opportunity to do something special, often with family members or friends. Gifts of doing require planning on the part of the person who gives the gift, and the hours of planning (plus the cost) are sure signs of concern. The Gifts of Doing can be simple, like going out to a special dinner, bowling, or taking a gang of children roller skating, or they can be more elaborate, such as going skydiving or on a vacation somewhere the child has always wanted to go. Sometimes parents will decorate the house and create a home-based special event that is full of surprise and fun. Other parents create annual family rituals, such as going to see the Nutcracker together or going to a concert. These events become incorporated into the child's sense of the holiday. These Gifts of Doing don't have to cost much, or they can be quite expensive. The purpose of all of them, however, is to plan to do something that the children will truly enjoy with people who love them.

Gifts of Necessity are not necessarily exciting, but they can provide a child with absolute relief, which can ultimately be joyful. Each season, my mother always made sure under the Christmas tree we found new pajamas, socks, and underwear. These are not exciting presents. However, they were ultimately some of the most used gifts we received, and we could always count on once a year getting a new supply of these essentials. Kitchen utensils, new hub-caps, bath-towels, or microwave ovens may help make our lives easier, but they just aren't thrilling gifts.

However, what is a gift of necessity for some children are perceived as gifts of delight for others. I work extensively with poor children, and can say that many find gifts like warm coats, new mittens, and a sleeping bag to be gifts of delight. Recently I worked with two sisters who were happy with the gifts they received, and they didn't feel slighted – except for one thing. The girls wanted snow pants so they could play outside more comfortably. Their father said he couldn't afford them, but their step-brother received a pair wrapped under the tree. The girls felt hurt over preferential treatment - their step-brother received a gift that would liberate him while they were forced either to stay inside or go out to play and be cold and wet. They felt a sense of injustice, of righteous indignation in the differential gifting. They weren't mad at Santa. They weren't being greedy. They just needed snow pants.

Sometimes people get upset when getting a Gift of Necessity when they really wanted a Gift of Delight. Often, Gifts of Delight win out even over Gifts of Becoming, since it takes a relatively sophisticated child to understand that Gifts of Becoming are probably the best gifts of all. Developmentally, children are naturally living more "at the moment", so it is logical that they may not be able to appreciate Gifts of Becoming until later on in their lives. Gifts of Doing are great because they allow children to do things for themselves, but also for others as they bond with people who they enjoy.

There are **Gifts of Bonding**. Giving other people gifts is a way to create a relationship with them. If you give me a gift, I will feel inclined to give you one, which makes you want to give me one back, and so on. Gift-giving is a way to establish social bonding with others. Reciprocity increases the chances of an ongoing relationship. When children get gifts from Santa, it conveys the message that they are unique, special, and deserving people. It also encourages children to leave Santa the best cookies so that there is an establishment of some sort of reciprocity and relationship. Hopefully, he will like those cookies enough to come back again next year!

There are also **Gifts of Forgiveness**. We all do things that we regret and we look for ways to make things right.

Sometimes it is hard to say the words or get the meanings across, especially to people who have closed down and are resistant. Sometimes a holiday gift will warm their soul and enable them to open their hearts. This is true among adults and children. Children may save their money for months to buy someone a gift that they hope will make a person love them more. Husbands may buy wives peace offerings in the shape of a nicely wrapped Christmas gift. People may say that "Santa" gave the gift in order to save face, even though everyone knows who actually bought and delivered the gift. Some people are particularly hard to reach, so finding the 'right' gift that will touch their hearts may be a way of softening that person so that a true and caring relationship can actually exist.

Sometimes we give each other very generous gifts as if the cost and brilliance of the gift will show the recipient how much we want to make up for the bad mistakes we have made in the past. Other times we carry guilt inside and use Christmas gifts as a way to right old wrongs. For instance, I have felt guilty for twenty years after making my son take back a bunch of Teenage Mutant Ninja Turtle characters after he spent over a hundred dollars from Grandma's Christmas money on them. At the time, I thought he should save some of the money his grandma had sent him for Christmas and he should buy some sensible things as well as a few toys. In hindsight, I regret that I was a party-pooper. It was his money. He had a right to spend it on whatever he wanted. He would have had a great time playing with so many figures at once. He could have had a feast of plenty. Instead, in my righteousness of being a responsible parent, I made him do the adult thing of saving and buying boring stuff along with a limited number of toys. I am so sorry I did this. I have carried this emotional burden for so many years that I found some of the ones he wanted so long ago in E Bay and bought them for him. I wrapped them up and put them under the tree a few years ago. As a young adult, he was surprised and confused by the gift, but he still liked his Turtle buddies. The giving of the gift enabled me to explain to him why I had done what I do so many years ago, why I was sorry, and it was a way to try to make amends. Has he played with the Turtles? No, at least not to my knowledge. But by the giving and receiving of this gift, I hope he understands that I recognize that I'm sorry. There is healing in such an act, and I am grateful for Santa to give me such an opportunity.

There are **Gifts of Deliverance**. Some parents use Santa as a vehicle to gift their children things they want that parents normally refuse to purchase. It allows the parent to save face, maintain their rules, and let Santa spoil them. Take for example Melinda's experience: "I told my son that I would not buy this one super-hero toy, and it got to be a matter of principle for me. The more Scotty asked the madder I got. I felt if I gave in, it set a bad precedent. There was really no major reason why he couldn't have it, except that he first asked me at a moment when I was feeling annoyed at him, so I took an overly firm "no" position on the toy. He really wanted the toy, his friends all had it, he was feeling left out, and I came to see some value in that particular toy. I felt I had been mean, but I couldn't back off. Santa came to my rescue. He delivered the toy, not me. Scotty got the toy he desired and I got to maintain my position. Thank you, Santa, for being there to help me!"

Reciprocal Gifts post a real problem for children. Children generally do not have money of their own. Therefore, they cannot go out and purchase gifts that are of equal monetary value to that which will be purchased by adults. Santa is a nurturing kind of guy, a grandfather type figure who expects, and receives nothing (except some cookies and milk) for his generosity. Adults usually expect that when they give a gift, they will get a gift that is of approximately equal value in return. But when it comes to children, adults are not to expect that children should gift them in an equitable way. Children generally don't have money. Some will make an art project or try their hand at cooking, or they will go to the store with crumpled dollar bills and a handful of coins to purchase something they think is of value. This gifting between adult and child is imbalanced, but that is totally acceptable and part of the Christmas ritual of gifting.

Often, what children want most is not material gifts but gifts that are much harder to come by. **Gifts For Others** are what some children want most. They may want their grandma to get out of the hospital, for their parents to reconcile from a divorce, or they may want their little brother to get over cancer that has left him bedridden. They may want their daddy to quit drinking or their mother to quit smoking. They may want their uncle to get asylum out of a war-torn country, or for their cousin to be found innocent at his court case. They may want their injured dog to regain the use of his leg, or for their neighbors to stop screaming at each other every night and keeping them awake. Children are often very generous of spirit, and what they want most isn't something that can be purchased. Sometimes, the anti-Santa folks forget this in their zeal to focus on the crass materialism of the holiday.

Gifts of Unconditional Love are of utmost importance. Children appreciate receiving gifts that have "no strings attached." If someone, like Santa, wants to give you a gift that is wonderful. They are not required to do anything special for it; the domain assumption is that the children get gifts because they ARE special. This means that if they don't give Santa a reciprocally equal-in-value set of gifts, it is acceptable. Santa doesn't need or want anything from children. He takes care of them, not the other way around. He is an adult. He is a caregiver. He CARES, so he puts other people's needs first, before his own. If he is tired and hungry after a long night of present delivery, that is too bad, but children don't have to feel responsible for his weariness. Santa is a fine role model of how adults ought to behave as he teaches children that they deserved to be cared for and beloved, not for what they do, but just because they are.

Gifts from Parents Vs Gifts from Santa.

It is important that parents make sure to give children gifts that are clearly acknowledged as from their parents. Some parents have put everything under the Christmas tree marked from Santa, and children may logically associate all gifts as coming from him. This is not true, and children should not be led to think that.

It is my opinion that Santa, due to his small sleigh and his propensity to be fair to every child, should only give a few presents to children that would fit into their stocking. Deciding that Santa presents would only go into a stocking would liberate parents from thinking that they have to many and costly items for their children in order to keep Santa alive and respectable. Stocking gifts would have to be small, like candy or sweets, small items like crayons or colored pencils, little games, books, or toys. Socks could fit into stockings, as could hair ribbons, bubble bath, and the like. There are zillions of fun and inexpensive items available that could fit into a stocking. At my house, stockings are my children's favorite things to open because we fill them with so much fun.

Big items like bicycles, skateboards, or rocking-horses could never fit into Santa's sleigh and should be marked as gifted from Grandpa or Mom. Santa's elves aren't techies, and electronic toys and items sometimes don't work properly and need to go back to the store or techie elves need to be consulted – so avoid saying electronic devices are from Santa.

The most important gifts should come from their parents so that the children know that the parents have given them wonderful gifts. This establishes a good transition for when children no longer believe in Santa, but want to experience a new meaning of Christmas and gift-giving. Children will come to know, over time, that the gifts they received were from the care, sacrifice, and hard work of their parents. This will help children to ultimately regard their holiday presents as gifts of love.

Making Santa's gifts arrive in stockings creates a greater sense of equality for all children in the community. Many parents are going through very hard economic times and to thrust upon them the expectation that they will be big gift-givers is unkind. But they could likely come up with enough creative ideas to put into their child's stocking that the child will feel pleasantly gifted by a Santa Claus. Having presents from family helps relieve the burden of expectation for everyone. If a child understood that money was tight at their home and their parents couldn't afford to get them something, the child would have an easier time accepting that or could devise a plan with the parents about how they could work together so they could come up with the money overtime to get the present. If a store had sold out of an item, then the child be taught about supply-and-demand economics instead of feeling rejected and unloved by Santa.

The Santa Stocking Pact

Imagine this - what if there was a pact among parents that in their family, school, or community that Santa would only deliver presents in children's stockings? If children were trained to expect that Santa only brought presents that would into stockings, it would eliminate much of the social class variation and poor children feeling left out and deprived. While it could be expected that some parents would go over-board and have bigger stockings into which they put Rolex watches or expensive items, children who learn early about some families having more money than others could feel that they shared a more equal Santa experience. If the Fire Department or civic organization collected toys for children, think of how positive it would make gifted children feel to know that there were people in the community who cared about them? Sticking "From Santa" on the present may be well-intended, but it keeps the Santa disparity going. A note that the present is from "Your Secret Santa Friend" would work, or "From the City of XXX", or even Anonymous. I'm all for making sure children feel gifted during the holiday – I just think that children may benefit more from keeping Santa in his place and helping children to know that living, breathing people in the community can also act in the Santa Spirit.

For more information on how to productively use stocking gifts to help transform Santa, see my books, *The Legend of the Santa Stocking, The Santa Spirit,* or *The ABC's of the Santa Spirit for Adults.*

What I Concluded

So is it OK for children to expect gifts? Absolutely. Gift-giving can allow people to reflect upon others, as well as themselves. There is a great deal of teaching that parents can incorporate into the gifting of others. Children can not only learn the value of money as they weight what material objects to buy, they can also learn the importance of relationships and how conspicuous consumption isn't necessarily satisfying, either for giver or recipient. The happiness and satisfaction that we all receive from the gifting is not necessarily related to the gift itself, but from the relationship that surrounds the gift. The manner in which the gift is given, the time, the place, the context, and the relationship all matter extensively in the gift-giving moment. To be like Ebenezer Scrooge and fail to give gifts to friends and family doesn't make you beloved. To be like the Grinch and wish to take away other people's delight only ends up hurting yourself.

In my home growing up, visitors knew that they came to our house they would never leave empty-handed. They may get help, common-sense advice, money, clothes, or food. The unexpected gift-giving was especially prevalent during the holidays. My mama started baking sweets shortly after she finished addressing her Christmas cards around Thanksgiving Day. By the time December 25 arrived, she had multiple card tables groaning from the weight of cookies, pies, cakes, and candies. Anyone who wandered into the house during that season would leave with a paper plate loaded with goodies. We were not taught to expect anything in return; our ability to give was not just other people's gift, it was our own.

The benefits of Santa for teaching children altruistic behavior is that the giving occurs just to make someone else happy; the giving doesn't have to cost much, and children can make items so they may be personally engaged in the altruistic action over an extended period of time. His arrival to come once a year can be counted upon and looked forward to, so there is a predictability that children can use to organize their lives. This helps families to integrate altruistic behavior into children's lives as part of their annual plans – and hopefully giving to others will replicate time and time again throughout the rest of the year.

Mahatma Gandhi quote

Gentleness,
self-sacrifice,
and generosity
are the exclusive possession of
no one race or religion.

Mahatma Gandhi

Gandhi: An autobiography. 1927. Public Affairs Press

Chapter 21

How To Explain Santa To Children

The Dilemma

Whether we should encourage children to believe in Santa is a dilemma for most parents. But since we created this problem, we can fix it so it doesn't have to be a problem anymore. Through conducting this research, I have come up with what I think could be a reasonable way to conceptualize and explain Santa Claus to children, and I want to share it with you.

What I Discovered

We (meaning society at large and us parents individually) created the crisis about whether to tell our children Santa Claus is real or not because we constructed him as a real person to begin with. If we had recast him not as a real person but as a representation of someone who embodies goodness in the first place, then we wouldn't be having this problem.

The overarching point I wish to make is that I think Santa should be conceptualized to be the *spirit* of altruism, joy, and loving-kindness. People dress up pretending to be Santa because they enjoy spreading positivity to others. Most do so feeling like it may help to bring joy and make the world a better place. There are many different people dressed up and pretending to be Santa Claus that children have a right to be confused on why there are so many Santas, and which one is the "real" one. Some had professional training on how to be a good Santa and some haven't; some are wonderful, some aren't, some are hired to represent Santa and some are self-appointed Santas. There are charity Santas, civic Santas, Santas-that-look-like-Grandpa, mall Santas, home-delivery Santas, street Santas, Salvation Army Santas, parade Santas, and more. But all of them – ideally - is to bring joy and happiness to people. Sometimes they may hand out presents or candy canes. But the big thing they bring is the opportunity to remind us all to be kind and generous to others and to find enjoyment in the company of others. It's the Santa Sprit that they are supposed to be delivered. You know the cliché – the best present is our presence when we are sharing happiness.

The issue of how to explain Santa gets complicated around the issue of whether parents are lying to children about whether he is real. As I discovered, lying about Santa is a very complicated, multi-dimensional issue. How do we best explain him to children in a healthy, positive, meaningful manner? I've thought long and hard about this and will give you my recommendations.

Together, these factors helped me to discover a way out of the annual Is-Santa-Real? dilemma.

Is Santa the Big Lie?

Deciding whether you tell children that Santa is real or not is not an easy decision, according to ethicists and experts in child development. This decision is full of conceptual and ethical struggles. There is a hearty amount of opinion from psychologists pertaining to whether parents who tell their children there is a Santa Claus is lying to them. Sooner or later children will figure out that there is no such person as Santa Claus, and depending on how he is presented, children could see their parents had lied to them about his existence – leading them to question what else their parents may have lied to them about and whether or not their parents are actually trustworthy. Frances Chaput Waksler's research indicates that when children get upset after learning "the truth" about Santa, their upset could occur because they feel their parents lied to them. Waksler (2002) alleges that parents, the community, the media, and society as a whole engage in an orchestrated deception to make Santa seem real. She regards this misleading of children to be harmful, especially when parents have to turn around later and admit they had all conspired to make children believe in something that simply wasn't true. If parents are to be trusted, they shouldn't lie – therefore, they should not encourage children to believe in Santa Claus. Waksler feels that such acts can undo the hard work that parents and teachers do to increase children's scientific knowledge of how the natural world works.

While Waksler seems convinced that believing in Santa is bad for children, in reviewing what other experts have to say about letting children believe in Santa Claus, it appears that the verdict is out and leaning heavily towards the view that believing in Santa Claus has more pros than cons for children. There are both positives and negatives about encouraging children to believe in Santa (Fetters 2018; Healthways 2017; Lewis 2013; Melbourne Child Psychology 2020; Prentice 1979; Sloat 2017). Some argue that encouraging children to believe in figures like Santa Claus could actually be good for both their mental health and cognitive well-being, such as views by Dr. Matthew Lorber, a New York City child psychiatrist (Lewis 2013):

"I don't think it's a bad thing for kids to believe in the myth of someone trying to make people happy....Imagination is a normal part of development, and helps develop creative minds."

Psychology professor Bruce Henderson's research found that learning that Santa Claus isn't real is a natural shift in thinking rather than a traumatic experience for children and that fewer than ten percent of young adults report having any negative repercussions from this realization (Cantrell 2016). Psychology professor Jacqueline Woolley (2014) concludes that it is alright to "let your children believe in Santa." Dr. Claude Cyr, a Canadian pediatrician (2002), investigated children's belief in Santa. Through his research, he concludes that awareness of Santa Claus was universal; all the children in this study were quite familiar with Santa Claus, even if they did not view Santa as real. His study demonstrated that children tend to believe (in one form or another) so long as their parents believe in Santa. So what is the truth about Santa Claus, according to Dr. Cyr?

"I agree with the famous reply of Francis Church who wrote in the New York Sun in reply to a letter from an 8-year-old girl, Yes, Virginia, there is a Santa Claus. He exists as certainly as love and generosity and devotion exist. Children whose ...parents... believed in Santa ... are more likely to believe in Santa Claus and, I hope, in love, generosity, and devotion."

The question of whether Santa Claus is true or false, real or not real, is the wrong question, or at least poorly phrased, according to sociologist Cindy Dell Clark (1995) who conducted extensive research on children's views of Santa. She feels that whether someone believes in Santa depends upon whether the person accepts the philosophic underpinnings of what Santa is. "Acceptance is up to the child – or perhaps the believing adult.... Faith, not reasoned skepticism, is the relevant mental experience" (Clark 1995:57). Faith and belief are paramount in the Santa experience. Marjorie Taylor's (1997; 1999) research on children and their imaginary friends indicates fantasy characters play an important role in children's development. Youngsters are introduced to the world of make-believe from an early age; parents introduce Santa, the Tooth Fairy, and the Easter Bunny, children are told fairy tales, taken to movies that portray talking animals, toys, mermaids, or aliens, and they are actively encouraged to engage in fantasy or imaginative play. Taylor asserts that children as young as four years old can distinguish between what is real and what is pretend, and they are comfortable with this dual world that often seems to exist simultaneously. When you talk with children, they can flip back and forth between these different worlds because they have developed a mental scheme that organizes them and makes sense. Because they are young, children may lack the conceptual sophistication to differentiate between exactly how nonexistent creatures like the dinosaur and the unicorn are really that different from each other. Children may not always be able to discern from television shows what is really real, such as when making distinctions between shoot-'em-up adventure films like Star Wars or like news clips of street violence or war. But then again, as H. G. Wells found out in his radio broadcast of the War of the Worlds, adults may have that same problem. Sometimes it is difficult, even for people who are older to discern between what is fantasy and reality. So when a community gets excited for Santa's arrival and the family gets caught up in that excitement, it is that much different than being excited over Star Wars, Harry Potter, or other collective social experiences in which we all can't wait for, even though we know that they are not "real"?

The Truth About Parents Lying

A big reason some parents report not wanting their children to believe in Santa is because they don't want to lie to them. **So don't!** If we don't lie to children in the first place, we aren't going to have to fix the secondary problem of how to get out of the lie.

Seriously, the truth is that parents lie to children all the time. Let's take a look at this. I ask you the following question directly – have you ever told a lie? Was it a teeny-weeny fib or a hum-dinger whopper of a lie? Did you try to color the lie by developing an elaborate context around it so that maybe people wouldn't know it was really a lie, or to justify your stretching of the truth?

And what was it that you lied about? According to psychologist Paul Ekman (2020), chances are that we lie for specific reasons. These include to: a) keep ourselves out of trouble; b) keep from hurting someone in some way; c) avoid being embarrassed; d) hide that we don't know something; e) get out of an awkward or uncomfortable situation; f) obtain a reward or admiration; g) exercise power and control over others or h) maintain privacy so others don't know something about you or what you really think or do. All of these pertain to why we lie to children about Santa. We lie when we change our story about Santa, we lie to shelter children from knowing that he isn't really real or to protect them from ridicule, we lie when we are with other parents who disagree and we don't want them to think badly of our parenting style, we lie to make ourselves feel like we are better parents, we lie because we know our children will believe whatever we say (for a while, anyway), we lie to protect others and we lie to protect ourselves. In the process of doing so, we re-conceptualize what we are doing not to be lies and we justify our actions because they serve some greater, more important purpose. Parents regularly teach children not to say things that are true, such as what they really think about something or somebody. Children are regularly admonished to "keep your mouth shut", or "don't you dare say that" out of fear they may repeat things that happened or statements others made. If they "spill the beans," that could get them – or their parents – in trouble. Adults may discount or demean Santa because they don't want children to see them s liars. Pretense and not telling the truth, the whole truth, and nothing but the truth is part of the American way of life.

So when is a lie a lie, when is the truth masquerading as a lie and when is a lie actually the truth? Ah, lying is complicated indeed.

Lying is regarded in most societies as disrespectful, self-serving, potentially dangerous, and just plain bad. In general, we view that people who lie cannot be trusted. Once someone lies, you never know when they will lie again; once they distort the truth, you can't be sure if what they're telling you is the truth about anything. In order to develop a healthy parent-child relationship, there must be trust on both sides. Parents need to trust children and children need to trust parents. Inherent in this assumption is the position that parents should never lie. It is unrealistic to expect the child to always tell the truth when they observe their parent telling lies. But most parents actually teach their children how to lie by their use of "white lies" and attempts to protect other people's feelings. Parents feel it is important to teach children how to be socially appropriate and therein is tension in their pressure to tell truth or lies.

Mom and Dad are caught when they want their children to appreciate the joy associated with Santa but don't want to lie to them. They don't want to tell them that Santa is real when he isn't, but they want children to have fun with him. But Santa isn't exactly a black-and-white thing that people can lie about. It all depends on how you define him. People can believe Santa is real, and they can believe that Santa isn't real; belief can be real even when there is no tangible proof for what it represents. If you say that Santa is real and you believe it, it's not a lie. If you say Santa is real and you don't believe it, well, it is a misrepresentation of truth as you know it.

Santa isn't the only predicament of this type that parents confront. Look at this common comparison: When parents address their children's question, "What is God?" or "Does God exist?" they face a similar contextual conflict. For people who believe in God and want their children to as well, they believe the signs that he exists are obvious. But to those who do not believe, they may dispute the meaning of the signs and offer proofs and arguments that could be just as valid. There is a long and lively debate on the fact between those who rely on faith and those who rely on science as they sort through the existence of God.

Parents are caught in this type of bind in other situations too. It is helpful to expand one's analysis of situations in which parents attempt to explain a "truth" to children. As pediatric sociologist David Kallen told me, you always have to tell the truth – but you don't always have to be telling the truth. When children ask questions, often all they want is a short and sweet answer. Parental thought may have jumped far ahead and they may be anticipating that the child wants to know more than they do. This results in parents launching into long and elaborate explanations, providing "too much information".

Consider the dilemma many parents feel when their young children ask them "where do babies come from?" Sooner or later they have to know, they MUST find out where babies come from - but they don't need all the details at one time, especially when they are too young to handle the information. Young children do not necessarily need to know about eggs and sperms, ejaculations and orgasms,

DNA or genetics, or the three trimesters of gestation. A simple explanation is quite sufficient when children are young. In another example, when the child's dog dies, parents may tell the child that the dog has become an angel in heaven. Or, they tell the child it "went sleep and never woke up" instead of telling the tyke that the dog's cancer was eating holes through its organs, that it was in excruciating pain, and that they took it to the vet who euthanized it, after which it was burned up and turned into ashes in a process called cremation. That may be a fact, but it is way too much information for a young child to handle. The issue of truth-telling is made a much more daunting for the anxious-to-say-the-right-thing-parent than it is for children, who are just looking for a simple, straightforward answer that they can understand.

In order to protect their children, parents give them smaller, symbolic variations of the truth that they can handle. Explanations such as "the stork brings children," or "we found him under the cabbage patch" surely aren't accurate, but do they harm children? What child will really grow up believing that flying birds carry babies, or that infants grow in gardens like vegetables? The explanations are sufficiently far-fetched that children will mull them over and ultimately come to the conclusion that another explanation must exist. Other parents may answer the baby question with answers like "God put the baby in mommy's tummy," or "the baby is a gift because mommy and daddy love each other so much" or later with statements like, "I guess the parents had unprotected sex," without giving the child any explanation about how exactly God put that baby in the mom's tummy or exactly what "unprotected" or "sex" might be. Often children accept such answers without discussion.

These ambiguous answers are a way of buying time until children are developmentally able to comprehend the realities of the phenomenon. Do you always really wanting to tell them the truth, the whole truth, and nothing but the truth? Are there better ways to explain the arrival of a baby brother or sister besides giving them the graphic particulars about how daddy's sperm and mommy's egg actually met up? Do you think there should come a later time when children would more appropriately learn the details about how babies get created? Most parents do. Children learn at a very early age that lying is acceptable, and expectable, in certain situations. It is a rare parent who hasn't told a mistruth, partial truth, or "white lie" around their children.

In fact, most parents encourage their children to lie, or at least not to say exactly what they think. Consider when children are told to tell Grandma how much they like a gift she gave them or that they enjoyed the food she prepared when the children don't care for it at all. Children are routinely ordered to apologize for things that they aren't sorry about. They may be taught to say something nice to someone they dislike, thereby engaging in polite but phony behavior.

Most parents role-model deceptive behavior for their children to observe, even though this may not be intentional. Children observe parents say unkind things about their boss at home but see them act all sweet and charming to their face in public. They watch their parents lie to avoid getting a speeding ticket after they are stopped by the police officer. They hear parents tell creditors on the phone that "I just put the check in the mail today" when they didn't. All too often, parents take the position of teaching children to "do what I say, don't do what I do" because they know their behavior isn't stellar – yet they expect that of their children to be.

The Relativity of Truth and Santa

Now back to the Santa question. Despite what the skeptics say, encouraging children to believe in Santa could be regarded quite differently than lying. If over many generations around the world their whole community and the family members who care and protect them all work so hard to promote the notion that Santa Claus exists, there must be something beneficial to justify that collective behavior.

Sociologist Peter Berger (1963) tells us that truth and reality are arbitrary constructs. Truth can be plural. There can be several different realities that exist simultaneously. Parents tend to agree that Father Christmas, St, Nicholas, or Santa Claus story conveys positive values with some kind of universal acceptance such as generosity, kindness, and caring. Theodora Papatheodorou's (2002) research found that parents themselves use the Santa story to transmit social and personal values and to facilitate their children's ability to make sense of the self and the world. The story and the children's experience of excitement and the sense of magic, wonder, and awe which it generates were regarded by parents as extremely important. In a different but similar example, look at the story *The Christmas Carol*. In it, Bob Crachit had nothing but gave everything; Ebeneezer Scrooge had everything and gave nothing. Yet thanks to the spirits, both came to come to a sense of balance on Christmas day.

"Christmas mediates between hedonism and selfless love, especially the love of children, upon whom material goods are lavished. On the face of it, hedonism (for example, lavish parties with fancy clothing) and selfless giving (in the form of charity toward children and others) are paradoxical values. Yet Christmas manages to encompass both indulgence and sacrifice at once." (Clark 1995:33).

Part of growing up is to decide what is true from what is not. This means that children must be exposed to untruths to derive what is truth. The use of their imagination and their cognitive skills to sort through information and make their own determination about what is real is a very important conceptual skill to develop. Children may not always be able to negotiate the boundary between what is real and what is not, but as Taylor (1999) alleges, children have a much greater grasp on reality and fantasy than adults may think. She feels they create conceptual places for imaginary figures and come to understand how to interpret the behavior of adults who are engaged in pretense. Children may come to understand that the mistruth their parents told them may have been for some greater good. Even babies know when people play peek-a-boo with them that it is a game of pretense. Has daddy disappeared for good when he's playing peek—boo? Of course not, and this is useful for a child to learn so in this regard, this deceptive play has benefit. Besides, learning to play along is fun.

When children inevitably ask parents directly if Santa is real or not, usually that is to confirm their own thinking patterns and the conclusions they have reached with their peers. Despite horror-filled testimonials of children who have found out that there is no Santa, there are countless other stories of children who are relieved to have processed the questions of what is real and what is a myth successfully. Many children are quite proud of themselves for figuring out their answer to the Santa situation successfully themselves. They have no need to even process that conclusion with parents, who may throw a wet blanket of their own notions onto the golden ones created by the children. Given that parents often try to take control of every aspect of their children's existence, it is a positive step toward independence when children attempt to resolve this major social question on their own. Figuring out who Santa Claus in their own way and on their own terms is an important step in their cognitive independence. They often do so within a social collective context where there is an entire age cohort of other children who are struggling with the exact issues at the exact time.

Children are vulnerable and cannot risk doing anything that will put their relationship with their parents at major risk. They do not know what the appropriate boundaries of communication are when it comes to imaginary figures. For example, if they say they believe in monsters, their parents may assure them that monsters don't really exist so they don't have to worry that one is under the bed or in the closet. Children pick up the message that things like the monsters, trolls, cyclopes, giants, and the Boogieman aren't really real, and they shouldn't believe in them. In fact, if they say they do believe in them they could be subject to ridicule. But if they say they do not believe in things that meet the same criteria as other imaginary figures they have heard about, such as a God that they cannot see or touch or talk with but who exists nonetheless, they may suffer their parent's wrath, especially if the parents are devout. The rules continue to change for children; dinosaurs were once real but they don't exist anymore, so how is that different for why a dinosaur is considered as real but a unicorn, mermaid, or centaur isn't? Children who may have figured out that Santa isn't delivering gifts by flying reindeer are not confident that they can say, "Oh, Mama, I know that Santa is a made-up guy, and I believe in him anyway." They're not sure they can be that direct. Santa communication rules have been totally unclear. Talking about what is real and what isn't can be more dangerous territory for adults than children.

The older children grow, the more sophisticated their scientific grip on what is real and what is not. But even younger children may develop their own conceptual schemes to make sense of such information. Should we interpret belief in Santa Claus as evidence that a child has a poor grasp of fantasy and reality? Most scholars don't think so. There are many reasons why children believe in Santa. Parents, other family members, and the community often go to great lengths to create a presence of Santa. They go out of their way to encourage children to believe. So when it comes to Santa, what is the truth?

Unwrapping Santa

Children have a right to be confused over the Santa Claus issue. They get taught that there is one true Santa, but when they see so many people walking around in Santa suits that it is mind-boggling. When parents ask their parents to explain why there are so many of them, inherent in the asking of the question is a compliment that parents should not treat lightly. Santa is a very user-friendly figure that allows for this type of skill development to occur in a natural and easy manner.

The issue of whether or not to tell children "the truth" about Santa depends upon two things – the way Santa Claus is presented to children in the first place, and the trustworthiness and stability of the relationship between the parent and child. Psychologists report that when parent-child relationships are secure, there is more room for children to accept the good intentions of the parent and to trust that the parent is telling them the truth, or some version of it. When relationships are insecure and the child figures out that Santa is not portrayed in the way the parents initially presented him, it becomes one more nail in the coffin. The more dramatic the revelation is that Santa isn't "real" for the child, the harder it will be on the child – and the more it can harm the parent-child relationship (Boyle and McKay 2016).

It seems to me that there is a very easy solution to this problem. That is for parents to portray Santa not as a real person but as a spirit that anyone can emulate. Parents may talk about Mickey Mouse being real – but certainly, he is not a real mouse. Children quickly learn that the Disney mouse is not the same kind that is rummaging through their cupboards. Children observe that there are different people dressed up as Santa Claus - thinking that each of them are trying to promote the Santa Spirit would negate parent's trying to explain why "this one" isn't the "real" Santa and why "that one" might be. Parents have caused their own difficulty because they contextualize Santa to be a blood-and-bones obese male who lives in the North Pole rather than a fantasy spirit of kindness and goodness. Reframing him in to embody a spirit of joy and goodness allows for more dialogue with children about positive attributes that someone with the Santa Spirit should emulate, and which attributes are counter-productive to it.

Sooner or later, families have to explain who Santa Claus is to their children. We may want to explain him differently to young children than to older ones. But we don't have to lie to any of them as we engage in the telling of the tale.

Usually, children know that Santa isn't real long before they have "the conversation" with their parents about it. Many children are generous in spirit and know their parents want them to believe in Santa, so they pretend to believe when they don't. "I'd hate to disappoint my mom," one boy confessed. "She likes making all the Christmas stuff. I don't know what she'd do if we said we didn't believe." Children may scaffold their beliefs in fantasy characters to go along with what they believe their parents want them to believe. They may know that Santa isn't real, but they may choose to play along because there are so many benefits to be gained. "After all, what would Christmas be like without Santa? All the magic would be gone," one girl observed. And a young man grinned as he told me, "I'd better believe in Santa, because if I stop believing, he'll stop coming!"

Here are some things to help guide you in your explanation of Santa Claus to children.

Babies are just learning words, people, and concepts, so introducing "Santa" by name is a reasonable thing to do. As they grow older, there is nothing inherently wrong about making the association between Santa as a person and the getting of a gift. Santa brings presents. The fact is, he could only bring one gift or just bring stockings of trinkets; there is no role requisite that he brings many or expensive gifts. (This is where parents can put a lid on what Santa delivers).

It's fun for kids as they get older to look at themselves with Santas. At the time the picture is made sometimes babies don't think it's so much fun. Pliable babies won't mind getting their picture made with Santa; those with more separation anxiety may not like it as much. A photo with Santa can create lifelong happy memories, as brothers showed in a 2013 Christmas internet sensation with 30 years of photos of themselves with Santa.[i]

Toddlers and preschoolers are at a prime time for enjoying Santa. This is when their imagination capabilities are skyrocketing. They are in the midst of enjoying playing with ideas and thoughts, and Santa provides fertile fuel of flying reindeer, workaholic elves, and a jolly old man who eats the cookies you've made for him after delivering you marvelous elf-made presents. Parents and families can have enormous fun together during this time, which benefits their solidarity with and for the child. Of course, Santa is real for toddlers. This is developmentally a reasonable answer.

There will come a point when toddlers or children who are bit older hear that Santa isn't real, or start to question the authenticity of him. The older a child is, the easier it is to talk about different dimensions of what is real. The younger a child is, the more speculative the reality talk is because cognitively they are just starting to build a foundation to understand it. We know that media, peers, siblings, or innocent slips by well-intended others may "spill the beans" about Santa. Sometimes kids put two-and-two together at the mall and wonder if the Santa there is the real one.

So what is the proper thing to do when things happen and the child directly asks you – is Santa real? I have a two-fold response. One is don't lie – if you think you are lying, then you will have the problem and intentionally or unintentionally you will foist it on to your child. There is no need to tell small children more than they need to know. There is no good in telling them information that they can't process or handle. The other is to tell the truth. So when it comes to Santa, what is the truth for toddlers and small children? Here are some things to say:

I think there is a real Santa somewhere. Lots of people want to be like Santa and dress up like him. He has a lot of helpers. So it's hard to tell which one is the real Santa. Do you want to be one of Santa's helpers? (This paves the way for you to talk about gifting others)

I've sometimes wondered that too! He's a lot of fun, isn't he? I like believing in Santa. (This switches the focus to the fun of believing)

No one I know has ever seen the real Santa, but he's existed for hundreds of years. (This is a historical argument that older children can appreciate)

Some people believe Santa Claus is real and some people don't. (Fact). Often that answer is enough. You don't need to go further - if your child doesn't ask you what you personally believe, you're off the hook.

But if your child directly asks you – *"Do YOU believe in Santa?"*, then you have to have an answer ready. Think about what you want to say. Have your answer ready, since sooner or later it could come.

Safe ones include:

I believe that Santa's spirit exists and helps people to be nice to each other.

I got presents from Santa when I was little, so I always figured he was real.

I think that Santa is real, but he may not be real like you and me. (Here you can explore fairies or things that exist that are hard to prove)

I believe in Santa (if you do, in some way).

If you come from a Christian orientation, you may also find Tony Canamucio's (2009) or Alan Barrington's (1997) books on how to explain Santa to children to be useful.

I think it is OK to let little children enjoy the mystery of Santa Claus if you feel comfortable doing so. Research indicates that there are a variety of conceptual benefits for this. Santa is a transition figure that helps children developmentally to move towards more abstract thinking. We have to remember that children are laying brain tracks down as they grow. They need to have a good grip on something tangible before they can gain the ability to develop the ability to extrapolate information to higher-order concepts and thinking.

The development of imagination is of utmost importance to children. The Santa characters and histories are rich with images to inspire imagination growth – flying reindeer, helpful elves, sleighs that can contain presents for millions of children, being able to travel around the world in a single night, all create wonder for children to ponder. Learning to be creative is an outgrowth of rich imagination. Does Santa have a factory with a conveyer belt where elves work to make so many toys? Astronauts today were children pondering space flight when they were little, and Santa contributed to that in some way.

Santa helps inspire a work ethic – he doesn't just wish all those toys into existence. He has to plan ahead, keep on schedule, and work as a team with others (elves) to make things happen. Mom and Dad have to work to pay for food, clothes, and a place to live. Everybody has to work. Learning this early is a valuable lesson. It helps to diffuse a sense of entitlement and inspires gratitude for receiving gifts that clearly someone else had to work hard to make.

By the time children get into elementary school, some will believe in Santa and some won't. First and second graders may hold on to belief longer than fourth or fifth graders. This is because of the difference in their cognitive abilities, as well as the pressure from peers who don't believe. Children in the older age group don't want to be ridiculed by their peers. They also want to believe in the precious things they learned as a child. They rely upon adults (parents) to know what to say. They have learned scientific principles but still have faith. This is a tough place for kids to be. An elaboration on the previous explanations is in order, including higher-level conversations the move into more abstract and conceptual thought.

The older and more inquisitive children become about Santa's reality lends itself into potentially fascinating, fun, and mind-growing opportunities for children. It allows for talk about belief and the benefits of believing versus not believing. Talking about flying reindeer and climbing down chimneys with a sack full of presents is pretty hard to understand – but could lead to discussions on whether children think they could be an analogy for something else, like giving to others. It's fun to think about the impossible being possible. Santa conversations can point to the historical and cultural facts about the traditions that all merged into our understanding of Santa. As a general rule, the younger the child, the shorter the explanation. Going on too long or too detailed is unnecessary except for older kids who long for that type of explanation.

By the time children turn into teenagers they have acquired a scientific mind that makes them not believe in Santa Claus. If they have younger siblings, they can easily be recruited into creating Santa for them. That gives them a powerful, more adult-role in the family that they appreciate. It also helps them to understand the commitment their parents made to them when they were small. If they are not socialized into an altruistic role, they may see Christmas as merely an opportunity to get presents. Toys have less cache than they did; electronics and expensive gifts have more. This time period is challenging for parents who still want to celebrate the magic of Christmas but whose children no longer believe in it. The question of how to help teens find the Santa Spirit within them to make magic for others is key.

The presence of younger children in the family helps teens engage the Santa Spirit. In the absence of younger children in the family, emphasis on volunteerism where the family works to bring holiday toys to other children (so the youth get to practice being Santa) is useful. Families can create traditions and transform their relationships to still be loving and magical without leaving out cookies or expecting Santa to arrive at midnight. But it will take more work and creativity, since teens are inherently skeptics and harder to recruit into family activities. But don't give up on them – secretly, teens want parents to still create holiday magic!

By the time we hit young adulthood, we have to figure out for ourselves what Santa is, and what he isn't. We have to decide whether he will have a place in our hearts and homes. That's why you're reading this book, right?

When do believers stop believing in Santa Claus? In my study of college students, the majority stopped believing in him by the time they hit age 11; only 14.4% of students said they believed in Santa after age 10. Most (46.6%) stopped believing when they were between 8 and 10 years of age. Slightly under a third (30.8%) reported they had stopped believing by the time they were 5-8 years old. Believing in Santa is most common for children under age 5.

So how did it come to pass that they stopped believing in Santa? Most of the students figured it out for themselves (46.6%), or in conjunction with friends around their age (25.3%). This means that 71.9% of students either figured out that Santa wasn't real either by themselves or in association with other children their age as they problem-solved the "is Santa real?" question. People older than the child were responsible for telling the child that Santa didn't exist in 29.5% of the cases. The media was only responsible for "spilling the beans" 4.1% of the time. None of the respondents reported being traumatized by learning that

Santa wasn't real. For many, their parents had paved the ground by providing a larger view of Santa than being a flesh-and-bones human. Allowing them to figure out the reality of Santa for themselves was reported to be a useful process that gradually let the students come to the conclusion that Santa couldn't possibly be real, at least in the way they thought when they were little. However, a process that allowed them to explore the issues associated with belief and reality for themselves was regarded to be very helpful. As one person reported, "Processing takes time and is gradual, so my understanding that Santa wasn't exactly real in the way I initially thought felt comfortable. I think it discovering what Santa meant on my own helped me discover myself."

Most people remember like Christmas morning better when Santa arrived than those holidays when he didn't. Santa Claus is not a threat to children's capacity for faith. Faith and hope are wonderful things for children to find within themselves; without them, it is very difficult to get through troubling times. And children do have troubles and they will experience problems that seem overwhelming as they grow through life. Faith, however one finds it, is a way to help us get through life's crises.

Santa Claus clearly means different things to us at different points in our life. The convenient thing about him is that he is a conversation-opener that has the potential of opening up real and meaningful conversations that are far more important than whether reindeer can fly. Because Santa is a symbol, conversation about him can open other abstract conversations that are even more important. In a personal correspondence with Dr. Cyr, he told me the following story:

"I work in pediatric palliative care and use Santa every year to enter the world of dying children. A few years ago, in preparation for this article, I entered a 12-year-old girl's room to discuss Santa Claus. She was in her last days, dying from myeloid leukemia. I asked her what was her thought about Santa. After a few seconds of silence, I was thinking that maybe she found me a little bit childish. She then smiled and asked me "is he here?" We had the best discussion a child and a doctor could have after that, talking about our memories, our gifts, and eventually the next Christmas that she would not attend".

I know well how important Santa Claus has been for sick, sad, abused, and mistreated children. While Santa Claus can be regarded as a momentary bandage to stop the bleeding, it seems we ought not to underestimate the importance of what he can do for children.

Perhaps it is parents who need Santa so much that they need their children to keep him alive for them. We all need fantasy, we need to dream, we need to hope. Mothers, in particular, start the Santa stories and keep them up long after the time that their children have given up their belief in the man in red. Research shows pretty conclusively that children don't have big problems finding out that Santa doesn't exist – it is the parents who have the problems. My own children told me that they wouldn't dare spoil my December good times by telling me that they have known for years since they know Santa and I "are close".

I wonder if parents get so obsessed about telling their children "the truth" because their disbelief will prevent parents from going back to a time when they felt anything was possible. Adult reality is filled with restrictions, obstacles, and a sense of chronic challenge. Adults are confronted routinely with logical explanations that are limiting and often don't make sense. Children's explanations of things are often much more hopeful, pleasant, and truthful in a different sort of way. Hope, for all of us, needs to be encouraged.

What I Concluded

Is Santa real? Is it appropriate to tell children that Santa doesn't exist? These questions have been with us for a long time. I believe that Santa, in different forms, does exist. In saying this, I do not believe I am lying. I decided I had lots more to gain by believing in Santa, and more to lose by not believing in him. You have to make a decision that you feel is wise in the long run. Sometimes wisdom means doing things that are unfamiliar or even uncomfortable. But it's important to help provide children with the opportunity to believe – in hope, in the goodness of others, and in the preciousness of themselves.

No matter what all of these Santas look like, they all help to advance the Santa Spirit. Perhaps having many Santas gives children the potential to see that there are many different types of people who care about them and that there are many different ways to show others that you care. Santa is the embodiment of the spirit of giving, of joy merely for delight's sake. I believe it is important that children learn that Santa is not a person but a state of mind. Santa is the spark that helps us not just to be alive, but to live. Santa is something that you can become, something you can learn as you watch others making the Santa spirit. The Santa spirit exists in all of us. It may look different and mean something different to each person. But the thing that unites them all is the same. And that thing is love.

Notes:

[i] http://www.hlntv.com/slideshow/2013/12/13/brothers-take-pictures-santa-34-years?hpt=hp_t3

Emerson, Lake and Palmer quote

I Believe in Father Christmas
I wish you a hopeful Christmas
I wish you a brave new year
All anguish, pain and sadness
Leave your heart and let your road be clear
They said there'll be snow at Christmas
They said there'll be peace on earth

*Hallelujah, Noel, be it heaven or hell
The Christmas we get we deserve.*

Emerson, Lake and Palmer
Greg Lake. 1975. BMG Rights Management

Chapter 22

Where This Leaves Me

Researching Santa became my life journey because it thrust me to the world's past, my past, analysis of who he is in the present and consideration of who he could be in the future. If it isn't obvious, I have spent years, countless hours and energy researching Santa Claus to figure out he was and why he's been so important. I have seriously tried to look at all sides of his construction in this book. I've wrestled over whether I think it's appropriate or good for my own or other children to enjoy him. I am left with two different strains of thought that I'd like to share with you. The first is micro-personal the second is macro-political.

On the micro-personal side, this project forced me to own my history with Santa. I had never realized that he proved to be one of the best parts of my childhood. Believing in Santa has given me far more than I ever imagined. When I was little, believing in Santa gave me assurance that once a year everything would be wonder-full. Contrary to adult rhetoric to the contrary, being a child is often hard – and for some of us, very hard. When we are little we are told to sit down, shut up, do as we are told, that we don't know enough, can't do this or that, that we have to wait, be nice, be good, and don't say or do anything to anyone that will get us in trouble. In many homes, money is hard to come by. Children hear parents talking about how there isn't enough money for rent or food or to buy certain things that other people seem to have. Children see the disparity between the haves and have-nots, even at an early age. Many are subject to being smacked, yelled at, and harshly reminded about all the things they are not, rather than being smiled-upon for all the things that they are. As children, we are often manipulated, conned, cajoled, lied to. Our lives as children are spent in "one day". One day we will grow up, one day we will be old enough to pour milk without it spilling, go to school, take a walk by ourselves, drive a car, meet a sweetheart, get a job, have our own house, and on and on the list grows. One day a year it will be our birthday and if we are lucky someone might remember. And once a year, Santa might come. But only if we are good, we are told. So every time we do something that big people define as naughty, we are at risk of Santa not coming. His not coming is proof positive that we aren't really good enough, not really loved, and that nobody really cares about us.

That's a lot for a young person to bear. We look for kernels of everlasting truths that we can cling to that will get us through those hard days.

For me, Santa Claus embodied a time when I believed there would be "enough". At the time when Santa was due to arrive, there wasn't just enough food, but fancy foods that were fixed only once a year. Family members came together at our house or we went to someone's house, where there was nonstop chattering and laughter. At least for that day, people seemed to enjoy and care about one another. The fact that they may gossip and back-bite the next day was the next day – but not allowed on Santa's day. The anticipation grew and grew as the hour when Santa would arrive, almost to the point that it was hard to stay in our skin, we got so excited. There were beautifully wrapped presents for everyone, and even if we got just a few, we felt happy for ourselves and gleeful watching others open and enjoy their gifts. It was a time when everyone mattered, everyone was included, and no one was forgotten.

The town dressed up with white lights on storefronts and colored lights strung around houses. Giant snowflakes and candles were hung on poles down the street. Strums of the same songs filled the airwaves, and every year I could count on hearing the long-dead Gene Autry still alive singing Here Comes Santa Claus, or Bing Crosby crooning Silver Bells. There were festive displays in the parks and on people's lawns, even contests to see who had the most light-up spirit. While putting up the tree was always prone to someone swearing, it was thrilling to hang my special ornament on the tree as everyone else hung theirs amongst the tinsel and glistening lights. Everyone worked hard to decorate with beauty. I believed it represented the beauty that they felt in the hearts towards all human-kind.

Santa's arrival filled my head with the possibility of magic. He filled my heart with hope. He knew what I needed and wanted, even if I never wrote him a letter and asked. There was a gentleness in Santa's smile, wisdom in his twinkly eyes, kindness to his touch. Once a year, the impossible became possible. Grumpy people could suddenly become kind. Not that everything I dreamed of came true, but enough and unexpected wonders occurred to assure my little spirit that anything could happen. And for that blessed moment, I knew in my heart of hearts that I mattered to him, to someone, and maybe to a lot of people. That lifted off the weight that my little shoulders carried so many days the rest of the year.

As I grew older and "one day when grow up" became reality, the sweet Santa memories etched into my childhood DNA remained. Nobody tells children that growing up will be a roller-coaster, with amazing highs and devastating lows. People rejoice over the high when we feel when we think we're on top of the world. It's when the lows come that we learn about aches and heart-breaks that wrack us to our core. No one can escape struggles, and unfortunate, hard, and bad things happen to everyone. Our souls long for relief, and when we think there is none, I remember the hope that goodness will come if I can just hold on. Remembering that even when I don't ask, someone is there who cares about me, and they may gift me by lifting my burden for a little while. Joy might be around the corner if I hold tight to the magic.

Belief in Santa isn't really about Santa at all. It is about something much bigger. Having the annual Santa joy-filled experience taught me that the realm of possibility always exists. Even if it is for one day a year, when everything is put right for that moment, it is often enough to keep us going for the other 364 days of the year. There is always a Santa Spirit around – we just have to look to see it. It's in the smiles, the twinkly eyes, the wise nod of someone's head as they gaze at us. Santa can be found in March or May, February or September, on a Tuesday or Friday, in the early morning or heat of the afternoon, at home or work or on a street-corner, from an old woman, a man weary from work, or in the beaming face of a small child when we least expect it. The Santa spirit is pervasive and can be brought by the solitary Santa trudging through the snow or in a sleigh pulled by eight tiny reindeer. This is what I discovered about myself in learning about Santa and why I loved him then, and love him still.

I discovered thatSanta is standing at a fork in the road. We can decide whether he will go down a path of transformation that makes him relevant for contemporary society or if we will push him to become irrelevant to future generations. While he has existed for decades, he has become a casualty in a cultural war on Christmas. "Should I let my children believe in Santa?" has become a normal question for parents. While some parents are Santafanatics and others are Santaphobes, most hover in the netherworld in between and aren't sure what they should do. As a pediatric sociologist who has done extensive research on him, I've concluded that either Santa must be transformed to have a positive place in the lives of children or he will become obsolete.

A thoughtful review of research on historical, psychological, cognitive, and sociological data has led me to this conclusion. Santa is a product of social construction. He can be anything we make him and mean anything we want him to. We have an opportunity to positively transform this figure for the good of children. He could become a universal symbol of joy, diversity, civility, and altruism if we let him. His history is a tapestry of different belief systems, figures, and messages that have been woven together and refined over time. He need not be a symbol of division, materialism, and opposition unless we make him into that. We have an opportunity to transform Santa Claus into a figure that represents the finest qualities and attributes that we want our children to emulate.

Should we let children believe in Santa? In doing the research on this question, the answer hit me between the eyes.

Yes, if Santa is portrayed as the essence of loving-kindness. Yes, if Santa is presented as a role-model for altruism who teaches children to be generous and thoughtful about caring for the needs of others. Yes, if Santa is a vehicle for learning that making dreams comes true takes planning, work, time, and patience. Yes, if Santa is the deliverer of joy, laughter, and delight who has no other purpose than making others happy. Yes, if Santa is seen as universal, a spirit not associated with any religion, nationality, or creed. Yes, when Santa is presented with no prescribed gender or race or ability or age so that everyone, children as well as parents and grandparents, can learn they can be Santas too. Yes, when Santa is used to bring people in the family and community together to see the goodness we all have inside, that is begging to be set free to limitlessly express caring and sharing at least one time a year.

No, not when Santa is presented as the fountain of corporate conspicuous consumption and materialistic greed. No, not if he is used to exclude some children. No, not when he is being used as by religious or political fanatics as a tool to separate us from one another. No, not when his gift-giving is associated with a values that make children who get a lot feel more entitled and worthy than children who receive little or nothing. No, not when Santa is used to be a symbol of competition of who is better than others. No, not when he is used by parents to control children or as someone who will punish them.

How we decide as adults to present Santa says much more about who we are as individuals and communities than it does about him. We can choose to grow Santa into a spirit that lifts us up instead of brings us down. Santa Claus can be transformed into the bringer of genuine well-being and care about others, instead of materialism and greed. Santa Claus has been ageless and universal because he has delivered to us something that we all desperately need – **hope that things will be better** in the future and that somebody, somewhere **cares about us**. Santa Claus has endured in the hearts and minds of people for hundreds of years because he has given us things of immense value. In my conclusion, what he provides children, families, and communities far outweigh things that people may find challenging. Santa can embody the best attributes of humanity, including hope, charity, selflessness, and love. These attributes need to be reinforced, not eliminated. What he has to offer children in today's divisive world could be even more important than what he delivered in the past – but only if we let him.

Santa Claus has always been a product of social construction that has meant different things to different people at different places at different points in time. It's time again to think differently about Santa. If people could recognize the constructive cognitive and emotional benefits delivered by Santa, this could help diffuse the confusion about whether or not to let children believe in him. The positive bonding that could be gained in families and communities around the Santa issue is important for cohesion and belongingness. Santa Claus can be transformed into a vehicle to make children feel as though they matter.

Shedding old preconceptions is difficult. Getting past negative experiences that trigger present emotions is challenging. Children deserve the right to experience the pleasure that is separate from the emotional baggage or agendas of their parents. Parents hold tremendous power over what children will think, believe, do, and feel. So do communities by what they establish as normative and acceptable. Santa provides children with a figure that adults can mobilize to help children learn how to be kind, loving, and accepting of others.

The fact is, no matter our age, we are all needy children. We need to know that we are loved and cared about. We need to know that people are good and go out of their way to bring goodness to others. We need to know that if we work hard and keep our values high that we will be uplifted, and we can uplift others. We need fantasy. We need to dream. We need to hope. We need to know that there is still magic in the world. We need to know that sometimes the impossible can be possible, especially if we engage ourselves to make it happen. Importantly, we need to remember that we need each other. Santa is merely a good reminder of this fact.

There is no substitute for love and the sheer delight we experience when we open our hearts, hands, and minds. It is in the giving that we truly receive – and that message is a fine one for us children of all ages to remember. If we can decide to keep the spirit of Santa alive in thought, word, and deed, imagine how his transformation can be used for the betterment of children's development and well-being. Imagine the fun that families could have together as they share the Santa spirit. One can dream about how supportive communities could be if everyone worked together with the singular mission of how to make life easier and happier for each other. Imagine preserving a worldwide legacy where people go out of their way to help others and to find joy. Santa is a vehicle to create child, family, and community bonds. Santa is an important figure in delivering universal values of hope, love, joy, and altruism. Creating in children a sense of possibility has benefits that far exceed any material item associated with the December holiday. Learning to make the impossible possible is a critically important lesson to learn in every aspect of our lives. Why on earth would we want to take that away from children?

Benefits of a Santa State of Mind

Usually, people assume that Santa is just for children, but actually, adults need Santa too. Studies indicate that the majority of adults profess to believe in Santa (Bump 2013). My own studies of young adults found that most thought believing in Santa Claus enhanced their childhood and they plan to have their own children believe in him as well. Why parents want their children to believe in Santa is just as much as the study of the adult needs and behaviors as it is of children. We all need hope, dreams, and the possibility of miracles.

You can watch the Santa Spirit all around you in December. You can see it in the bundles that people carry out of stores to be wrapped at home before they are delivered with delight to someone who is beloved. You can see it in the faces of the tots who sit on Santa's lap. You can see it in the giggling eyes of children as they sit icing cookies with family. It can be found when teenagers share favorite music with their friends; it's there when children paint pasta they will string on yarn for a necklace to give to their grandma. You can see it in the sacrifice of the mechanic who is working late to earn enough for the necklace he wants to give that someone special; you can see it in the tired back and rough hands of the janitor who has worked an extra shift to make sure his children get the gifts they deserve. People who normally forget about the hungry, sick, and homeless suddenly remember them during the holidays in radiant acts of kindness. The Santa spirit is everywhere, at least for a short period of time. According to Charles Smith (2009), Kansas State University child development specialist, Santa Claus represents a wonderful spirit of kindness. And, you don't have to believe in Santa per se to benefit, since the need for kindness is universal. It is the spirit that Santa represents that is of importance.

"The magic of Santa Claus is no lie....Santa Claus is a shared cultural image of benevolence and kindness and you don't want to undermine that. With Santa Claus, you are trying to enrich the child's life by sharing something that

you both enjoy. Santa Claus embodies the whole idea of the Christmas season as a time of caring, togetherness, and magic....a child's belief in the story of Santa Claus enables the child to develop a sense of wonder about the jolly character and use their imagination. Using their imagination to consider the possibilities is key to problem-solving and other mental tasks down the line. Santa Claus is a loving, merry person who cares about kids so much that he wants to bring toys to kids throughout the whole world. If you take Santa Claus out of the picture, you diminish that child's sense that they are special. We know that Santa is not real, but the truth of Santa is the shared cultural commitment to kids, to bring happiness into children's lives." (Smith 2009).

Santa enables parents to relive their youth in positive ways. Inside of us exists a whole bunch of "us" – us when we were four when we were ten, us when we got our first car when we got our first kiss, our first job. We remember our first Christmas together with someone special, and the year we had our first baby. When we celebrate Christmas, we remember our past, who we have been, and who we are now. We remember people who are dear to us who are no longer with us, and the season reminds us of conversations, activities, and outings, like when we rode in the horse-drawn wagon through the snow to cut down our tree as we listened to the horses' bells jingle. Memories help us to recall people that were especially dear to us or times when a moment of perfect wonder and love enveloped our hearts. Santa gives us an opportunity to build positive memories in our children. He is a vehicle so they can one day remember that we dearly loved them and had so much fun with them.

In this way, holidays are just as important to adults as to children. Children help adults to feel the magic of the season more intensely. We long to recapture those days of innocence when we believed that anything was possible. We want to believe that our dreams will still come true. Adults may find themselves beaming with delight as they listen to children's interpretations of the nature of Santa and how he comes to do the things he allegedly does. Children's unique interpretations and creative tales are often beyond our comprehension since most adults gave up real creative imaginations a long time ago.

When it comes to Santa, we have replaced magic with scientific rationality and "facts". It's we, the adults, who are the ones who have politicized him. Children are not constrained by our mental boundaries and they come up with hysterically funny scenarios, brilliant insights, and tender explanations for why Santa does certain things. Their tales make us laugh until we cry, reflect our own reasoning, and touch our hearts. Children's views of Santa help make Christmas a special time not just for themselves, but for the adults around them. Many people travel far and wide to be with friends or family who have children because as many people will testify, "Christmas just isn't as much fun without kids." We like interweaving our own childhoods into the lives of new generations through cherished rituals, silly as they may be.

Children are such sweet creatures that they willingly accept about anything that well-intended, beloved adults tell them. Parents hold tremendous power over how they think and feel, and these early holiday experiences can last a lifetime inside them. Research indicates that people remember things best when they are associated with emotional experiences. Adults who had wonderful Santa experiences may still be able to smell pine trees or cookies baking, even as they recall the holiday in the middle of summer. We can almost be able to taste special sweets we enjoyed or smell the perfume from an aunt who hugs too much. We can feel the frost in our minds that once danced on our windowpanes. I like sitting on the couch staring at the lights on the tree; blurring the lights into a kaleidoscope of color reminds me of Christmases long ago.

Maurice Reidy (1999) talks about how sad he is that the routine of Christmas has changed once they were no longer children. "For a kid who believes in Santa Claus, there is no bigger night than (Christmas Eve)." He missed the wonderful Christmases of his youth but found he could recapture them when his nieces and nephews came home for the holidays -until they too became "too old" to appreciate Santa.

"When my nieces and nephews were younger, I would be with them, sitting at the top of the stairs, waiting for the green light to be given so we could slide down the banister together and into the living room, branching out in every direction until our piles of goodies were found. Skis. Kitchen sets. Stockings stuffed with oranges. Although Santa had long since stopped leaving me anything -- I blame my father for this because of those still-warm embers on Christmas Eve of 1958 -- I still enjoyed being part of the scramble. As they say, it's all about the journey, and heading down those stairs with my young relatives put me back in my flannel Dr. Denton's, the built-in feet gripping the hardwood floor, my heart once again pounding with excitement. And then, a few years ago, it all changed. For some reason, someone in the family decided delayed gratification was what the Wilson clan

needed on Christmas morning. Instead of waking up early and descending upon the living room and having everything opened by 8 a.m., the family decided we needed breakfast before presents. Eggs. Bacon. Coffee. Restraint. No one accepts blame for this decision now, but someone obviously made it, and it wasn't me. It smacks of my sister-in-law, always one for self-improvement programs, always reciting the "It'll make you a better person" mantra, although I don't know for the life of me how having a leisurely breakfast before opening presents makes anyone a better person. If anything, it causes anxiety, heartburn, and hair loss. I know because I suffer all three. Maybe this year I'll sleep in, joining my nieces and nephews, now all young adults in college who have discovered the pleasures of 18 hours of sleep, rarely rising before noon. Then again, maybe I'll just get up early by myself, sit at the top of the stairs and wait for the green light. For old time's sake."

Just as adults can remember holidays fondly, they may dread holidays if they've had unpleasant experiences at them in years past. Sometimes, family members fight during the holidays; people may drink too much and say things they shouldn't, or hurt other's feelings. Because memories of holidays may be unconscious as well as conscious, family rituals, foods, music, or objects may evoke emotions that are highly charged. Adults may respond to holiday exchanges with responses that are way out of proportion. Instead of dreading the holidays for the rest of their lives as they deal with injustices of the past, adults can transform Santa in their psyche so that they are able to heal and become whole. Michigan pediatrician Theodore Miller taught me that having children enables adults to re-live their childhood in a new and positive, constructive way. Everyone has parts of our pasts that have left us with scars and wounds; it is impossible to grow into adulthood without experiencing at least some amount of trauma. But we don't have to keep reliving those abuses and wrongs. Through our children, and through joyful celebrations like those promoted by the presence of Santa, we can make strides to re-do our past and write a new future for ourselves.

Dr. Miller knew it is vitally important for adults to play, and to become children with their children. Adults may go out of their way to give their children things they wanted and never got – and those "things" may be emotional and relational as well as material. For instance, I made sure my kids got the Lite Brite because I always wanted but never got from Santa. I never got a stocking filled with silly treats to delight me – but in making them for my children, I finally did get them. And when I became a parent, I bought my daughter the pony that I always wanted but never got. And I loved him as dearly as she did.

When adults give their children healing experiences, they get them too. As adults lick the frosting out of the bowl, careen down a snow-covered hill on a sled with their little one tucked safely between their legs, or build sandcastles on the beach, they are able to laugh and play, doing silly things that on the surface seem to have no value – but which actually contain immense emotional meaning. While sharing experiences with children they may touch a tender spot in the heart of the adult, and the ice that once formed around their heart may melt as adults allow themselves the full experience of remembering past pains and appreciating current pleasures. This type of simple engagement, according to Ray Helfer, MD, one of the founding fathers in the field of child abuse and neglect, truly enables adults to heal. Once that child inside of us is healed, adults can move forward with their lives in a more positive and productive manner. Make no mistake about it – adults need Santa just as much as children do.

Why are parents so obsessed with telling children "the truth" about Santa? When children quit believing in Santa, it is often their parents who are the saddest because their disbelief denies parents the opportunity to go back to a time when they felt that anything was possible. Adult reality is filled with restrictions, obstacles, and a sense of chronic challenge. Which view is more comforting? Which is going to get you through life more easily? Hope, for most of us, needs to be encouraged. Adults are confronted routinely with logical explanations that are limiting and actually don't make sense while a child's explanations of things are often much more hopeful, pleasant, and just as truthful in a different sort of way.

Parents, and mothers, in particular, are often the ones who don't want children to stop believing in Santa. Christmas is often cherished as the premiere nostalgic and sentimental time because it allows for adults to go back into their golden age of childhood when they remember the joy instead of the challenges that so often accompany childhood. Making Santa helps adults to leave behind the here and now as they revisit their early childhood when life was magical and they could receive gifts just because they were good. When parents create Santa in the minds of their children, they also create him on their own. For a brief glimmer in time, Santa sails through the snow with absolute delight as he delivers long-awaited toys to dear girls and boys. Parents get to "be Santa." They ARE Santa, in every way, with everything that entails. What a marvelous gift for adults Santa is! So it is understandable, logical, that when their children quit believing, their opportunity to play and fantasize often stops. But it doesn't have to. Parents have found something wonderful in themselves as they have discovered the adult Santa Claus. They don't want to let go of it. And why should they? For them, Santa is a way for them to express love, and love is real. **Real love lasts forever.**

During the COVID-19 lock-down, I created not just this book but a five-book series on the Santa Spirit. This **Re-Imagine Santa** book was for savvy adults, there was a shorter version for busy adults (**The ABCs of the Santa Spirit for Adults**) that accompanied a children's picture book so that they could learn **The Santa Spirit**. I created **The Legend of the Santa Stocking** so that children could relate to other children and families who struggled with how to make a truly happy holiday, and **The Santa Spirit Advent Calendar Book: COVID Edition** that gave families fun, free, family-oriented things to do each day of December to create a "feastival" (or combination feast and festival) for Santa's arrival. Doing this and getting them out for the December 2020 holidays became an obsession, one time-wise that made it best for me to self-publish.

As I poured heart and soul into creating the Santa Spirit series, I realized that I was doing this for a deeper reason than re-creating dreams about how I wished my childhood was, or more exactly could-have-been. I think transforming Santa to showcase the Santa Spirit is essential to helping create a kinder, more humane world. I am watching adults of all sorts taking a stand for who they are and what they believe. There are millions who are acting in the Santa Spirit who are going out of their way to bring loving-kindness to the world. And yet there are countless more who aren't. They are Team Krampus instead, saying mean-spirited words and doing mean-spirited, punitive actions that are not for the benefit of others – and certainly not or the benefit of children who will become the parents and leaders of tomorrow. What children experience today surely guides the direction tomorrow will take. So for them, and for all humanity, let's value and invest wisely in what has the biggest, best, long-term benefits.

I hope that you will open the power of the Santa Spirit. Famous words remind us that "The glory of God is within us, not just in some of us but in everyone...so let (your) own light shine[1]". "There is no day but today"[2] to "Become the change you want to see in the world." [3]. Gordon Fellman's book, *Rambo and the Dalai Lama*, reminds us that we have a choice about how we greet each other. We can see each other as someone to be angry at, frightened of, someone we must conquer and control - or we can see others with compassion, a listening ear, and an open heart as we find ways to honor our collective humanity. I believe that children are beautiful and the world is a grand and glorious place. We have more that unites us than divides us. Learning how to be kind and respect one another's human rights is essential for the world's survival. Now that this book is over, I realize that helping children to learn the art of loving-kindness is why I have written it. As adults, parents, and leaders, we can use the Santa Spirit to show them the way. This is my contribution to helping to make the holidays more joyful, peaceful, and kind, with the hope that love and justice will rain upon the world and wash away the sadness and despair that has the potential of growing if we don't do something about it today.

[1] Nelson Mandella 1994 Inaugural speech excerpts
[2] RENT
[3] Mahatma Gandhi

Final quote to Remember

So this is Xmas
And what have you done
Another year over and a new one just begun
And so this is Xmas, I hope you have fun
The near and the dear one, the old and the young.
A very merry Xmas and a happy new year
Let's hope it's a good one without any fear
And so this is Xmas
For weak and for strong, for rich and for poor ones
The road is so long. And so happy Xmas
For black and for white, for yellow and red ones
Let's all stop the fight.
***
Imagine all the people living in peace.
A brotherhood of man.
Imagine all the people sharing all of the world.
You may say I'm a dreamer
But I'm not the only one. I hope you will join us
And the world will live as one.

Excerpts from Happy Xmas by Paul McCartney and John Lennon, and Imagine by John Lennon,who must have understood the importance of The Santa Spirit

References

Here is a list of some of the materials that I used for my research that helped me come up to the conclusions provided in this book to help you if you wish to read them.

ABC. (2019). Made in America Christmas. https://abcnews.go.com/WN/mailform?id=14998335

Alcántara, Ann-Marie. (2020). The 2019 holiday season saw digital sales grow. https://www.adweek.com/retail/the-2019-holiday-season-saw-digital-sales-grow-to-723-billion/

Allen, Samantha. (2017). Is Mrs. Claus Santa's real beard: Who made Santa straight? *The Daily Beast*. https://www.thedailybeast.com/is-mrs-claus-santas-real-beard-or-who-made-santa-straight

American Battlefield Trust. (2020). Christmas during the Civil War. https://www.battlefields.org/learn/articles/christmas-during-civil-war

American Psychological Association. (n.d). *What Makes Kids Care? Teaching Gentleness in a Violent World*. Retrieved from https://www.apa.org/helpcenter/kids-care

Anderson CJ., & Prentice NM. (1994). Encounter with reality: Children's reactions on discovering the Santa Claus myth. *Child Psychiatry and Human Development, 25*, 67–84. https://doi.org/10.1007/BF02253287

Andreae, Giles. (2013). *I love you Father Christmas*. London:Orchard.

Arthuriana. (2002). America and the creation of Santa Claus. Arthuriana. http://www.arthuriana.co.uk/xmas/pages/santa.htm

Arthuriana. (nd). The History of Santa Claus and Father Christmas. http://www.arthuriana.co.uk/xmas/pages/folklore.htm.

Assembly of Yahweh, Cascade. (n.d). Christmas is not for Christians. Assembly of Yahweh. http://assemblyoftrueisrael.com/Documents/Christmas.html

Barak, Azy, Engle, Cathy, Katzir, Liora, & Fisher, William. (1987). Increasing the Level of Empathic Understanding by Means of a Game. *Simulation & Games,* 18(4), 458-470. https://doi.org/10.1177/0037550087184002

Barksdale, Nate. (2014). Who Was St. Nicholas? History. www.historychannel.com

Barnett LA. (1990). Developmental benefits of play for children. *J Leis Res.*1990;22 :138– 153

Barnett, Mark A., & Thompson, Shannon. (1984). The role of perspective taking and empathy in *children's* Machiavellianism, prosocial behavior, and motive for helping. *The Journal of Genetic Psychology,* 146, 295-305. https://doi.org/10.1080/00221325.1985.9914459

Barnett, James Harwood. (1976). The American Christmas: A Study in National Culture. New York: Arno P.

Barnett, James H. (1949). The Easter Festival--A Study in Cultural Change. *American Sociological Review* 14.1 (1949): 62-70.

Bates,Katherine.(1889).*GoodySantaClaus.* http://www.hymnsandcarolsofchristmas.com/Poetry/Goody_Santa_Claus/goody_santa_claus.htm

Baxter JM & Sabbagh MA.(2005, October). Examining young children's changing theories about Santa Claus through parent-child conversations. [Presented at the biennial meeting of the Society of Child Development]. San Diego, CA.

BBC. (2020). What will COVID-19 mean for Christmas events? https://www.bbc.com/news/uk-wales-53496428

BBC. (2020). St. Lucy. https://en.wikipedia.org/wiki/Saint_Lucy

Becton,D.(2004). The Real Meaning of Christmas. *Xavier Herald.* http://www.xula.edu/herald/issues/20041209/editorials.html

Belsie, Laurent. (2010). Cyber Monday Deals: Worth Waiting For?. *Christian Science Monitor* 26 Nov.

Bengtsson, H., & Johnson, L. (1992). Perspective-taking, empathy and prosocial behavior in late childhood. *Child Study Journal,* 22, 11-22.

Belk, Russell W. (1987). A Child's Christmas in America: Santa Claus as Deity, Consumption as Religion. *The Journal of American Culture* 10 (1987): 87-100.

Belk, Russell W. (1989/2000). Materialism and the Modern U.S. Christmas." *Advertising & Society Review* 1.1 Project MUSE.

Benediktsdottir, Helga. (2014). The impact of fairytales. https://skemman.is/bitstream/1946/17819/1/BAessay.Helga.Benediktsdottir.pdf

Berk, L. E., Mann, T. D., & Ogan, A. T. (2006). Make-believe play: Wellspring for development of self-regulation. In D. Singer, R. Golinkoff, & K. Hirsch-Pasek (Eds.). Play = Learning: How play motivates and enhances children's cognitive and social-emotional growth. New York: Oxford University Press

Berger, Peter. (1963). Invitation to sociology: A humanistic perspective. Garden City, N.Y: Doubleday.

Berger, Peter L, and Thomas Luckmann. (1966). The *Social Construction of Reality*: A Treatise in the Sociology of Knowledge. Garden City NY: Doubleday.

Blanc, Jon. (2002, December) *Christmas in Africa.* US – Africa.org. http://us-africa.tripod.com/xmass.html

Blizard, Paul and Pat Blizard. (2019). Watchtower 101: 101 Strange Beliefs and Practices of Jehovah's Witnesses. http://www.geocities.com/Heartland/2919/reasons.html

Boerger, Elizabeth, Tullos, Ansley, & Woolley, Jacqueline. (2009). Return of the Candy Witch: Individual differences in acceptance and stability of belief in a novel fantastical being. *Br J Dev Psychol, 27*(Pt 4), 953–970.

Bongiorno, Laurel. (2020). 10 things parents should know about play. https://www.naeyc.org/our-work/families/10-things-every-parent-play

Bornstein, M. H., Haynes, O. M., Legler, J. M., O'Reilly, A. W., & Painter, K. M. (1997). Symbolic play in childhood: Interpersonal and environmental context and stability. *Infant Behavior and Development*, 20, 197-207.

Bouldin, Paula & Pratt, Chris. (2001). The ability of children with imaginary companions to differentiate between fantasy and reality. *British Journal of Developmental Psychology, 19*(pt1), 99–114. https://doi.org/10.1348/026151001165985

Boyer, Pascal. (2002). *Religion Explained: The Human Instincts That Fashion Gods, Spirits and Ancestors.* William Heinemann: London.

Boyle, Christopher & McKay, Kathy. (2016). A wonderful lie. *The Lancet Psychiatry.* 3. 1110-1111. 10.1016/S2215-0366(16)30363-7. https://www.researchgate.net/publication/310789588_A_wonderful_lie

Breen, Lynda. (Nd) Santa. http://www.discussanything.com/forums/archive/index.php/t-68431.html

Brock Chisholm. (1956). The Family: Basic Unit of Social Learning. *The Coordinatior*, 4(4), 2-15. https://www.jstor.org/stable/581287

Broom, Douglas. (2019). Christmas by the numbers. https://www.weforum.org/agenda/2019/12/christmas-holiday-season-shopping-retail-gifts/

Brown, Jacob. (1896). *Brown's Miscellaneous Wri*tings. Cumberland, Maryland: JJ Miller.

Buller, Tom. (2005). Can we scan for truth in a society of liars? *American Journal of Bioethics*, 5(2), 58 - 60.

Bulleit, Mark. (n.d). Mommy, Daddy – Is there really a Santa Claus? Streetdirectory.com. https://www.streetdirectory.com/travel_guide/10851/parenting/mommydaddyis_there_really_a_santa_claus.html

Burns, Thomas. (1976). Dr. Seuss' How The Grinch Stole Christmas. *New York Folklore*, 2, 4, 191-204

Cantrell, Geoff. (2016). Psychologists study impact of children finding truth about Santa. https://news-prod.wcu.edu/2016/12/psychologists-study-impact-children-finding-truth-santa-claus-will-cry-pout/

Caplow, Theodore. (1982). Christmas gifts and kin networks. *American Sociological Review*. 47 (June_ 383-392.

Caplow, T. (1984). Rule Enforcement Without Visible Means: Christmas Gift Giving in Middletown. *American Journal of Sociology*, 89(6), 1306-1323. Retrieved May 25, 2020, from www.jstor.org/stable/2779184

Caron, Andre. (1975). Gift decisions by kids and parents. *Journal of Advertising Research*. 15: 15-20

Carlsson-Paige. Nancy. (2008). *Taking Back Childhood*. Hudson Street Publishers.

Carver, Sally. (1982). Santa Claus: A man for all seasons. Hobbies. 95, 104-110.

Catholic Online. (2020). St. Lucy. https://www.catholic.org/saints/saint.php?saint_id=75

Centers for Disease Control. (2020). Disability impacts us all. https://www.cdc.gov/ncbddd/disabilityandhealth/infographic-disability-impacts-all.html#:~:text=61%20million%20adults%20in%20the,is%20highest%20in%20the%20South.

Cheal, David. (1986). The social dimensions of gift behavior. *Journal of Social and Personal Relationships.* 3, 423-429.

Chisholm, Brock. (1956). The Family: Basi.c Unit of Social Learning *Coordinator,* 4(4), 2-15.

Choose Your Cyprus. (2020). Christmas customs of Cyprus. https://chooseyourcyprus.com/christmas-customs-of-cyprus.html

Christmas Archives. Chronology of Santa *Claus.* (n.d). Christmas Archives. http://www.christmasarchives.com/santa.html

Christmas.com. (1978). The True Story of Santa Claus Begins With Nicholas. http://www.christmas.com/pe/1978

Christmas.com. (nd). Christmas in Japan. http://www.christmas.com/worldview/jp

Christmas Around the World. (n.d) Santa's Net. Retrieved from http://www.santas.net/africanchristmas.htm

Christmas Around The World. (nd).Christmas by country. http://www.soon.org.uk/country/christmas.htm

Christmas in Asia. (nd). http://www.cvc.org/christmas/asia.htm

Christmas in Syria. (n.d) Christmas World. Retrieved from http://christmas-world.freeservers.com/syria.html

Christmas FunDoo Times. (2020). Commercialization of Santa Claus. http://christmas.fundootimes.com/santa-claus/santa-commercialization.html

Christmas Traditions. (Nd). Christmas traditions. http://www.soon.org.uk/christmas.htm

Chronology of Santa Claus. (n.d). Christmas Archives. http://www.christmasarchives.com/santa.html

Chua, Amy. (2011). *Battle Hymn of the Tiger Mother.* NY: Penguin.

Church, Francis. (1897). Yes, Virginia there is a Santa. *New York Sun.*

Clark, Cindy Dell. (1995*). Flights of Fancy, Leaps of Faith: Children's myths in contemporary America.* University of Chicago Press: Chicago, IL.

Clark, Richard. (nd). Santa Claus. The Spirit of Christmas. Source no longer available.

Clifford, Stephanie. (2010). Black Friday Expectations Are High. *New York Times* 26 Nov.

Clifford, Stephanie. (2010). Why Wait? This Year, Retailers Push Black Friday Into October. *New York Times* 28 Oct.

Cline, Foster and Jim Fay. (1990). Helicopter parent in *Parenting with Love and Logic*. Nav Press.

Coates, Ta-Nehisi. (2013). What we mean when we say race is a social construct. The *Atlantic*. https://www.theatlantic.com/national/archive/2013/05/what-we-mean-when-we-say-race-is-a-social-construct/275872/

Coca Cola. (Nd). 5 things you never knew about Santa Claus and Coca Cola. https://www.coca-colacompany.com/news/five-things-you-never-knew-about-santa-claus-and-coca-cola

Coolahan K, Fantuzzo J, Mendez J, McDermott P. Preschool peer interactions and readiness to learn: relationships between classroom peer play and learning behaviors and conduct. *J Educ Psychol*.2000;**92** :458– 465

Corcoran, Kieran. (2014, December 26th). *Merry Christmas from America to unfortunate Britain.* Daily Mail. https://www.dailymail.co.uk/news/article-2887988/Merry-Christmas-America-unfortunate-Britain-1914-U-S-Navy-Santa-Claus-ship-sailed-England-5MILLION-Christmas-presents-children-fathers-died-WWI.html

Corsaro, William. (2005). *The Sociology of Childhood.* Pine Forge Press.

Cotton, Kathleen. (1992). *Developing Empathy in Children and Youth.* Northwest Regional Education Laboratory.

Cousins, Norman. (2005). *Anatomy of an Illness as Seen by the Patient.* W.W. Norton & Company; Twentieth Anniversary edition.

Crampton, Gertrude. 1947. The Golden Christmas Book. New York:Golden Books

Cyprus Alive. (2020). Christmas in Cyprus. https://www.cyprusalive.com/en/cyprus-chistmas

Cyr, Claude. (2015). Personal communication.

Cyr, Claude. (2002). Do reindeer and children know something that we don't? Pediatric inpatients *belief* in *Santa Claus. Canadian Medical Association Journal, 167*(12), 1325-1327.

Daughtery, Greg. (2017). *In World War II America, Female Santas Took the Reins.* Smithsonian. https://www.smithsonianmag.com/history/world-war-ii-america-female-santas-took-reins-180967580/

Dautovic,G . (2019).Deck the halls with boughs of money. https://fortunly.com/statistics/christmas-spending-statistics/#gref

Deas, Gerald. (1999). *Santa* Rx. *New York Amsterdam News*; 12/23/99, Vol. 90 Issue 52, p14, 1/5.

Deas, Gerald. 2011. Take a pause with a black Santa. *New York Amsterdam News*. http://amsterdamnews.com/news/2011/dec/14/take-a-pause-with-a-black-santa-claus/

Dierker, Lisa C., Sanders, Barbara. (1996). Developmental differences and individual differences in children's ability to distinguish reality from fantasy. *Imagination, Cognition, and Personality*. https://doi.org/10.2190/KEKG-5P6C-G153-5E86

Dr. Seuss. (1957). *How the Grinch Stole Christmas!* Random House Books for Young Readers.

Elkind D. (2001). *The Hurried Child: Growing Up Too Fast Too Soon*. 3rd ed. Cambridge, MA: Perseus

Ekman, Paul. (2020). Why do people lie? https://www.paulekman.com/blog/why-do-people-lie-motives/

Egan, Bill. (2001). Christmas In Venezuela. Christmas Around the World. http://christmas-world.freeservers.com/venezuela.html

Egan, W. C. (n.d). Christmas in Scotland. Christmas World. http://christmas-world.freeservers.com//scotland.html

Eisenberg, Nancy. (1983). *The Socialization and Development of Empathy and Prosocial Behavior*. National Association for Human and Environmental Education: East Haddam, CT.

Elkind, David. (2007). *The Power of Play*. Da Capo.

Elves. (2015). *Letters to Santa*. Bloomington: Indiana University Press.

Encyclopedia.com. (2020). Processions. https://www.encyclopedia.com/religion/encyclopedias-almanacs-transcripts-and-maps/processions-religious

Engelbreit, Mary. 1998. *Believe*. Kansas City:Andrews McMeel Publishing

Erikson, Erik. (1993). *Childhood and Society*. W.W. Norton & Company, Reissue Edition.

Erickson RJ. (1985). Play contributes to the full emotional development of the child. *Education*.1985;**105** :261– 263

Eriksson, Stig. (2002) Christmas traditions and performance rituals: a look at Christmas celebrations in a Nordic context. *Applied Theater Researcher*, 3. https://www.medievalists.net/2011/12/christmas-traditions-and-performance-rituals-a-look-at-christmas-celebrations-in-a-nordic-context/

Evert, Lori. (2013). The Christmas Wish. New York:Random House.

Federation of American Scientists. (n.d). *NORAD at 40 Historical Overview.* Retrieved from https://fas.org/nuke/guide/usa/airdef/norad-overview.htm

Fein, G. G. (1981). Pretend play in childhood: An integrative review. Child development, 52, 1095–1118

Fellman, Gordon. (1998). *Rambo and the Dalai Lama*: The Compulsion to Win and Its Threat to Human Survival. New York: SUNY Press.

Ferland, Francine. (2009). *My Child's Development.* Montreal: Chu Sainte-Justine

Fetters, Ashley. (2018). Should parents protect their children's belief in Santa Claus. *The Atlantic.* https://www.theatlantic.com/family/archive/2018/12/parents-kids-belief-santa/577819/

Fields, Samantha.(2019). Lots of Americans go into debt over the holidays. Marketplace. https://www.marketplace.org/2019/11/26/lots-of-americans-go-into-debt-over-the-holidays/

Flaxman SG. (1999). Play: an endangered species? *Scholastic Inc.*1999;**110** :39– 41

Flynn, Tom. (1993). *The Trouble with Christmas.* Prometheus Books: Buffalo, NY.

Foster, Don. (2000). Author Unknown: On the trail of Anonymous. Henry Holt & Company: New York City: NY.

Forster, Mark. (2002). *How To Make Your Dreams Come True.* Hodder & Stoughton.

Francis, Heather. (Nd.) Native American culture of giving. https://www.learningtogive.org/resources/native-american-culture-giving

Franklin Institute (nd). The science of Santa's reindeer. https://www.fi.edu/flying-reindeer

Free Gifts.com. (2006). Stop Child Abuse: Tell Your Children The Truth. www.free-gifts.com/Santa_Claus.htm .

Fulghum, Robert. (1988). *All I Ever Needed To Know I Learned In Kindergarten.* NewYork:Villard Books.

Gannon, Megan. (2016). Race is a social construct. *Scientific American.* https://www.scientificamerican.com/article/race-is-a-social-construct-scientists-argue/

Garvey, C. (1991). *Play* (2nd ed.). Cambridge, MA: Harvard University Press

Genome News Network. (2003). Genome Variations. http://www.genomenewsnetwork.org/resources/whats_a_genome/Chp4_1.shtml

Gershaw, David. (2020) *Altruism and the Holiday Spirit*. [pdf file]. http://drdavespsychologypage.homestead.com/Altruism__Holiday_Spirit.pdf

Gerstner, Lisa. (2010). What You Need to Know About Holiday Shopping. Kiplinger's Personal Finance 64.12 (2010): 87..

Ginsburg, Kenneth. (2007).The importance of play in promoting healthy child development and maintaining positive parent-child bonds. *Pediatrics* January 2007, 119 (1) 182-191; DOI: https://doi.org/10.1542/peds.2006-2697 https://pediatrics.aappublications.org/content/119/1/182

Gittins, Diana. (1997). *The Child in Question*. St. Martin's Press.

Goffman, Erving. (1959). *The Presentation of Self in Everyday Life*. Garden City NJ: Doubleday.

Golby, H. and W. Purdue. (1986). *The Making of the Modern Christmas*. Athens: University of Georgia Press.

Grassl, Gary. (n.d). *Does Santa harm children?* 2think. Retrieved from http://www.2think.org/hii/santa.shtml

Grills, Nathan J., & Halyday, Brendan. (2009). Santa as a Public Health Pariah. *BMJ: British Medical Journal (Overseas & Retired Doctors Edition), 339*(7735), 1424-1426.

Grueber, H. A. (1895). *Myths of Northern Lands* (Ed published in 2010). Kessinger Publishing, LLC: Whitefish Montana. From https://www.amazon.com/Myths-Northern-Lands-H-Guerber/dp/1169775497

Gruber, H. A. & Thor, A. (2011). *Norse Gods, Goddesses, Giants, Dwarves, Elves & More* – A Complete Guide. Amazon.

Hagstrom, Warren. (1966). What is the meaning of Santa Claus. American Sociologist. 1(Nov):248-252

Haładewicz-Grzelak, Malgorzata. (2011). Cultural codes in the iconography of St Nicholas (Santa Claus*). Sign Systems Studies 39*(1), 105-146. https://doi.org/10.12697/SSS.2011.39.1.04

Hall, C. Michael. (2008). "Santa Claus, Place Branding and Competition." *Fennia* 186.1 (2008): 59-67.

Haller, Sonja. (2018). What type of parent are you? *USA Today.* https://www.usatoday.com/story/life/allthemoms/2018/09/19/parenting-terms-explained-lawnmower-helicopter-attachment-tiger-free-range-dolphin-elephant/1357612002/

Hanson, Keri. (2017). The History of Macys. https://www.visitmacysusa.com/article/history-macys-humble-beginnings-stunning-success

Harbaugh, William & Krause, Kate. (2000). Children's Altruism in Public Good and Dictator Experiments. *Economic Inquiry, 38*(1), 95-109.

Harris, Aisha. (2013). Santa should not be a white man anymore. *Slate.* https://slate.com/human-interest/2013/12/santa-claus-an-old-white-man-not-anymore-meet-santa-the-penguin-a-new-christmas-symbol.html

Harris, Paul L., Pasquini, Elisabeth S., Duke, Suzanne, Asscher, Jessica J., & Pons, Francisco. (2005). Germs and angels: the role of testimony in young children's ontology. *Developmental Science, 9*(1), 76-96.

Harris, P. L., & Kavanaugh, R. D. (1993). Young children's understanding of pretense. Monographs of the Society for Research in Child Development, 58(1).

Harvey, Ian. (2016, February 27th). The Santa Claus ship- United States gave English children the Christmas they never had during World War 1. *The Vintage News.* https://www.thevintagenews.com/2016/02/27/58091/

Healthyway. (2017). Ho ho hoax: the psychology behind the myth of Santa Claus. https://www.healthyway.com/content/ho-ho-hoax-the-psychology-behind-the-myth-of-santa-claus/

Heinselman, Craig. (1999, December). *His Reindeer Drive This Frosty Night.* Crypto.

Helfer, Ray E. (1984). *Childhood Comes First: A crash course in childhood for adults.* Helfer self- published.

Helsel, Phil. (2018). Do you still believe in Santa? Trumps approach to a child's Christmas. NBC. https://www.nbcnews.com/news/us-news/president-trump-first-lady-take-calls-children-about-santas-n951751

Hendricks, Trisha..2020 (July12).Will Christmas be called of due to COVID-19? 12 News. https://www.12news.com/article/news/local/valley/will-christmas-be-called-off-due-to-covid-19/75-485fcdfd-4a61-4336-a327-8473abe0201a

Henry M. (1990). More than just play: the significance of mutually directed adult, child activity. *Early Child Dev Care.*1990;60 :35– 50

Hessinger, Shawn. (2015). How did Christmas become commercialized? https://smallbiztrends.com/2015/12/christmas-become-commercialized.html

Hirschman, Elizabeth. (1998). *Interpretive Consumer Research*, Provo, UT: Association for Consumer Research

Hirsh-Pasek, Kathy & Roberta Golinkoff. (2004). *Einstein Never Used Flashcards: How our children really learn-and why they need to play more and memorize less.* Rodale Books.

History.com. (2020). Santa goes to war. https://www.history.com/news/santa-goes-to-war

Hodapp, Eleanor. (2016). Evil isn't born, it's made, as communicated in Once Upon A Time. https://scholarworks.bellarmine.edu/cgi/viewcontent.cgi?article=1035&context=tdc

Holiday Traditions (n.d). Holiday Traditions. Welcome to a world of holiday traditions! From http://www.californiamall.com/holiday-traditions/

Holpuch, Amanda. (2012). Meet Santa Claus, the presidential candidate running on children's rights. *The Guardian.* https://www.theguardian.com/world/us-news-blog/2012/oct/25/santa-claus-us-election-candidate

Horowitz, Kate. (2016). The secret history of Mrs. Claus. https://www.mentalfloss.com/article/90113/secret-history-mrs-claus

Howes, C., Unger, O., & Mattheson, C. C. (1992). *The collaborative construction of pretend: Social pretend play functions.* Albany, NY: SUNY Press

Howes, C., Unger, O., & Seidner, L. B. (1989). Social pretend play in toddlers: Parallels with social play and solitary pretend. *Child Development,* 60, 77-84.

Hughes, Christopher. (1998). Negative existentials, omniscience, and cosmic luck. *Religious Studies, 34*, 375-401.

Hughes, F. P. (2009). *Children, play, and development* (3rd ed.). Boston: Allyn and Bacon

Hurwitz SC. (2002). To be successful: let them play! *Child Educ.*2002/2003;79 :101– 102

Illes Judika. (2009). Encyclopedia of Spirits. Occult World. https://occult-world.com/gaude-frau/

Isenberg J, Quisenberry NL. (1988). Play: a necessity for all children. *Child Educ.*1988;64 :138– 145.

Jablonski, Nina. (2018). The Biology of Skin Color. https://www.biointeractive.org/sites/default/files/SkinColor-Educator-film.pdf

Jacobson, Lisa. (2004). *Raising Consumers: Children and the American mass market in early twentieth century.* New York: Columbia University Press.

Jacoby, Jeff. (2004, December 19). *A Jew Says Merry Christmas.* Boston Globe. Retrieved from http://archive.boston.com/news/globe/editorial_opinion/oped/articles/2004/12/19/a_jew_says_merry_christmas/

James, Allison and Prout, Alan. (2015). *Constructing and Reconstructing Childhood.* London: Routledge.

Juchniewicz, Melissa. (2007). Asking the hard questions: Giving children's literature a critical reading. *New England Reading Association Journal.* 43(2). https://www.questia.com/library/journal/1P3-1490385911/asking-the-hard-questions-giving-children-s-literature

Kageleiry, Jamie. (2019). Where was the first department store Santa? *New England Magazine.* https://newengland.com/today/living/new-england-history/first-department-store-santa-claus/

Kane, Amy. (n.d) Who Is Santa Claus? *Foster's Daily Democrat.*

Kibblesmith, Daniel. (2017). *Santa's Husband.* New York: Harper.

King, David. (2017). How religion motivates people to give and serve. *The Conversation.* https://theconversation.com/how-religion-motivates-people-to-give-and-serve-81662

Kee, Susan. (2019, December 16th). Santa Claus was much more than a Santa. Facebook. https://www.facebook.com/susankeewriter/posts/1189759357881629

Kelly, R., & Hammond, S. (2011). The relationship between symbolic play and executive function in young children. *Australasian Journal of Early Childhood*, 36, 21- 27.

Kilkell Marge. (1995) A Child's Christmas in Lebanon. The Diaspora Potrezebe. http://almashriq.hiof.no/lebanon/300/370/371/acs/pot/1-96-christmas.html

Klara, Robert. (2007).The Making of a Must-Have. Brandweek 48.44 (2007): 18

Klein, Christopher. (2019). When Santa Claus was deployed in Wartime. History. https://www.history.com/news/santa-goes-to-war

Koch, Pat and Ammeson, Jane. 2006. Holiday World. Charleston, SC: Arcadia.

Koch, Pat and Emily Weisner Thompson. (2013). *Santa Claus*. Charleston, SC: Arcadia.

Krebs, D., & Russell, C. (1981). Role taking and altruism: When you put yourself in the shoes of another, will they take you to the owner's aid? In J. P. Rushton & R. M. Sorrentino (Eds.), *Altruism and helping behavior: Social, personality and developmental perspectives* (pp. 167-187). Hillsdale, NJ: Erlbaum.

Krythe, Maymie Richardson. (1962). *All About American Holidays*. New York:Harper.

Kurdek, L. A., Krile, D. (1982). A developmental analysis of the relation between peer acceptance and both interpersonal understanding and perceived social self-competence. *Child Development,* 53, 1485-1491.

Ladd GW. (1990). Having friends, keeping friends, making friends, and being liked by peers in the classroom: predictors of children's early school adjustment. *Child Dev.*1990;61 :1081– 1100

Landover Baptist Church. (n.d) *The Devil is In Your Chimney. Is Santa Claus Satan? Retrieved from* https://www.landoverbaptist.org/news1299/santy.html

Leatherati. (2009). Santa Claus is gay. https://leatherati.com/is-santa-claus-gay-5896282d9cf3

Lee, Katherine. (2020, March 5). *How Parents Can Raise a Good Child*. Verywell family. Retrieved from http://childparenting.about.com/od/emotionaldevelopment/a/altruisticchild.htm

Lego Foundation. 2020. Learning through play. https://www.legofoundation.com/media/1063/learning-through-play_web.pdf

Lemmens, Koen. (2017) The dark side of 'Zwarte Piet': A misunderstood tradition or racism in disguise? A legal analysis, *The International Journal of Human Rights*, 21:2, 120-141, DOI: 10.1080/13642987.2016.1276448 https://www.tandfonline.com/doi/abs/10.1080/13642987.2016.1276448?scroll=top&needAccess=true&journalCode=fjhr20

Leone, Melissa. (2011). Commercialization in American Society. https://ufdc.ufl.edu/AA00060082/00001

Leone, Vikki. (2002 Dec. 11.) Santa on the Outer. http://www.education.theage.com.au/pagedetail.asp?intpageid=1005&strsection=students&intsectionid=0

Levin, Diane. (2010). Defending the Early Years. https://dey.org/resources/dianes-page/

Levins, Hoag. (2008). 146 Years Later, Macy's Windows Still Pull Huge Audiences. *Advertising Age.* 25 Nov.

Lewicki, Lillian. (1956). *Christmas Tales: Legends from many lands.* Golden Press: New York.

Lewis, Tanya. (2013). Kids belief in Santa myth is healthy. Livescience. https://www.livescience.com/42089-kid-s-belief-in-santa-is-healthy.html

Lillard, A. S. (1993). Young children's conceptualization of pretend: Action or mental representational state? *Child Development,* 64, 372-386.

Lillard, A. S. (2011). Mother-child fantasy play. In A. Pellegrini (Ed.), *The Oxford handbook of the development of play* (pp. 284-295). New York: Oxford University Press.

Lillard, A. S., Lerner, M. D., Hopkins, E. J., Dore, R. A., Smith, E. D., & Palmquist, C. M. (2012). The impact of pretend play on children's development: A review of the evidence. *Psychological Bulletin.* doi: 10.1037/a0029321

Liusuwan,, Nicholas. (2017). Generosity in Buddhism. *Huffington Post.* https://www.huffpost.com/entry/generosity-in-buddhism_b_14487312

Logan, Jim. (2018). Worry about commercialization of Christmas goes way back. Futurity. https://www.futurity.org/commercialization-of-christmas-1939892-2/

Lothrop-Green, Patricia. (2002). Retelling Myths for Children. *School Library Journal, 48*(5), 38-40.

Lythcott-Haims,Julie. (2015). *How to Raise an Adult: Break Free of the Overparenting Trap and Prepare Your Kid for Success.* St. Martins Press.

MacDonald KB. (1993). *Parent-Child Play: Descriptions and Implications.* Albany, NY: State University of New York Press

Marofsky Myrna. (Nd.). Tips for Handling the December Dilemma: Should Santa Be Invited? Pro-Group Diversity Innovation Solutions. http://www.progroupinc.com/site/page/pg2360-pn_The_December_Dilemma.html

McAfee, Tierney. (2017). Presidents who believe in Santa. *People Magazine.* https://people.com/politics/presidents-first-ladies-santa-claus-christmas/

Mead, George Herbert. (1934). *Mind, Self and Society*. Chicago: University of Chicago Press.

Melbourne Child Psychology. (2020). Believing in Santa Claus: Harmless or Hurtful? https://www.melbournechildpsychology.com.au/blog/believing-in-santa-claus-harmless-or-hurtful/

Mendelsohn, Michaela & Gil Straker. (1999). Social Perspective Taking. *Journal of Genetic, 160* (1), 69.

Montanaro, Domenico. (2016). I saw first ladies kissing Santa Claus. *NPR.* https://www.npr.org/2016/12/25/506420373/i-saw-first-ladies-kissing-santa-claus-and-a-first-dog-dressed-as-him

Moore, Clement. (1988). The Night Before Christmas. New York: Putnam.

Morton, Ella. (2015). Does Mrs. Claus have a life of her own? https://www.atlasobscura.com/articles/does-mrs-claus-have-a-life-of-her-own

Moschetti, Greg. (1979). The Christmas potlatch: A refinement on the sociological interpretation of gift exchange. *Sociological Focus.* 12 (Jan) 1-7.

Nast, Thomas. (1862). Christmas Eve. Illustrations in Harper's Weekly

National World War I Museum and Memorial. (2020). Christmas during World War I. Retrieved from https://www.theworldwar.org/christmas-during-war

Nelms, BC. (1996). Santa Claus: Good or bad for children? *J Pediatr Health Care, 10*(6), 243

Neuendorf, David. (1994). The True True Meaning of Christmas. NeuSys, Inc. Retrieved from http://www.neusysinc.com/columnarchive/colm0004.html

Novak, Matt. (2014, December 23rd). How Santa Claus became a cold-war icon. Gizmodo. Retrieved from https://paleofuture.gizmodo.com/how-the-u-s-military-turned-santa-claus-into-a-cold-wa-1664149776

Oakes, Robert A. (1972). Pragmatism, God, and Professor Matson: Some Confusions.
Philosophy and Phenomenological Research, 32(3), 397-402.

O'Barr, William M. 2006. Advertising and Christmas." *Advertising & Society Review* 7.3

Oberg, Alcestis "Cooky". (2004, December 22). *Santa?* Here's coal in your stocking. *USA Today*

Office of the United Nations High Commissioner for Human Rights. (1989). Convention on the Rights of the Child. General Assembly Resolution 44/25 of 20 November 1989. Available at: www.unhchr.ch/html/menu3/b/k2crc.htm

Oliver, Keenya H. (2004) Ascension to Humanism. *Free Inquiry*, *24*(2), 39-41.

One North Pole. (Nd). Famous Letters to Santa. http://www.onenorthpole.com/Post%20Office/famousletters.html

Orlet, Christopher (2003, December, 23). Yule Never Stop them from Shopping. *The American Spectator.* http://www.spectator.org/dsp_article.asp?art_id=7547

Orwell, George. (*1984).* New York, NY: Published by Signet Classic, 1977.

Oxfam. (2006). Holiday celebrations. http://www.iyp.oxfam.org/news/newsletter/Newsletter%2050%20Celebration.doc.

Papatheodorou, Theodora. (2002). Father Christmas: just a story? *International Journal of Children's Spirituality*, *7*(3), 329 – 345.

Parten, M. (1932). Social play among preschool children. *Journal of Abnormal and Social Psychology,* 28, 136-147

Passantino, Gretchen. (1986). *Santa Claus and the Gospel.* Answers in Action. Retrieved from http://answers.org/issues/santa.html

Paul, Kari. (2018). Here's how long it will take Americans to pay off their Christmas debt. Marketwatch. https://www.marketwatch.com/story/heres-how-long-it-will-take-americans-to-pay-off-their-christmas-debt-2017-12-29

Pedler, Caroline. (2001). My Treasury of Christmas Stories. New York:Paragon Books

Pellegrini, A. D. (2009). *The role of play in human development.* New York: Oxford University Press

Penhollow, Steve. (2014). Use of Santa in advertising through the years. *Medium.* https://medium.com/marketing-and-advertising/the-use-of-santa-claus-in-advertising-through-the-years-29f883bcd762

Perkes, Alden. (1982). *The Santa Claus Book.* Lyle Stuart Inc.

Perton, Marvin H. (n.d). Celebrating Christmas in Mexico. MEXonline.com. http://www.mexonline.com/christmas.htm

Piaget, J. (1929). *The Child's Conception of the World.* Harcourt, Brace Jovanovich: New York.

Piaget, J. (1932). *The Moral Judgement of the Child.* Harcourt, Brace Jovanovich: New York.

Piaget, Jean C., & Inhelder, Barbel. (1959). *The Growth of Logical Thinking from Childhood to Adolescence.* Routledge and Kegan Paul.

Piaget, Jean. (1962). *Play, Dreams, and Imitation in Childhood.* The Norton Library.

Piaget, J. (1969). *The Mechanisms of Perception.* Rutledge & Kegan Paul: London.

Pilkington, Brian. (2001). Yule Lads: A celebration of Iceland's Christmas folklore. Reykjavik:Gudrum

Polacco, Patricia. (1996). Trees of the Dancing Goats. NY: Simon and Schuster.

Premack, Rachel. (2017, December 20). Welcome to the paradoxical world of Korean Christmas. *Forbes.* https://www.forbes.com/sites/rachelpremack/2017/12/20/welcome-to-the-paradoxical-world-of-korean-christmas/#6d9e43427ca8

Prentice, Norman. (1979). Children's belief in Santa Claus. *American Academy of Child Psychiatry.* https://www.jaacap.org/article/S0002-7138(09)62213-5/pdf

Prentice NM, Manosevitz M, & Hubbs L. (1978). Imaginary figures of early childhood: santa claus, easter bunny, and the tooth fairy. *Am J Orthopsychiatry, 48*(4), 618-28.

Prentice NM, Schmechel LK, Manosevitz M. (1979). Children's belief in santa claus: a developmental study of fantasy and causality. *J Am Acad Child Psychiatry, 18*(4), 658-67.

Quartz. (2018). Christmas sermon: Pope Francis condemns modern materialism. https://www.newtimes.co.rw/news/christmas-sermon-pope-francis-condemns-modern-materialism

Rabie M. (2013) Social Transformation. In: *Global Economic and Cultural Transformation.* Palgrave Macmillan, New York. https://doi.org/10.1057/9781137365330_4

Rachel's Ruminations. (2018). Is Black Pete racist? https://rachelsruminations.com/is-black-pete-racist/

Reidy, Maurice. (1999). Santa's Helper. *Commonweal, 126*(22), 10.

Restad, Penne.(1995). Christmas in America: A History. New York:Oxford.

Restadt, Penne.(1995). How Christmas became the most commercialized holiday. http://www.santaswhiskers.com/how-christmas-became-the-most-commercialized-holiday.html

Reuters. (2020). Biden will cancel Christmas. https://www.reuters.com/video/watch/idOVD0STZHB

Ricks, Deanna. (n.d). Overgifting. The Dollar Stretcher. Retrieved from http://www.stretcher.com/stories/99/991101k.cfm

Robinson, B. A. (1999, December 24). Other Information About Santa Claus. Religious Tolerance. Retrieved from http://www.religioustolerance.org/santa3.htm

Rogoff, Barbara (2003). *The Cultural Nature of Human Development.* Oxford University Press.

Romero, Skylar.(2019). What is bulldozer parenting? https://parentology.com/what-is-bulldozer-parenting/

Rosengren, Karl S., & Hickling, Anne K. (1994). Seeing is believing: Children's explanations of commonplace, magical, and extraordinary transformations. *Child Development, 65*(6), 1605-1626.

Rosengren, Karl S., Kalish, Charles W. Hickling, Anne K., & Gelman, Susan A. (1994). Exploring the relation between preschool children's magical beliefs and causal thinking. *British Journal of Developmental Psychology, 12*(1), 69–82.

Rother, Steve. (2002). The Gift: Secret of the Magi. Astrostar. Retrieved from http://www.astrostar.com/articles/TheGift.htm

Ruffino, Dave. (nd). The Santa Files: A Counterfeit Jesus Christ . Source unavailable.

Rumela.com. (2006). Christmas and Santa. www.rumela.com/events/christmas_santa.htm.

Russiapedia. (2020). Snegurochka. https://russiapedia.rt.com/of-russian-origin/snegurochka/

Sade, Vivian. (2015, November 10th). Korean War Veteran, Santa Claus portrayer, recalls service. KCP News. Retrieved from https://www.kpcnews.com/news/latest/northwest/article_26c22a4c-a154-5f8b-986b-ffdf3ee4bcfb.html

Santa's Christmas Around the World. (n.d). Santa Claus. From http://www.santaclaus.com/world.html

Santa Claus. (nd) http://www.cdnbiz.net/xmas/santa.html

Santa Claus. (n.d). Novareinna. From http://www.novareinna.com/festive/santa.html

Santa Claus: An Engineer's Perspective. (2006). Baltimore MD. Retrieved from http://www.baltimoremd.com/humor/santaengineer.html.

Santa Claus Hall of Fame. (2010). Jim Yellig. https://www.santa-claushall.com/2010-inaugural-class/raymond-joseph-jim-yellig/

Santrock, John W. (2008). *A topical approach to life-span development.* McGraw-Hill Higher Education, New York City

Saracho, O. (2002). Young children's creativity and pretend play. *Early Child Development and Care,* 172, 431-438.

Sari, Yuliani. (2011). The commercialization of the myth of Santa Claus. https://core.ac.uk/download/pdf/16506909.pdf

Schenkman, Jan. (1850). *Sint Nikolaas en zijn Knecht* (Saint Nicholas and his Servant). G. Theod. Bomb, Pub.

Schmidt, Leigh Eric. (1995). *Consumer Rites: the Buying & Selling of American Holidays.* Princeton: Princeton

Schmidt, Leigh Eric. (1991). The Commercialization of the Calendar: American Holidays and the Culture of Consumption, 1870-1930. *Journal of American History* 78.3 (1991): 887- 916.

Schmidt, Leigh Eric. (1992). Christianity in the Marketplace: Christmas and the Consumer Culture." *Cross Currents* 42.3 (1992): 342. 27

Schobert, Matthew. (2003). Beyond Candy Cane Lane: 76-82. Academic Search Premier. EBSCO.

Sheehan, George. (1993). Play is life lived. https://www.behance.net/gallery/57001735/George-Sheehan-Play-Is-Life-Lived

Shoemaker, Nancy. (2015). A typology of colonialism. https://www.historians.org/publications-and-directories/perspectives-on-history/october-2015/a-typology-of-colonialism

Shonkoff JP, Phillips DA. (2000). *From Neurons to Neighborhoods: The Science of Early Childhood Development.* Washington, DC: National Academy Press

Schwartz, Barry. (1967). The social psychology of the gift. *American Journal of Sociology.* 73(1):1-11.

Sereno R. (1951). Some observations on the Santa Claus custom. *Psychiatry, 14*(4), 387-96. DOI 10.1080/00332747.1951.11022841

Sharon T. & Woolley JD. (2004). Do monsters dream? Young children's understanding of the fantasy/reality distinction. *British Journal of Developmental Psychology, 22*(2), 293-310.

Shorr, D. (1993). *Children's* perceptions of others' *kindness* in helping: The endocentric motivations of pride and guilt. *The Journal of Genetic Psychology, 154*(3), 363-374. DOI: 10.1080/00221325.1993.10532189

Singer, D, R. Golinkoff, & K. Hirsch-Pasek (2006). *Play = Learning: How play motivates and enhances children's cognitive and social-emotional growth*. New York: Oxford University Press.

Sloat, Sarah. (2017). The psychology of Santa Claus. https://psmag.com/social-justice/the-psychology-of-santa-claus-christmas-71679

Smid, M. (2001). Please fix The World. *National Edition, 28*(1), 54.57.

Smith, Charles. (2009). K-State child development expert says the magic of Santa Claus is no lie. https://www.k-state.edu/media/newsreleases/dec09/santa120709.html

Smith, Charles. (2000). Santa's Best Gift Universal. http://www.oznet.ksu.edu/news/sty/2000/santa2000.htm

Smithsonian. (2020). Modern Human Diversity: Skin color. https://humanorigins.si.edu/evidence/genetics/human-skin-color-variation/modern-human-diversity-skin-color

Smolucha, Larry & Smolucha, Francine. (1986). L. S. Vygotsky's Theory of Creative Imagination. [Paper presented at Annual meeting of the American Psychological Association]. Retrieved from http://eric.ed.gov/?id=ED274919

Snyder, Michael T. (n.d). Mystery of the pagan origins of Christmas. Unexplained Mysteries of the World. http://unexplainedmysteriesoftheworld.com/archives/the-mystery-of-the-pagan-origin-of-christmas-jesus-was-not-born-on-december-25th-but-a-whole-bunch-of-pagan-gods-were.

Snyder, Phillip. (1985). *December 25: The joys of Christmas past*. NY: Dodd, Mead & Co.

Sobel, David. (2006). How fantasy benefits young children's understanding of pretense. *Developmental Science, 9*(1), 63-75.

South East Asia. (n.d). Merry Christmas. Retrieved from http://www.twilightbridge.com/hobbies/festivals/christmas/southpacific.htm

St Nick OR Fake God? (n.d). Islam Newsroom. Retrieved 7/3/2014 from http://islamnewsroom.com/news-we-need/2163-santa-was-no-saint-fake-god.

Stec, Carley. (Nd). 24 iconic Santa Clause advertisements. https://blog.hubspot.com/marketing/santa-claus-advertisements

Stockman, Farah. (2019). Who gets to join a Santa society? *New York Times*. https://www.nytimes.com/2019/12/20/us/santa-claus-international-brotherhood-members.html

Stieb, Matt. (2020). Leaked Recording of Melania Trump: 'Who Gives a F**k About Christmas Stuff?' *New York Magazine.* https://nymag.com/intelligencer/2020/10/melania-trump-who-gives-a-f-k-about-christmas-stuff.html

Stronach, Ian & Hodkinson, Alan. (2011). Towards A Theory Of Santa. *Anthropology Today, 27*(6), 15-19.

Suiter, Triona. (2019). The Santa Claus effect: An assessment of colonized pop-culture. https://www.teentix.org/blog/the-santa-claus-effect-an-assessment-of-colonized-pop-culture

Sullivan, Robert. (1996) *The Flight of the Reindeer.* MacMillian: NY.

Sundblom, Haddon, Taylor, J., R., and Fans, Charles Barbara. (1992). *Dream of Santa: Haddon Sundblom's Vision.* Staples & Charles Ltd: Alexandria VA.

Sugirtharajah, Sharada. (2001). Traditions of giving in Hinduism. https://www.alliancemagazine.org/feature/traditions-of-giving-in-hinduism/

Tavares, Izalina. (2004). Black Pete. Humanity in Action. https://www.humanityinaction.org/knowledge_detail/black-pete-analyzing-a-racialized-dutch-tradition-through-the-history-of-western-creations-of-stereotypes-of-black-peoples/

Taylor, Marjorie. (1997). The relation between individual differences in fantasy and theory of mind. *Child Development, 68*(3), 436-55.

Taylor, Marjorie. (1999*) Imaginary Companions and the Children Who Create Them.* Oxford University Press: New York.

The Time-Life Book of Christmas. (1987). Prentice Hall: New York.

Thomas, Garwin. (2014, February 27). *12 Year Old Creates Low Cost Braille Printer out of Legos.* NCB Bay Area. Retrieved from http://www.nbcbayarea.com/news/local/Santa-Clara-12-Year-Old-Creates-Low-Cost-Braille-Printer-Out-Of-Lego-247716461.html

Thomas, W. I. and D.S. Thomas. (1928). *The child in America: Behavior problems and programs.* New York: Knopf

Thomson, Paul. (2010). A Christmas fairy tale. *European Journal of Psychotherapy and Counseling, 5*(2), 149-169.

Todres, Jonathan and Higgenbotham, Sarah.. (2016). Human Rights in Children's Literature. London: Oxford.

Tullos, Ansley., & Woolley, Jacqueline. D. (2009). The development of children's ability to use evidence to infer reality status. *Child Development, 80(1)*, 101-114.

Twilight Bridge. (n.d). Christmas in Southeast Asia. Retrieved from http://www.twilightbridge.com/hobbies/festivals/christmas/south-pacific.htm

Twitchell, James B. (2001). Twenty Ads That Shook the World: The Century's Most Groundbreaking Advertising and How it Changed Us All. Crown Publishers: New York.

UCDSB Virtual Learning Commons. 2020. What is Santa Claus's wife name?

http://ucdsb.libanswers.com/studentsK6/faq/197362

USA Today. (1992, December). Don't Curb Belief in Santa. *USA Today, 121*(2571), 12.

Unexplained Mysteries of the World. 2020. Mystery of the pagan origins of Christmas. http://unexplainedmysteriesoftheworld.com/archives/the-mystery-of-the-pagan-origin-of-christmas-jesus-was-not-born-on-december-25th-but-a-whole-bunch-of-pagan-gods-were.

Vissing, Yvonne. (2020). The Santa Spirit. Vissing & Associates.

Vissing, Yvonne. (2020). The ABCs of the Santa Spirit for Adults. Vissing & Associates.

Vissing, Yvonne. (2020). The Santa Spirit Advent Calendar Book: COVID edition. Vissing & Associates.

Vissing, Yvonne. (2020). The Legend of the Santa Stocking. Vissing & Associates.

Vissing, Yvonne. (2007). *How To Keep Your Children Safe.* University Press of New England.

Vissing, Y. (2011). *Introduction to Sociology.* Bridgepoint Education.

Vygotsky, L. S. (1967). Play and its role in the mental development of the child. *Soviet Psychology*, 5, 6-18.

Vygotsky, L. S. (1978). *Mind in society: The development of higher psychological processes.* Massachusetts: Harvard University Press

Wade, Peter. (2019). People are saying Merry Christmas again, thanks to Trump. *Rolling Stone.* https://www.rollingstone.com/politics/politics-news/people-are-saying-merry-christmas-again-thanks-to-trump-930898/

Waits, William Burnell. (1993). *The Modern Christmas in America: A Cultural History of Gift Giving.* New York: New York UP

Waits, William. (1978). *The many-faced custom: Christmas gift-giving in America. 1900-1940.* Rutgers University Department of History.

Waksler, Frances Chaput. (2002).Let's Pretend Santa is Real. *Education Digest*; February, Vol. 67 Issue 6, p62-4. 2002.

Walansky, Aly. (2020). The dark hidden truths in fairy tales and what we can learn from them. https://www.goalcast.com/2020/01/08/fairy-tales-dark-truths-and-lessons/

Wallace, Kelly. (2014, June 5). Slenderman stabbing case: When can kids understand reality vs. fantasy? CNN. http://www.cnn.com/2014/06/03/living/slenderman-stabbing-questions-for-parents/

Wang, Shirley. (2009, December 22). The Power of Magical Thinking. *Wall Street Journal*. http://online.wsj.com/news/articles/SB10001424052748703344704574610002061841322

Weber, Louis. 2002. Christmas Stories. Longwood, IL:Publications International.

Weber, Max. (1958). *The Protestant ethic and the spirit of capitalism*. New York: Scribner.

Wenz, Phillip. (2008). *Santa's Village*. Mount Pleasant, SC: Arcadeia Publishing. https://santaclausoath.webs.com/jimyellig.htm

Watters, Pat. (1978). *Coca-Cola: An illustrated history*. Garden City, NJ: Doubleday.

Whitesell, S. (2013) Why you should believe in Santa Claus even if he doesn't exist. https://christandpopculture.com/why-you-should-believe-in-santa-claus-even-if-he-doesnt-exist/

Wikipedia. (2020). St. Lucy. https://en.wikipedia.org/wiki/Saint_Lucy

Wikipedia. (2020). Mrs. Santa Claus. https://en.wikipedia.org/wiki/Mrs._Claus

Wikipedia. (2020). Le Befana. https://en.wikipedia.org/wiki/Le_Befana

Wikipedia. (2020). Winter solstice. http://en.wikipedia.org/wiki/Winter_solstice

Winncott, Donald.(1965). *The Child, the Family, and the Outside World*.

Winncott, Donald. (1971). *Playing and Reality*

Why Christmas.com. (2019). Christmas around the word. *Christmas in Ireland*. (n.d). and

Whychristmas?com. https://www.whychristmas.com/cultures/ireland.shtml and *Christmas in Greece*. (n.d). whychristmas?com. https://www.whychristmas.com/cultures/greece.shtml

Wilbur Bock, E. (1966). Symbols in Conflict: Official versus Folk Religion. *Journal of the Scientific Study of Religion*, 5(2), 204-12.

Wilber Bock, E. (1972). The Transformation of Religious Symbols: A Case Study of St. Nicholas. *Social Compass, 19*(4), 537-549.

Wilson, Craig. (2003). True believers never outgrow their Christmas spirit. *USA Today*; 12/24/2003.

Woodard, Joe. (1995). The Enduring Power of Saint Nicholas. Alberta Report / Newsmagazine 23.Wooley, Jacqueline. (2014). Children's concepts of reality. http://www.utexas.edu/cola/depts/psychology/faculty/jwoolley

Woolley, Jacqueline. (2014). Let your children believe in Santa Claus. https://news.utexas.edu/2014/12/19/let-your-kids-believe-in-santa-claus/

Woolley, J. D., & E Ghossainy, M. (2013). Revisiting the fantasy-reality distinction: children as naïve skeptics. *Child development, 84*(5), 1496–1510. https://doi.org/10.1111/cdev.12081

Woolley, Jacqueline D., & Van Reet Jennifer. (2006). Effects of context on judgments concerning the reality status of novel entities. *Child Development, 77*(6), 1778-1793. https://doi.org/10.1111/j.1467-8624.2006.00973.x

Worland, Justin. (2014, December 24). *Here's how Santa Claus was rewarded during World War II*. Time. Retrieved from https://time.com/3636048/fdr-santa-claus/

Yahoo.com 2917. How many letters addressed to Santa Claus does the Post Office receive each year? What do they do with them? http://ask.yahoo.com/ask/20021213.html

Yao, Margaret. (1981). Gift-giving spirit haunts some people who can't afford it. *Wall Street Journal*. Dec. 24:1

Yates, Ronald. (1985). Japanese merrily leave the Christ out of Kuisumasu. *Chicago Tribune.* Dec 22:1,16.

Yogman, Michael, Andrew Garner, Jeffrey Hutchinson, Kathy Hirsh-Pasek, Roberta Michnick Golinkoff, (2018). The power of play. *Pediatrics.* September 2018, 142 (3) e20182058; DOI: https://doi.org/10.1542/peds.2018-2058. https://pediatrics.aappublications.org/content/142/3/e20182058.short

Yule in Iceland. (nd). http://www.simnet.is/gardarj/yule5.htm

Zelizer, Viviana.(1992). Pricing the Priceless Child. Princeton, NJ: Princeton University Press.

Zipes, Jack. (2006). Fairy Tales and the Art of Subversion. New York: Routledge.

Zmuda, Natalie. (2010). Shoppers, retailers divided on the timing of seasonal onslaught. Advertising Age 81.40

End Notes

[1] Black Pete. *"VN wil einde Sinterklaasfeest - Binnenland | Het laatste nieuws uit Nederland leest u op Telegraaf.nl [binnenland]"* . Telegraaf.nl. 22 October 2013. *Retrieved 19 December 2013.*
[1] South Park. 2013. Jesus vs Santa. https://www.youtube.com/watch?v=olMsAy8HTUo
[1] Wrestling Examiner. 2015. https://www.youtube.com/watch?v=1E0jVcTf4fo
[1] Jack the Musical 2014. https://www.youtube.com/watch?v=60Ay97EHjV4
[1] Makem and Clancy. 2007. https://www.youtube.com/watch?v=NcG1JNpazN4
[1] Liberty Land Santa. 2001. http://joart515.tripod.com/id38.html 2001.
[1] http://about.usps.com/corporate-social-responsibility/letters-to-santa.htm#p=1[1]
[1] http://www.thelivingmoon.com/41pegasus/02files/Proof_that_Santa_Claus_is_Real.html
[1] Van Kuijen, Anne-Marie, Milstein, Dan, Yuruk, Koray, Folkow, Lars, Fokkens, Wytske, and Blix, Arnoldus. 2012. Why Rudolph's nose is red. https://www.bmj.com/content/345/bmj.e8311
[1] Halvorsen, Odd. 1986. Epidemiology of reindeer parasites. Parasitology Today. Volume 2, Issue 12, December 1986, Pages 334-339. https://www.sciencedirect.com/science/article/abs/pii/0169475886900530?via%3Dihub
[1] https://santaclausoath.webs.com/
[1] Poushter, Jacob and Fetterolf, Janelle. 2019. How people around the world view diversity. https://www.pewresearch.org/global/2019/04/22/how-people-around-the-world-view-diversity-in-their-countries/
[1] Maher, Matt. 2020. Children are at the forefront of change. PRB.org. https://www.prb.org/children-are-at-the-forefront-of-u-s-racial-and-ethnic-change/

[1] Community Solutions. 2020. https://community.solutions/analysis-on-unemployment-projects-40-45-increase-in-homelessness-this-year/

[1] Kristof, Nicolas. 2020. Crumbs for the hungry but windfalls for the rich. New York Times. https://www.nytimes.com/2020/05/23/opinion/sunday/coronavirus-economic-response.html?smid=em-share

[1] http://gilmichelini.com/acceptable-list-songs-public-school-winter-concerts/

[1] https://santacon.nyc/ and https://www.cnn.com/2019/12/14/us/santacon-nyc-trnd/index.html

[1] https://nymag.com/tags/santa-con and https://www.santacon.info/locations.html

[1] https://santahustle.com/

[1] http://www.hlntv.com/slideshow/2013/12/13/brothers-take-pictures-santa-34-years?hpt=hp_t3

Picture Credits

Picture Credits*
(in order of appearance)

Cover photo: Girl looking out window   Yuganov Konstantin
Chapter 1 Scroll Marisha
Santa hand dividing parts rangizzz
Church quote Sergey Nivens
Chapter 2 Garland   marilyn barbone
Irving quote elenabsl
Chapter 3 Walking Santa Victorian Traditions
Mabie quote
Chapter 4 St. Nicholas hans.slegers
Buber quote HelgaLin
Chapter 5 Female Santa Subbotina Anna
Englebreit quote S_Photo
Chapter 6 Santa in field   Alexander Raths
Girando quote Kiselev Andrey Valerevich
Chapter 7 Santa with poster Kiselev Andrey Valerevich
Miller quote Mimka
Chapter 8 Santa pulling bag   IfH
Toyland quote Victorian Traditions
Chapter 9 Santa and Jesus Tomacco
Deloria quote Curioso.Photography
Chapter 10 Santa and scroll Sunny studio
Whittier quote 4 PM production

Chapter 11 Writing table Romolo Tavani
Irving quote   Yuganov Konstantin
Chapter 12 Red holly scroll marilyn barbone
Dickens quote Monkey Business Images
Chapter 13 Wood words Steve Collender
Grayson quote weedezign
Chapter 14 Belly sign kurhan
Chase quote 4 PM production
Chapter 15 Greenery with red berries marilyn barbone
Field quote PCH.Vector
Chapter 16 Snowy Santa and sign Subbotina Anna
Bob Hope quote tommaso lizzul
Chapter 17 Indie Santa Kiselev Andrey Valerevich
Englebreit quote elenabsl
Chapter 18 Santa and world map Ollyy
de Saint Exupery quote Yuganov Konstantin
Chapter 19 Santa blowing magic Romolo Tavani
Haley quote   ingibiork
Chapter 20 Santa opening box   TierneyMJ
Gandhi quote Yvonne Vissing
Chapter 21 Santa in snow   Milles Studio
Emerson, Lake and Palmer quote Victorian Traditions
Chapter 22 Santa pointing Romolo Tavani
Beatles quote Olga Hmelevskaya
Chapter 23 Santa walking away wavebreakmedia
Santa with tree over shoulder Victorian Traditions

- These pictures were purchased from Shutterstock and approval to use them in this book was given. The author wishes to express gratitude to the photographers and graphic artists who contributed to the beauty of this book. Thanks for sharing the Santa Spirt with our readers!

About The Author

About the Author

Dr. Yvonne Vissing is a pediatric and community sociologist and the US child rights policy chair for the Hope for Children UN Convention on the Rights of the Child Policy Center in Cyprus. She is the founding director of the Salem State University Center for Childhood & Youth Studies in Massachusets, where she is a Professor of Healthcare Studies. She is a former National Institute of Mental Health Post-Doctoral Research Fellow, a fellow at the University of New Hampshire Family Research Lab, a Whiting Foundation Fellow where she studied child and youth studies programs in Europe and is a Democracy and Dialogues Initiative Fellow at the University of Connecticut Dodd Center, Humility & Conviction in Public Life Project. Dr. Vissing is a fellow at Times 4 Homes and a former board member of the National Coalition for the Homeless. She is on the Human Rights Council for the American Association for the Advancement of Science and on the Steering Committee for Human Rights Educators USA. As a consultant with the American Sociological Association, she works with colleges around the nation to develop strong higher education programs and departments. She has three children who she adores, plus a large family of assorted animals.

You can learn more about her consultations, publications and services at yvonnevissing.com

About the Book

About the Book

The dilemma we face about Santa Claus isn't about Santa at all. Rather, his character is symbolic of larger cognitive, relational, and political tensions that impact the lives of children, parents, and society. The study of Santa is not a childish topic but one ripe with scholarly factors and implications. Around this singular fantasy figure are institutions that include the family, religion, politics, the economy, media, education, and recreation. The intersection of the fields of child development, psychology, sociology, anthropology, political science, economics, family studies, religion, communication, and contemporary cultural studies has become apparent. There is a huge set of social forces to be influenced by this socially constructed character, forces that seem to be both cause and effect variables.

Transforming Santa will have significant benefits for children and society if the Santa Spirit is highlighted. Focusing on loving-kindness, generosity, altruism, and joy is good for children, good for adults, and holds significant benefits for society as a whole. The book explains how this was the original intent of the Santa Claus figure, how it got co-opted by those seeking to fulfill economic, political, religious, and ideological agendas. It is time to re-imagine all the wonderful things that a Santa figure could bring to children of all ages.

Other Books in the Santa Spirit Series

The Santa Spirit
The ABCs of the Santa Spirit for Adults
The Santa Spirit Advent Calendar Book: COVID edition
The Legend of the Santa Stocking

Other Books by Dr. Vissing

Changing the Paradigm of Homelessness
Women Without Children: Nurturing Lives
Going Gluten Free: A Cooking, Eating and Dining Guide
Introduction to Sociology
How to Keep Your Children Safe: A Guide for Parents.
Finding Information About Children: Using Human and Electronic Resources
Out of Sight, Out of Mind: Homeless Children in Small Town America.

and coming soon:

The Rights of Unaccompanied Minors: Perspectives and case studies
Mother Muckers
Children's Human Rights

Santa

www.ingramcontent.com/pod-product-compliance
Lightning Source LLC
Chambersburg PA
CBHW020036120526
44589CB00032B/357